United States Foreign Policy: Perspectives and Analysis

United States Foreign Policy: Perspectives and Analysis

William P. Gerberding
Assistant Professor of Political Science
University of California, Los Angeles

McGraw-Hill Book Company
New York, St. Louis, San Francisco, Toronto,
London, Sydney

To Ruth

Preface

In an age of specialization, inexhaustible paperbacks, and rapid change, anyone presumptuous enough to write a textbook should explain why he has engaged in such unfashionable behavior. I wrote this book for a variety of reasons, but the most important was my conviction that most students—and other citizens as well—do not know *how* to think about foreign policy. They may approach the purchase of a car or the choice of a profession—or, less often, even marriage—with a cool, analytical eye, assessing advantages and disadvantages. But when they begin to talk or think about foreign policy, they become emmeshed in slogans, pseudo principles, half truths, and emotional traps.

This book is an effort to provide the interested reader with a rather systematic and analytical method of thinking about foreign policy. It endeavors to provide the reader with a realistic grasp of the often painful and usually difficult choices confronting policy makers. The emphasis is on analysis, on *how* to think, not *what* to think, about foreign policy. It stresses the importance of asking the right questions; it is less concerned with providing the right answers.

It must be conceded, however, that the author's own opinions and policy biases are apparent. In the innocent early days of writing this book, a determined effort was made to avoid all prescription. It not only failed; it was deliberately abandoned as unsound and artificial, to say nothing of being impossible. But this book is not primarily an explication of the author's policy preferences. They are set forth, but never—or, alas, seldom—insisted upon. The reader is almost entirely free to draw his own conclusions.

For those who want to find out what the author's biases are before —or without—reading the book, a few statements may be helpful. I believe the major elements of United States policy in the postwar world have been and are sound; therefore, this book is *not* the outraged outcry of an angry academic. In other words, I do not believe there are any American policy changes which could transform fundamentally and advantageously today's international arena. This general stance does not, of course, mean that I endorse every specific policy since 1945. I do not, as the text makes abundantly clear. Finally, I am profoundly impressed—some would say too impressed— with the complexity of foreign policy problems and impatient with those who would have us believe otherwise. For many of these problems, I see no solutions at all in the foreseeable future.

The book is divided into two parts. Part I has an introductory chapter which endeavors to present some important concepts and modes of analysis; two chapters dealing with the policy formulation process in the United States; and two chapters on the origins of the cold war.

Part II deals with some of the major foreign policy problems that confront the United States in the contemporary world, such as, for example, Cuba, Berlin, and the underdeveloped areas. A book such as this can be fatally dated even before it is published if it attempts to discuss these constantly changing contemporary issues in an up-to-the-minute fashion or to engage in much prediction. Moreover, there will be new and different issues in the years ahead. Part II does not, therefore, concentrate on given problems so much for their own sakes but rather utilizes them as appropriate objects of analysis and suggests that they are illustrative of broader and continuing policy problems of the United States. The book was finished in June, 1965. It is up to the readers and the instructors to fill in the unavoidable gaps.

I have avoided the "encyclopedic approach." I am astonished at the breadth of information and understanding apparently acquired by writers of books that deal with all foreign policy problems all over the world. This book is selective. Even so, if anything, it errs on the side of trying to write sensibly about too much, not too little.

This book is not heavily footnoted. I gave up very soon trying to acknowledge all or even most of the sources of the facts, ideas, and opinions expressed. It goes without saying that I, like everyone else, am intellectually deeply indebted to many people. Anyone interested in these roots can get a fairly accurate impression by looking at the Selected Bibliography at the end of each chapter, especially if he or she should happen to notice the names of Hans J. Morgenthau, Robert E. Osgood, Inis L. Claude, Jr., and George F. Kennan. The names of two seminal influences do not appear, because they labor in somewhat different vineyards: Thomas E. Hill, Professor of Philosophy, and G. Theodore Mitau, Professor of Political Science, both of Macalester College.

I have three special debts at UCLA. Good students stimulate a professor and—of equal importance—tend to keep him honest. I have had scores of first-rate students, undergraduate and graduate. My department, besides affording an intellectually exciting atmosphere, has let me teach the courses I want to teach, an invaluable asset. And the Committee on Research of the Academic Senate has subsidized some of the research for the book.

At a recent end-of-the-semester party given by the graduate students at UCLA, my wife Ruth was presented with an award "for producing four children while her husband was producing one book." Amen.

William P. Gerberding

CONTENTS

Chapter Eight: FOREIGN AID AS AN INSTRUMENT OF POLICY 305

Chapter Nine: EPILOGUE 363

INDEX 377

Part One

Chapter One

Some Perspectives on American Foreign Policy

PEACE CORPS
WASHINGTON 25, D.C.

chapter 1 Most of the people who read this book have grown up in a United States heavily involved in international politics. When the Japanese attacked Hawaii on December 7, 1941, they shattered once and for all the illusion that even in the twentieth century the United States could effectively isolate itself from what was going on in the rest of the world. From that day to the present, there has not been any serious doubt in the minds of most Americans that the values, security, and well-being— i.e., the interests—of the United States are affected, and often endangered, by developments in world politics. That the United States should, therefore, attempt to play an influential role in international affairs—that it should, in other words, pursue "internationalist" rather than "isolationist" foreign policies—has been nearly universally accepted.

But what should this "influential role" be? What *can* the United States reasonably expect to be able to accomplish outside its borders? What *should* the United States attempt to accomplish? How? These questions do not lend themselves to easy answers, and the result is that there are many different and sometimes contradictory answers offered by individuals, groups, governmental institutions, and, sometimes, political parties. These differences are prompted by the diverse interests, intelligence, levels of information, and attitudes toward political affairs that characterize a free society.

Many specific controversies over policies and policy objectives will be discussed in this book. At the outset, however, it is desirable to ask some rather fundamental questions about the nature and purposes of this nation's foreign policy. In the years following World War II, the United States sought to define its new position in international politics and to establish some coherent and manageable objectives. The ensuing debates took many forms and covered a wide range of issues, but perhaps the most significant debate took place between the "idealists" and the "realists."

Idealism versus Realism

The idealists took the position that the United States should use its great prestige and power in the immediate postwar period to transform fundamentally international politics. Some of the most optimistic idealists called for the abolition of the nation-state system and its dangerous game of "power politics," and for the establishment of a world government, which could control or eliminate altogether the conflicts among nations. Another and slightly less utopian set of idealists called for the establishment of an international police force stronger than any national military force, which could impose peace in accordance with the decisions of the United Nations and "international law."

At a more sober and serious level, idealists argued that the United States could help decisively to create an unprecedentedly harmonious international arena, without surrendering its sovereignty to a world government or an international police force. The specific policies proposed to achieve this goal varied extensively. But they were all marked by the distinguishing characteristics of the idealists' mentality. The core of idealistic thought and assumptions was as follows:

> Man is basically good. The root of most of his difficulties in living with his fellow man is a lack of understanding. The impulses to dominate, to fight, to exploit are largely the product of misunderstandings; they are defensive, springing out of a fear of largely imaginary aggressive intentions on the part of someone else. Most of the rest of these destructive impulses spring from economic considerations: rich nations competing for greater riches, and poorer nations seeking to improve their economic conditions.
>
> These impulses can be eradicated or weakened by eliminating these causes. Through conscious effort, understanding can be increased and fear substantially reduced. Modern industrial achievements have now made it possible to create enough wealth that no nation is doomed to a debased standard of living.
>
> Insofar as man does by nature have antisocial or aggressive instincts, these can be controlled or made manageable by the creation of institutions designed to make aggressive behavior unprofitable.
>
> Therefore, the old game of power politics—of incessant rivalry and frequent wars between nations to achieve security or economic or territorial or prestige goals—can be eliminated; it is not a law of nature.
>
> Moreover, the goal of a peaceable and orderly world cannot and need not be regarded as an achievement for the distant future. Substantial and crucial reformations can be achieved now or at least in the foreseeable future.
>
> As for the United States, it is uniquely equipped and especially responsible for effecting fundamental reforms of international politics. As a rich, free, and relatively secure nation, the most powerful nation on earth owes it to itself and to the world to change the pattern and direction of international politics; to turn it away from hostile competition, unbridled rivalry, and frequent armed conflict and to turn it toward cooperation and peace.

The "realists" took a quite different position, based on radically dissimilar assumptions. The core of the postwar realists' position was as follows:

> Man has an enormous capacity for evil. This is an ineradicable fact of life. Conflict and tension between men and societies are quite natural and have existed since the dawn of time. It may be possible to mitigate some conflicts and in specific circumstances to change hostility into tolerance or even respect or friendship. But such achievements will always be limited and conditional.
>
> Under these circumstances, no nation can afford to expend much of its energies or to place much of its trust in schemes or proposals which are designed to transform international politics fundamentally. The United States must look to its own survival and well-being in an often-hostile environment. It should seek understanding and harmonious relations with other nations, but it should expect in some important instances to be disappointed. When necessary, it should seek defensive alli-

ances with nations whose interests broadly coincide with its own. It should, when feasible, use its power and resources to help less developed or war-devastated nations, but not because it has a moral obligation to do so or because of an illusory belief that such policies are likely to alter radically international politics. Rather, it should do these things when they serve the legitimate interests of the United States.

This may not be a morally exciting or a politically exhilarating definition of America's role in world affairs, but it has the advantage of taking into account the world as it is, as it always has been, and as it almost certainly will remain.

Obviously, the summaries presented above are oversimplified. Moreover, most individuals did not fit neatly into such categories. Nonetheless, the summaries do suggest broad tendencies of thought that were—and are—represented at all levels of American life.

For the most part, American foreign policy in the postwar period has reflected substantially more of the realists' assumptions than those of the idealists. Soviet policy after the war had a sobering effect on the United States, as wartime dreams of a harmonious postwar world were shattered by the protracted conflict of the cold war (see Chapter 5).

But this is a rather recent development, and it should be recognized that the idealistic strains in American thought and policy have a long history and exhibit great tenacity and recuperative powers. Much, but by no means all, of the earlier internationalist thought in this country was idealistic in tone and substance. Its struggle with isolationist thought often took on the appearance of a moral crusade. In retrospect, it often seems as if the American public was being asked to choose between those who wanted to reform the world—the idealistic internationalists—and those who wanted to ignore it—the isolationists. On those terms, it is understandable that the isolationists were dominant. The American people had been told that they were entering World War I "to make the world safe for democracy" and that it was "a war to end all wars." When the war ended and it became clear that these goals were not likely to be achieved, the disillusionment with idealistic internationalism provided a fertile ground for isolationism.

Isolationism also had an idealistic element in it, however. For the most part, it represented a rather hard-headed and self-serving—but impractical—attitude toward foreign policy. But it also drew much of its strength from somewhat loftier motives. Since the founding of the Republic, there has always been a widely held conviction that the best service the United States could perform for the world was to set an example of a peaceful, prosperous, and free society. Other nations would eventually see the merits of the American system, adopt it, and the result would be a peaceful, prosperous, and free international arena. The responsibility of the United States, therefore, was to stay out of the traditional rivalries, alliances, and wars, and to lead the way by example to a different and better world order.

The idealism that persists to this day has, of course, been chastened by the long and bitter experience of the cold war. Only a few persons any longer believe that it is possible in the near future to create a harmonious international order; and even fewer believe that the major responsibility of the United States is to withdraw from the international arena and merely perfect its own society, important and desirable as such domestic reforms may be.

The surviving remnant of idealism manifests itself in rather different ways. It seeks wherever possible to civilize policy and diplomacy, and it continues to look forward hopefully to a day of reduced tensions and genuine peace. It doggedly and patiently seeks honorable understandings with our adversaries rather than abandoning all hope and treating them as incurably evil and hostile. And it insists that however primitive or grave the struggle may become, the United States should continue to show a decent regard for moral considerations in its policies and actions.

The realists, having won most of the argumentation and finding their attitudes and assumptions broadly accepted, have also been forced by events to adjust some of their thinking. The cold war has dampened the ardor and faith of the idealists and made them more realistic; modern technology has sobered the realists into an appreciation of the desirability of somehow softening and ameliorating the harsh patterns of international politics. In a sense, therefore, the great debate has lost its relevance. A broad consensus has emerged that embraces most of the realist position and some of the idealist position. The realists salute the Peace Corps; the idealists support a $50 billion defense budget.

To talk of a broad consensus, however, is not to imply that the two strains of thought discussed above do not still represent different tendencies and emphases; they do. Moreover, they underlie many of the specific foreign policy disputes, which, of course, are as numerous as ever.

Some Basic Assumptions

Any book, but especially a book dealing with policy matters, reflects the basic attitudes and beliefs of its author. These should be made explicit, at least in general terms. What follows is a brief attempt to fulfill this obligation.

The author's basic assumptions and predispositions tend to fall more in the "realist" category. It is assumed in this book that conflict and tension between nations are a normal state of affairs. Nations, like individuals, have values and interests that they seek to preserve or expand. It is inevitable that the values and interests of various nations will often conflict, no matter how circumspectly and judiciously they may be defined by one or all nations. This would be true even if there were no Communist governments; their presence merely accentuates this unavoidable fact of international political life.

Whether these clashes of interests or values become armed conflicts depends on a number of factors. One is the intensity of the conflict. If it involves matters that one or more of the contending governments regard as being of fundamental importance—as, for example, the Western presence in Berlin—the possibility of war is clearly present. Lesser conflicts, of course, are less likely to provoke war. A second factor is the extent of the perceived risks and costs that any initiating of war would incur. It is, for example, undeniably true that the awesome presence of nuclear weapons on the other side has restrained the activities of both the United States and the Soviet Union in recent years. A third important factor in determining whether conflicts will lead to war is the level of skill and prudence of the leadership. Many wars that might rather easily have been avoided have occurred because of the laziness or stupidity or imprudence of a national leader who failed to acquaint himself with the facts or to ponder carefully the alternatives and consequences. A classic and tragic example of a war that skilled statesmanship might have avoided is World War I.

But conflict and tension are constants in international affairs, and the problem is not how to eliminate them—that is impossible—but how to control them and keep them at tolerable levels. This is a difficult enough objective for any nation's foreign policy, and it is foolish and sometimes reckless to ask it to achieve any more.

This view is not a cynical or a pessimistic one. It does not preclude the possibility of achieving a low level of tension, and it most certainly does not affirm that large-scale war is inevitable, especially in the day of the H-bomb. But it does suggest that every nation must keep a wary eye on other nations, especially those who for some reason or other, sound or unsound, choose to make themselves its adversaries. It emphasizes the *limitations* on what any given set of policies can achieve. It stresses the uncertainties, ambiguities, and imponderables in international politics and the prudent necessity of bearing in mind the countervailing power of adversaries or potential adversaries. Above all, it acts as a brake on the construction of panaceas, on idle enthusiasms, and on grand designs and ambitious dreams.

Specifically with respect to the United States, this view suggests that despite its great power and its generally honorable intentions, it must expect to be misunderstood, maligned, threatened, and perhaps even physically attacked. Therefore, it should take care to formulate its objectives and its policies with prudence and a sense of the possible; it should not let its enthusiasms rule over its more sober judgments; and it should maintain enough military strength to discourage any attempts to violate its security.

Some Important Concepts

In discussions and writings about international politics and foreign policy, certain words and phrases recur frequently; most of them have already appeared in this chapter. They express basic concepts that will be introduced rather sketchily in the following paragraphs.

The central concept is "the national interest." It is generally accepted that any government pursues foreign policies that it believes will be in its nation's best interests. The basic criterion for any policy or proposal, then, is whether it serves the national interest. Whether this ought to be the basic criterion of policy, and what the concept "national interest" actually means—either in general terms or in specific circumstances—are matters in endless dispute. At this point, however, the main problem is one of meaning. As used in this book, "the national interest" means the security and well-being of the nation and its citizens. Whatever protects or promotes these conditions is said to be "in the national interest."

"Security" means physical safety, territorial integrity, and political independence. "Absolute security" is obviously unattainable in today's world; perhaps it always was. Therefore, the term "security" should be understood to refer to the "maximum security possible under any given set of circumstances."

"Well-being" is much more difficult to define. It surely has an economic dimension, but it is more than that. The well-being of a citizenry requires the preservation of its culture and values, of its "way of life." In the case of the United States, this "way of life" includes such nonmaterial things as the enjoyment of nearly unlimited civil liberties and the right and capacity to select political leaders democratically.

The national interest is sought for its own sake; it is not a means to another end. In order to serve their national interests, governments establish *objectives*, or goals. These are instrumentally important—that is, they are means to another end: the national interest—and they are temporary in character, adjusting to the changing international picture. Examples of American objectives today are the creation and preservation of a strong, non-Communist Western Europe, and the avoidance of thermonuclear war. Among Soviet objectives today are the preservation of a Communist Eastern Europe and the avoidance of thermonuclear war. To some extent in both cases, these objectives—or ends, or goals, or purposes—are sought for their own sakes. The United States presumably desires and would be willing to assist in the creation or preservation of a free, prosperous Europe even if such a condition were not so clearly desirable from the standpoint of American security. Similarly, the Soviet leaders may actually believe it intrinsically desirable for Eastern Europeans to live under a Communist regime even if the Soviet Union had no stake in it. But the central reason for these objectives is not their intrinsic desirability, but their presumed connection with other goals that are desired for their own sakes. These other goals have been referred to above as the security and well-being of the nation—the national interest.

Objectives are not *policies*. To be in favor of peace, for example, is not by itself a policy. Foreign policies are devised to achieve specific objectives. Policies, therefore, are still further removed from the characteristic of being pursued for their own sakes. They are, even more than objectives, instrumental and temporary in character. The United States does not, for example, have a policy of providing South Korea with military assistance just because it likes to provide military assistance. It does so in order to achieve certain objectives that are deemed to be in the national interest.

The preceding distinctions are useful, but they are also somewhat artificial. The vocabulary of foreign policy cannot be so neatly categorized. It is used in different ways by different people. A striking example of this is the so-called "policy of containment." Strictly speaking in terms of the categories provided above, the containment of communism is not a policy at all; it is an objective for which policies must be designed.

Another difficulty inheres in the suggested distinction between those values that are desired for their own sakes and those that are instrumental in character. In the realm of values, one man's set of priorities may bear little or no relationship to the next man's. As intimated above, the objective of preserving a non-Communist Western Europe is purely a defensive expedient to some Americans, whereas for others it constitutes an intrinsically important objective, which should be pursued at great cost simply for its own sake, regardless of its bearing on American security. The fact is, of course, that both perspectives on the matter contribute to the fact that a non-Communist Western Europe ranks among the highest American objectives.

For analytical purposes, however, these distinctions are useful and will recur throughout the book.

Some Essential Questions

In the following paragraphs, a method of thinking about, or analyzing, foreign policy and objectives will be put forward. Anyone who wants to think seriously and sensibly about such complicated and contentious matters must begin by developing an awareness of which questions are relevant and pertinent and which are not. It is necessary, in other words, to learn *how* to think about foreign policy before one can intelligently determine *what* to think about foreign policy. Much of the rhetoric and debate about foreign policy is not intellectually respectable—that is, it is not, on its merits, worthy of serious attention—because it deals in matters that are either wholly irrelevant or are mere fragments of the broader perspective from which wise and prudent policy must derive.

The national interest is an abstract notion, which specific objectives and policies are designed to serve. Therefore, it is the objectives and policies that lend themselves to careful analysis and understanding. The following scheme of analysis attempts to focus attention on basic questions. Whether it evokes wise answers is entirely up to the person providing the answers. Its only purpose is to focus on the right questions.

Regarding any objective or proposed objective of foreign policy, the following questions should be asked:

1. How, if at all, can it be achieved?
2. If it can be achieved, what are the risks involved?
3. What are the costs involved?
4. Does the objective, or the means of achieving it, violate any moral principles that *should* be taken into account?
5. Are there any acceptable alternative objectives that are achievable, involve fewer risks and/or less cost, and are more in accord with moral principles?
6. On balance, after considering all the questions above and weighing their relative importance, is the objective worth pursuing? Or, to put it another way, is its pursuit in the national interest?[1]

There would probably be universal agreement that questions 1, 2, 3, 5, and 6 are meaningful and important questions to be asked of any objective or proposed objective. Regarding question 4, however, there would be much disagreement. Whether moral considerations are relevant to an

---

[1] The questions that should be asked about any policy or proposed policy are only slightly different. Question 1 is ordinarily not very helpful; most policies are achievable. The policy, for example, of providing India with military assistance with which to resist Chinese demands and incursions is easily achievable; the question is whether it is desirable. Questions 2, 3, and 4 are already addressed to policies, or means of achieving objectives, and are precisely the most pertinent ones. Question 5 is also appropriate concerning policies: Are there any acceptable alternative methods of, or policies for, achieving the objective that involve fewer risks and/or less cost, and are more in accord with moral principles? Question 6 should be reworded as follows: On balance, after considering all the questions above and weighing their relative importance, is the policy worth pursuing? If a policy is indeed deemed to be the best available means of achieving the desired objective, a final judgment on whether it should be pursued should depend on whether the achievement of the objective outweighs the costs and risks involved in pursuing the suggested policy.

There is no suggestion here that even the most conscientious and orderly policy makers actually follow such a rigid and systematic method of analyzing foreign policies and objectives. It is contended, however, that intelligent and responible policy making must at some point come to grips with the suggested questions. A failure to do so could result—and sometimes has resulted—in seriously and perhaps even disastrously misguided policies.

analysis of foreign policy objectives is a serious question. And any attempt to effect a reconciliation between ethics and politics, or even to describe their relationship, is bound to be controversial and ultimately beyond proof or demonstration. Nonetheless, an effort, perhaps a brash one, is made in the following paragraphs to suggest some guidelines. If nothing else, at least the author's position on this important matter will be made explicit.[2]

Ethics and Foreign Policy

Foreign policy has been misunderstood or badly formulated for a variety of reasons, and prominent among them in the United States has been confusion about the proper role of morality in international politics. Some maintain that international politics is and/or should be conducted without regard to ethical considerations. Others, including the author, believe that moral considerations do and should play some role in the formulation of foreign policies. Exactly what that role should be is, of course, a knotty and contentious question.

It is often said of a policy that it is immoral because it involves actions that are ordinarily regarded as unprincipled and "the end doesn't justify the means." This is a popular cliché but in practice is regarded as an appropriate guide to action by very few people. Nearly everyone judges acts, or means, in terms of the ends they serve, and properly so. Otherwise, there would be no moral distinction, for example, between various kinds of killing. If a man shoots and kills another person in self-defense, this act surely has a different moral status from an act wherein a man shoots and kills another person out of sheer malice or in order to gain some reward. In both instances, the act is the same: A man shoots and kills another man. The first act, however, is morally acceptable to most people, whereas the second is not; it is murder. The difference obviously has to do with the end or purpose of the act. In one case, the purpose *justifies* the act; in the other it does not. The moral status of an act, therefore, is dependent upon the purpose for which it is done. Some ends justify some means.

To take an example from an area more directly related to foreign policy, consider the morality of a soldier who kills an enemy soldier. Why is this any different from murder? It is different because the larger purpose or end—winning the war, or defending the nation, or perhaps even a lofty end such as "defending freedom"—justifies the means.

This delicate and paradoxical relationship between morality and policy

---

[2] No one is more aware than the author that the following analysis does not dispose of a question which has occupied thinkers for centuries. In writing a book such as this, one is confronted with the choice of ignoring this basic problem or of treating it too summarily. The latter course was chosen as the lesser of two evils.

is frequently misconstrued. It is sometimes said, for example, that the President had to order some action or other because the security of the nation required it, but that the action was clearly immoral. Such remarks are often heard, for example, in connection with American espionage or military activities. The implied standard of judgment in such a remark is an abstract, formal standard: Some acts are intrinsically immoral, regardless of the context within which they take place or the purposes they may be serving at any given time.

A few people, and even a few who have thought seriously about the matter, actually do have such a simple, rigid, formalistic ethical code. Most people, however, do not; and any government that faithfully followed such an abstract ethical code would soon find itself menaced from without, if not from within. Only those who are prepared to defend the proposition that any kind of violence at any time and for any purpose is immoral are in a position to say that "the end doesn't justify the means."

Most people, including the author, are at least as interested in the consequences, or ends, of actions as they are in the actions themselves. They make ethical judgments more in terms of results than in terms of whether an action accords with some abstract or formal ethical code. From this perspective, then, the difficult moral problem is to determine which ends justify which means.

This book is based on the assumption that the United States, as the strongest Western democracy, is the primary defender of the highest principles and most noble values known to man.[3] These values are eminently worth preserving and they are unquestionably under attack today, as they presumably always will be in one way or another. Many policies and actions which are ordinarily undesirable or even unsavory are morally justified if they serve to protect these values. Hence, it is an unconvincing moral argument to claim, for example, that *under no circumstances* should the United States support a dictatorial regime abroad or invade a country with which it is not at war. If such unpleasant expedients are necessary to help preserve the greater good—the principles noted above—then they are morally defensible.

Do good ends justify *any* means? No. At some point, a good end becomes so corrupted by unprincipled means of achieving it that it no longer justifies such means. Means should, in other words, be both necessary and

---

[3] It would be inappropriate and, presumably, unnecessary to go into an extended explication of these principles, or values, at this point. It is assumed that they are generally understood and include such things as a profound respect for human dignity, self-government, and political, religious, and cultural freedom. It should perhaps be acknowledged that these principles are quite obviously not universally observed or respected in Western nations or, more particularly, in the United States. What is being contended, however, is that they are meaningful ideals, meaningfully pursued and often achieved in the West; and that they are neither in Communist countries.

appropriate to the end being served. It might be argued, for example, that a massive nuclear attack on key Chinese cities and installations would so effectively cripple China's capacity to make war that it would serve the long-range interests of world peace and of freedom. Even if it is assumed, for the sake of argument, that such an attack would in fact serve such praiseworthy ends without involving attendant costs that would outweigh them, many people—including the author—would nevertheless still object to such attack. The objection would be based on some elemental moral sense which finds such actions so horrible and so disproportionate to the problem as to be immoral. The difficult problem, of course, is to know where to draw the line. Needless to say, even morally sensitive people draw the line at different places, some willing to condone more than others. The problem of appropriately relating ends and means is a perennial and basic one for moral philosophy and political practice.

However, if one assumes, as the author does, that the greatest immorality of all would be to permit the enemies of freedom and human dignity to gain control of international affairs, many actions that otherwise would be unpalatable become not only morally tolerable but morally imperative.

This kind of reasoning is risky, of course, both morally and intellectually. It can easily be corrupted into a self-serving, hypocritical, and self-righteous rationale for any and all foreign policies. It lends itself to a crude, "good guys versus bad guys" view of international politics. But it is not intended that way. Any sensitive person, particularly in the twentieth century, is aware of his and his nation's capacity for self-deception and, more importantly, for evil. There is no presumption here that the United States and Western civilization are morally untainted or that their principles are universally adhered to in practice. This is obviously not true. Nor is there any presumption that the Soviet government and its Communist associates are irremediably evil and motivated by wholly immoral impulses.

It is, however, insisted that the struggle between the West and the Communists is not merely a struggle for power, or an unfortunate misunderstanding. On the contrary, great moral as well as political issues are at stake, and the West, led by the United States, represents and is defending what for the most part are morally sound principles. It is morally incumbent upon the West to defend those values, and if in their name some ordinarily opprobrious actions must be taken, so be it: the end *does* justify many otherwise unjustifiable means.

In our day, the most serious challenge which can be made of the preceding line of argument has to do with the presence and possible employment of nuclear weapons. These instruments of mass destruction raise special ethical problems because the physical survival of large sections, if not all, of humanity is involved. Is their use *ever* morally justifiable? Could *any* end justify a resort to that desperate means? And, at a somewhat less apocalyptic level, is it morally defensible even to maintain such weapons for deterrent purposes? A small percentage of Americans would answer the last question in the negative; we shall have more to say about nuclear pacifism in the last chapter. As to the preceding question regarding their actual use, no suggestions will be offered. Any answer to that question will reflect the answerer's most fundamental attitudes toward the meaning and purpose, if any, of human existence.

One other thing perhaps needs to be said on this difficult and controversial subject. One of the most menacing aspects of recent history has been the development of "political religions." Secular creeds—fascism, communism, and other varieties of totalitarianism—have arisen which make extraordinary claims regarding their own possession of truth and righteousness. They are impelled by messianic drives, and they launch crusades on behalf of what they claim to be immortal truths. They create national systems of self-righteousness that purport to justify the most monstrous evils imaginable, including genocide.

Some persons in the democratic West, when confronted by nations possessed of such a political religion, believe that the only safe response is to launch a crusade to extirpate the evil, root and branch. In the process, they run a very severe risk of embracing a political religion of their own.

The preceding assertions regarding the moral necessity of defending Western values unavoidably partake of some of the flavor of such morally dubious crusades. They can easily be twisted or misunderstood. In the hands of a morally insensitive person, the position outlined can become a perverse apologia for unbridled self-righteousness and even outright aggression. It can, in short, be perverted into an effort to justify a crude and morally indefensible political religion.

In the hands of a morally sensitive person, on the other hand, it can combine the often harsh facts of life with an ethical concern and produce statesmanship of the highest order.

Two Proposed Objectives Analyzed

To illustrate how the questions listed above can help a person think critically and intelligently about foreign policy objectives, two frequently proposed objectives will be analyzed below: "a world rule of law" and "total victory over communism."

Many men of good will and some estimable organizations have argued for many years that the United States should lead the way to achieving the objective of a "world rule of law." The precise meaning of these words is usually left unclear, but their general import is apparent. Stable domestic societies have largely controlled violence and antisocial behavior by establishing laws and enforcing them. Especially since the appearance of thermonuclear weapons, it is imperative that international society come together in an analogous fashion, accept a certain code of behavior, or laws, and then enforce it, or them.

The proposal begins to come apart, however, when the first question is asked: How, if at all, can the objective be achieved? There are at least four characteristics of a functioning legal system that would have to be created on the international level before it could be regarded as analogous to a domestic legal system: (1) a generally accepted body of laws, (2) a generally accepted source of new laws, (3) a generally accepted court system to interpret the laws, and (4) an instrumentality of enforcement.

None of these things currently exist on the international scene; each of them would have to be created. There is something that in Western countries is called "international law," which purports to establish the boundaries of legal and illegal behavior between nations, but it has at least two fatal flaws as a candidate for an acceptable body of laws for the world: its content and scope are constantly in dispute in the West, and it is not recognized as valid in much of the rest of the world, most particularly in Communist countries. Moreover, and similarly, there is no recognized source for such a world law. And thirdly, although there is a World Court —the International Court of Justice—which hears a few cases, mostly of little consequence, its authority is severely limited by most states—including the United States—which technically accept its jurisdiction, and there is little or no chance that any nation would regard as binding a disagreeable decision affecting its vital interests.

Even if all the above difficulties could be removed—and they almost certainly cannot be—the fourth one would still frustrate the achievement of the objective. How would this newly constituted law be enforced? This brings us back to the staggering problem of how the United States or any other nation or group of nations could lead the way toward an international military force that could impose its will on any recalcitrant state. Very few nations, and certainly no major nation, are willing to turn over to an international agency, however constituted, the power to control their national affairs or impose its judgment on matters which affect their vital national interests. The nation-state system may not be the permanent method of organizing the world politically, or the best, but its demise is unlikely to occur in the near future.

The critical question is "How?", and the plain truth is that there are no answers to this question that offer the slightest chance of success in today's world. If international politics should ever be so radically altered that major powers were willing to turn over the ultimate characteristic of sovereignty—armed forces—to an international agency, this astonishing act would merely be a reflection of a transformed international system. It could not be its *cause* because under present circumstances, no self-respecting nation would take such a risk, and, if it did, it would probably be the only one.

One has only to contemplate what would happen in the United States Congress if any administration dared to propose turning our defense responsibilities over to the United Nations. Not today and not tomorrow is such a proposal likely to be seriously made, much less approved, by practical men in this or any other major country.

The proposed objective of a "world rule of law" is clearly utopian. It bears no practical relationship to the world in which we live. It may be a noble idea—that would depend on the character of the law to be adopted and enforced—and it may even come to pass some day in a distant future. But it is important not to confuse the support of lofty goals and noble sentiments with statesmanship. The statesman must deal with the here and now, with the harsh realities of an international system that does not resemble a stable, orderly domestic system with its admirable "rule of law." If analogies with domestic orders must be made, the international system most resembles a domestic system in a state of anarchy. On the international level, there is no government to impose law and order, and each of the individual actors—nation-states—is restricted in its actions only by its own sense of morality and responsibility or by its fear of the power and reactions of others. This anarchic system cannot be wished or willed away, nor can it be dissolved by moral fervor or passionate rhetoric.

The above proposal is a striking example of what can be called "the utopianism of the left." It is a legalistic prescription for a political problem, and it disintegrates upon a careful consideration of the first-suggested question. The other proposal to be analyzed—"total victory over communism" —requires a rather more extensive analysis.

"Total victory over communism" is a stirring challenge, an obviously desirable objective. It is put forward as an alternative to present national objectives. With brief rhetorical interludes—which will be referred to below—the central objective of American foreign policy since shortly after the end of World War II has been the containment[4] of communism. For some people, the word "containment" has carried too defensive a connotation. For others, it has seemed to be defeatist: either we win or we lose. For still others, it has seemed downright immoral, involving a tolerance of evil. "Total victory over communism" suffers from none of these liabilities: it implies positive action, it resolves the problem, and it eliminates the evil. It appeals especially to those who find the uncertainty, inconclusiveness, tension, and menace of the cold war intolerable.

How, if at all, can it be achieved? Several possibilities suggest themselves.

---

[4] The word "containment" as used in this book refers to a set of ideas about American foreign policy that emphasizes the need for stopping, or containing, Communist encroachments into the non-Communist areas of the world but that views with caution and skepticism any schemes that purport to show the way toward eliminating existing Communist regimes. Containment does not, however, rule out this latter possibility, especially in areas—such as Cuba, for example—where the Communist regime is not clearly linked with Soviet security interests and/or by itself constitutes a serious menace or potential menace to the security of the United States. It is not, in other words, a wholly defensive concept, although it does tend to emphasize the limitations on what American foreign policy can achieve inside the Communist bloc.

The most obvious one—and the one that most exponents of the objective deny is necessary—is to defeat the Communist nations in war. This would surely not eliminate communism as an ideology, but it would serve the admirable purpose of eliminating, at least for the time being, the military threat to the United States posed by these Communist nations, especially the Soviet Union.

The proponents of "total victory" are not talking about some dim and distant prospect. They are talking about the proximate future. Therefore, since the Soviet Union has shown little disposition to launch an all-out attack on the United States,[5] a military solution would require that the United States take the initiative and attack the Soviet Union.

Assuming for the moment that such an attack would be successful, it nonetheless seems reasonable to assume that the Soviet leaders would use every means at their disposal to win such a war. This raises the question of risks. Modern technology changes rapidly, and it is hazardous to make any flat statements about the comparative military capabilities of any nations. Nonetheless, it is an indisputable fact that the Soviet Union has a highly sophisticated delivery system—featuring intercontinental ballistic missiles (ICBMs)—and a large supply of thermonuclear warheads. It is distinctly within the range of the possible that the United States would be hit very hard by Soviet retaliatory blows. How much damage are we willing to absorb as the cost of destroying the Soviet Union? How sure are we of how much destruction would in fact occur in the United States?

There is also the risk that the United States, even if it began the war, might lose it. From what is publicly known about the comparative capabilities of the two superpowers, this is an unlikely but not an impossible outcome.

There are other risks. What would be the response of other nations to this kind of action by the United States, especially since the action would not have been provoked by an earlier Soviet attack? It is highly likely that the United States would become an outcast nation, despised and feared by the rest of mankind because it had wreaked the greatest destruction in history on a nation that had not even attacked it. Would this be a more desirable, or even in the long run a more secure, world than the one in which we now live?

There are also certain inescapable costs involved in such an action. Much of American society would be repelled by such an action and would become alienated from the government and the society that produced it. Even

---

[5] The question of whether the Soviets would launch such an attack if conditions were favorable is not under consideration. The fact is that they have not done so under the conditions prevailing since the onset of the cold war. Barring some major technological breakthrough, the risks and costs of such an attack will probably increase in the future for the Soviets.

among those who approved the action in advance, the psychological consequences would almost certainly be deleterious. It is one thing to talk about wiping out millions of human beings in an afternoon; it would be quite another actually to do it. In sum, it would be a disunited, troubled, and nearly universally hated nation that would then try to face the challenges of the future, even if it were lucky enough to escape serious retaliatory blows.

Does this means of achieving the desirable objective of "total victory over communism" violate any moral principles that should be taken into account? In this case, does this end justify this means? As suggested above, every person must ultimately answer this question for himself. If, however, one takes the position that moral standards should have some bearing on the conduct of foreign policy, several considerations should be taken into account.

To fight back in response to an aggressive attack and to maintain weapons of colossal destruction as a deterrent are morally defensible actions by most standards. But to *initiate* a thermonuclear attack, no matter how "selective," falls into another category. To justify the action on moral grounds would take an enormous amount of self-righteousness and a very simplistic view of good and evil and their distribution in the world. To justify the slaughter of millions of human beings in the name of morality is a difficult task in any event; under the conditions described, it seems impossible.

It is sometimes argued that we *should* not coexist with evil. This, like the objective under consideration, has a certain flamboyant appeal. But it is, of course, an absurdity: we cannot avoid coexisting with evil. It cannot be eliminated from human existence; to call for its repeal or elimination is to betray at once a touching innocence and an arrogant self-righteousness. This is not to say that a person or a nation should tolerate *any* evil, but merely to suggest that the real problem is to determine which evils are tolerable, which are not, and what the alternatives are. This brings us back to a more tactical level, where costs and risks must be considered.

A somewhat different version of this argument is that we *cannot* coexist with evil for very long, because in the foreseeable future either the Communist nations or the West will triumph. We are told that the only alternative to victory is defeat. But this is as fatuous an argument as the preceding, and it betrays the same kind of simpleminded, black and white, "either-or" mentality. Life and therefore history are full of evidence to the contrary. Clear-cut victories and neat solutions may be the stuff of soap operas and westerns; they bear little relationship to the ambiguous, uncertain, and compromised character of human existence. As for the specific question of whether the West and the Communist states can coexist for an indefinite period, there seems to be little doubt in the minds of most informed observers that they both can and will.

All things considered, a military attack on the Soviet Union—and China and the rest of the Communist nations—appears to be intolerably risky, terribly costly, and morally indefensible. As a matter of fact, there doesn't seem to be much dispute about this when it is stated in these terms. The proponents of "total victory" deny that their objective requires war. Unfortunately they are not at all clear on what it does in fact—and instead— entail. The following is an attempt to discover other possible answers to the first question: How, if at all, can it be achieved?

It is hypothetically possible that economic sanctions might endanger the existence, or at least soften the policies, of Communist governments. In fact, however, this is an idle dream. It may be that the West strengthens Communist regimes by trading with them, and perhaps this is an unwise policy. But there is no evidence whatever that their continued existence is dependent upon their trade with or economic assistance from the West. Boycotts of Communist nations have been attempted, and the results have been minimal. It might even be argued that they strengthen the regimes by forcing them to develop their own productive facilities more rapidly.

Another possibility is the instigation and support of revolutionary forces in Communist countries. It used to be generally accepted that a revolution in a modern state was highly unlikely or even impossible. The argument was, briefly, that governments possess a near-monopoly of the instruments of force, and they can effectively crush any revolutionary efforts. The original success of the Hungarian revolution in 1956 rather effectively demolished this theory. But what happened thereafter—namely, the Soviet intervention that crushed the rebellion—raised the problem in other terms. Would the Soviet Union stand aside if one of its satellite regimes were overthrown? Probably not. What, then, would the West do about Soviet intervention? Hungary demonstrated that it is highly unlikely that the West would force a showdown with the Soviets over such an issue. So, successful revolutions in even the satellite countries are dim possibilities at best.

But suppose that some satellite revolutions were successful. The major center of Communist power, the Soviet Union, would remain, and virtually no reputable observer believes that the Soviet regime can be overthrown from within.

Communist China presents a different problem. It is not a satellite country anymore—if it ever was—and *perhaps* a revolution could be effected there and *perhaps* this could be achieved without provoking Soviet intervention. This is highly unlikely, but not entirely implausible. But even if such an enormous and dramatic operation could be successfully engineered, the West would still be confronted with the Soviet Union.

The victory would surely not be total until the leading Communist nation was liberated.

It should be noted in passing that since the prospects that economic sanctions or internal subversion could be effective means of toppling Communist regimes have been judged to be dim or nonexistent, these policies have been discussed without reference to the risks and costs that they would entail. It is worth mentioning that these risks and costs would be very sizable. Among other things, they would increase tensions in the world, thereby increasing the possibility of reckless action, and they would alienate large segments of humanity, who would regard them as cruel or reckless. Even if one regards the preceding analysis as incorrect and believes there is a slight chance of such policies' succeeding, would the unavoidable incurrence of such costs and risks be worth it?

We have now analyzed several conceivable methods of achieving total victory over communism. It has been suggested that there is no way of accomplishing this in the foreseeable future short of an attack on the Soviet Union. Therefore, the objective will have to be judged in terms of this means of achieving it.

The fifth question asks whether there are any acceptable alternative objectives that are achievable and involve fewer risks and/or less cost and are more in accord with moral principles. The one that immediately suggests itself, of course, is the existing objective of the containment of the Communist empire. For reasons that have already been touched upon, many people find this objective unacceptable. But the burden of proof is upon the dissenters. If they can suggest a more promising objective—one that is more likely to maintain both peace and freedom—so much the better.

So, the final question is reached: On balance, in view of the above considerations, is the proposed objective of "total victory over communism" preferable to the existing objective of containment? It has been assumed in this analysis that the proposed objective is not merely a rhetorical flourish or regarded by its exponents as a desirable but admittedly very distant goal. The proposal has been taken seriously on its face as an alternative objective for American policy here and now. In those terms it is difficult to escape the conclusion[6] that it is an alternative emphatically *not* worth pursuing.

---

[6] The word "conclusion" may suggest too logical or deductive a procedure. A more precise term for this final step would perhaps be "judgment." Policy formulation is not a science or a matter of pure logic. Intelligent men, when confronted with identical information and choices, may render conflicting judgments. Policy making necessarily involves estimates and guesses about the consequences of various alternative policies. This is why a leader's capacity for sound judgment is at least as important as his intelligence.

To be comprehensive about this analysis would require a similar examination of the objective of containment, and, finally, a judgment about the comparative merits and demerits of the two objectives. This, however, would be much too lengthy a procedure at this point in the book. In a sense, the objective of containment will be under scrutiny for much of the rest of the book. Judgments about its utility should be put off at least until the end of the book. Suffice it to say at this point that it has been the operative objective of every postwar administration, Democratic and Republican. It has been criticized, pilloried, misrepresented, and even, at one time, officially abandoned. But it persists for two reasons: It has worked tolerably well in maintaining peace and freedom, and, more importantly, there are no practical alternatives.

The abandonment mentioned above occurred during the 1952 presidential campaign when the Republican party and its candidates announced that hereafter the American objective would be the "liberation" of the captive peoples under Communist rule. Containment was denounced as unworkable, cowardly, and immoral. The sobering responsibilities of office cast a rather different light on the matter, however, and "liberation" was quietly buried. Anyone who doubts its demise as official policy need look no further than the Hungarian revolution. Here was liberation achieved by a captive peoples' own efforts and presenting itself to an astonished world. Four years after the campaign rhetoric of 1952, the United States had not yet liberated any Communist country, but here was one that liberated itself. Then the Soviets, after pulling out, reintervened, and the new Hungarian government called for help. The United States and the West gave no help, for the obvious and sound reason that we were unwilling to go to war with the Soviet Union over Hungary. But the cruel myth of liberation was brutally exposed.

"Total victory over communism"—the direct descendant of "liberation" —is a utopian idea, a prime example of what can be called the "utopianism of the right." Like other utopian ideas—for example, the world rule of law—it may have some relevance for a distant and obscure future. But for the present and the foreseeable future, it has little or no utility and can create illusions and foster unwise policy judgments. These characteristics are not harmless in the thermonuclear age.

Both of the utopian ideas suggested above spring from basic misunderstandings of the realities of international politics. The utopians of the right argue that an international solution of our problems is impossible and that the United States should impose its own solution. By abandoning sentimentality and a fuzzy-minded internationalism, and exerting its great power unilaterally, the United States could effectively—and, they seem to imply, easily—solve the manifold problems confronting it in this un-precedented era and achieve a peaceful and secure world. The utopians of the left fear and despise the use of national power; they would like somehow to renounce it or abolish it. Whereas one group demands and even glorifies the use of national power, the other deprecates and abhors it.

In different ways, both of these groups share what has been aptly called "the Illusion of American Omnipotence." This illusion has taken many forms, and it crops up in diverse places and from widely differing sources; it has a strange and compelling quality. If something has gone wrong in the world, which affects American interests, the United States must be at fault or, at the very least, heavily implicated. Did the Chinese civil war result in a Communist victory? It must have because there were Communists or Communist dupes in the American Department of State. Was President Eisenhower disinvited to Japan in 1960 because left-wing mobs threatened his security? It must have been because Eisenhower's policies regarding Japan were poor ones.

The common thread that runs through these positions and this kind of reasoning is that the United States is in the final analysis responsible for nearly everything that goes on in the world. The fact that the Chinese civil war was a massive upheaval with largely indigenous roots and causes that had a dynamism of its own over which the United States had and could have had little control is either forgotten or denied. The fact that Eisenhower's policies did not create and were not responsible for traditional left-wing student activities in Japan is dismissed as irrelevant. The Illusion of American Omnipotence is a powerful and persistent element in contemporary discussions of American foreign policy. We shall have occasion to refer to it again.

The purpose of suggesting the six questions and then asking them of two currently proposed objectives for American foreign policy has been threefold. First of all, it is to be hoped that this rather lengthy and some-what tedious exercise will help to prepare the reader to make his own careful analysis of existing or proposed objectives and policies. A proposal or an existing objective or policy should not be judged on the basis of its instinctive or emotional appeal. It must be able to withstand the kind of criticism and analysis that the two superficially appealing proposals discussed above were unable to survive.

Secondly, the analysis seeks to emphasize the great complexity of foreign policy problems. To understand *and accept* the proposition that there are no easy solutions—and, in many areas, no solutions at all—is the beginning of wisdom.

Thirdly, it must be acknowledged that the choice of the two proposals for examination was by design, and it was hoped that they would be effectively laid to rest at the outset. In one form or another, they represent two states of mind that the author believes to be deadly dangerous to the Republic in this modern age. It has been emphasized that this book is based on the assumption that both "idealism" and "realism" have a role to play in American foreign policy; that both the impulse to bend every effort to create a less tense and divided world and the impulse to resist hostile nations by a strong and deterring policy are honorable and appropriate responses to the international situation in which we find ourselves. However, like any legitimate or even noble ideas or instincts, they can be corrupted or grossly distorted by men who, however admirable their intentions may be, are not capable of thinking soberly and clearly about them or the specific issues of the day.

The purpose of this chapter then has been to sensitize the reader to the complexity and intractability of international politics. To be an intelligent student of American foreign policy is to get behind the easy slogans and the glib rhetoric and to come to grips with the difficult and often insoluble problems of the real world; to understand the limitations as well as the potentialities of American foreign policy.

Selected Bibliography

Carr, Edward Hallett: *The Twenty Years' Crisis, 1919–1939*, Macmillan & Co., Ltd., London, 1946. (Available in a paperback edition, published by Harper & Row, Publishers, Incorporated, New York, 1964.) Written in 1939 in an effort to explain the impending disaster in Europe, this book remains an insightful introduction to international politics. See especially chap. 9, "Morality in International Politics."

Claude, Inis L., Jr.: *Power and International Relations*, Random House, Inc., New York, 1962. The author assumes the permanence of power in international relations and addresses himself brilliantly to the problem of establishing and maintaining reliable control over the exercise of such power.

Kennan, George F.: *American Diplomacy, 1900–1950*, The University of Chicago Press, Chicago, 1951. (Available in a paperback edition, Mentor Books, New American Library of World Literature, Inc., New York, 1964.) A devastating assault on naïveté and self-delusion in American foreign policy.

Morgenthau, Hans J.: *Politics Among Nations*, 3d ed., Alfred A. Knopf, Inc., New York, 1960. The basic work by the most influential scholarly writer on international affairs in the postwar world.

Osgood, Robert E.: *Ideals and Self-interest in America's Foreign Relations,* The University of Chicago Press, Chicago, 1953. (Available in a paperback edition, same publisher, 1964.) An analysis of the competing claims of ideals and self-interest in United States foreign policy from the late nineteenth century to World War II. The book concludes with a sophisticated effort at reconciliation.

Wolfers, Arnold: "Statesmanship and Moral Choice," *World Politics,* vol. 1, no. 2, January, 1949, pp. 175–195. Perhaps the best contemporary treatment of the dilemma implied in the title.

Chapter Two

The Formulation and Administration of American Foreign Policy: Formal and Informal Congressional Roles

chapter 2   Who makes American foreign policy? There is, of course, no simple or universally applicable answer to that question. In a tense and rapidly unfolding crisis in Berlin, an American general or lieutenant or sergeant might have to make a quick decision that would, in effect, be American policy. And when a relatively minor official in the administration makes a binding judgment about some detail in a foreign aid agreement, he is making policy.

Such decisions may or may not be trivial, and they may or may not reflect a faithful pursuit of the basic American objectives at any given time. Nonetheless, it does make sense to ignore these "details" at least temporarily and ask the broader question of who makes *major* foreign policy decisions in the United States. To raise such a question immediately brings into view the historic struggle for power between the executive and legislative branches of government.

The Constitution was written by men who sought to divide power. Their concern for "the separation of powers" is nowhere more clear than in the area of foreign policy. The President is designated the Commander in Chief of the Armed Forces. He is empowered to appoint American ambassadors and to receive foreign diplomats. And he negotiates and proposes treaties to the Senate.

The Congress, on the other hand, also has quite an impressive array of formal constitutional responsibilities. It alone has the power to declare war. The Senate accepts or rejects ambassadorial appointments, and it ratifies or rejects proposed treaties. In the latter instance, the approval of two-thirds of those present and voting is required. In addition, Congress's general power to legislate affects vital aspects of foreign policy such as trade and tariffs, immigration, and the taxation of overseas investments. Finally, and most importantly, Congress has "the power of the purse": it appropriates or fails to appropriate the money sought by the President to support his proposals.

This is all the Constitution has to say on the subject. It is characteristically brief and ambiguous, encouraging an endless rivalry between the executive and legislative branches of government. The actual distribution of power and responsibility between them in foreign affairs has evolved pragmatically in response to practical necessities, common sense, and the lasting impact of major political leaders, especially Presidents.

In this evolution, the President has become indisputably the chief formulator of American foreign policy. He sets the broad outlines of policy and determines most of the important specific actions and policies. For the most part, this is the result of practical necessity. The formulation and conduct of foreign policy, especially in modern times, require centralized authority, a chain of command, specialized knowledge, access to diverse and systematic sources of information, secrecy, efficiency, and, oftentimes, speed. These are characteristics that are hard to come by in any organization, but they are conspicuously lacking in Congress, which is organized for and pursues different objectives. Authority is widely dispersed; there is no chain of command; specialized knowledge is fragmentary and unsystematically acquired; much of its information comes from the executive branch; secrecy is seldom achieved; efficiency is frowned upon; and speed is nearly unattainable.

On the other hand, Congress does have a considerable impact on the formulation, administration, and content of American foreign policy. In this chapter, the formal and informal roles of Congress in the policy process are described and, very briefly, evaluated. An effort is made to communicate some of the "flavor" and subtlety of the congressional role, as well as the salient facts about it.

The Power to Declare War

Some of the formal powers granted to the Congress have eroded over time. The power to declare war, for example, is not as significant in practice in the twentieth century as it was in the eighteenth. If the United States should ever become involved in a major war, there would almost certainly not be enough time to seek congressional authorization. The President, as Commander in Chief, would have to take immediate action. Even more limited wars have been and probably would be entered largely at the discretion of the President. The United States has been heavily involved in the warfare in Vietnam in recent years without any declaration of war. It fought in Korea for over three years in a rather large-scale conventional war without Congress's ever officially declaring war. The Korean experience merits special attention in this connection.

The armies of Communist North Korea invaded South Korea on June 24 (Washington time), 1950. The United Nations Security Council was hurriedly called into session the following day and quickly passed a resolution demanding an end to hostilities and the withdrawal of the North Korean invaders. It requested all United Nations members "to render every assistance to the United Nations in the execution of this resolution. . . ." The Soviet Union was boycotting the Security Council at that time in protest against the Council's failure to seat the new Chinese Communist government in place of the Chinese Nationalist government. (The Communist military victory on the mainland was completed in late 1949.) It was not present, therefore, to cast a veto against the resolution.

The next day, June 26, President Truman and his advisers decided to use American naval and air forces to support the retreating South Korean forces. The following day, June 27, congressional leaders were *informed* of the decision; they had no role in it whatever. A few Senators challenged the President's authority to commit armed forces in this fashion, but for the most part the reaction in and out of Congress was favorable.

That evening, the Security Council passed another resolution, proposed by the United States. It recommended that member nations furnish such assistance to South Korea as was needed to repel the attack and restore peace. Again, passage was made possible by the absence of the Soviet delegate. On June 30, the President ordered American ground troops into the battle. Again, congressional leaders were merely *informed.*

In sum, Congress did not formally or informally participate in these important decisions, which in effect committed the United States to war.

The decision to intervene was, at the time, a popular one. Most of those who disapproved of the President's failure to obtain congressional authorization nonetheless supported the intervention itself. Moreover, Congress readily appropriated funds for the prosecution of the war. Partly for these reasons, the episode did not immediately become the occasion for a major constitutional crisis or even for much of a debate.

The main lesson of this experience is that a President who is so inclined is clearly able to commit the United States to battle. This was underlined once again by President Kennedy's independent handling of the Cuban missile crisis in October, 1962 (see Chapter 7).

The power to declare war is not, however, altogether a dead letter. Its force in any given circumstance depends upon a wide variety of factors, including a President's conception of his powers and responsibilities, his desire to cultivate good relations with Congress, his need for appropriations to support a given action, and the specific conditions under consideration. It may be that all of these factors will combine in such a way as to suggest that a President should seek congressional sanction for a particular policy. Something like this apparently happened during the Indochina crisis of 1954.[1] The French had been engaged for many years in a losing battle against indigenous nationalists and Communists who sought to end French colonial rule. By the spring of 1954, the French position had deteriorated to the point where apparently only an intervention by the United States could reverse the trend. A weak and uncertain French government made an appeal to the United States for such an intervention. The highest echelons of the Eisenhower administration, including the President, at one point apparently were prepared to accede to this request. The Korean War had been over less than one year, and the relatively new Republican officials were not anxious to drag the United States back into an armed conflict. But they were even less willing to sacrifice Indochina.

The memory of what had happened politically to President Truman, after the Korean War had turned into a long and bitter stalemate, was,

---

[1] The following account is based on an article by Chalmers M. Roberts, "The Day We Didn't Go to War," *The Reporter*, vol. 11, no. 4, pp. 31–35, Sept. 14, 1954. This extraordinary piece of journalism may or may not be entirely accurate, but it is at the very least a highly plausible and instructive account of an important episode in recent American foreign policy.

however, very much alive. As time wore on, Truman had been increasingly criticized for having taken the United States into the war without a formal declaration of war by Congress. Moreover, most of this criticism had, naturally enough, come from Republicans, many of whom began to refer to the conflict as "Truman's War." For this and other reasons, the Eisenhower administration decided that a congressional resolution authorizing the use of American air and naval forces should be requested. As a preliminary to a formal request, Secretary of State John Foster Dulles and the Chairman of the Joint Chiefs of Staff, Admiral Arthur Radford, invited the leaders of Congress to a meeting at the Department of State. Eight congressional leaders—three Republicans and five Democrats—attended the meeting.

Secretary Dulles and Admiral Radford announced their intention to seek the authorizing resolution and explained their reasoning. It was hinted that the passage of such a resolution might by itself eliminate any need for its implementation. Then the congressmen began to ask a series of questions. They wanted to know whether it was not likely that American ground troops would be needed in addition to air power. The answer given was indefinite. They wanted to know what the other three members of the Joint Chiefs of Staff thought of the idea of intervention. It developed that all of them opposed it. They wanted to know whether our European allies had been consulted. They had not.

The congressional leaders were unimpressed, and the meeting came to an inconclusive end. The administration then proceeded to attempt to line up support among its European allies. These efforts proved fruitless, with Great Britain's refusal to support intervention the most significant development. A few weeks after the original meeting with congressional leaders, the United States advised the French that we would not intervene. One of the reasons given was that such action would require congressional approval. And that approval had never been formally sought.

The decision not to intervene was doubtless the product of a variety of factors, as all decisions are. But there is little doubt that the probing questions and demonstrated reluctance of congressional leaders affected that decision significantly. There is, in other words, a real possibility that the United States, wisely or unwisely, would have gone to war in Indochina in 1954 but for the restricting influence of prominent congressional opinion.

The significance of this can, of course, be overrated. If the administration had been more confident about its original decision to intervene, it could have done so, with or without the support of allies or Congress. In technical, legal terms it probably had the constitutional authority to do so; in practical terms, it certainly had the power. But largely for domestic political reasons, it chose not to do that, and then, in part because of congressional resistance, it decided not to intervene. The final subtlety is that there is little doubt that Congress would have passed an authorizing resolution if it had been formally asked to do so. To refuse to grant such a request would seriously compromise a President's stature before the world; prudence would have dictated acquiescence. On the other hand, prudence also dictated that the request not be made in the face of strong congressional opposition, even if privately expressed. Such are the complexities of "the war power" in executive-congressional relations.

A somewhat similar situation arose a few months later, and this time the President did formally seek congressional authorization in advance of possible actions. In January, 1955, President Eisenhower asked for and received congressional sanction for military action if it should be needed to protect Formosa and the Pescadores Islands from the Chinese Communists. Needless to say, many members of Congress—especially Democrats, of course—who voted for the resolution disapproved of this request, arguing that the President as Commander in Chief already had such authority. Moreover, many felt that the request put undue pressure on Congress, which could scarcely repudiate the President once he made public his wishes.

If by now the reader is thoroughly confused about the precise distribution of power and responsibility between the President and Congress regarding the initiation of hostilities, this is as it should be. In talking about our system of divided or separated powers, we sometimes give the impression that one can draw neat and clear-cut lines between the powers of the executive and legislative branches. But this is not true. A more accurate, if less understandable, way to describe our system of government is to say that a few powers are clearly executive, a few are clearly legislative, and the rest are *shared* powers. Moreover, the precise distribution of power varies over time and from issue to issue.

A consideration of other constitutional grants of power will further illustrate these propositions.

The Power to Approve or Reject Appointments

The Senate, as noted above, can reject a presidential ambassadorial or cabinet appointment. Under some circumstances, such a repudiation might have important policy implications.[2] Yet the Senate has never rejected an ambassadorial nomination, and it has rejected a nomination to the Cabinet on only eight occasions—only twice since 1867. None of these eight rejections involved a nomination for Secretary of State. The general prin-

---

[2] The rather sensationalized and crudely oversimplified best-selling novel by Allen Drury, *Advise and Consent*, Doubleday & Company, Inc., Garden City, N.Y., 1959, dealt with precisely such a situation: Senate consideration of a President's controversial nomination for Secretary of State. Although the particular foreign policy dispute related in this novel is not likely ever to occur, some such confrontation between an innovating President and a resistant Senate is well within the realm of the possible.

ciple has been that a President should be permitted to appoint whomever he wishes in these positions of considerable authority.

Here again, however, it would be a mistake to conclude that the congressional—in this case, senatorial—power is of no importance. Although no ambassadorial nomination has been formally rejected, some have been withdrawn in the face of strong opposition in the Senate. And undoubtedly many more have never been formally proposed for fear of the reaction that would be provoked in the Senate.

Oddly enough, this power has a positive dimension as well as the more obvious negative one. Quick and overwhelming confirmation of an appointment can have the effect of bolstering a man or even a policy. In April, 1959, the cancer-stricken John Foster Dulles was forced to retire as Secretary of State. President Eisenhower, after much delay, reluctantly forwarded the nomination of Christian Herter as the successor. The Democratically controlled Senate acted with unusual dispatch in confirming the appointment unanimously. Majority Leader Lyndon Johnson told the Senate that "I want the world to know that this nation is united behind the Secretary of State whose nomination is about to be confirmed."

What is the significance of this senatorial power to approve or reject appointments? Again, there is no simple answer. There is no way of knowing how much this latent power affects presidential judgments in nominating ambassadors and Secretaries of State and Defense. Moreover, it is by no means certain that there will never be an outright rejection of a nominee. In recent years, a few serious efforts to this end have been made; one day one of them might be successful. In sum, it is probably fair to say that this power, largely latent, has been of only marginal significance and is likely —but not certain—to remain so.

The Power to Approve or Reject Treaties

In policy terms, a more important senatorial role is involved in the constitutional requirement that two-thirds of the Senators present and voting must concur in a treaty proposed by the President. This constitutes a formidable veto power, irrespective of the fact that it is seldom invoked. Its most famous use, of course, was the Senate's failure to ratify the Treaty of Versailles after World War I. Opinions differ regarding the precise impact that this had on American foreign policy and international politics generally in the 1920s and 1930s, but there is little doubt that its effects were substantial.

It should be noted in passing that most agreements between governments nowadays are "executive agreements" rather than formal treaties. An "executive agreement" is any international agreement other than a treaty. It may be made solely by the authority of the executive branch or it may be authorized by an act of Congress or by a provision of a treaty. Executive agreements range in importance all the way from the specific accord establishing a cultural exchange program to the historic exchange in 1940 between the United States and Great Britain of 50 overage American destroyers for a 99-year lease on British naval bases in the Western Atlantic, and the Yalta agreements. Neither the courts, nor Congress, nor the executive branch has ever officially declared what categories of agreements should be treaties and what can appropriately be negotiated as executive agreements.

This has naturally given rise to fears that a President can commit the nation on fundamental matters without obtaining congressional or at least senatorial approval. That possibility does in fact exist, but it is a slim one for several reasons. First of all, Presidents are likely to honor and respect the clear intention of the Constitution that the Senate ratify major international accords. Second, political prudence requires that they do so. Any President who failed to respect the unwritten boundary between what he can appropriately do alone and what requires senatorial or congressional sanction would be undermining his position with Congress and the public. Finally, and closely related to the last consideration, many important agreements require implementation by statute or appropriation of money or both. In these instances, of course, Congress will effectively retain its power to thwart the President.[3]

In sum, the respective appropriate spheres of treaties and executive agreements are technically obscure but politically and practically rather clear. Perhaps the most conspicuous policy area where this statement applies is disarmament. In 1963, for example, President Kennedy conceivably could have made an executive agreement with the Soviet Union and Great Britain banning nuclear testing everywhere but underground. He chose, however, to make the agreement as a formal treaty, thereby necessitating a two-thirds concurrence in the Senate. Aside from any desire that he may have had to respect the Senate's judgment on such a grave matter, President Kennedy was driven by the demands of political life in the United States to submit the matter to the Senate.

So, the treaty remains an important device in United States foreign relations, and the Senate's power to accept or reject a treaty is important and respected. On the other hand, and for reasons unrelated to the issue just discussed, it should be recognized that this negative power is somewhat circumscribed in practice. Only the most irresponsible of Senators would want to use it lightly. To reject a presidential proposal, negotiated and

---

[3] For a learned and persuasive discussion of this intricate issue, see Arthur E. Sutherland, Jr., "Restricting the Treaty Power," *Harvard Law Review*, vol. 65, no. 8, pp. 1305–1338, June, 1952. This article is reproduced in Robert G. McCloskey (ed.), *Essays in Constitutional Law*, Alfred A. Knopf, Inc., New York, 1957, pp. 216–251.

agreed upon with a foreign government, is a serious matter. In other words, the Senate often feels obligated to ratify a proposed treaty, because to do otherwise would be to humiliate the President at home and abroad. Except for a few reckless ones, Senators will assume such a responsibility only when they are convinced that a proposed treaty is clearly and dangerously not in the national interest. Such occasions, obviously, are bound to be rare, and the result has been that only fourteen treaties have been rejected by the Senate, and only two of these rejections occurred in the twentieth century.[4]

To accept or reject a proposed treaty is not, however, the only choice open to the Senate. The Senate can attach reservations to its acceptance, as it did, for example, in 1946 when agreeing to accept the "compulsory jurisdiction" of the International Court of Justice. It specifically exempted three categories of disputes, including those "with regard to matters which are essentially within the domestic jurisdiction of the United States of America as determined by the United States of America. . . ." The last eight words of that quotation constitute the famous Connally Reservation, and they involve a substantial dilution of the United States' acceptance of the World Court's jurisdiction.[5]

Moreover, the Senate can make its approval conditional upon some alteration of the terms of the treaty, thereby necessitating its renegotiation. Or, less formally, a group of Senators can request an administration to provide certain specific assurances in connection with a treaty. This happened in 1963 regarding the partial nuclear test ban treaty. There was, of course, widespread concern that the Soviet Union might break the treaty and disadvantage the United States technologically. Accordingly, during the hearings a group of Senators asked the administration for a written

---

[4] One of these two was the Treaty of Versailles alluded to above, and the other was a 1934 treaty between the United States and Canada for a joint development of the St. Lawrence River. It is interesting to note that the essential provisions of this latter treaty ultimately became law in 1954 when the House and the Senate approved an executive agreement to establish a St. Lawrence Seaway.

It should be noted in passing that voting it down is not the only way to reject a treaty. The Senate can simply refuse to vote on a proposed treaty. The President is then faced with the choice of withdrawing the treaty or of letting it remain before the Senate. As of July, 1963, there were twenty-eight treaties still pending before the Senate. Major proposals are, however, almost always brought to a vote.

[5] The resolution that accepted "compulsory jurisdiction" was not technically a treaty. In endorsing the United Nations Treaty in 1945, the Senate had already approved of the United States' becoming a member of the International Court of Justice. The resolution before them was to go further and permit the President to declare that the United States would accept the compulsory jurisdiction of the Court. After some debate, the Senate decided to treat it as a treaty, taking it up in "executive session" and requiring a two-thirds vote for approval. This interpretation has persisted, incidentally, and it is generally assumed that efforts to repeal the Connally Reservation to the resolution would have to receive the support of two-thirds of the Senate rather than a simple majority.

pledge that certain specified steps required for a continuing high state of readiness to resume tests would in fact be taken. These Senators were in effect making a separate agreement with the administration, not technically attached to, but inextricably bound up with, the treaty itself.

One other aspect of this constitutional provision merits attention. The Constitution provides that the President shall have the power to make treaties "by and with the advice and consent of the Senate." The words "by and" are superfluous and need not concern us; the consent aspect has just been discussed. But the word "advice" raises some interesting possibilities. It could be argued that this provision requires the President formally to seek the advice of the entire Senate before or during the negotiation of a treaty. This would be difficult to do in practice, and no one seriously expects it to be done. What does frequently happen, however, is that the President seeks the advice of leading Senators regarding specific aspects of a proposed treaty or executive agreement.

The motive for such consultation, however, is usually more tactical than substantive; that is, a President is usually more interested in finding out what the Senate is likely to accept or in giving the appearance of being solicitous about senatorial opinion than he is in the independent judgments of the Senators about the substance of the treaty. One result of this provision and the practical activity that it suggests is that Senators are often found on United States delegations to treaty-making sessions, such as the sporadic and tedious negotiations on disarmament.

Occasionally, however, senatorial participation in the drafting of a treaty is much more substantial. In 1948, the United States, Canada, and many European governments began the negotiations that led in the following year to the historic North Atlantic Treaty. Several conditions combined to induce President Truman to bring leading Senators into the negotiation process at the outset. In the first place, the projected treaty would mark a revolution in American foreign policy: it would be our first peacetime military alliance, and it would effectively commit us in advance to the defense of Western Europe. Moreover, a presidential election was coming up in the fall, and the President wanted to assure the Republican-controlled Congress that the treaty would not become associated only with the Democratic administration. This nonpartisan approach to the matter had been facilitated in June of 1948 by Senate passage of the Vandenberg Resolution. This resolution, among other things, expressed it as "the sense of the Senate" that the United States should associate itself with "regional and other collective arrangements for individual and collective self-defense. . . ."

Partly because of this, Senators Vandenberg and Connally—the ranking Republican and Democrat, respectively, on the Foreign Relations Committee—were asked to work closely with representatives of the State Department as negotiations progressed. Because of their formal positions of authority and because their views were broadly representative of the Senate, these two men were almost in a position to speak for the entire Senate. To a considerable extent, the treaty negotiations were triangular. The State Department sought concurrence for each major provision with the Senators as well as with the other nations. When the long and intricate procedure was concluded in early 1949, the treaty was nearly assured of passage. It is not clear how much the two Senators—and their colleagues on the committee, who were also consulted from time to time—affected the final provisions of the treaty. Apparently, their role was primarily to legitimate the treaty, not to take the initiative in formulating its provisions.[6] Nonetheless, this episode was an unusually literal fulfillment of the constitutional requirement that the President seek the advice, as well as the consent, of the Senate.

An even more striking and atypical example occurred in 1952 under similar conditions. The Truman administration, soon to leave office, was negotiating a peace treaty with Japan. The chief negotiator was John Foster Dulles, the leading Republican spokesman on foreign policy. Dulles met frequently with the Foreign Relations Subcommittee on Far Eastern Affairs and discussed alternative proposals with the members. Just prior to the treaty's formal submission to the Senate, there developed a strong concern in the Senate over whether Japan might negotiate a separate treaty with Communist China. The two Senators who had worked most closely with Dulles made a trip to Japan and, along with Dulles, told the Japanese Premier that fear in the Senate over such a separate treaty was endangering the prospects of ratification of the United States–Japanese treaty. The Premier thereupon sent a formal letter to Dulles advising him that Japan did not intend to negotiate a peace treaty with the Peking regime. The treaty then passed the Senate easily.[7]

As in the earlier case, it is not clear how much initiative the Senators assumed in the formulation process. It is clear, however, that their advice was sought from the earliest stages and that they met frequently with Dulles. Moreover, they actually performed a diplomatic function in talking with the Japanese Premier and inducing him to write his letter to Dulles. In sum, the "advice" aspect of the Senate's role was taken much more seriously than usual.

---

[6] See James A. Robinson, *Congress and Foreign Policy-Making*, The Dorsey Press, Inc., Homewood, Ill., 1962, pp. 46–48. Robinson relies heavily for his account on Stephen K. Bailey and Howard D. Samuel, *Congress at Work*, Holt, Rinehart and Winston, Inc., New York, 1952, pp. 387–388.
[7] See Robinson, *op. cit.*, pp. 50–52. Robinson cites Bernard C. Cohen, *The Political Process and Foreign Policy: The Making of the Japanese Peace Settlement*, Princeton University Press, Princeton, N.J., 1957.

The General Power to Legislate

Another constitutionally ordained role for Congress noted above is its general power of legislation. A large percentage of the basic American objectives and policies in international affairs requires supporting legislation. Included herein is the specific constitutional provision that "The Congress shall have the power . . . to regulate commerce with foreign nations. . . ." Throughout much of our history, Congress guarded its prerogatives in this area with great jealousy and specificity. Recently, beginning with the Reciprocal Trade Act of 1934 and continuing through the historic Trade Expansion Act of 1962, Congress has shown itself more willing to delegate large responsibilities in this area to the executive branch. Despite a narrow escape in the House of Representatives in 1955 this trend is not likely to be reversed. It is, however, impossible to predict what would happen, for example, in an economic crisis when great pressures would be brought to bear on Congress to establish more restrictive tariffs and quotas. But whatever the future may hold, the fact remains that Congress retains the power, even if unused, to do whatever it pleases in this area which so crucially affects the conduct of foreign affairs.

Similarly, it was Congress that initiated the famous neutrality legislation beginning in 1935. Congress was determined to keep the United States out of any war that might develop out of the emerging clash of policies among the European powers. A substantial percentage of the population was convinced that our entry into the Great War (World War I) had been a mistake and one that could have been avoided. It was determined not to repeat this experience, and Congress sought to accomplish this by passing laws that, among other things, prohibited the sale or shipment of arms to any belligerent power. President Roosevelt did not share this interpretation of history, and, more importantly, he believed that such a total ban might endanger American security. He sought to have the proposed ban disposed of in committee, but he failed. So did all his efforts to make the embargo discretionary—that is, enabling the President to authorize the sale of arms to certain belligerents (France and Great Britain, for example). Congress was dictating foreign policy in a vital area that had a substantial—and unfortunate—effect upon the situation in Europe. It was not until after the outbreak of hostilities in the fall of 1939 that Roosevelt was able to induce Congress to alter the legislation so as to permit belligerent nations to purchase arms in this country.

The modern counterpart to this is the congressional urge to involve itself in trade policy as it affects Communist nations. While the trend, as noted above, has been toward the reduction of trade barriers and the delegation to the executive branch of vast powers in this field, the special problems raised in trading with Communist countries have engendered

great congressional interest. As in the case of the earlier neutrality legislation, congressional concerns are political, not economic. In the present
instance, it is feared that trading with the Communist nations strengthens
them, thereby reducing the possibility of eliminating the existing regimes
and also contributing to their capacity to wage the cold war or a hot war
against non-Communist nations. Thus it was that the only important setback suffered by the Kennedy administration in the passage of the 1962
Trade Act had to do with this issue. The act directed the administration
"as soon as practicable" to withdraw the "most favored nation" treatment—
by which a nation is granted any tariff concessions granted to any other
nation—from any country "controlled by Communism." This directly
affected trade with Poland and Yugoslavia, and was strongly resisted by
the administration, which argued that such a provision would only serve
to push these countries into closer dependence on other Communist countries. But feelings against trading with and providing aid to Poland and
Yugoslavia were running especially high in 1962, and the administration
suffered defeat in both areas.

The most impressive example of congressional influence in a matter
impinging on foreign policy has to do with immigration. Congress has
jealously guarded its prerogatives here and actually has succeeded in retaining the initiative. Presidential proposals regarding immigration policy
have traditionally been discarded. Congress—and within Congress, certain
key members—has initiated as well as determined the final details of immigration legislation. As this is written (in early 1965) the McCarran-
Walter Act of 1952 is still the basic law in this field. [Its popular name
comes from its two principal sponsors, the late Senator Pat McCarran
(D-Nev.) and the late Representative Francis Walter (D-Pa.), two unusually conservative non-Southern Democrats.] It was vetoed by President
Truman, but the veto was overridden by Congress.[8]

Not only has Congress initiated and determined immigration legislation,
it has also controlled how and by whom the legislation will be administered. This phenomenon merits special attention because it applies, in less
extreme fashion, to many other policy areas. It is generally recognized that
the President and his administration—the executive branch of government
—participate in the legislative process. The President is often referred to,

[8] There are some indications that both the law and the locus of influence regarding
immigration policy may be altered soon. In 1963, soon after the death of Representative
Walter, President Kennedy proposed a radically different immigration program. It
failed to reach the floor of either house. But in January, 1965, President Johnson proposed similar legislation and there appeared to be some chance for its passage in the
liberal atmosphere of the 89th Congress. If it does pass in roughly the same form as
that proposed by the President, it would fundamentally alter immigration policy and
suggest that at least the initiative, if not the final authority, regarding such policy had
shifted to the executive branch. Such changes could be ephemeral, however.

with much accuracy, as the "chief legislator."[9] But what is less often under-stood is that Congress—or, more precisely, individual members of Con-gress—often controls the details of administrative decisions. Administra-tion, like legislation, is a shared responsibility in the United States.

The most conspicuous example of this in recent years was the control that the late Representative Walter exercised over the administration of the immigration law that bore his name. Walter was for many years the chairman of the Immigration and Nationality Subcommittee of the House Judiciary Committee. From this position, he not only controlled legislation affecting immigration, but he also effectively controlled the Bureau of Security and Consular Affairs in the Department of State, which was re-sponsible for administering immigration and nationality laws, and issuing passports and visas. He did not exercise a case-by-case control over these matters, but he was able to impose his judgment on almost any specific matter in which he became interested. His power in this domain was never more effectively demonstrated than when he opposed President Kennedy's initial suggestion for the position of Administrator of the Bureau. This appointment was not subject to senatorial approval and when the new President went through with the appointment, it appeared that Walter's authority had been effectively undermined and that executive independ-ence had been established. But the appearance was illusory. The new administrator soon resigned, and some months later a man supported by Walter was appointed. In all, it took Walter about one year to reestablish his control.

The above is, of course, an extreme example. A more ordinary pattern is for members of Congress to have a considerable influence on adminis-trative decisions but not to control them. One notable example of this is in the area of defense policy. Constituencies, and therefore members of Congress, develop an interest or stake in a military facility or a defense contract, and they naturally seek to protect this interest. The location of military installations in this country has a demonstrable relationship to the geographical areas best represented on the House and Senate Armed

---

[9] It is assumed that the reader understands at least in general terms the reasons for this appellation. Almost all important legislation originates in the executive branch. It con-stitutes "the President's program." The President thereafter attempts to influence legislative action through a wide variety of techniques. He may appeal "over the head of Congress" to the nation over radio and television in an effort to drum up "grass roots" support; he may more subtly seek to have local pressures brought to bear on a congressman; he can send messages and emissaries to Capitol Hill to argue the merits of his proposals (to assist in this operation, the White House and all the major depart-ments and agencies have liaison personnel assigned to Congress; they are, in effect, lobbyists for the administration); he has weekly meetings with the congressional leaders of his own party and occasional meetings with leaders of both parties; he has a declining but nonetheless tempting amount of patronage to negotiate for votes with; and he can attempt to invoke the prestige of his office by making personal appeals to legislators. Presidents view this role with varying degrees of enthusiasm and have varying amounts of success in exercising it.

Services Committees. The chairmen of these committees are both from Georgia, which is liberally sprinkled with military installations. One wag predicted that "one more base would sink the State."[10]

The awarding of defense contracts to industries is also a matter that engages the attention of many members of Congress. It is impossible to document the proposition that decisions regarding which company should be awarded a given defense contract are seriously influenced by pressure from members and committees of Congress. But it is surely true that such contract awards take place in a highly politicized context, and it would be astonishing and unique if congressional wishes were ignored. Much of the sound and fury, for example, surrounding the 1963 congressional investigation of the Department of Defense's decision to award the contract for the "TFX"—tactical experimental fighter—airplane grew out of suspicions on both sides that considerations other than monetary and technical ones had motivated the other side.

The distribution of military installations and defense contracts around the country does not have an obvious or necessary connection with defense or foreign policy. But it is suggestive of the extent to which congressional influence pervades what might appear to be purely "administrative" decisions. Moreover, major foreign policy decisions cannot escape this complex and subtle congressional influence. Decisions about which weapons systems—and, therefore, which defense strategy—should be adopted or further developed or abandoned are not always made for exclusively technical or strategic reasons. They are sometimes affected by the vested interests that develop in a massive defense establishment and that are guarded by congressional watchdogs.

It is not being suggested here that this kind of influence based on reasons not directly related to foreign or defense policy considerations is generally decisive; it seldom is.[11] But it does serve to illustrate further that members of Congress can and do affect the administrative process.

Returning to the more traditional question of how much power Congress has in the original formulation of policy—as distinguished from how much influence it exerts over its administration—it needs to be emphasized that there are no constitutional prohibitions against Congress's playing an ever-widening role and assuming the initiative beyond such relatively peripheral matters as immigration. And occasionally this latent power is exercised. One of the most conspicuous examples in recent years led in 1958 to the passage of the Monroney Resolution.[12] The Senate resolution

[10] As quoted in "The 'Military Lobbying'—Its Impact on Congress, Nation," *Congressional Quarterly*, vol. 619, no. 12, p. 469, March 24, 1961. This is a valuable article.
[11] See the broader discussion of this problem in Chap. 3.
[12] See James A. Robinson, *The Monroney Resolution: Congressional Initiative in Foreign Policy Making*, Holt, Rinehart and Winston, Inc., New York, 1959, and Robinson, *Congress and Foreign Policy-Making, op. cit.*, pp. 61–62, 70–92.

urged the Eisenhower administration to investigate the possibility of co-operating with other governments in the creation of an international development fund based on less conservative fiscal policies and interest rates than those prevailing in the International Bank for Reconstruction and Development (or World Bank). Monroney's original proposals were opposed by the administration, but, with several revisions, they prevailed, and the International Development Association was launched in 1960 with the United States participating.

So the possibility of congressional initiatives in foreign policy does exist and conceivably could be exercised more frequently and on matters of more importance than the one just described. It seems almost certain, however, that in practice nearly all the initiatives will continue to come from the executive branch.

One other dimension of the general legislative power should be mentioned. As noted above, the Constitution empowers the President to send and receive ambassadors. This implies that the President alone shall determine which states and which governments shall be formally recognized by the United States. And, in fact, this interpretation is accepted by all concerned. But Congress is not without its weapons even here. Nearly every year now, for example, the House and Senate adopt unanimous resolutions expressing their opposition to the recognition of Red China. It has become a ritual that few people take very seriously, but it unquestionably inhibits any reappraisal of American policy regarding the Far East.

Moreover, although an administration could theoretically recognize Red China anyway, it would then be faced with a hostile Congress, which might refuse to appropriate any funds to set up an embassy in Peking, or might retaliate in some other area. The upshot of it is that even when power is apparently clearly separated and assigned to one branch, the other branch is not powerless.

The Appropriations Power

We turn now to the most potent congressional power of all: the power to appropriate or not appropriate money. Even aside from defense expenditures—which Congress seldom balks at and sometimes, in a reversal of ordinary roles, urges on the executive branch—foreign policy is an expensive aspect of the American budget. By far the largest item is foreign aid. This has been a central part of American foreign policy since 1947 and will be discussed at length in Chapter 8. For present purposes, the central point is that the program of assistance is entirely dependent upon the willingness, or lack of it, of Congress to provide the funds. And, unlike its attitude toward defense appropriations, Congress exercises this authority with considerable independence. For fiscal 1964, for example, the President requested $4.52 billion, and Congress appropriated $3.0 billion, a huge cut of just over one-third.

Moreover, sometimes in the authorization process and sometimes in the appropriations process, Congress vitally affects the character and purpose, as well as the size, of the foreign aid program. Congress becomes involved in the smallest specifics of foreign aid policy formulation. Although most of the details bear the basic imprint of their executive branch origins, on some matters Congress goes well beyond mere adjustment. As might be expected, the issues most often affected by such legislative initiative are those that touch emotional responses tied directly or indirectly to the cold war.

In 1962, for example, Congress made an especially determined effort to impose its judgment on foreign aid policy. In addition to cutting the President's request by over $1 billion—to just under $4 billion—it imposed, among others, the following restrictions on the use of foreign aid funds: No aid[13] could be given to nations that either provided items of "strategic value" to Cuba, or permitted ships under their registry to do so. Unless the President decided to make an exception that he deemed would be in the national interest, no aid could be given to a nation that was providing Cuba with economic aid or whose ships were carrying economic aid to Cuba. (The House wanted to eliminate the presidential waiver power.) Congress also continued several earlier restrictions that it had imposed, such as barring military aid to any Communist nation, and barring aid to any nation that provided military aid to Cuba. In addition, Congress ordered the suspension of all aid to nations that expropriated American-owned property without "just compensation." The administration opposed most of these significant restrictions on its discretion.

These examples of congressional involvement in the formulation of American foreign policy are by no means exhaustive. In 1962 alone, for example, Congress also affected foreign policy in the following ways: It approved the purchase of up to $100 million worth of United Nations bonds; it appropriated $59 million for an expanded Peace Corps; it authorized the administration to lend up to $2 billion to the International Monetary Fund; it appropriated $73 million to pay World War II damage claims by the Philippines; it extended the President's authority to regulate the imports of certain agricultural commodities and textiles; it adopted resolutions expressing congressional attitudes toward Communist threats against Berlin and from Cuba; and it authorized the President to call up 150,000 more reservists without declaring a national emergency.

Congress gives the executive branch nearly everything it wants in only one area: national security. It has already been noted that defense budgets are seldom trimmed these days. Even more unusual is Congress's willingness to appropriate untold billions of dollars for secret operations that it

---

[13] "No aid" as used in this section is not an altogether accurate phrase. In all foreign aid bills, the President is provided with a modest "contingency fund," which he may use in any manner he sees fit. This discretion is usually subject only to restrictions on the amount of such funds that any one nation may receive.

knows little or nothing about. During World War II, the atomic bomb was developed and built with funds hidden in appropriation bills in such a manner that only a few members of Congress were aware of their existence. During World War II, Senator Harry S Truman had been chairman of the Senate Committee to Investigate the National Defense Program, a committee that earned a reputation for the thoroughness of its investigation into defense expenditures. And he was elected Vice President of the United States in 1944. Yet he did not find out about the atomic project until he suddenly became President in April, 1945.

The most striking contemporary example of congressional complaisance of this kind has to do with the Central Intelligence Agency (CIA). This organization has a sizable budget and a large bureaucracy, but its exact size and cost are known only to a few people. Congress has thus far been satisfied with this unusual condition, but a few Senators and Representatives have insistently proposed that a joint congressional committee be established to oversee the CIA, much as the Joint Committee on Atomic Energy serves as a watchdog over the Atomic Energy Commission (AEC).

The Investigative Power

Implicit in the power to legislate and the power to appropriate is the right to have access to the kinds and amounts of information necessary to the formulation of an intelligent and independent judgment. Members of Congress have many sources of information about foreign affairs, including the press, radio, television, their travels abroad, and their formal inquiries to and informal contacts with members of the executive offices that administer programs and policies. All executive departments have liaison staffs charged with keeping Congress informed about their operations and, when possible, seeking congressional support. The Department of State, for example, has an Assistant Secretary of State for Congressional Relations. He and his rather substantial staff spend much of their time in congressional offices, and all of their time is devoted to establishing good relations and policy agreement between "downtown"—that is, the executive branch; in this instance, the Department of State—and "the Hill"—that is, Capitol Hill, where the capitol and other congressional offices are located.

A special word needs to be said about the "informal" contacts between executive officials, including military officers, and members of Congress. These contacts have varying degrees of importance and "legitimacy." Some are merely innocuous departures from the formal channels of communication, as when a congressman calls a friend in the State Department to get his judgment about a minor policy matter. Sometimes, however, the formal channels are wholly circumvented by executive branch officials who develop and cultivate congressional allies—or vice versa—for some project or policy that they vigorously support. Unauthorized releases of information—

"leaks"—to the press and to friendly congressmen are common in Washington. Judged in terms of their contribution to the rational formulation of policy, they range all the way from the courageous and admirable to the petty and irresponsible. Most fall somewhere in between. All contribute to the further blurring of any neat separation or division of responsibility between the executive and legislative branches of government.

But none of these sources, nor all of them together, are sufficient to provide Congress with enough information to formulate an independent judgment about foreign policy. For this purpose, among others, congressional committees hold extensive hearings and receive testimony from a wide variety of people, including officials of the executive branch, fellow congressmen, representatives of interested groups, specialists, and ordinary citizens. Most of these hearings are held in connection with a specific piece of legislation. Others are held with no specific or immediate legislative object in view. These latter are usually called "investigations," and often are accompanied by extensive field investigations by a trained staff, which operates along the lines of the Federal Bureau of Investigation (FBI). The distinction between hearings and investigations is not especially important, however; they all have as their ostensible purpose[14] the gathering of information that will better enable Congress to legislate intelligently. For the purposes of this book, no attempt will be made to distinguish carefully between ordinary hearings and investigations.

These hearings affect policy indirectly in that they provide members of Congress and interested segments of the public with information and insights into official policy. But they also play a more direct role in the policy process. There are several reasons for this. First of all, the mere fact that such hearings are inevitable acts as a restraint upon any administration. It knows that whatever it does or proposes to do will, sooner or later, be held up to congressional and public gaze and scrutiny. The existence of a free press makes this unavoidable to some extent, but the existence of Congress makes it much more certain. Congressional interest in American foreign policy—as distinguished from congressional influence over American foreign policy—knows no bounds, and the congressional capacity to publicize its questions and findings is impressive. More than the executive branch of any other major nation, an American administration has reason

[14] Some hearings, of course, have no real legislative purpose; or at least that purpose is of secondary importance. The variety and purposes of congressional hearings and investigations are as diverse as the motives of those holding them. Members of Congress are not merely, or even largely, objective pursuers of facts, figures, and judgments. They are also politicians, and hearings can serve such purposes as providing publicity for committee members, harassing private citizens or groups who may hold unpopular or subversive views, or embarrassing a past or present administration. It follows, therefore, that congressional hearings run the gamut from sober and intelligent inquiries to sensational and even reckless publicity stunts. The latter receive more public attention, but the former are more typical.

to fear the scrutiny and possible disfavor of the legislative branch. "How do they feel (or will they feel) about this on the Hill?" is a question that no prudent American executive official, including the President, can afford to ignore.

Secondly, some hearings are specifically designed to affect policy by forcing a lackadaisical or reluctant administration to alter some specific policy or set of polices. A recent example of this occurred in the late 1950s when the opposition Democrats, who controlled Congress, held a variety of hearings that had as their objective the intensification of America's space program after the first Soviet sputnik was sent into orbit. The hearings were not designed merely to acquire information to support the appropriation of more money for space programs; there was already sufficient sentiment in Congress for this. Nor were they designed primarily to make partisan gains against the Republican administration, though this was certainly an element in their motivation. They sought primarily to goad the reluctant administration into adopting a sharply more ambitious space program and to do so quickly.

Thirdly, some hearings—usually, in this instance, officially labeled "investigations"—are designed for less specific and more comprehensive purposes. They may be sober and responsible inquiries into the general character and direction of American policy, such as the Senate Foreign Relations Committee's occasional "Review of Foreign Policy" hearings. Or they may be reckless and irresponsible exercises in demagoguery, such as the productions staged by the late Senator Joseph R. McCarthy in the early 1950s. Responsible or irresponsible, these hearings are not designed to serve any immediate or specific legislative purpose; rather, they seek to stimulate public concern and discussion and to affect the basic assumptions and directions of foreign policy. Their impact ranges from imperceptible to substantial. It is impossible to measure the precise impact that Senator McCarthy had on American foreign policy in the early 1950s prior to his condemnation by the Senate in 1954, but it was certainly considerable. The damage done to the Foreign Service alone by his unsubstantiated charges of subversion was little short of disastrous. Recruitment of high-quality officers fell off sharply, morale was very low, and a spirit of caution, even fear, permeated our diplomatic corps. In addition, and of greater short-range importance, his investigations and the public hysteria provoked by them so poisoned the well of thought and discussion that American policy itself became moribund. Finally, the Senator succeeded in partially undermining the authority and prestige abroad, as well as at home, of the Truman administration after 1950 and of the Eisenhower administration during its first year and a half in office.

Finally, some hearings have no legislative intent whatever but act as a sort of safety valve in releasing and controlling public frustration. The hearings conducted by the combined Senate Armed Services and Foreign

Relations Committee in 1951, which looked into the recall of General Douglas MacArthur during the Korean War, were among the most important hearings of this kind ever held. Feelings were running high in the United States and in the Congress regarding the frustrations of the Korean War and the policies being pursued therein by the Truman administration. When General MacArthur, a national hero and symbol of military strength and victory, was relieved of his command in April, 1951, by President Truman, whose popularity and authority had been seriously undermined by developments in Korea and at home, there were informed and intelligent observers who feared that the authority of the administration might be undermined.[15] At the very least it can be said that the country was deeply divided over issues going to the heart of the military operations in Korea, and that this is not a propitious background in a democracy for the conduct of a war or of foreign policy generally.

Under the chairmanship of the respected Senator Richard B. Russell (D-Ga.), the combined committees conducted lengthy and exhaustive hearings in May into MacArthur's recall and, more generally, American policy in the Far East. The hearings were kept secret, but the press and public were kept advised of what was going on by means of a transcript that was censored a page at a time as the hearings progressed and then immediately released. As the hearings droned on and the issues were ventilated in a calm and restrained atmosphere, some of the emotionalism surrounding the matter was dissipated. The critics of the President had the feeling that "something was being done," and MacArthur himself did exactly what he said he would do: he faded away.

Hearings thus serve a wide variety of purposes relating to American foreign policy. What follows is a brief account of which committees hold these hearings and of the power structure among congressional committees.

The Committees

The most powerful and prestigious committee is the Senate Committee on Foreign Relations. More Senators seek appointment to it than any other committee; it has a long history not only of high status but also of great influence both inside and outside the Senate; and it holds the hearings on high executive appointments relating to foreign affairs and on treaties. Its recommendations to the Senate are not often overturned.

The chairman of this august group has often played a leading role in the formulation of American policy. Perhaps the most prominent example in recent years was Arthur H. Vandenberg (R-Mich.). He became chairman in 1947 as a result of the Republican capture of Congress in the 1946 elec-

---

[15] See, for example, William S. White, *The Citadel*, Harper & Row, Publishers, Incorporated, New York, 1956, pp. 241–252.

tions, which undermined President Truman's authority and sapped his power. Truman adopted the practice of consulting extensively with Vandenberg, seeking his support for specific policies, and in turn altering those policies to fit the Senator's wishes. The result was that on major issues the President and Congress were able to present a common front to the rest of the world at a time when vital decisions bearing on the breakup of the wartime alliance were required. In recent years, the chairman of the committee has been J. William Fulbright (D-Ark.). Fulbright is a man of high intelligence who enjoys an enviable reputation in the Senate, in the bureaucracy, and among the well-informed public generally. He has maintained his independence of each succeeding administration, Republican and Democratic, and has from time to time been among their most severe critics. On the other hand, he has frequently been critical of some of the less responsible critics of official policy. Because of his chairmanship and because of his use of it, therefore, Fulbright plays a unique and valuable role in the public and congressional debates that surround most policies in this free and diversified democracy. And when called upon to consult with the President or his advisers, his judgment is treated with considerable respect. It is impossible to weigh or measure his influence. But it exists, and any attempt to describe the power and role of Congress must take such factors into account.

The technical counterpart to the Senate Foreign Relations Committee in the House of Representatives is the Committee on Foreign Affairs. In earlier and quieter days, the House had comparatively little to do with foreign affairs. Appointments and treaties have always been strictly senatorial concerns. As foreign policy has become more expensive, however, the responsibilities of the House have grown. This has increased the importance and stature of the Foreign Affairs Committee, but not to the point where it has achieved anything like the prestige and power of the Foreign Relations Committee. Aside from the fact that it is not involved in approving appointments or treaties, and aside from the fact that the Foreign Relations Committee is a traditionally powerful committee in a tradition-conscious Congress, the primary cause of the Foreign Affairs Committee's comparative weakness is the congressional system of appropriating money. It places enormous power in the hands of the House Appropriations Committee at the expense of the Foreign Affairs Committee.

The congressional appropriations process is cumbersome and complicated. First, an "authorization bill" must be passed by both chambers. This bill originates in the "legislative committee" in each chamber that has jurisdiction; regarding foreign policy, these committees are the Senate Foreign Relations and the House Foreign Affairs Committees. The "authorization bill" authorizes the appropriation of a certain amount of money for certain stated purposes. But the appropriation of the money itself requires another bill, an "appropriation bill." Both chambers have a Committee on Appropriations, which deals with these bills, usually after extensive hearings. It goes without saying that these committees are among the most powerful committees in Congress. They embody and symbolize "the power of the purse," which Congress guards so jealously. Actual appropriations are usually lower than the authorizations that preceded them. Many observers have come to regard the authorization process as merely a kind of dress rehearsal for the more important process of actually appropriating funds. The result, obviously enough, has been to reduce the power and significance of the legislative committees such as Foreign Relations and Foreign Affairs.

The Constitution requires that all revenue (taxation) bills originate in the House. Traditionally, all appropriations bills have also originated in the House. The Senate has begun to resist this tradition, but whatever may come of this skirmishing, the House Committee on Appropriations has developed a position of enormous power in Congress. Its Subcommittee on Foreign Operations has more impact on the size of the foreign aid appropriation each year than any other group within Congress. It is respected and feared by the administration and by other committees in both chambers that deal with foreign policy.

Hearings before the subcommittees of the House Appropriation Committee are invariably closed (secret) hearings. They are subsequently published, minus any classified information. These hearings are lengthy ordeals for representatives of the executive branch seeking to justify their requests for funds. Moreover, they are frequently conducted by subcommittee chairmen who are hostile to the programs under consideration. The most conspicuous example of this in recent years has been Representative Otto Passman (D-La.) who heads the Foreign Operations Subcommittee and is an outspoken opponent of almost all foreign aid.

The Senate Appropriations Committee has traditionally been less powerful and more lenient than its House counterpart. Its hearings, incidentally, are ordinarily open to the public. It has acted as a kind of court of appeals for the administration and others who feel that the House has dealt unfairly with some appropriation or other. On foreign aid, for example, the Senate committee usually recommends a higher figure than that passed by the House. The Senate usually accepts the recommendations—or something like them—of its committee, and then the differences between the two chambers have to be compromised into acceptable form by a conference committee. This latter consists of representatives of the committees of both chambers.

Thus far we have discussed four committees, the responsibilities of which are either wholly or partially in the area of foreign policy. They are the most important ones, but there are others. The foreign policy responsibilities of the two Armed Services Committees and the Joint Committee on Atomic Energy are clear enough. In addition, there are many others, the concerns of which touch substantially or slightly on foreign affairs, as shown below.

In the House of Representatives: Agriculture (disposal of surplus agricultural products); Government Operations (administration of foreign and military operations); Interior and Insular Affairs (territorial possessions); Interstate and Foreign Commerce; Judiciary (immigration and naturalization); Science and Astronautics (control and use of outer space); and Ways and Means (tariffs, trade agreements, taxation of overseas investments).

In the Senate: Aeronautical and Space Sciences (outer space); Agriculture and Forestry (disposal of surplus agricultural products); Finance (tariffs, trade agreements, taxation of overseas investments); Government Operations (administration of foreign and military operations, including relationships between the United States and international organizations); Interior and Insular Affairs (territorial possessions); and Judiciary (immigration and naturalization).

Nor is this all. The House Committee on Un-American Activities and the Internal Security Subcommittee of the Senate Judiciary Committee often carry on investigations that have a direct or indirect bearing on foreign policy. Their mandates are sufficiently flexible to permit inquiries into alleged subversion in executive departments dealing with foreign policy, for example. The Internal Security Subcommittee has been especially active in recent years in matters affecting foreign relations. During the early days of the Castro regime in Cuba, for example, the subcommittee offered its platform to some notable defectors who declared that Castro had betrayed the revolution. The Eisenhower administration was sufficiently embarrassed by this to issue a formal statement dissociating itself from the hearing. It is not easy for foreigners, however, to understand our complicated governmental system, and many of them take the statements of individual congressmen or even of witnesses before committees to be official American policy.

One other subcommittee merits special attention. For the last several years, a subcommittee (currently called National Security Staffing and Operations) of the Senate Government Operations Committee has conducted extensive hearings relating to the administration of "national security" affairs.[16] These hearings and the periodic reports and recommenda-

---

[16] The term "national security" embraces many aspects of foreign policy. Central among these, of course, is military defense policy (strategy), but also included are such activities as intelligence (the gathering, ordering, and interpreting of information about other nations and their policies) and diplomacy (the conduct of foreign relations). Primarily, the term suggests an emphasis in foreign policy on the security of the nation and the need to coordinate policy in all agencies to this end. In 1947, as we shall see, the National Security Council was formed; it can—but does not always— serve as a kind of supercabinet for foreign affairs.

In a sense, the term is the obverse of "internal security," which has to do with internal threats to the security of the nation and its institutions, such as subversion and espionage.

tions issued by the subcommittee and its chairman, Henry M. Jackson (D-Wash.), have occasioned considerable discussion inside and outside the government and have unquestionably served an educational purpose; whether they have prompted anything other than minor adjustments in the administration of national security affairs is an open question.

Constitutional Amendments

The President has no formal responsibilities in the process prescribed for amending the Constitution. The Presidency and its accumulated powers, therefore, are technically in a vulnerable position. If two-thirds of the Congress and three-fourths of the states decide to alter the existing system, they can do so. This rather implausible possibility actually became quite a serious matter in the 1950s with the proposed Bricker amendment, named after Senator John Bricker (R-Ohio), its principal sponsor. This amendment, which was very narrowly defeated in the Senate in 1954, would have required that all executive agreements with foreign powers be ratified by Congress and would also have restricted the subject matter of treaties. Its passage would have had a crippling effect on the conduct of American foreign policy. Although the Bricker amendment failed of passage and no similar proposal is likely to be approved in the foreseeable future, that experience underlined dramatically the ultimate power that Congress retains. The power to amend the Constitution—with the concurrence of three-fourths of the states—is not likely to be exercised, but it stands as potentially the most powerful congressional weapon of all in the struggle for control of foreign policy.

Some Observations on the Role of Congress

As money has become more and more important in the conduct of American foreign policy, the role of Congress in setting that policy has also increased. It may even be true to say that in relative terms Congress is now more powerful and the executive branch less powerful in the formulation of policy than was the case a generation ago. Such speculations are interesting, but they are impossible to quantify and verify, and they draw attention away from the more important fact that the domain and significance of foreign policy for the United States have increased immensely since the 1930s. Moreover, as any casual reader of a good newspaper can sense, the role and power of the President are still vastly greater than those of Congress. "Presidential primacy" in foreign policy is a well-understood fact in our political system. American voters "feel it in their bones" when they elect a President: that man, that mortal and fallible human being, will be called upon to make decisions vitally affecting their freedom and their very survival. The President is the man with his hand on the trigger.

His preeminence is also understood overseas. Indeed, it is sometimes overrated by those who do not understand our system of shared powers.

When enough people ascribe power to an individual or an office, he or it acquires it. The original ascription may have been faulty, but if enough people believe it and act as if it were true, it becomes true in fact. The Presidency has a good deal of this "ascriptive power" in addition to its already awesome formal array of powers. In other words, the general presumption that "the President makes foreign policy" helps to make this largely true. If that presumption should ever be questioned by enough people, the President's preeminence would be partially undermined, but it would, short of revolution, never be overturned.

Many of the conditions that would be most propitious for a congressional attempt to assume greater control over foreign policy seemed to be present in the late 1950s. President Eisenhower was in his second term and could not succeed himself. He had always taken a more restrictive view of presidential responsibility and power than his immediate predecessors; he had been unusually deferential to congressional prerogatives. Moreover, Congress had been controlled by the opposition Democrats for all but the first two years of his tenure in office. And, finally, these Democrats had, by 1958, become more and more outspokenly critical of some of the popular President's policies.

In June, 1958, the Senate Foreign Relations Committee held hearings that were ambitiously called *Review of Foreign Policy, 1958.* In the course of those hearings, Senator Fulbright, who probably knows more about this matter than anyone else, made the following remarks to a witness who was calling upon Congress to exert a greater influence over foreign policy:

> I do not think there is the remotest chance for congressional and Senate control of foreign policy. Leadership in the Department of State must control it. That is the tradition of this country. . . .
>
> In a way I am flattered that you think the Senate can do something about this [United States policy in Europe], and in another way I am a little disappointed that you should have such illusions about your own Government. You should understand it better than that.[17]

The contemporary role of Congress, *in foreign policy,* in practice, is to amend, to question, to apply pressure, to air criticisms, to support, and, occasionally, to reject. It seldom initiates, though it conceivably could. It does not administer, though occasionally it meddles in administration. It sits as a kind of board of directors, but it doesn't have the power to fire the management, and on the most critical decisions it often is not even consulted.

---

[17] *Review of Foreign Policy, 1958, Hearings of the Senate Committee on Foreign Relations,* 85th Cong., 2d Sess., June, 1958, pt. 4, p. 774.

This is not the place to attempt a detailed evaluation of the manner in which Congress carries out its responsibilities regarding foreign policy. That would require a separate volume, and even then any conclusions would unavoidably be somewhat arbitrary. However, it does seem appropriate at this time to make a few remarks with some evaluative content.

Congress is a frequent target of criticism. It is inefficient, difficult to understand, frequently stubborn and even petty, and members of Congress have not always reflected the noblest sentiments or the highest intelligence in the nation. Congressmen are busy people; most of them have little time to develop a sophisticated appreciation of foreign policy matters, and by no means all of them arrive so equipped. One of the most prominent characteristics of the institution is its diffuseness: power and responsibility are widely and bewilderingly dispersed. It is, moreover, incurably parochial in tone, and sometimes in output as well. It is composed of politicians, men and women whose political survival depends on local and state constituencies and political parties, who owe little or no allegiance to a national party, and whose views may or may not reflect a serious concern for the public interest.

It is, in sum, easy to criticize, even to ridicule. But there is another side to the story, as well. Its slowness is often the result of a legitimate and useful desire to weigh matters carefully. The dispersal of authority has often served to protect minority interests in this huge and variegated country, and to foster a healthy diversity in thought and policy. The sometimes crude and even absurd level of debate, and even occasionally of decision, is one of the costs of democracy. Congress is sometimes blamed for not reflecting "the people"; more often, it is blamed for doing precisely that.

The best standard for judging Congress, however, is its actions. By this standard, Congress does not come off badly. Since the end of World War II, American foreign policy has undergone a fundamental transformation, *and Congress has supported that transformation.* It supported the historic gesture of providing economic and military assistance to Greece and Turkey in 1947 when the independence of those nations was threatened by Communists; it supported the Marshall Plan and NATO, which helped revive and protect Western Europe; it supported the unpopular war in Korea; and it has appropriated over $70 billion for foreign aid since 1945. *It has not seriously undermined a single major postwar American policy.*

Moreover, Congress provides a useful public forum for dissent. It is valuable in a democracy to have an institution that jealously checks and criticizes the administration. The administration has the expertise and the information; this helps, incidentally, to explain the "pro–executive branch bias" that is so evident among intellectuals and journalists. But Congress has some worthy qualities, too. Because members of Congress are politicians, they bring a type of shrewdness and experience and discernment to the formulation of public policy that is not always conspicuous in large bureaucracies. This is reflected in the probing questions that they often put to those who testify before congressional committees.

The overwhelming majority of the members of Congress are intelligent men and women, and a goodly percentage are brilliant. Over the years many of them become uniquely knowledgeable about certain areas of American policy, ranging from atomic energy through the intricacies of the organization of the Department of Defense to the subtleties of European politics. Many of them have been closely associated with such matters for a longer period of time than anyone in the executive branch. In recent years, members of Congress have traveled extensively overseas to observe American programs and policies. Some of these journeys have been merely vacations at the expense of the taxpayer—such excursions have acquired the label "junkets"—but many of them have served to educate the traveler and make it easier for him to legislate intelligently.

The role of Congress is inevitably more negative than that of the administration. The character of this negativism is often overrated or otherwise misunderstood, however. It would be a mistake, for example, to assume that the presidential proposals always reflect precisely his aspirations. This is particularly true in an area such as foreign aid where it is understood by all concerned that Congress will unquestionably cut the President's request. It is often, in some respects, a game: the original request is inflated so as to absorb the inevitable cut, and the cutters (Congress) attempt to gauge just how much can be eliminated without seriously damaging the program. The President understands the need of congressmen to represent themselves as tough-minded and frugal; Congress understands that the requested figure is not really as "rock bottom" as advertised. In this connection, the following true story is related, under the general heading of "In Watching Executive–Legislative Combat, Remember That There Is Often Less There Than Meets the Eye":

A new Senator arrived in Washington and shortly after he assumed office, the President, who was of the same political party, sent his budget to Capitol Hill. The press asked the Senator what he thought of the budget, and he remarked that it was fine. He and his staff thereafter noted that many of his colleagues had criticized the budget and had received a good deal of publicity; the Senator's approving remarks had not.

The following year, the not-so-new Senator attacked the budget, saying there was "fat" in it that he intended to help eliminate. He received large headlines in his state's press, which was surprised and delighted that the Senator was displaying "independence and a critical eye."

Shortly thereafter, the Senator attended a reception at the White House. Upon taking his leave, he was overcome with guilt feelings and remorse, and he apologized to the President for having attacked the budget. The President, who had heretofore been unaware of the attack, said that no apologies were necessary. The Senator persisted, however, embarrassing both himself and the President. Finally the President asked if the attack had earned the Senator any publicity. When informed that it had, he slapped the Senator on the back and said, "Good boy,———!"

Selected Bibliography

Carroll, Holbert N.: *The House of Representatives and Foreign Affairs*, The University of Pittsburgh Press, Pittsburgh, Pa., 1958. A somewhat dated but essentially valid description and analysis of the enlarged role of the House in the formulation of foreign policy.

Congressional Quarterly Weekly Reports and *Almanac* (annual). The authoritative and comprehensive account of congressional affairs.

Dahl, Robert A.: *Congress and Foreign Policy*, Harcourt, Brace & World, Inc., New York, 1950. (Available in a paperback edition published by W. W. Norton & Company, Inc., New York, 1964.) A rather hoary but solid and instructive book.

Hilsman, Roger, Jr.: "Congressional-Executive Relations and the Foreign Policy Consensus," *American Political Science Review*, vol. 52, pp. 725–745, 1958. A perceptive analysis of the requirements and techniques of achieving policy consensus between the executive and congressional branches of government.

Hughes, Thomas L.: "Foreign Policy on Capitol Hill," *The Reporter*, vol. 20, no. 9, pp. 28–31, Apr. 30, 1959. An insider's description of some of the frustrations and opportunities occasioned by Congress's role in foreign policy.

Robinson, James A.: *Congress and Foreign Policy-making*, The Dorsey Press, Inc., Homewood, Ill., 1962. A valuable account of how Congress has influenced and failed to influence many foreign policies and a description of the processes involved.

Shils, Edward A.: "The Legislator and His Environment," *University of Chicago Law Review*, vol. 18, pp. 571–584, 1951. A sensitive treatment by a renowned scholar of the legislator's milieu.

chapter 3   The power to make basic American foreign policy is a shared power, but it is not shared equally. The President has most of it. He is not an absolute ruler, and he must therefore endeavor to persuade Congress and, to a lesser extent, even the executive agencies to accept his policies. But most of the basic decisions and virtually all of the major decisions made in a crisis are presidential decisions. To assist him in this awesome responsibility and sometimes to act in his stead, a modern President is surrounded by a vast array of people and institutions. The purpose of this chapter is to identify his most important sources of advice and information and to sketch the outlines of the activities and responsibilities of the bureaucracy around him.

If the primary concern of this book were administration rather than policy, it would be necessary to set forth in detail the formal and informal organization, responsibilities, and interrelationships of the various persons and agencies involved in this policy process. And it is of course true that administrative arrangements vitally affect policy. They affect the character of the advice and information reaching the President and other high-ranking officials, the quality of the decisions made below these top levels, and the general conduct or execution of established policy. But to attempt to trace the organizational details of this vast bureaucracy or any of its constituent parts is beyond the scope of this book. Even further removed from our present concerns is the alluring exercise of prescribing cures for the administrative ills that permanently trouble the executive branch. These somewhat technical and contentious matters will be left to others. The purpose of this chapter is, rather, to set forth the central facts about the governmental and nongovernmental institutions that affect policy and to suggest something of their interrelationships and impact on policy.

What we most need to know about the policy process is not what the formal organization charts show—although this may be helpful—but rather what the actual, often informal, patterns of influence are. In other words: Who talks to the President, about what, and with what consequences? Who influences the President's top advisers, and, in turn, what is their actual influence on the President? Answers to these kinds of questions would go a long way toward explaining how foreign policy is made in the United States. To a considerable extent, that is what the rest of this chapter is about.

It should be stressed at the outset that the role and importance of the various offices and agencies discussed below vary considerably over time and from administration to administration. In order to bring some order into the discussion, these offices and agencies will be taken up separately and in some kind of hierarchal order, but their interrelationships and fluctuating significance should be borne in mind.

Formal Sources of Advice and Information for the President

The Department of State

By comparison with most other Federal agencies, the State Department is a small organization. In 1963, it consisted of just under 14,000 American employees, about half of whom were stationed overseas. (In addition, it employed nearly 10,000 foreign nationals overseas.) Only about 3,750 of these people were Foreign Service Officers, that is, career diplomats. The cost of administering the Department was a mere $155 million in fiscal 1963, and overall departmental expenditures came to only $414.3 million. This included $100 million for the purchase of United Nations bonds, $50.2 million for educational exchange programs, and $72.5 million for international organizations and conferences. During that year, the Department maintained embassies in 105 foreign countries and legations in 4 others.[1]

Its organization is designed to serve five basic purposes: to represent, formally and symbolically, the United States; to serve as a point of contact with the United States for foreign governments in order to facilitate or actually negotiate political, commercial, and other agreements; to render services to foreigners interested in immigrating to or visiting the United States; to assist Americans abroad, especially business representatives; and to acquire and transmit to the rest of the United States government—especially the President—information and advice about political and economic affairs in foreign countries.

For these purposes, the Department is organized primarily along two different but complementary lines: functional and geographic. Examples of the former are the Bureaus of Economic Affairs, Intelligence and Research, and Security and Consular Affairs. The geographic Bureaus are as follows: African Affairs, Inter-American Affairs, European Affairs, Far Eastern Affairs, Near Eastern and South Asian Affairs, and International Organization Affairs. The heads of most of these Bureaus have the title of Assistant Secretary of State.

Between the Secretary and these Bureaus there are a number of high-ranking officials. The second in command is the Undersecretary and the third is the Undersecretary for Political Affairs. In addition there are such positions as Deputy Undersecretary for Administration, Deputy Undersecretary for Political Affairs, Assistant Secretary for Policy Planning,

---

[1] For comparative purposes, the following rounded-off figures are of interest (the number of civilian employees being as of June 30, 1963, and the amount of expenditures being for fiscal 1963): Department of Agriculture, 115,000 employees, $7,735 million; Department of Defense, 1,050,000 civilian employees, $51,000 million; Department of Justice, 32,000 employees, $317 million. *Source:* U.S. Department of Commerce, Bureau of the Census, *Statistical Abstract of the United States, 1964,* Washington, D.C., 1964, pp. 391, 406–407.

Assistant Secretary for Congressional Relations, Legal Adviser, and Counselor.

All of these top-level officials are political appointees. They may or may not be career diplomats, but their tenure in these top policy-making positions is dependent upon the wishes of a given administration. The purpose of this, of course, is to ensure that the Department adjusts to different administrations pursuing different objectives and policies; to ensure, that is, that the bureaucracy is responsible to elected officials and their appointed representatives. This purpose is not always entirely achieved, of course, but the principle is a desirable and necessary one.

On formal charts depicting the responsibilities of the various governmental agencies, the State Department is usually identified as the agency primarily responsible for the formulation and conduct of foreign affairs, and the Secretary of State is identified as the President's chief foreign policy adviser. These conditions may or may not obtain in practice. In some periods of our history, the State Department has had very little to do with formulating American foreign policy and even less to do with executing it. The Secretary himself, moreover, may have much or little access to the President and considerable or little influence over policy. Two fundamental questions, among many, deserve special attention in this connection: What is the Secretary's relationship to the Department? What is the Secretary's relationship to the President? The answers to these questions have ranged from "nominal" to "intimate"; they will undoubtedly continue to vary as drastically in the future.

Cordell Hull was Secretary of State for nearly twelve years under Franklin Roosevelt (1933–1944). He had been a highly respected member of Congress for a generation before becoming Secretary in 1933, and he retained the respect and confidence of the Congress and the public throughout his long tenure. When he resigned because of ill health in late 1944, his relations with the Department were excellent as they had always been, and the President was, as always, cordial and friendly.

Was Cordell Hull, therefore, an influential Secretary of State? The answer would depend, of course, on what criteria were applied, but in terms of the large issues of the day—and there were plenty of them during that period—he was not influential. He had been appointed in the first instance because his views broadly coincided with those of President-elect Roosevelt and because he commanded the respect and affection of Congress. This latter qualification is a matter of some importance for any administration; Roosevelt was especially sensitive to its significance. Moreover, neither of these preconditions ever changed much. Hull was for the most part agreeable to Roosevelt's foreign policies, and he retained his prestige in Congress. But the foreign policies were emphatically Roosevelt's, and, on grave issues, Hull was not one of the President's principal advisers or confidants. Roosevelt's style of leadership made this kind of relationship not only possible but, some would argue, nearly inevitable. He relied heavily on informal channels of communication and constantly used unofficial persons for various tasks, including vitally important ones. He preferred administrative disorder and unclear lines of authority because he believed that they facilitated his own control of the vast machinery of government.

But this alone would not have precluded a relationship of intimacy between Roosevelt and his Secretary of State, one in which the Secretary served in fact as well as in name as the President's chief adviser. The vital missing ingredient was the President's confidence. Roosevelt did not have complete or even substantial confidence in Hull's judgments, and consequently their relationship was cordial and correct, but not intimate. In sum, a Secretary's *actual* role may or may not conform to his *formal, legal* role.

The case of John Foster Dulles (1953–1959) was the reverse. His relationships with the Department were nominal; those with his President, Dwight D. Eisenhower, could scarcely have been closer. Dulles came into office in 1953 convinced that the State Department had become something less than a brilliant instrumentality after twenty years under the opposition Democrats, and he was not comfortable about it or with it. This tendency was heavily reinforced by Dulles's overweening self-confidence and by his unwillingness to associate himself and the new administration with an agency that had been a favorite target of his party for many years. The result was that the Department's role declined as the Secretary assumed staggering responsibilities while relying relatively little on the career officers of the Department. Whereas Hull had trusted and used the Department, Dulles was suspicious of the Department and used it much less. The claim that Dulles "carried the Department around in his hat" is, of course, grossly misleading. Much of the Department goes about its business unaffected by whether or not it is having any appreciable effect on policy; much of it is not even designed for such a purpose. But the phrase does suggest how little the Secretary depended on the Department.

Dulles's relationship with President Eisenhower constitutes one of the most remarkable episodes in recent American history. The two men scarcely knew each other before 1952. Dulles, however, had long been regarded as the Republican party's leading specialist in foreign affairs, and it was generally believed that the politically inexperienced Eisenhower would automatically select Dulles as his Secretary of State. Whatever Eisenhower's private thoughts on the matter may have been,[2] he loyally nominated Dulles, and the latter made excellent use of his opportunity.

[2] For a suggestion that Eisenhower may have been somewhat reluctant to appoint Dulles, see Emmett John Hughes, *The Ordeal of Power*, Atheneum Publishers, New York, 1963, pp. 37, 51.

Despite their differing personalities and styles, and also despite their somewhat divergent attitudes toward international politics, the two men developed an impressive rapport. By all accounts, the President leaned heavily on the judgment of his Secretary; some would say Dulles was nearly the President's *exclusive* adviser, not merely his chief adviser. Some critics, in fact, have gone so far as to suggest that the President abrogated his constitutional responsibilities by delegating too much of his authority to his Secretary. It is almost certainly an exaggeration to claim that Dulles, not Eisenhower, made American foreign policy from 1953 until Dulles's retirement because of cancer in 1959; but the exaggeration grew out of a hard core of fact.[3]

Secretary of State Dean Acheson (1949–1953) presented still another combination of traits. He respected and used the Department and enjoyed good relations with it. Moreover, he was unquestionably President Truman's principal adviser on foreign affairs. Apparently, neither man wanted a relationship as close as that which subsequently grew up between Eisenhower and Dulles, but there was a strong mutual respect and loyalty between them.

Apparently, Dean Rusk (1961–   ) enjoys the confidence and respect of the Department and relies on it heavily. His relationship to President Kennedy was less clear. He had powerful and skillful competitors for the President's attention and confidence, notably Attorney General Robert Kennedy, Special Assistant for National Security Affairs McGeorge Bundy, and Secretary of Defense Robert McNamara. Whether he, a somewhat colorless but reputedly able man, had managed to make his own and his Department's influence felt above all others is a question that probably will not be answerable for several years. The same must be said regarding his impact on President Johnson.

These examples serve to underline several important facts about the policy process in the United States. The influence of the Department of State varies sharply over time. It depends in good measure on the Secretary's attitude toward the Department.[4] Similarly, the Secretary of State's role may be of enormous or of little consequence. Finally, these examples suggest that there are many other people and agencies that play a role in formulating basic policy because they also have access to the President and they also have expert opinion and specialized knowledge to offer. The

---

[3] In any event, the distinction between being strongly influential and being in actual control is a difficult one to make. A persuasive Secretary of State may be able to influence a President on nearly any subject. But if the President continues to reach his own conclusions based on his own judgments, and does not simply accept the Secretary's opinion without question, the President is still in control. In the final analysis, it is impossible to identify the sources of a President's decisions.

[4] This is not, however, the only consideration. Hull respected and relied on the Department, but Roosevelt did not. As a result, the Department's influence was sharply reduced during Roosevelt's twelve years in office.

determination of basic policy in any administration is made by the President. The character and quality of that policy depend not only on the President—his knowledge, intelligence, and judgment—but also on whom he sees and trusts and respects. To repeat, the patterns of influence are never the same from one administration to the next and they vary over time within the same administration.

Besides being the head of a major department and at least nominally the President's chief adviser, a modern Secretary of State has many other responsibilities. He is often the nation's chief diplomat.[5] This means that he must have or develop the subtle arts of diplomacy. At major international conferences, much can depend upon the negotiating skill of the major participants. A Secretary of State who is ineffective or unpleasant could damage the country's reputation and even endanger its interests. Americans often expect too much of diplomacy and diplomats, and are prone to exaggerate the extent to which their activities have affected events, but it is nonetheless true that diplomacy does have a bearing on the failure or success of policies. This places a heavy burden on a Secretary of State and his highest ranking subordinates, who, in an age of supersonic jet aircraft, often replace ambassadors as the nation's foremost representatives and negotiators.

In addition, a Secretary and his chief subordinates are frequently called before congressional committees for briefings, explanations, and defense of policy or practice. This can be time-consuming and, perhaps more importantly, it makes great demands on a person's patience and intelligence. Congressional inquiries can be quite brutal, and State Department representatives are called upon to be patient, courteous, and full of answers. Anything less may get the Department into trouble.

Like most large organizations, the State Department is often cumbersome and inefficient. One of the most celebrated alleged instances of bureaucratic inertia occurred in the summer of 1961. In June, 1961, President Kennedy met with Soviet Premier Khrushchev for the first time. During their meetings, Khrushchev handed the President an *aide mémoire* regarding Berlin, which demanded that the West come to an agreement with the Soviets by the end of the year or else lose all rights there. Aside from the six-month ultimatum, the Soviet note was unexceptional, and yet it allegedly took the State Department six weeks to draft a reply. The product was unnecessarily long, imprecise, and generally unimpressive. The number of people who would have an interest in such a matter is so large and the bureau-

[5] The words "diplomat" and "diplomacy" are used in a variety of ways. Herein they are given a narrow meaning: "diplomacy" is the process of representation and negotiation between nations, and a "diplomat" is a person who participates importantly in that process. "Diplomacy" can also be used to include the substance of policy itself, but this detracts from its utility as a word referring to the process or mechanics of international representation and negotiation.

cratic demands for thoroughness and deference to expertise are so compelling that such policy statements can easily spend weeks going from person to person and committee to committee and back again. Sometimes this institutional caution is desirable, but often it is not.

Another aspect of the administrative problem plaguing the State Department is the flood of messages that come in from overseas every day. The reporting function of the Foreign Service is among its most crucial, but important information is in constant danger of being lost amidst the less vital communiqués. Embassies transmit information by mail and by telegraph, and the telegraphic traffic alone between the Department and the embassies is more than 300,000 words a day. How to ensure that this is properly digested is obviously an important and difficult matter.

There are regular appeals, in and out of the Department, for administrative reforms. Some call for a vast reduction in staff and a closer identification of responsibility. Some put their faith in reorganization plans, and the Department has been reorganized several times in the last generation by experts in administration. The problem persists.

Another celebrated State Department problem is its vulnerability to attack by politicians and the press. The Department is a favorite whipping boy because it deals with a policy area that is full of opportunities for mistakes and where final solutions are rare. Foreign policy is not a traditional concern for the American public, and its contemporary preeminence is often resented. Whenever something goes wrong abroad—and it often does—it requires little imagination and virtually no supporting evidence to blame the State Department.

This vulnerability to irresponsible attack is most serious in the area of internal security. An adversary's foreign service is an obvious target for espionage, and there is therefore a legitimate concern about the loyalty of State Department employees. In actuality, the Department has an almost perfect record in this respect, but there has been enough successful Soviet espionage in the government as a whole to keep suspicions alive. As noted earlier, this has given rise to some sensational and irresponsible congressional investigations. These inquests have turned up precious few Communists or fellow travelers, but they have severely affected the morale and quality of the Foreign Service. They inhibit honest reporting and exchange of views, they focus attention on minor and misleading questions, and they endanger the quality of the Service by causing gifted people to resign and by scaring off potential recruits to the Service. This problem has receded in recent years, but it is an ever-present threat to an already harassed organization.

Another problem that touches on morale is the practice of appointing ambassadors who are not career Foreign Service Officers. No other major nation does this with any regularity, but it is traditional in the United

States. Many of these appointments are simply rewards for persons who have helped pay for or have otherwise assisted in political campaigns. Others go to persons with special competence in a given area, such as businessmen or intellectuals. Approximately one-third of the present United States Ambassadors are not Foreign Service Officers. The percentage of career ambassadors has ranged from 56 to 69 since 1945. In May, 1963, the percentage figure was 63.

One of the reasons for noncareer appointments has been the unwillingness of Congress to supply sufficient funds to support the necessary social activities of an Ambassador. Congress appropriates only small amounts of money for "representation allowances," which critics refer to as "the whisky fund." It refuses to support the extensive and expensive social responsibilities that are an unavoidable aspect of an Ambassador's life in the major European capitals. The result has been that, with a few exceptions, the Ambassadors to Great Britain, France, Italy, and West Germany have had to be wealthy men who were willing and able to incur these expenses themselves. This has not always resulted in quality representation, and it damages the morale of the diplomatic corps, which cannot aspire to such premium appointments. This niggardly behavior by the wealthiest nation in the world has become increasingly absurd, and there are some indications that this tradition is being abandoned. Two recent Ambassadors to France, for example, were not wealthy men, and one was a senior Foreign Service Officer.

There seems to be little dispute, on the other hand, that it is a healthy thing for some Ambassadors to be drawn from outside the career ranks. Some of these appointments have been notable successes. Moreover, any organization can profit from the periodic infusion of new talent and techniques. In sum, it is generally agreed that strictly political appointees are unfortunate and largely unnecessary, that representation allowances should be raised to reasonable levels, and that ambassadorial appointments should be concentrated within, but not restricted to, the career Foreign Service.

The Department of Defense

Any major nation's foreign policy is, or should be, closely related to its military capabilities. Or, to turn it around, any major nation's military policy is, or should be, closely related to its foreign policy. The two are intimately connected because policies are ordinarily more or less successful in accordance with how much power a nation is able to bring to bear in their support; and a nation's power—the capacity to influence the behavior and policies of other nations—is in large measure defined in terms of military strength. In other words, the success or failure of the foreign policies of the United States depends in considerable measure upon whether the American military forces are capable of supporting them.

It is appropriate and necessary, therefore, that the military establishment should be closely associated with the formulation of American policy. This intimate connection between foreign and military policy had no formal institutional and sometimes very little informal recognition in the United States until after World War II. Then, in 1947, Congress created the National Security Council (NSC) to advise the President on American foreign and military policy and to coordinate the two. The NSC and its variants will be discussed below, but first the prominent role of the Defense Department and the Secretary of Defense will be underlined.

The Defense Department, housed in the vast Pentagon, is by far the largest and most expensive Federal agency. It employs several million civilians and military personnel, and spends nearly $50 billion a year. These enormous figures are, of course, the product of the felt requirements of the cold war. The United States is determined to protect its independence; and, in order to deter potential aggressors from attacking either the United States or one of the many areas of the world in which it has vital interests or serious commitments, it maintains this huge military establishment.

There is, however, no obvious formula for accomplishing these defensive and deterrent purposes. What kinds of forces and weapons are required and where? To put it another way, what are we defending against? An all-out attack on the United States? On Europe? A more limited attack in a peripheral area? All of these and more? The attempt to answer these questions gets us into the area of defense strategy, which will be discussed as a policy matter in Chapter 7. For now, suffice it to note that whatever strategies or plans are adopted, they will have important implications for foreign policy, and vice versa. The State Department is interested in the Defense Department's policies because they vitally affect what the United States can and cannot expect to be able to do in the world; therefore, they affect foreign policy. The Defense Department is interested in the State Department's—or the Government's—policies because it needs to adjust its defense policies to those overall foreign policies and objectives.

It would be difficult to look at any area of foreign policy today and not discover a military dimension to the problem. The strength and credibility of our policies regarding Berlin, for example, are intimately related to our military policies. In this and most other areas, what we want to do and what we can do may be two very different things.

The person who, besides the President, is primarily responsible for making our military policies responsive to our foreign policies is the Secretary of Defense. Some have taken this responsibility lightly or have not even understood it; they viewed their job as primarily technical and administrative. In this view, defense policy is a matter for the specialists, the military themselves. Others have taken their responsibilities in the field of strategy very seriously and have made their influence felt throughout the government. Perhaps the most spectacular example of this latter type has been Robert S. McNamara, who was appointed Secretary of Defense by President Kennedy and whose influence has been enormous. There has even been some concern that his unquestioned brilliance and great energy resulted in his becoming too powerful, dominating the vast defense establishment and also eclipsing the position of the rather more bland Secretary of State.

Like a Secretary of State, any given Secretary of Defense may or may not succeed in deeply influencing the policies and practices of his department, on the one hand, and the President, on the other. But his opportunities and responsibilities are immense.

The National Security Council and Associated Agencies and Officials

The composition of the National Security Council (NSC) suggests its purpose. The statutory members are the President, the Vice President, the Secretary of State, the Secretary of Defense, and the Director of the Office of Emergency Planning. (The Office of Emergency Planning is the successor to a long list of predecessor agencies concerned with planning and preparing for the emergency use of industrial capacity, natural resources, manpower, and so forth. It attempts, in sum, to develop reasonable plans for adjusting the civilian economic sectors of American life to the anticipated requirements of a national emergency.) In addition, the President invites participation as he sees fit from such sources as the Joint Chiefs of Staff, the Director of the Central Intelligence Agency (CIA), and the Chairman of the Atomic Energy Commission (AEC). Also associated with the Council and regular attendants at its meetings are the Special Assistant to the President for National Security Affairs, his Deputy, and the Executive Secretary of the NSC.

The Council has, with some justification, been referred to as a "super-Cabinet" for foreign affairs.[6] When fully operational, it brings together formally and regularly and with an independent staff those officials and agencies that are most closely concerned with American security against external threats. Like most agencies or coordinating bodies, it has had a a varied career. It was never intended to be an entity with independent

---

[6] The Cabinet itself—the heads of the ten executive departments, plus the Ambassador to the United Nations—has no formal legal status and appears to be of declining significance despite its traditional and symbolic importance. Whatever its future may be regarding domestic affairs, it is almost certainly destined to have little or nothing to do with foreign policy deliberations. The Secretary of the Interior, to cite only one example, is not vitally concerned with such matters.

authority or operating responsibilities. In the words of the authorizing act, it is to advise the President "with respect to the integration of domestic, foreign, and military policies relating to the national security so as to enable the military services and the other departments and agencies of the Government to cooperate more effectively in matters involving the national security."

Like all such efforts, its impact on policy has depended largely on how much the President chooses to rely on the Council, and this, of course, has varied over time. When President Kennedy assumed office, for example, he believed that the Council was an artificial construct, which produced more bland agreement than it did successful policy, and he virtually ignored the Council and its staff for several months. He of course met and counseled with the individuals who collectively comprised the Council, but he chose not to call the Council together in formal session. After the disastrous experience at the Bay of Pigs in April, 1961, however, the President began to call meetings with some regularity. He evidently felt that it had been a mistake to ignore this formal mechanism.

When the Cuban crisis of October, 1962, broke, the President created an *ad hoc* advisory group, which he called the "Executive Committee of the National Security Council." This was a rather standard procedure. In times of crisis, any President tends to call in his most trusted advisers. This particular informal grouping included all of the regular NSC members (except the Director of the Office of Emergency Planning) and an indicative list of other key officials. An analysis of this list and what agencies and offices these people represent will go a long way toward explaining how major foreign policy is made in this country. Besides the NSC members, the President chose to counsel with the Attorney General, the Special Assistant to the President for National Security Affairs, the Director of the CIA, the Chairman of the Joint Chiefs of Staff, the Secretary of the Treasury, a Special Adviser to the President on Soviet Affairs, the President's Special Counsel, and the second-ranking officials in the Departments of State and Defense.

The Attorney General has few formal responsibilities in the area of foreign affairs. In this instance, however, he happened to be the brother and most intimate associate of the President. He was not attending these meetings or talking privately with the President as the Attorney General. He was acting as the President's brother and most trusted adviser. This kind of unofficial advisory role is not at all unprecedented in American history. In fact, some Presidents have had close advisers who held no governmental position whatever or merely a nominal title. Harry Hopkins, for example, was Franklin Roosevelt's closest associate and most influential adviser for years, especially during World War II, yet he never held a title that even suggested such great influence. Presidents seek information and advice in many different ways and from many different and often unorthodox sources.

The Special Assistant to the President for National Security Affairs in this instance was McGeorge Bundy. A former dean at Harvard, he was broadly trained in foreign policy and had a forceful personality. Special Assistants and their very small staffs have their offices in the White House itself. Their responsibilities are exclusively advisory; they do not direct and are not formally associated with any agency. They are part of a small —approximately twenty-two in number—and elite group that is called the White House staff. Bundy's role was to maintain a detached view of national security affairs and to advise the President regarding any gaps or shortcomings in either policy or administration. He was reputedly highly regarded by the President, and some observers suggested that he was more influential with the President than the Secretary of State. However that might be, his formal position and the President's confidence made him a central figure in the drama.

The Director of the CIA, in this instance John McCone, heads a semi-secret agency, the primary purposes of which are the gathering and evaluation of intelligence about foreign nations, especially hostile ones. The CIA is one of the most controversial of all Federal agencies. As mentioned above, the amount of its annual expenditures and size of its staff are known to only a limited number of people, including only a few congressmen. It is widely believed, however, that it employs more people and spends more money than, for example, the State Department.

The CIA is controversial on several grounds. A minority of Americans are opposed in principle to the maintenance of an organization whose reason for being is to spy on foreign nations. Many more citizens object to the secrecy that surrounds the size, expenditures, and operations of the CIA. There is, they argue, something undemocratic about the furtive character of such an organization, and some fear that it might become too powerful and abuse its influence. Many members of Congress, as mentioned earlier, have urged Congress to establish a joint committee to oversee the activities of the CIA, along the lines of the Joint Atomic Energy Committee's responsibilities regarding the AEC. Finally, there is a widespread concern that the practice of giving the CIA operational responsibilities in addition to its responsibilities for gathering and evaluating information is unwise and has not worked well. The CIA was, for example, heavily involved in the Bay of Pigs fiasco in 1961, and in 1963 there was widespread concern that the CIA was working at cross-purposes with the State Department in South Vietnam.

However that may be, it goes without saying that there is an urgent need for information about the activities and intentions of one's adversaries, and the presence of the Director of the CIA on this *ad hoc* committee in

October, 1962, was natural enough. Much depended on what was going on in Cuba before and during the missile crisis, and presumably the CIA had more information on such matters than anyone else.[7]

The Chairman of the Joint Chiefs of Staff was there for obvious reasons and for less formal but equally important ones. The Chiefs of Staff are the highest-ranking military officers in each of the three armed services, plus occasionally the top-ranking Marine officer. The Chairman is chosen by the President from any of the services, and he presides over the meetings of the Joint Chiefs. He is technically and often practically as well the nation's most influential military officer.

The Chairman of the Joint Chiefs of Staff in October, 1962, was Army General Maxwell Taylor. His presence on the Executive Committee of the NSC was decidedly more than a mere formality. General Taylor had been Army Chief of Staff for four years during the Eisenhower administration, but wide policy divergencies developed between him and the President. Upon leaving the Army in 1959, he wrote a book that attacked administration policies and called for vastly increased expenditures for limited war forces. Taylor's book joined a growing list of dissents which were being published in the latter years of the Eisenhower administration, and, perhaps inadvertently, he therefore became a "political general." Soon after President Kennedy assumed office, he called General Taylor out of retirement and made him a special adviser. Later on, he appointed him Chairman of the Joint Chiefs of Staff. By all accounts, Taylor had become one of the President's most trusted advisers. His role on the Executive Committee was, therefore, not simply that of a top professional adviser but was in addition that of a person whose judgments on policy matters had a special affinity with the President's and had strongly influenced the President in the past.

The Secretary of the Treasury would not *ipso facto* be presumed to have a role in this crisis. In this instance, however, the Secretary of the Treasury was C. Douglas Dillon, a prominent Republican who had served as Undersecretary of State during the Eisenhower administration. Dillon personifies that kind of public official that keeps cropping up in the opposition party's administrations. He was a favorite of the Democrats during his years with the Republican Eisenhower administration and President-elect Kennedy

---

[7] The failure of the CIA to discover the missile installations earlier has been attributed by some analysts to the fact that official policy at the time was based on the assumption that the Soviets would not take such a dangerous step. This raises some interesting questions about the techniques and effectiveness of the CIA.

The CIA is not the only intelligence operation maintained by the government. The State and Defense Departments maintain separate intelligence programs, and the Defense Intelligence Agency is primarily responsible for gathering and evaluating military intelligence. For an analysis of some of the problems of the United States intelligence apparatus, see Hanson W. Baldwin, "The Growing Risks of Bureaucratic Intelligence," *The Reporter*, vol. 29, no. 3, pp. 48–52, Aug. 15, 1963.

asked him to stay in Washington, this time as Secretary of the Treasury. Appointments of this kind are, of course, the product of diverse motivations, but aside from the simple fact that such men are often very capable, three considerations stand out. They provide some continuity between departing and incoming administrations, and in our system of government, where most changes are less than fundamental, this is feasible and worthwhile. Moreover, an incoming President, especially one who has narrowly won the election, may find it expedient to facilitate a sense of national unity by appointing partisan opponents to high office. Finally, a President partially protects himself from partisan attacks if he has opposition members in prominent positions in his administration. Dillon is a typical "nonpartisan Republican," and his presence on the Executive Committee was testimony both to his extensive experience and to the nonpartisan character of national crises.[8]

The Special Adviser to the President and the Secretary of State on Soviet Affairs was Llewellyn E. Thompson, who had recently returned from Moscow after serving for five years as United States Ambassador there. The reasons for this specialist's presence are obvious.

The President's Special Counsel was Theodore Sorenson. He was the President's chief speech writer, and his responsibilities were reputed to be largely domestic in character, but his presence on this committee came as no surprise. He had been a close associate of the President's for nearly a decade. Such a relationship requires a great deal of mutual trust and respect, and when a major crisis develops that requires decisions of incalculable importance, Presidents invoke such relationships.

Another individual, not listed as a member of the Executive Committee of the NSC, who participated importantly in the deliberations of that fateful week was the Ambassador to the United Nations, Adlai E. Stevenson. The role that Stevenson played became the center of an intense controversy afterward, but the only relevant point at this juncture is to note that he did participate and actively. This was not inevitable. Despite the feverish activity that the missile crisis set off at the United Nations, it is quite conceivable that the United States Ambassador could have been completely isolated from the policy decisions being made in Washington. In this, as

[8] It is more difficult to name "nonpartisan Democrats" who served in the Eisenhower administration. There were a few, mostly Southerners, but nothing like the number of opposition figures employed by Roosevelt, Truman, Kennedy, and Johnson, for example. The primary reason for this is probably historical: The Republicans had been out of the White House for twenty years when they captured the Presidency in 1952. They were, therefore, anxious to clean the slate. Roosevelt operated in much the same way until the war clouds descended and he sought national unity. Kennedy, as already remarked, won a narrow victory in 1960, and could not afford to take a sharply partisan stance. Moreover, the Democrats had only been out for eight years, and their appetites were presumably less demanding. Whatever the reasons, four of the twelve officials listed as part of the Executive Committee in October, 1962, were Republicans. Two others were not identifiable on partisan grounds.

in all of the other examples cited, what really counts is whom the President cares to consult, irrespective of position or title.

The same thing can, of course, be said about the vice presidency. Every recent administration has proudly announced that its Vice President has assumed unprecedented responsibilities. President Truman had come into office woefully uninformed in 1945 upon President Roosevelt's death, and he was determined that that mistake would not be repeated. After his election in 1948, he made a considerable effort to take Vice President Alben Barkley into his confidence and to keep him informed about developments at home and abroad. Vice Presidents Richard Nixon and Lyndon Johnson were assigned important responsibilities as well as kept close to the basic decisions by participation in most of the vital discussions and briefings. The Vice President is, therefore, a person who is quite likely to be found close to the levers of power and decision, but not necessarily so.[9]

Other Agencies Affecting Foreign Policy

It can be argued that virtually all the major governmental agencies today have an impact on American foreign policy. This is technically true. The U.S. Department of Labor, for example, sends representatives to international conferences on labor, and their performance could conceivably affect, for example, the development of labor movements in the underdeveloped areas. The focus in this book, however, is on those agencies and persons that participate in the formulation or execution of *major* foreign policies.

The most important agency that has not yet been mentioned is the Bureau of the Budget. It is the central coordinating agency for a President's budget proposals to Congress; that is, it is the clearing house for a President's program. The other agencies annually submit budget proposals to the Bureau, and it annually cuts them back and presents the President with an overall proposed budget, or program. The general magnitude of this budget and some of its elements are ordinarily the product of negotiations among the many interested parties, particularly the President, the Director of the Bureau of the Budget, and the major departments and other agencies. It is seldom large enough to suit the agencies or small enough to suit the Bureau or the Treasury Department. Whether it will contain projected deficits—less anticipated revenue than budgeted expenditures—or surpluses is a related and major policy decision that has to be worked out.

As with all other agencies, the amount of influence that the Bureau is

[9] At the risk of forsaking good taste, the reader is reminded that John Nance Garner, Vice President from 1933 to 1941, is reported to have advised Lyndon Johnson in 1960 that the vice presidency "is not worth a pitcher of warm spit." In the case of Johnson, that opinion turned out to be tragically erroneous. But that version of the office may become valid again some day if a President and a Vice President encounter insuperable personal or policy barriers between them and the President's life is spared.

able to exert in this grim struggle varies over time. But the Bureau is the only designedly disinterested party,[10] and its voice has often been quite prominent. Its impact is typically greater in a conservative administration that is deeply worried about large budgets and/or large budget deficits; the Bureau's role was almost certainly greater under Eisenhower than under either Kennedy or Johnson, for example. But in all recent administrations, its great experience and high prestige has assured it a prominent voice in budgetary matters and therefore in policy questions of the first magnitude.

The Department of the Treasury often has an impact on the character of American foreign policy. Aside from the obvious fact that the Treasury is interested in all matters involving governmental expenditures, there is the growing complexity of international monetary affairs. International affairs affect the dollar, and vice versa. As in the case of the Bureau of the Budget, the Treasury Department tends to wield more influence during Republican than during Democratic administrations. George Humphrey's influence during Eisenhower's first term, for example, was very great in all policy areas. It would be impossible to name a Treasury Secretary in a recent Democratic administration with similar power.

The Agency for International Development (AID) and the Peace Corps are technically agencies within the State Department. Their foreign assistance policies reflect changing emphases in American foreign policy, and, in turn, their experiences help to shape that policy. How much assistance should be offered, of what kind, and where, are matters undergoing constant analysis and change. The whole problem of foreign aid will be taken up in Chapter 8.

The Arms Control and Disarmament Agency was created in 1961. It occupies a somewhat anomalous position in the government. Its assigned policy area is so intimately connected with the responsibilities of the major departments concerned with foreign policy that it cannot possibly operate as a truly independent entity. Furthermore, its mere existence is viewed with disdain by powerful officials in the executive and legislative branches. The result has been that the agency has exerted little influence. When the Senate Foreign Relations Committee held hearings on the partial nuclear test ban treaty in 1963, the Arms Control and Disarmament Agency did not even testify. The key administration witnesses were, appropriately enough, the Secretaries of State and Defense and the Joint Chiefs of Staff.

---

[10] The Bureau is not, of course, really a "disinterested party." Depending upon the policy preferences of its leadership and also, in part, of its career specialists, the Bureau will deal kindly or harshly with specific proposals, will press for higher or lower overall expenditures, and will reflect one of the many possible attitudes toward deficit financing. Beyond that, the Bureau is composed of human beings who behave much as other human beings. Therefore, once the Bureau's priorities and proposals are set, its representatives will fight for them with something like the same tenacity that the other and more directly interested agencies bring to the struggle.

The Commerce Department promotes trade and has representatives all over the world. The Agriculture Department also has an interest in trade and plays a leading role in negotiations affecting the export and import of farm commodities.

Finally, the United States Information Agency should be mentioned. It has a marginal impact on the formulation of policy by virtue of its polling of sentiment abroad, but its primary significance is as an instrument of established policy. It attempts to influence public opinion in foreign nations by disseminating information about the United States and its policies. It does this through such means as radio broadcasting (the Voice of America); maintenance of libraries; distribution of books, magazines, and motion pictures; and personal contact. It maintains a total of over 200 field offices in over 100 countries. Like the CIA, it is engaged in an activity—in this case, propaganda—that is not traditional for the United States and that requires great skill and subtlety. It is, predictably, a frequent target of criticism.

It remains to note the existence of a vast and growing array of technical specialists who are employed by various governmental agencies to supply advice and information. They range in number and cost from the experienced private citizen who contributes his advice and counsel from time to time on specific issues to the huge research organizations (or "think tanks") that are technically nongovernmental but that depend largely or entirely upon contracts with the Federal government. These organizations, such as the RAND Corporation and the Hudson Institute, are a postwar phenomenon, a natural outgrowth of the government's extensive peacetime involvement in international affairs and the felt need to retain and develop expertise in a wide variety of technical and nontechnical fields. They are hired by various agencies in the executive branch to work on various kinds of problems, and their employees often become prominent and influential advisers to the government. Moreover, they constitute a training ground for high-level governmental positions. Several men from these types of organizations became officials in the government, for example, when the Kennedy administration assumed office.

Informal Sources of Advice and Information for the President

Political agitators and alarmists like to talk about "the invisible government." They paint dark and foreboding pictures of sinister, unseen forces, which they allege *really* control official policy in this country. There is no such invisible government, but there are many persons and institutions that affect policy while having no official responsibility.

Mention has already been made of the influence of personal friends and trusted counselors of the President who occupy no governmental position. Another recent example involves Dean Acheson, who was Secretary of State during Truman's last term. Since his party returned to office in 1961, Acheson has taken on a variety of limited official responsibilities, but for the most part he has remained a private citizen. He still lives in Washington, however, and maintains high-level contacts abroad. He had periodic conversations with President Kennedy about foreign affairs and was one of the first persons consulted by President Johnson in those dark days in late November, 1963. As long as Presidents and other high officials continue to seek or listen to his counsel, he will have at least a marginal effect on American policy.

Another informal source of influence on policy is partisan politics. No administration is so sure of continuing popular support that it can ignore the inevitable attacks from the domestic opposition party. This generally introduces a cautious or conservative strain into American foreign policy because new departures may prove to be unsuccessful, thereby creating an opportunity for the opposition party to condemn the innovation and the innovators.

Any administration in power seeks to foster "bipartisanship" in foreign policy. It trots out old slogans such as "politics stops at the water's edge" in an effort to muffle criticism. Conversely, the party not controlling the White House emphasizes the undeniable fact that a healthy democratic society not only permits but actually requires vocal and energetic voices of dissent.

The term "bipartisanship" is highly ambiguous. Does it mean that the parties *should* not disagree about foreign policy? Or, more incredibly, that they *do* not disagree? Or that they have not disagreed in the past? It is used in each of these senses, but of course the appropriate answer to each of the questions is "no." The term originated in the postwar period and is most often associated with Senator Arthur Vandenberg (R-Mich.). Vandenberg had been a typical Republican isolationist prior to World War II but was converted to internationalism during the war. As the most senior Republican member of the Senate Foreign Relations Committee, he became an influential Republican spokesman on foreign policy. Before and after the Republicans captured both houses of Congress in 1946, he cooperated with Truman on such vital matters as the establishment of the United Nations Organization, aid to Greece and Turkey, the Marshall Plan, and the creation of NATO. He never liked the phrase "bipartisan" because it implied erroneously that foreign policy was or should be wholly outside the partisan arena. He preferred "nonpartisan," which merely suggested that foreign policy positions should be based on a rational calculation of the national interest and not on what might work for partisan advantage at any given moment; partisan debate, in other words, should be restrained and responsible.

This generalized kind of sentiment works well enough when there is in fact a broad consensus about objectives and policies. If this consensus is ever seriously challenged, bipartisanship will be undermined. In its place we shall have two sharply divided party positions competing for public acceptance. As it is today, the foreign policy divergencies between the parties sound rather substantial during campaigns but turn out to be rather marginal in practice. It is instructive to note that the Secretary of State, the Undersecretary of State, and the Ambassador to the United Nations during the last years of the Republican Eisenhower administration were all employed by the subsequent Democratic Kennedy administration in positions of considerable responsibility. Secretary of State Christian Herter became President Kennedy's Special Representative for Trade Negotiations, Undersecretary of State Douglas Dillon became Secretary of the Treasury, and United Nations Ambassador Henry Cabot Lodge in 1963 became Ambassador to South Vietnam. There were many other less visible holdovers.

There are some signs that this combination of practical consensus and rhetorical skirmishing may be giving way to a more sharply differentiated set of attitudes and assumptions about objectives and policies. But even if, as seems more likely, the consensus should prevail, it is quite clear that partisan politics about what goes on beyond "the water's edge" will go on as always and that the foreign policies of all administrations will continue to be influenced by this fact.

The struggle over policy *within* parties is sometimes nearly as significant as the struggle *between* parties. When President Eisenhower assumed office, for example, he and his Secretary of State sometimes found more support for their internationalist policies among Democrats than they did among Republicans. The strongly nationalistic and naïvely militant element of the Republican party is periodically pronounced dead, but it survived the nomination of moderate candidates by the party from 1936 through 1960, and, despite the debacle of 1964, it promises to persist as a potent minority within the party for many years to come. This has historically been less of a problem for Democrats, but it could become more critical. The deep fissures opened up in the party by Democratic President Johnson's policies in 1965 in South Vietnam and the Dominican Republic may portend a new era in this regard.

Another and closely related informal source of influence on foreign policy is public opinion. If anything, this phrase is even more ambiguous and imprecise than the one just discussed. There is, of course, no monolithic public attitude about any policy question. There are many "publics" with differing levels of interest, information, and political strength, and they shift from issue to issue. Opinion polls may or may not address themselves to significant questions, and they may or may not accurately reflect the public temper at any given time. But they invariably report the public divided in its views, and they often show a widespread absence of opinion as well. These facts alone should caution against any simplistic notion that governments either do or should respond slavishly to "public opinion." Moreover, most polls have revealed a very permissive attitude within large segments of the public regarding what foreign policies an administration should pursue. When public sentiment is strongly united on some issue, however, few administrations would dare to defy it. Perhaps the most conspicuous recent example of a strong public sentiment setting American policy today relates to the nonrecognition of Red China.

What is the proper role of public opinion in a democracy? Given the complexity of foreign policy problems, any democratic system that made its government beholden to the spasmodic and often ill-informed whims of "the public" would seriously endanger its own security. Democratic theory does not—or should not—require a close popular control over policy. It requires only that the public be enabled to express opinions freely, including and especially dissenting ones, and that it retain the right to vote the administration out of office at regular intervals. Political leaders and experts have often been wrong, but so has "the public." No one has a monopoly on political judgment, and it is a romantic and dangerous notion to assume otherwise. Any administration that merely responds to what it believes public opinion to be is not assuming its responsibilities. It is elected to govern; it should do so.

Historically, among the most conspicuous kinds of influence was that wielded by the "hyphenated Americans": Irish-Americans, German-Americans, and so forth. With the sharp reduction in immigration in this century, that kind of influence is declining. Third- and fourth-generation Americans are much less likely to have emotional ties with "the old country."

There are two important exceptions to this, however. The most obvious is the impact of American Jews on United States policy toward Israel. The United States supported the establishment of a Jewish nation, quickly recognized Israel in 1948, and continues to aid and protect that beleaguered country. None of these policies were clearly dictated by long-range American national interest. A cool, detached appraisal might very well have come to quite different conclusions, emphasizing the desirability of cultivating good relations with the vastly larger, more populous, and oil-rich Arab states. The pressure of American Jews was, of course, reinforced by a general moral sense of obligation to Jews, especially after the unspeakable horrors perpetrated by Hitler. But the fact remains that the existence of a substantial and well-endowed Jewish population fundamentally affected American policy.

The other, less noticeable, exception is the increasing sensitivity to

African aspirations that the United States has displayed in recent years. This sensitivity would exist in any event, but it is powerfully reinforced by the decision makers' awareness that one-tenth of the American population is Negro.

The mass media—newspapers, magazines, radio, and television—are also a significant informal source of influence. Their impact on the lives of all of us scarcely needs underlining here. Regarding foreign policy, however, a specialized kind of influence is at work. Its purveyors are largely columnists and several newspapers.

There are about a half dozen widely respected or feared syndicated columnists, who, over the years, have an impact on official and unofficial thought. Walter Lippmann is perhaps the most prominent example. He has been writing about public affairs for over fifty years and has become something of a national institution or resource. His sources of information, whatever the administration, are extensive and highly placed; his judgments are widely respected. There is a reciprocal relationship between such a prominent "leader of opinion" and the government. Government officials provide him with information and attempt to influence his opinions. He, in turn, informs and tries to influence the government through his columns.[11] Lippmann is probably a unique case, but there are others of nearly equal stature, such as James Reston, Joseph Alsop, and Arthur Krock. President Kennedy reportedly read each of these gentlemen with regularity, and although such high-level access may or may not exist at any given time, these and other columnists always play a role in the Washington community within which the top policy makers live.

Newspapers play a similar but less personal and direct role. In Washington, *The New York Times*, the *Washington Post*, and the *Washington Evening Star* are the three most influential papers. What they report and in what way, what their editorials support or denounce: these things affect official Washington and are bound to have a subtle long-range impact on the quality of official thought and, therefore, official policy. (Fortunately, these are all excellent newspapers; *The New York Times* is probably the best newspaper in the world.)

It goes without saying that foreign governments affect American foreign policy. Their actions, their stated policies, and their official communiqués all have a bearing on what an Administration decides to do or say. Stronger nations, of course, have more influence than weaker ones; and allies or friends are presumably treated with more regard than adversaries.

All the informal sources mentioned above affect major policy; none of them come anywhere near controlling it. There is little disagreement about

---

[11] Sometimes the contact is more direct. No one was surprised, for example, to learn that nine days after he became President, Lyndon Johnson spent about an hour at Lippmann's home.

that, but there is much disagreement about the extent of influence wielded by economic interest groups or even certain individual companies.

For the Marxists, this is no problem at all. American foreign policy is simply and unavoidably the creature of the monopolists and imperialists who control the government. The absurdity of these assertions should not blind us, however, to the fact that official American policy in the past has occasionally been the servant of private economic interests. Historically, for example, much of our policy in Latin America has concerned itself largely or exclusively with creating and preserving opportunities for American private investments. This has sometimes been done out of the highest motives and sometimes not, but it frequently put the government in the position of protecting exploitative enterprises from which the local population derived little or no benefit. Rightly or wrongly—actually, it is some of each—there is a widespread conviction in Latin America that United States policy is concerned primarily with protecting lucrative private investments that may or may not be welcome.

Whatever may have been our motives in the past, it is quite obvious that we can no longer take that narrow a view of our relations with these nations in the future. Since this is generally understood, it seems unlikely that private economic interests will be able to control United States policy in these areas in the future. Unlikely, but not impossible. It seems certain, to cite an emerging problem, that many private overseas investments of American citizens and firms are going to be expropriated by militant and nationalistic governments. If "due and just" compensation is not paid promptly, is the United States going to respond to private pressures (or general indignation) by sending in the Marines, or cutting off economic assistance, or severing diplomatic relations? Those are not likely to be very prudent responses from the standpoint of our long-range interests, but it is conceivable that the expropriated interests may be able to help goad the government into such actions. To the extent to which they will be able to accomplish this, they will be controlling United States policy.

Overseas investments are only one aspect of the problem. Another and potentially more serious problem has to do with the relationship between American producers and United States trade policies. There is general agreement these days about the desirability of maintaining low or no traiff barriers, but as the barriers come down, some protected industries will be hurt, and even put out of business. Will they be able to induce the government to raise—or not to lower—the barriers? If they do—as some already have even under the unprecedentedly liberal 1962 Trade Act—they will be controlling United States policy in that limited, but significant and consequential, area.

By far the most widespread concern about the possibility of private interests' influencing United States policy unduly has to do with defense expenditures. Although this concern has resulted in some absurd and hysterical outbursts, it is quite legitimate. The government spends over $50 billion a year for defense and has been spending at least $35 billion a year since the Korean War. Quite naturally, there has developed a multitude of industries and even geographic areas that are largely or wholly dependent upon this gigantic enterprise. They have a vested interest in the cold war. More precisely, they have a vested interest in some particular aspect of the cold war: missiles, ships, tanks, military installations, or whatever it happens to be that their livelihood depends upon. On the governmental side, these private interests find allies in Congress—as noted in Chapter 2—and in the executive branch, especially, of course, in the Department of Defense.

This is so serious a matter, actually and potentially, that President Eisenhower made it the primary subject of his farewell address to the nation as President. He said:

> This conjunction of an immense military establishment and a large arms industry is new in American experience. The total influence—economic, political, even spiritual—is felt in every city, every State House, every office of the Federal government. We recognize the imperative need for this development. Yet we must not fail to comprehend its grave implications. Our toil, resources and livelihood are all involved; so is the very structure of our society.
>
> In the councils of government we must guard against the acquisition of unwarranted influence, whether sought or unsought, by the military-industrial complex. The potential for the disastrous rise of misplaced power exists and will persist. We must never let the weight of this combination endanger our liberties or democratic processes. We should take nothing for granted. Only an alert and knowledgeable citizenry can compel the proper meshing of the huge industrial and military machinery of defense with our peaceful methods and goals, so that security and liberty may prosper together.

The primary emphasis in the above statements was on the threat to our traditional liberties. This is surely a matter of the greatest importance, but our concern at this point relates more to how this "military-industrial complex" may affect our foreign policies. General Eisenhower evidently felt that he, as a professional military person and one with vast experience at the highest policy levels in government, had been able to cope with these pressures, but he was apparently concerned about the strength or wisdom of his young and inexperienced successor.

There are many specific and vital areas of foreign policy that might be affected by these kinds of private and intragovernmental pressures. First and foremost is the fundamental question of what official attitudes toward the cold war should be. Is it interminable? Should we continue to seek means of reducing tensions? However one answers these and related kinds of questions, it is vitally important that the official answers be disinterested ones. The fact that many people and organizations and even regions have a large economic stake in the perpetuation of the cold war should not have any bearing on the answers. Too much is at stake for that.

This is not to suggest that such interested parties invariably favor prolonging the cold war; many of them rise above their own immediate interests. Nor is it meant to suggest that disinterested answers would necessarily be different from interested ones; they very often are not. But it is of transcendent importance that official attitudes and policies have as their criteria what is good for the nation as a whole and in the long run.

Secondly and relatedly, overall defense policy might be affected by such pressures. Questions such as the following are involved: What types of missiles should be developed? How fast? Should bombers be largely discarded? If so, when? How should the defense budget be distributed among the competing armed services? Each one of these questions is loaded with strategic implications, and each one of them touches vested interests. The nation's very survival may depend on the top leadership's ability to make such basic decisions on objective grounds.

Thirdly, and perhaps even more directly related to the first question, what should United States disarmament policy be? Do we favor any kind of disarmament? If so, what kind and under what conditions? A favorite Soviet line is that the United States economy could not survive disarmament and that therefore the United States government really does not want it. There is no doubt that the economic adjustments to serious disarmament would be severe. And it may also be true that the only kinds of disarmament that are likely to be negotiated would be inimical to United States security. But again, the important thing is that official policy not be the product of interested pressures.

There are subtler problems involved, as is suggested by General Eisenhower's use of the term "spiritual." A rational formulation of foreign policy in a democracy is possible only in an atmosphere of freedom, where dissent is not only possible but respected. It is not only those persons and institutions that have a direct economic interest in "the military-industrial complex" whose vision may be blurred from time to time as the long period of tension persists. The whole society runs the risk of adopting rigid and doctrinaire attitudes that are almost certain to hinder, if not prevent altogether, the objective formulation of wise policy. Such trends are unquestionably encouraged by the mammoth presence of a "military-industrial complex." It is the responsibility of the persons most directly involved and of the rest of society as well to see to it that they are held in check.

The above paragraphs are not meant to be alarmist. The Eisenhower warning was not meant to and did not describe an existing condition, and there is no sign that the subsequent administrations have lost control of official policies. Nor is any future administration likely to abdicate its responsibility to make policy for the whole country. But the problem is a real one, and it will persist.

The Problem of Coordination

The President is only one man, and the time that he ordinarily can devote to foreign policy is limited. This, plus the unavoidable complexity and interrelatedness of all aspects of foreign policy, gives rise to the difficult problem of coordinating—or making internally consistent and complementary—the nation's major foreign policies. Given the facts that American policy interests cover nearly the entire globe, involve economic, military, political, and cultural considerations, and are formulated by diverse elements of our complicated government, this problem of coordination is a central one. It is not at all uncommon for some aspects of American—or Soviet—policy to be working at cross-purposes; indeed, it is virtually unavoidable. The importance of keeping such contradictions at a minimum is obvious.

From among a wide range of possible examples, consider the matter of United States relations to the nations of Europe, especially its military dimension. Europe is changing rapidly these days; the direction this change will finally take is not clear, but the fact of change is. American policy must adjust to these changes or become outmoded and ineffectual. A central issue that has emerged is the control of nuclear weapons. The United States and, in lesser degree, Great Britain have provided and controlled these weapons, the major military means of keeping the Soviet Union out of Western Europe. As Soviet capabilities in this respect have advanced to the point where they now could inflict catastrophic blows on the United States, many Europeans have begun to fear that the United States, whatever its intentions, cannot be relied upon to enter a war involving only Europe, since that involvement would invite a Soviet attack on the United States. As the Europeans have revived economically and grown in self-confidence, this fear of United States withdrawal has grown apace; the result, reasonably enough, has been a growing demand for an independent nuclear capability.

The United States is not pleased with this development for a variety of reasons, to be discussed in Chapter 7. The substantive question is: What policies should the United States adopt to meet this growing problem? The procedural, or administrative, question is: Who should formulate these new policies? The problem is surely military. Should it, therefore, be turned over to the Department of Defense? But it is also political because the manner in which it is handled will affect the whole gamut of United States–European relations; the Department of State is therefore an interested party. In addition, the President's domestic political advisers will be concerned because anything involving nuclear weapons can have partisan repercussions. Finally, Congress is implicated because it might or might not be asked to change the laws affecting United States control over nuclear weapons.

Could the National Security Council and its staff work out an acceptable policy on such a delicate matter? Could an *ad hoc* committee of lower-level officials from both Departments and the White House staff do it? Could the Secretaries of Defense and State reach an agreement? The answers to these questions vary from issue to issue. In the one under discussion, it appears that the State Department has played the leading role in hammering out a policy. In another instance, it could be the Defense Department. (In either case, the President's approval would, of course, ultimately be necessary.) Oftentimes, the rivalries between agencies become so intense that it is virtually impossible for any one of them to "play a leading role" in working out a policy. It requires little imagination to understand what happens in the executive branch over a major issue such as a disarmament proposal, for example. The Departments of State and Defense, the Arms Control and Disarmament Agency, the Atomic Energy Commission, and the CIA are only the most prominent agencies with a stake in such a matter. The wrangling between them can become intense and even bitter.

When George Kennan, career diplomat and distinguished historian, resigned as Ambassador to Yugoslavia in 1963, he told a Senate subcommittee that he had been severely handicapped by the inability or unwillingness of his superiors in Washington to make sensible and coordinated responses to his problems and requests. His testimony is worth quoting in some detail.

A . . . serious limitation on my own effectiveness in shaping policy towards the country in which I was stationed was presented by my inability to get recommendations accepted in Washington. I rarely had difficulty in this respect when it was a case of policy matters on which the Department of State had discretion to act, although, of course, there were such cases, too. The trouble usually occurred where the Department of State, or at least its central organs, did not have primary responsibility for the decision. The difficulties were greatest, it seemed to me, when the matters in question were ones considered to lie within the primary competence of AID, of the Pentagon, of the budgetary or fiscal authorities, or of those authorities (I am ashamed to say that I do not know exactly who they are) which backstop the Department of State in, and in some respects control, such matters as the issuance of passports, visas, re-entry permits, etc.

With these latter, in particular, I felt the lack of any effective liaison. They included, I suppose, people in the Immigration Service, and in the FBI. I was never sure that they understood, or shared, or respected, the policy determinations of the Department of State with relation to Yugoslavia. . . .

In budgetary and fiscal matters, again, the Ambassador was sadly powerless. In general, he simply took what he got. The Department of State might receive his recommendations sympathetically; but the Department itself was too lacking in flexibility and authority to put them into effect with any firmness or promptness. Such recommendations had a habit of trailing off into the mysteries of the Budget Bureau, or the Treasury, or congressional appropriations committees, to a point where all track of them was lost, where months and years went by, and the Ambassador eventually either was transferred or forgot he had made them. . . .[12]

As if this weren't complicated and obstructive enough, there is the additional fact that these agencies are usually divided internally on contentious issues. At best, this results in delays; at worst, it causes immobilization.

There is therefore a premium in our government on strong leaders who are able to control their agencies and coordinate their policies or, when necessary, impose a solution by the exercise of authority or influence.

---

[12] *Administration of National Security, Hearings of the Subcommittee on National Security Staffing and Operations of the Senate Committee on Government Operations,* 88th Cong., 1st Sess., Dec. 11, 1963, pt. 5, p. 359.

The problem of coordination might also be defined to include the issues raised in the preceding chapter about congressional participation in the formulation of policy. Kennan had some angry things to say on this subject as well. For example:

> With respect to matters falling under the competence of AID, I found our governmental procedures slow and inflexible to an alarming degree. In general, I felt that the time for aid to Yugoslavia had passed. The aid programs were, in fact, generally dismantled during the period of my service there; and this was in accordance with my own recommendations. But there were times when a minor area of discretion on the part of the Ambassador would have yielded dividends from the standpoint of national interest, and when the absence of it was frustrating and embarrassing. This, again, was primarily a matter of congressional policy— particularly of the existence of sweeping and rigid restrictions on aid, or anything that smacked of aid, toward Yugoslavia. As an example, we were seriously handicapped by these legislative restrictions when it came to trying to render assistance in the case of the Skoplje earthquake. This was surely unnecessary. If the legislative stipulation had only allowed us a relatively small sum, to be used at the discretion of the Ambassador or the Secretary of State in instances when there appeared to be special need, we would have been spared this sort of embarrassment.
>
> I mention with some hesitation these instances of the limitations placed by legislative action on the ability of the Ambassador to play his part effectively. I have no choice but to do so; for these were the main impediments I experienced to the full deployment of my usefulness at my post. I do not need to remind you of the restrictions placed last year, not only on the extension of anything under the heading of aid, but even on the extension of normal trading facilities to Yugoslavia. These restrictions were adopted in the face of the most solemn and formal sort of warnings and objections on my part, conveyed to congressional leaders on many occasions and in many ways. It seems to me that a problem is arising here to which we shall, all of us, have to give attention sooner or later.
>
> If I had known, for example, when I was offered the position of Ambassador in Yugoslavia, how little value the Congress would assign to my own judgment, in the light of an experience of nearly 30 years in the affairs of the Eastern European area, I would not have accepted the appointment; for without the support of Congress it was impossible to carry out an effective policy there. I do not know how this sort of a situation can be avoided; but I think Members of Congress might wish to bear in mind that there is usually a price to be paid, not just in terms of the peace of mind of the person most affected, but in terms of the national interest itself, when an Ambassador's recommendations are wholly disregarded on the legislative side of the Government; for it is not just his usefulness in the given question, but his usefulness as a whole, which is thereby affected.[13]

[13] *Ibid.*, p. 360.

Policy coordination is not impossible to achieve despite the grim possibilities outlined above. Much depends upon the strength of and the personal relations between such persons as the Secretary of State and Secretary of Defense. If effective department heads get along well together, policy coordination is much easier to achieve. But when one of these men is not conspicuously in control of his department, or when they do not like and respect each other, difficulties are almost certain to arise. For example, in the early part of President Truman's second term, State-Defense relations were poor, and policy coordination was therefore difficult. When General George C. Marshall became Secretary of Defense in 1950, the Secretary of State was Dean Acheson, who had earlier been Undersecretary of State under Marshall. The two men admired and trusted each other and were both strong leaders; the result was a considerable amount of agreement and cooperation on foreign policy, especially and importantly regarding the war in Korea.

If no one else is able to impose or induce an acceptable policy in a given area, either the President does it or it does not get done at all. In matters as knotty as the ones mentioned above, that last possibility is by no means ruled out. Sometimes no acceptable policies can be worked out for emerging issues. For the moment, the central point is that very often foreign policy problems touch on a range of issues that draw in both the legislative and executive branches of government and, within each of them, competing and maybe even hostile elements.

Coordination, therefore, is not merely an intellectual challenge that can be assigned to experts in administration or logic or accommodation. It requires strong leadership that, by one means or another, is capable of inducing an intelligent common agreement or of imposing a settlement. A strong President will go a long way toward accomplishing this purpose. A weak or indecisive President will invite incessant rivalry and competition, and, unless some major figure such as the Secretary of State or Secretary of Defense is able to fill this leadership role, the result is likely to be contradictory and ineffectual policies.

Different administrations use different methods for attempting to coordinate the formulation of policy. During the Kennedy administration, there was considerable use of the *ad hoc* interagency task force for such purposes. There was, for example, a Berlin task force consisting of representatives of the interested agencies, which met regularly in an effort to achieve a united governmental policy regarding American policy in Berlin. This group also endeavored to coordinate American and Western European policies regarding Berlin.

But the problem of coordination is only partly that of imposing from above or agreeing upon an overall policy. Once such a strategy is worked out, it is by no means self-executing. Of the great numbers of people who must participate in its execution, many are in a position to undermine it.

This is not the place to go into the question of why bureaucracies are unavoidably difficult to control, but that they are is beyond dispute.[14] It is usually not impossible for a President to impose a major policy on a reluctant or hostile agency, but it is seldom easy. Agency heads encounter the same difficulties, most conspicuously the Secretary of Defense. It is often said that Robert McNamara became the first Secretary of Defense who really controlled the defense establishment. However that may be, the statement accurately suggests the magnitude of the task.

The problem of coordination is perhaps most acute in Washington, but it is by no means absent overseas. A typical American diplomatic mission today includes not only the traditional representation of the Foreign Service and military attachés, but also employees of the Agency for International Development (AID), the United States Information Agency (USIA), the Central Intelligence Agency (CIA), and, often, a Military Assistance Advisory Group (MAAG). These are the elements of what has come to be called "the country team." They are supposed to be under the general policy direction of the Ambassador but it is obvious that this is often little more than a "polite fiction."[15] The representatives of these other agencies often feel very little responsibility for coordinating their policies with the Ambassador. They have problems of their own, and they have superiors in Washington to whom they are more likely to turn for advice and support on budgetary and operational matters. This is especially true of the MAAG officers and, to a lesser degree, of the CIA as well. And there have been instances where the foreign assistance chief has undercut the position of the Ambassador in nations that are heavily dependent upon American aid. It takes a strong and willful Ambassador to weld these disparate elements together despite the fact that repeated Presidential orders have made it clear that the Ambassador is supposed to be in charge.

But even assuming that the President and the agency heads agree and assuming further that they control the agencies, the problem of coordination is still present. Unforeseen and unprecedented situations arise, often of very great complexity, which induce spontaneous and contradictory responses within and between agencies. The classic instance was the U-2 episode of May, 1960. Two weeks before a celebrated summit meeting was to take place in Paris, an American spy plane, a U-2, was shot down near Sverdlovsk, a city deep inside Russia. The U-2 was an unusual aircraft

---

[14] Among the most important books dealing with this problem is Richard E. Neustadt's *Presidential Power: The Politics of Leadership*, John Wiley & Sons, Inc., New York, 1960.

[15] This phrase and much of the accompanying discussion are drawn from an excellent staff report of the Subcommittee on National Security Staffing and Operations of the Senate Committee on Government Operations, entitled *Administration of National Security: Basic Issues*, Washington, D.C., 1963. See also a study prepared by the Historical Studies Division of the Department of State entitled *The Ambassador and the Problem of Coordination*, which was published by the same subcommittee in 1963.

designed to fly at extremely high altitudes and equipped with sensitive cameras and other complex instruments capable of measuring the effectiveness of Soviet radar and sampling the air to help determine whether the Soviets were testing nuclear weapons and, if so, what kinds. U-2s had been flying over the Soviet Union unmolested for nearly four years before this one was shot down by a powerful Soviet missile on May 1. When the Soviets first announced the shooting down of an unidentified American plane, the National Aeronautics and Space Administration (NASA) asserted that it must have been a weather plane operating from Turkey, which might inadvertently have strayed over into Soviet air space. The State Department piously announced that no American planes had ever been deliberately sent over Russian territory. When the Soviets then put their evidence on public display, the State Department responded by saying that no such flights had been authorized by officials in Washington, thereby suggesting that some intelligence officials were independently carrying on this spectacular and dangerous espionage activity. When it became clear that the domestic political opposition would be able to use such incredible negligence as a weapon in the forthcoming presidential campaign, President Eisenhower intervened and announced to a bewildered and embarrassed nation that he had indeed authorized such flights. Moreover, just before the President left for the summit meeting, his press secretary announced that reports suggesting that such flights had now been canceled were false. Three days later, in Paris, the President said that the flights had in fact been suspended and were not to be resumed.

Premier Khrushchev proceeded to turn the summit conference into a shambles, demanding an official apology and punishment for those responsible. What his immediate motives were and whether a U-2 flight should have been permitted at that particular time are arguable questions. What is inescapable, however, is that the whole episode revealed in stark terms how high the price can be for administrative chaos and policy confusion. Faced with this crisis, the administration lied at least once, made two diametrically opposed policy statements regarding continued flights, and wound up violating a fundamental canon of intelligence: the President assumed personal responsibility for the flight. Such a performance raises doubts at home and abroad about the ability of the United States government to conduct its foreign policy with intelligence, discretion, and a firm sense of purpose.

Finally, although not strictly relevant, it should also be noted that official policy, however clear and agreed upon, is not always regarded as binding by adventuresome and dissident citizens. Sometimes, private ventures in foreign policy become so important that the question arises of who is really in charge. The most obvious contemporary examples relate, as one might expect, to the hotly controversial matters of how the United States should conduct relations, if any, with Communist countries. Such things as private raids on Cuba, a union's refusal to unload goods from certain Communist countries, and a Los Angeles mayor's uncordial treatment of a Soviet premier are largely outside the control of the Federal government, yet the United States is held responsible for them. Such episodes are usually embarrassing and could conceivably be dangerous. It is, of course, nonsense to argue that it is incumbent upon a democratic system to permit every citizen to formulate and execute his own foreign policy.

The Execution of Policy

Thus far we have dealt mostly with the formulation of policy; it remains to focus on its execution. This is important for two basic reasons: The skill or lack of skill with which policy is carried out can be of decisive importance; and the line between formulation and execution is partly an artificial one anyway.

Regarding both of these points, consider for example the role of the United States delegation to the United Nations. It is the official policy of the United States to support the demands for independence of colonial peoples; and this has been a major issue at United Nations meetings for years. Since the official United States position accords with that held by almost all United Nations members, there might appear to be little diplomatic finesse required. Actually, however, the matter is quite delicate and requires considerable diplomatic skill.

The general policy of support for independence demands must be applied in specific circumstances; this is where the difficulties begin. Suppose the African and Asian nations are proposing an economic boycott of Portugal in an effort to induce Portugal to grant independence to its African colonies. Suppose also that European nations are opposed to the proposal on the grounds that this is beyond the United Nations' legitimate authority and/or that it would not be effective anyway. The United States Ambassador would be in a difficult position. He would not want to alienate either our European allies or the newly independent nations of Asia and Africa. If he is skillful and energetic, he might be able to negotiate a compromise resolution. Or he might be able to persuade the African and Asian delegates unilaterally to soften their proposal to a mere denunciation of Portugal. Whatever he does, and even if he does nothing, the manner in which he conducts himself—whether he demonstrates good will or the reverse, whether he acts with intelligence and understanding or the reverse, whether he can be trusted or not—may well be as important as what he does. Especially on such emotional matters, a diplomat's style and bearing can be critically important.

As suggested above, the example used also demonstrates that it is often quite difficult in practice to distinguish between formulation and execution of policy. Given modern communications facilities, United States Ambassadors are often not as free to act on their own initiatives as they once were. But Washington cannot control everything that its diplomats do; there is bound to be an area of discretion. In this area of discretion, important decisions may have to be made. When, for example, our Ambassador is seeking to work out a compromise on an issue such as this one, he may or may not have detailed instructions on what is acceptable in Washington; and he may or may not have time to consult with Washington. But even if he has detailed instructions and time to consult, he is still in a position to affect the outcome by his own performance. And his performance in effect constitutes American policy.

Most United States representatives abroad do not vote or negotiate about votes as in the example above. Nonetheless, the responsibilities in the execution of policy can be very considerable. Consider the case of a United States Ambassador to France. For a variety of reasons, United States–French relations have been strained in recent years. There is a natural temptation under such circumstances to give way to pique and the expression of hostilities that have developed. The long-range interests of the United States nonetheless call for cooperation with France, and it is therefore incumbent upon American representatives there to conduct themselves with patience, restraint, tact, and a sense of proportion. The common meaning of the word "diplomatic" suggests what is required of diplomats.

The importance of a high-quality diplomatic corps should be nearly self-evident. Beyond the importance of having the nation well represented and symbolized abroad, and beyond also the obvious desirability of having skillful negotiators at the conference table, it is vitally necessary to have diplomats who can report accurately on developments in the country to which they are assigned. The reporting function alone demands intelligence and judgment to ensure that enough—but not too much—information is sent to Washington and to provide for sophisticated and policy-oriented analysis.

To emphasize the continuing role of the regular diplomat is not to deny the increased role of higher-level officials. There has been a good deal of controversy in recent years over the extensive travels of American Secretaries of State. It has been alleged, among other things, that these travels undermine the importance and morale of the regular diplomatic corps. Of equal or perhaps greater importance is the suggestion that such frequent high-level confrontations between allies and between adversaries results in the adoption of unnecessarily rigid positions and an unfortunate tendency to use the attendant glare of publicity for propaganda purposes rather than serious diplomatic discussions. All of these criticisms are undoubtedly justified, as are the additional allegations that a Secretary in an airplane or in a diplomatic conference is not in a good position either to tend to his department or to retain a broad view of the nation's policies or of his responsibilities. Nonetheless, there seems to be no way out of these demands on a Secretary's time and presence. The character of diplomacy has, along with everything else, been altered by modern technology.

A question of graver importance is what role the President himself should play in negotiations. The pressure for "summit" conferences is often quite substantial. The Soviets frequently call for summit meetings—to engage in propaganda or to test Western intentions or for some other reasons—and sometimes Western governments do also. The natural longing of people everywhere for a relaxation of cold-war tensions gives rise to periodic demands that the top leaders get together and iron everything out on the spot. The leaders themselves, usually less optimistic about international consequences, often want such conferences as a means of bolstering their own prestige at home. It is no small thing to sit down with a Soviet premier and talk about world affairs. If nothing comes of it, you have demonstrated that you cannot be bullied by the Russians. If some sort of accord results, no matter how insignificant, you have shown yourself to be a man of peace.

Despite these attractions, real and imagined, summit conferences are risky affairs. The most telling argument against them is that they bring together people who in a very special way symbolize and represent the antagonistic nations. With such weighty figures, there is less disposition to engage in the subtle and often lengthy art of negotiation. Instead, there is a propensity toward posturing, clinging to fixed positions, and demanding concessions. Even more important is the fact that they represent the final authority: when they disagree, there is nothing left to say or do about an issue. When their subordinates disagree during routine negotiations, on the other hand, there is always the possibility, however dim, that when the results are reported to their superiors, some adjustments might ensue that would resolve the problem. The sense of finality that hangs over a summit conference is potentially dangerous and not only because one of the protagonists might lose his temper.

It should also be borne in mind that Presidents are not necessarily effective diplomats. If the experiences of, for example, Woodrow Wilson, Franklin Roosevelt, and Dwight Eisenhower are at all representative, it is by no means obvious that using Presidents as diplomats is a prudent practice.

Finally, conferences between heads of state take place under even less auspicious circumstances than do those between foreign ministers, as noted above. The enormous amount of publicity that is generated by such an event is not conducive to serious discussion. The eyes of an anxious world are focused on the conference, and the journalists outnumber the diplomats several times over. There is an insatiable demand for news. In the absence of anything promising to report, the delegations may begin to suggest to the press that the other side is being obstructionist. It does not take many such releases to eliminate any possibility for diplomatic progress.

And this assumes that the participants came to the conference prepared for serious discussions. Such an assumption is, of course, not necessarily in accord with reality and, indeed, very often is not. There is a much greater likelihood that one or all of the participants came to the conference primarily for propaganda purposes. Once the competition for favorable press coverage begins, any chance for productive negotiation is destroyed or, at best, sharply reduced.

It is, of course, conceivable that these risks, so conspicuous in the postwar summit meetings, might be overcome if conditions were favorable. In this as in most other matters affecting foreign policy, a fixed and dogmatic position would be unwise. It would not, for example, be likely to be in the interests of the United States to resist all summit meetings as a matter of principle. Even when the conference is likely to prove a failure, it may hurt the United States more to refuse to attend than actually to attend. Moreover, there is always the possibility that someday such a conference might accomplish something. Unless agreements were worked out in advance by subordinates and were merely ratified amidst much fanfare by the top leaders, such a result is unlikely in the extreme. But it should not be ruled out altogether.

But whatever may be the prudent attitude toward such things as summit conferences and secretarial travels, the fact remains that the style and tactics with which foreign policy is conducted are often nearly as important as the substance of the policy itself. Such things as an indiscreet reply at a press conference, a premature publication of a policy position, or an imprudent bluff can have serious implications. The U-2 episode discussed above was only partly a matter of poor coordination among various policy makers. It was also a sad example of clumsy diplomacy. Conversely, skillful diplomacy can earn rewards.

This last sentence seems rather obvious, but nonetheless there are some who mistrust the whole diplomatic function, especially as it involves negotiations with the nation's adversaries. It is, of course, true that the diplomatic exchanges between the United States and the Soviet Union are of a different order than those between, say, the United States and Great Britain. In the former instance, diplomacy often takes on the aspect of "a dialogue of the deaf." Each side rejects the basic purposes and values of the other. Nevertheless, in this thermonuclear age, both sides have one overriding common interest, the avoidance of war against each other. As President Kennedy said in November, 1961:

> The essential fact . . . is that diplomacy and defense are not substitutes for one another. Either alone would fail. A willingness to resist force, unaccompanied by a

willingness to talk, could provoke belligerence—while a willingness to talk, unaccompanied by a willingness to resist force, could invite disaster.

But as long as we know precisely what comprises our vital interests and our long-range goals, we have nothing to fear from negotiations at the appropriate time, and nothing to gain by refusing them.

At a time when a single clash could escalate overnight into a holocaust of mushroom clouds, a great power does not prove its firmness by leaving the task of exploring the other's intentions to sentries or those without full responsibility.

Nor can ultimate weapons rightfully be employed, or the ultimate sacrifice rightfully demanded of our citizens, until every reasonable solution has been explored.

In Conclusion

"American foreign policy today is everybody's business." The fate of the entire world is bound up in an unprecedented manner with the foreign policies of the Soviet Union and the United States. The burdens and responsibilities of the Presidency, therefore, have become awesome. Perhaps "monstrous" would be a better word because it suggests both size and something of the potential for horror or disaster, as well. Richard Neustadt has spoken of the "irreversibility" of some of the risks that a President must take. He then adds the chilling thought that such risks are not only irreversible, they are irremediable.

The sitting President lives daily with the knowledge that at any time, he, personally, may have to make a human judgment—or may fail to control someone else's judgment—which puts half the world in jeopardy and cannot be called back. You and I will recognize his burden intellectually; he actually experiences it emotionally. It cannot help but set him—and his needs—sharply apart from all the rest of us. . . .[16]

Selected Bibliography

Almond, Gabriel A.: *The American People and Foreign Policy,* Frederick A. Praeger, Inc., New York, 1960. (Originally published in 1950 by Harcourt, Brace & World, Inc., New York. The later edition contains a new introduction.) The classic but unfortunately rather dated treatment of how the American public perceives and responds to foreign policy issues.

Cater, Douglas: *The Fourth Branch of Government,* Houghton Mifflin Company, Boston, 1959. A thoughtful and revealing discussion of the intimate relationship between the government and the press.

[16] Administration of National Security, *Hearings before the Subcommittee on National Security Staffing and Operations of the Senate Committee on Government Operations,* 88th Cong., 1st Sess., Mar. 25, 1963, pt. 1, p. 76.

Cohen, Bernard C.: *The Press and Foreign Policy*, Princeton University Press, Princeton, N. J., 1963. A scholarly attempt to explain how the press affects foreign policy.

Graebner, Norman A. (ed.): *An Uncertain Tradition: American Secretaries of State in the Twentieth Century*, McGraw-Hill Book Company, New York, 1961. (Available in a paperback edition, same publisher.) A collection of essays describing and evaluating the performances of the twentieth-century Secretaries of State, through John Foster Dulles.

McCamy, James L.: *Conduct of the New Diplomacy*, Harper & Row, Publishers, Incorporated, New York, 1964. A detailed analysis and evaluation of the way in which contemporary American foreign policy is made and executed.

Neustadt, Richard E.: *Presidential Power: The Politics of Leadership*, John Wiley & Sons, Inc., New York, 1960. (Available in a paperback edition, same publisher.) A political science classic, and deservedly so, with much of the analysis devoted to presidential conduct of foreign policy.

Price, Don K. (ed.): *The Secretary of State*, Spectrum Books, Prentice-Hall, Inc., Englewood Cliffs, N. J., 1960. An uneven collection of essays; see especially those by Dean Acheson, Henry M. Wriston, and William Y. Elliott.

Rosenau, James N. (ed.): *International Politics and Foreign Policy*, The Free Press of Glencoe, New York, 1961, selections 22, 23, 24, and 25. The cited selections deal with the policy-making process in the United States.

Scott, Andrew M., and Raymond H. Dawson: *Readings in the Making of American Foreign Policy*, The Macmillan Company, New York, 1965. A well-chosen collection of articles dealing with virtually every aspect of the policy-making process.

Sorenson, Theodore C.: *Decision Making in the White House*, Columbia University Press, New York, 1963. (Available in a paperback edition, same publisher, 1964.) These lectures were given by President Kennedy's close associate while the late President was still alive.

Subcommittee on National Policy Machinery and Subcommittee on National Security Staffing and Operations of the Senate Committee on Government Operations, Henry M. Jackson, Chairman. The first-named subcommittee held hearings in 1960 and 1961; the second-named held hearings in 1963 and 1964. Both sets of hearings were concerned primarily with the efficiency and efficacy of the policy-making process in the executive branch. In addition to voluminous hearings, both subcommittees published a bibliography, extensive staff studies, and other background materials.

Selected extracts of the later material are available commercially in separate volumes: Senator Henry M. Jackson (ed.), Frederick A. Praeger, Inc., New York, 1964 and 1965.

Thayer, Charles W.: *Diplomat*, Harper & Row, Publishers, Incorporated, New York, 1959. A wise and lively book by a retired career Foreign Service Officer.

ALASKA

TREATY OF PORTSMOUTH

Chapter Four

The Roots of the Cold War

chapter 4   The most important and pervasive political fact in the world today is the cold war. The cold war is the sum total of all the rivalry, suspicion, and hostility that divide the major powers of the West and the Soviet Union. It is based on radically conflicting ideologies, values, purposes, and interests. It is characterized by the mutual pursuit of political, military, economic, ideological, and propaganda advantages. What distinguishes the cold war most sharply from preceding struggles for values, security, and power is the ominous presence on both sides of thermonuclear weapons and the capability of delivering them with intercontinental missiles.

In view of the fact that from 1941 to 1945, the Soviet Union, Great Britain, and the United States fought as allies and won World War II, questions naturally arise as to how and why the cold war began. While it would have betrayed an absence of historical sensitivity to believe that the wartime alliance would naturally survive the demise of the common foe and would usher in an era of cooperation, nonetheless there were high hopes in 1945 that the common experience of a colossally destructive war coupled with the dawning of the atomic era would induce a new civility in international politics. There is some evidence that these hopes were not merely products of Western liberalism and sentimentality but were indeed shared by the Soviet leaders, who are neither liberal nor sentimental.

Trying to isolate and define the roots of the cold war is an ambitious and perhaps ultimately an impossible task. Simple or single-cause explanations of great historic developments are easy to construct, but they do not increase understanding or show a decent regard for truth. Many factors contributed to the conversion of the triumph of World War II into the tragedy of the cold war. Communist ideology, Russian history, Western history, the personality of Stalin, Western—especially American—unwillingness to acquiesce quietly in the Sovietization of Eastern Europe, and the specific political issues that arose in the aftermath of the war: all of these factors and more played a part. This book makes no pretense of accounting exhaustively for so complex a phenomenon. But some background to contemporary affairs is essential to an understanding of them, and what follows is an attempt to describe *some* of the more important strands in the emergence of this fateful confrontation.

Some Historical Considerations

The United States and Russia have never fought a war against each other. This suggests that historically their interests have never seriously clashed. The United States has, after all, become involved in armed conflict with most of the major powers in the world, including England, Italy, Spain, Japan, and, of course, Germany.

On the other hand, the two nations had very little to do with each other prior to the Bolshevik seizure of power in 1917. There were sporadic political contacts over the years, such as the friendly appearance of a substantial number of Russian warships in New York and San Francisco harbors during the Civil War, which contributed to the North's victory by giving pause to those European states that were considering recognition of the Confederate government. Shortly thereafter, Secretary of State Seward unwittingly but luckily made his strategic contribution to the future cold war by overcoming strenuous domestic opposition and purchasing Alaska for the allegedly exorbitant sum of $7,200,000.

As the United States began to play a more active role in international affairs in the late nineteenth century, Russian and American interests clashed in China. The Czar was seeking to extend Russian control into Manchuria and Korea, and the United States sought instead to gain acceptance of its "Open Door" policy regarding China. Neither side trusted the motives of the other, but their contradictory aims suddenly became obsolete with the Japanese attack in 1904 on a Russian naval base in Manchuria. After Russia's crushing naval and military defeats, President Theodore Roosevelt eased Russo-American relations by playing a leading role in working out a peaceful settlement in 1905—the Treaty of Portsmouth (New Hampshire)—which satisfied both the combatants and the United States.

For the most part, however, contacts between the two emerging giants were relatively insignificant and cannot be regarded as providing the roots for either harmony or disharmony.

There has occasionally been some rather mysterious writing to the effect that the two vast continental powers were basically different from the European nations and were in some fundamental way very much alike. Those who like to speculate grandly about "the soul of a nation" have sometimes declared that Russians and Americans have a great deal in common and share a common or similar destiny. It is hard to come to grips with notions of this kind; their validity is beyond proof or disproof, and their relevance to practical affairs is doubtful. Tocqueville's famous comment—first published in 1835—has some of this flavor but is, characteristically, also more refined and instructive:

> There are at the present time two great nations in the world, which started from different points, but seem to tend towards the same end. I allude to the Russians and the Americans. . . .
>
> All other nations seem to have nearly reached their natural limits, and they have only to maintain their power; but these are still in the act of growth. . . . The American struggles against the obstacles that nature opposes to him; the adversaries of the Russian are men. The former combats the wilderness and savage life; the latter, civilization with all its arms. The conquests of the American are therefore gained by the plowshare; those of the Russian by the sword. The Anglo-American relies upon personal interest to accomplish his ends and gives free scope to the

unguided strength and common sense of the people; the Russian centers all of the authority of society in a single arm. The principal instrument of the former is freedom; of the latter, servitude. Their starting-point is different and their courses are not the same; yet each of them seems marked out by the will of Heaven to sway the destinies of half the globe.[1]

For our purposes, the central and still valid message of this quotation is that whatever the superficial similarities between the two nations may be, their historic experience—especially the development of their political institutions—has been fundamentally different. The one has been an open society, with democratic governments and great personal freedom; the other has been a closed society, with despotic governments and no substantial tradition of freedom. This does not, of course, preclude the possibility of their existing harmoniously together, but it does make it more difficult. Those who dismiss as irrelevant to foreign policy the character of the governmental system of any given nation are unable to explain, for example, the special relationship that has existed for so many years between the United States and Great Britain, or the United States and Canada. The special affinities—and the unguarded borders—are the result of something more basic and intangible than the cold calculations of power made by shrewd statesmen or the accidents of geography. And so, conversely, the absence of a shared political and philosophic tradition between the United States and Russia has almost certainly contributed to the present hiatus.

The following are excerpts from dispatches sent to the State Department by the United States Ambassador to Czarist Russia in the 1850s.

This is a hard climate, and an American finds many things to try his patience, and but few that are capable of winning his affections. One of the most disagreeable features that he has to encounter is the secrecy with which everything is done. He can rarely obtain accurate information, until events have transpired, and he may rely upon it, that his own movements are closely observed, by eyes that he never sees. The Russian mind seems naturally distrustful, and this is especially so with the Government officials. Everything is surrounded with ceremony, and nothing is attainable, but after the most provoking delays. Nothing is more striking to an American here on his first arrival, than the rigor of the police. It would seem that the capital was in a state of siege; and among all the astringents put into requisition for the preservation of peace and order none is so abhorrent, as the censorial power. As a proof of the extent to which it is carried I may mention, that the late message of the President of the United States, was not regarded in all its parts as a safe document for Russian readers, and came to their hands scathed with the censors' knife.

It is difficult in many instances to see the reason of the application of this power,

[1] Alexis de Tocqueville, *Democracy in America*, Vintage Books, Inc., Random House, Inc., New York, 1954, vol. I, p. 452.

and no doubt it is often capricious. I know but one book on Russia, of foreign origin, that is admitted into the Country. Nor do I know of a single one of domestic production, from which a stranger can derive any certain information, touching the revenue, the expenditures, the strength of the army and navy, or any other matter having a political bearing. . . .

I had a good deal during last winter to try my patience, for the Government possesses in an exquisite degree, the art of worrying a foreign representative without giving him even the consolation of an insult. The position as an Ambassador here is far from being pleasant. The opinion prevails, that no communication, at least of a public nature, is safe in the Post Office, but is opened and inspected as a matter of course. Hence those Legations that can afford it, maintain regular couriers, and never send anything by mail. The opinion also prevails, that Ministers are constantly subjected to a system of espionage, and that even their servants are made to disclose what passes in their households, their conversations, associations, et cetera. . . .

Display is a policy as well as a passion with the Russian Government. The popular mind is well adapted to this sort of finesse. A strange superstition prevails among the Russians that they are destined to conquer the world. . . .

These and other excerpts from dispatches of that period were revived and sent again in 1936 by the American Ambassador. He commented that they present "an accurate picture of life in Russia in 1936" and then wryly observed that the more things change, the more they remain the same.[2]

The Soviet Union of the 1960s is not the Soviet Union of either the 1850s or 1936, but the central points still obtain: The two nations have fundamentally different traditions, societies, and systems of governments, and these facts contribute significantly to the contemporary scene.

The New Russia

As the twentieth century dawned, czarist rule in Russia was being challenged from within by forces representing a wide spectrum of political beliefs. After the humiliation of the Japanese victory in 1905, Russia's costly and demoralizing participation in World War I against Germany provided the revolutionaries with a favorable political atmosphere, and in March, 1917, the Czar was overthrown. A Provisional Government led by genuine democrats assumed nominal control in a chaotic internal setting that was aggravated by the continuing war. There ensued an intense struggle for ascendancy among the many hostile factions and parties which characterized anticzarist political life in Russia. In November, 1917, a fanatical group of Marxists who were known as Bolsheviks overthrew the Provisional Government and seized power. They and their adherents still have it, and in the meantime the international position of Russia has

[2] U.S. Department of State, *Foreign Relations of the United States, Diplomatic Papers, The Soviet Union, 1933–1939*, Washington, D.C., 1952, pp. 289–291.

changed from that of a comparatively ineffectual major power among many powers to that of a "superpower" in a world where there are only two such powers.

The Bolsheviks were doctrinaire ideologues. Their kind of Marxism, as enunciated by their leader, Vladimir Ilich Ulyanov (known as Nikolai Lenin), was not simply revolutionary in terms of Russian economic, social, and political institutions; it presented a radical and ominous challenge to the whole international political system. It is incautious to believe that even messianic revolutionaries believe every word of their ideology and are motivated solely by its precepts. But in the case of the Marxist-Leninists —or Bolsheviks, or Communists—it is equally incautious to regard the ideology as a mere rationalization for the seizure of power or simply grand rhetoric designed to deceive the masses and foreign governments. Their ideology struck most Westerners as preposterous nonsense, but to some considerable extent it was the basis and inspiration of their actions and policies.

No attempt will be made here to set forth in any detail the ideology of the founders of the Soviet Union. Aside from the question of its importance or lack of it as a guide to action, there is the equally forbidding problem of determining precisely which version of the holy writ was in favor with the elite at any given time. Ideological ferment and the accompanying polemical internal debates have characterized Communist movements from the beginning, and still do today. Any effort to understand the roots of the cold war, however, must come to grips in at least a cursory fashion with this slippery and rather opaque subject.

Marxism-Leninism has scientific pretensions. It claims to have discovered a pattern in history that explains the past and the present and shows the "wave of the future." It holds that all of human history can be explained in terms of class struggles. One class has used the state, or government, to suppress and exploit all other classes. Inevitably, an exploited class revolts and seizes power. The last such revolutionary class was the capitalist entrepreneurs, the bourgeoisie, who overturned the feudal nobility and who in turn exploited the workers, or proletariat. The historical process makes inevitable the worldwide revolution of the proletariat against their oppressors. The precise timing will vary from country to country, but this revolution will be the last one. It will usher in the classless society where no one will exploit or be exploited.

In the final stages of the capitalistic epoch, there will be an increasing need for new markets and raw materials. This will lead to imperialism and intense rivalries—"contradictions"—within the capitalistic world and to great wars. In these wars, the exploited proletariat will become increasingly disillusioned and disadvantaged. This will facilitate its organization by a conscious elite, a vanguard, which alone understands and is facilitating the process of history. This vanguard is, of course, the Communist Party, and its historic task is to lead the proletarian revolution, everywhere.

World War I appeared to Lenin and his followers to be a classic imperialistic war, and the ensuing bourgeois revolution in Russia in March, 1917, loomed as a supreme opportunity. When the Bolsheviks seized power in November, they believed that revolutions were imminent throughout the capitalist world. Although these did not occur, despite Bolshevik urging and aid, Lenin was nonetheless successful in consolidating Bolshevik power within Russia and in devising means of ensuring its survival despite its encirclement by hostile capitalistic powers.

Marxism-Leninism is militantly atheistic. It teaches that belief in God is an especially deleterious aspect of the bourgeois mentality, wrong in fact and designed for the purpose of keeping the exploited workers fearful and peaceable. Religion, Marx had declared, "is the opium of the people."

The extent to which this ideology set the Bolsheviks apart from the rest of the governments of the world cannot be understood, however, exclusively in terms of their view of the pattern of history or of their atheism. It is necessary, in addition, to look briefly at another of their central concepts: materialism. The Bolsheviks believed that the basic fact about any period in history is the prevailing mode of economic production and exchange. The entire organization of society is based upon this, and so is its "superstructure"—its law, morality, religion, and philosophy. The Bolsheviks, therefore, expected to create an entirely new and unique society by taking the means of production and exchange out of the hands of the capitalists and assuming control themselves as the vanguard of the proletariat. The resultant new society would create its own values, its own art, and its own morality. A new man would emerge, with different motives and responsive to different and more socially useful incentives.

This view of history and of the nature of human thought and values struck—and strikes—most Westerners as pretentious and absurd. This reaction, coupled with the apparent seriousness with which the ideology was regarded by the Bolsheviks themselves, demonstrated the fact that men possessing a radically different view of the world had seized the government of one of the world's great powers. International politics was bound to be vitally affected.

There are those who argue that Marxism-Leninism is an unchanging dogma, a veritable blueprint for Communist world domination. They picture Communist leaders as diabolically clever, unchanging, dogmatic, and unified instruments of a Communist master plan that gives every promise of being, in fact, "the wave of the future."

There are others who argue that ideology has always been a mere façade and rationalization for a typical totalitarian regime controlled by tough, cynical men. This view dismisses as irrelevant all the policy implications and grandiose pretensions that can be derived from the ideology outlined above.

Most observers have avoided both of these polar positions about the relationship between ideology and policy in the Soviet Union. They believe that ideology is neither decisive nor irrelevant as a source of Soviet policy. On the subtle question of precisely how much ideology accounts for and under what circumstances, however, a consensus is difficult to achieve. There is obviously a lot of room for disagreement among those who believe that neither all nor none of Soviet behavior can be attributed to ideology. Among them, there is a general agreement that Soviet ideology is subject to change and that "in the long run" it may erode away entirely, thereby permitting Western and Soviet leaders to view their relations from a somewhat shared perspective rather than as representatives of irreconcilably hostile systems and radically dissimilar views of life. In this view, Marxist-Leninist ideology has played a substantial, and deplorable, role in shaping the mentality and policies of Soviet leaders, but it is not an eternal obstacle to better East-West relations and is, even "in the short run," malleable. What constitutes "the long run" is, of course, variously interpreted. Some believe ideology is already an insubstantial element in Soviet calculations, whereas others insist that it is still potent.

This book is based on this third view of the relationship between ideology and policy, with a tendency to lean toward the pessimistic side in judging the present impact of ideology and also the duration of its hold on Soviet leaders. In any event, we shall have occasion to return to this vital and unresolvable issue.

The First Contacts

The new Russian government was as a matter of basic principle hostile to all the governments then engaged in the carnage of World War I. On November 8, 1917, the second day of the Bolshevik Revolution, Lenin issued a "Decree on Peace." It proposed "to all the warring people and their governments that they immediately enter into negotiations for a just, democratic peace . . . an immediate peace without annexations . . . and without indemnities." This proposal was unexceptional and, of course, without any practical significance. What followed in the decree, however, was more suggestive of the style and direction of the new government's foreign policy. Lenin announced that "The Workers' and Peasants' Government" was abolishing "secret diplomacy"; it would conduct "all negotiations entirely openly before the entire people." Moreover, it announced its intentions to publish the secret treaties ratified or concluded between Russia and her allies during the brief reign of the Provisional Government, and it declared all of them to be rescinded. The treaties were "for the most part to the advantage and privilege of the Russian landlords and capitalists and to the maintenance or the increase of the annexations of the Great-Russians."

Any government that would go to these lengths to embarrass and insult several major nations on the second day of its existence was clearly no ordinary government.

Nor was this all. The decree concluded with a nearly explicit appeal for proletarian revolutions in England, France, and Germany. It expressed confidence that "the class-conscious workers" of these nations "will understand the tasks, now before them, of the liberation of humanity from the horrors of war and its consequences, and that these workers will help us, by their comprehensive, decisive and devotedly energetic activity, to carry to a successful conclusion the work of peace, and with it, the work of liberating the toiling and exploited masses of the population from every form of slavery and exploitation."[3]

This thinly veiled appeal for revolution was a reflection of the current Bolshevik conviction that the historic moment for the collapse of capitalism and its regimes in Western countries was at hand. The Bolsheviks at that time believed that such revolutions were essential to the success of their own revolution, and it was a short step from believing in their necessity to believing in their imminence. Needless to say, this conviction and the resultant Bolshevik efforts to foster such revolutions were regarded as offensive and intolerable by Western governments. (It should perhaps be added that this and subsequent appeals from the first "socialist"[4] govern-

---

[3] This document appears in George F. Kennan, *Soviet Foreign Policy, 1917–1941*, D. Van Nostrand Company, Inc., Princeton, N.J., 1960, pp. 116–119.

[4] Perhaps it needs to be emphasized that the words "socialist" and "Communist" are among the most ambiguous in modern political terminology. Sweden, Britain from 1945 to 1951 and 1964–, Communist Russia, and the United Arab Republic all have, or had, governments that call, or called, themselves "socialist." It is obviously necessary, however, to understand that the democratic socialists in the West have very little in common with the totalitarian "Marxist-Leninist," socialists of the Soviet Union or China, and, conversely, that they have a great deal in common with other democratic individuals and parties in the West. No one understands this better than the Soviet leaders, who often regard Western democratic socialists with even more scorn than they reserve for Western liberals and conservatives. As noted later on in this chapter, the Russian Communists were a radical and wholly distinct group of Marxists, who split off entirely from the mainstream of European socialism. Most of the latter movement has always been democratic and in recent years has also become conspicuously less doctrinaire.

How to define the self-styled "socialism" of such modern rulers as Gamal Abdel Nasser of the United Arab Republic or Kwame Nkrumah of Ghana is a more troublesome matter. These men are not democrats—i.e., they do not tolerate such democratic essentials as political opposition or a free press—and, therefore, they cannot be regarded as socialists in the Western sense. Nor can they be called Communists. Like many leaders in the underdeveloped areas of the world, they are strongly attracted to the term "socialism." They associate it with a rationally planned, centrally directed, and developing economy, with heavy overtones of a humanitarian and/or paternalistic regard for the citizenry. Moreover, it emphasizes their rhetorical—if not practical—rejection of "capitalism," a term that is associated in their minds with colonialism. Beyond such vagaries, the term "socialism" when applied to such persons and regimes has little meaning.

In recent years, even the word "Communist" has lost much of its precise meaning. It is no longer possible to restrict its usage to those parties and individuals all over the world who faithfully follow the party line as laid down by the Soviet Communist Party. There is no longer a single center of authority in the Communist world, and the resultant varieties of communism are increasingly difficult to define and understand. This is a problem that will recur frequently in the following pages.

ment were greeted with apathy or hostility by most of the "toiling and exploited masses" to whom they were addressed.)

Neither peace nor further revolutions were realized, and Lenin and his associates quickly set about seeking more practical objectives. They wanted to withdraw from the "imperialist war," of course, but the Russian armies were in such a weak and chaotic condition that they were in no position to demand favorable terms from the Germans. Even in such inauspicious circumstances, however, the extraordinary characteristics of the Bolshevik mentality were apparent. The ensuing negotiations with Germany that began at Brest-Litovsk in December, 1917, were conducted with the very government that the Soviet leaders were simultaneously trying hardest to overthrow. Soviet negotiators engaged in lengthy propaganda harangues, which had little or nothing to do with the substance of the questions under consideration. Despite their role as supplicants, they treated the German representatives with contempt and distributed revolutionary pamphlets to German soldiers in the vicinity. And then they infuriated Germany's foes by signing a treaty, which in March, 1918, effectively closed the eastern front of the war, thereby permitting a large transfer of German troops to the west, where the war was still very much alive. (In late March, the Germans launched a major offensive on the western front.)

Not all the new Russian leaders favored acceptance of the harsh terms of the Treaty of Brest-Litovsk. But Lenin did, and his persuasive arguments on its behalf demonstrate the strength and adaptability of Communist thought. He told the Seventh Congress of the Russian Communist Party on March 7, 1918, that his answer to the question of whether the "humiliating" and "predatory" treaty should be ratified was "absolutely yes." "Here we must know how to retreat. . . . If you do not know how to adapt yourself, if you are not inclined to crawl on your belly through the mud, then you are not a revolutionary but a chatterbox. . . ."[5] A willingness "to crawl on your belly through the mud," literally and figuratively, has sometimes given dedicated Communists an important advantage over their more fastidious and comfortable adversaries in the West.

For their part, the Western governments were rather bewildered by developments in Russia. Their concern was primarily to keep the eastern front activated, but this was a hopeless aspiration. Beyond that, they were unable to achieve anything like a concerted and rational policy for dealing with the portentous developments in Russia. The British and the French secretly supported some anti-Bolshevik forces in Russia— the so-called Whites—who were favorably disposed toward continuing the war, but these efforts did not substantially hurt either the Bolsheviks or the Germans. In sum, the Western governments did nothing in those early days to earn the respect or confidence of the new Russian leaders, and vice versa.

[5] Kennan, *op. cit.*, pp. 120–121.

The chasm soon widened and deepened. During the summer and fall of 1918, small numbers of British, French, and American troops were landed in northern Russia and in Siberia. The motives of the intervening powers were, of course, mixed. Partly because of exaggerated estimates of the capabilities of the White forces, British and French military leaders were anxious to lend them support. Some emphasized the intrinsic desirability of helping the Whites eliminate the Reds, who were clearly an affront and a challenge to all established systems of government. Others were more concerned with reactivating the eastern front and looked on a victory for the Whites as a feasible means of accomplishing this.

Another argument used in behalf of intervention was the fact that large quantities of military equipment were stored at Archangel, a northern Russian port city. This equipment had been sent there by Western governments for use by Russian troops on the eastern front. After the Bolsheviks seized power and took Russia out of the war, this unpaid-for equipment became something of a prize, and the British and French were anxious at least to keep it out of Bolshevik hands. They already had some troops in another northern Russian port city, Murmansk, which in 1918 was controlled by a local faction that was not altogether sympathetic to the new Red regime in Moscow.

The American role in the affair was that of a reluctant ally. President Wilson was adamantly opposed to participation in the civil war, but under constant Allied pressure, he finally consented to the dispatching of an expedition to Archangel for the purpose of guarding the military equipment there. It was a regrettable concession made by a harried man, who was preoccupied with other and apparently more grave matters relating to the prosecution of the war.

The British and French troops arrived in Archangel in August, 1918, only to discover that most of the equipment had already been taken away by the Bolsheviks. Because of the multiplicity of purposes behind their intervention, however, they stayed on and were joined in September by a larger American contingency. A British military commander was in charge, and he sent most of the American troops inland, away from the city, where they had sporadic and minor skirmishes with Red troops.

When the war ended in November, the continued presence of Western troops became more conspicuously interventionist in character. The only conceivable rationale for their staying on—beyond the obvious one of looking for a means to participate in the civil war—was a concern for the fate, once the Bolsheviks took over, of those who had been collaborating with the Westerners in Archangel and Murmansk. This was a serious problem, and it contributed to the delay of the Allied departure; many were ultimately evacuated along with the troops. But all the troops were not out until the summer of 1919, and the conclusion seems inescapable that the flickering hope that they might help unseat the Reds was the major reason for this imprudent delay. The debacle ended as ignominiously as it began.

The American contingent left in June and July, 1919. The British were less inclined to leave and actually sent fresh troops there that summer, ostensibly to secure the withdrawal of their small forces. However, by the end of September, all Western troops had left northern Russia.

The intervention in Siberia was, impossible though it may seem, even more poorly conceived and executed. When the czarist regime collapsed, the struggle for secession went on all over the vast territory of Russia. This weakened condition invited the concerns, legitimate and illegitimate, of other nations. Japan had long been interested in northern Manchuria, which Russia effectively controlled by virtue of its ownership and protection of that portion of the trans-Siberian railroad that went through Manchuria. There were German prisoners of war scattered around Siberia in sufficient numbers to raise the specter, however fantastic, of a German seizure of power in the area. And the British and French military leaders viewed the chaos in Siberia in much the same fashion as they viewed the situation in northern Russia: an opportunity to aid anti-Bolsheviks and perhaps reactivate the eastern front.

The most bizarre element in this whole picture, however, was the existence of a substantial number of Czech prisoners of war, who were delighted at the breaking up of the Austro-Hungarian empire and were anxious to join the fight against the Germans. They formed the Czech Corps, about 40,000 strong, and their adventures in Russia in 1918 and 1919 constitute what surely must be one of the strangest episodes in the long annals of warfare. With Allied encouragement and material support, they set out for Vladivostok, the Siberian seaport on the Pacific Ocean. Their purpose was to get around to the western front to fight against the Germans. They constituted one of the best, if not the best, fighting units in all of Russia in 1918, and, perhaps inevitably, friction between them and the Bolsheviks developed. The latter suspected that the Czechs were agents of the British and French and that their real objectives were not anti-German but anti-Bolshevik. Fighting broke out between them, and the plight of the Czechs drew the sympathetic attention of President Wilson.

As recounted, the British and French were eager for intervention in Siberia, and they had been pressing Wilson for his approval for some time. Again Wilson rejected involvement in the civil war as a reason for putting Allied troops on Russian soil, but again he finally intervened, this time unilaterally. His stated purpose was to assist the beleaguered Czechs. He was under the mistaken impression that they were fighting freed German prisoners of war in Siberia, not Bolsheviks, and he didn't understand the extent to which they had involved themselves in the civil war against the Reds.

About 7,000 American troops arrived in Vladivostok in August and September, 1918, and a much smaller number of British and French troops arrived shortly thereafter. These Western troops had a couple of very minor skirmishes with Bolsheviks in the course of their one and one-half year stay. They accomplished little or nothing, either in terms of their stated purpose or of whatever unstated purposes their governments may have had.

These unfortunate interventions are among the weirdest episodes in the history of American diplomacy. If someone had set out to prove that Communist beliefs about hostile capitalist encirclement were correct and at the same time wanted to do nothing that would seriously endanger the infant Red regime, he could scarcely have dreamed up a better chain of events. Subsequent Soviet claims that these interventions were large-scale, carefully planned Western efforts to overthrow the Bolsheviks are gross exaggerations, but there is enough truth in them to lend them some plausibility. Moreover, the interventions contributed to the poisoning of Soviet-Western relations in their infancy. Soviet policy probably would have developed pretty much as it did without this impetus, but then at least the difficult questions relating to responsibility for this state of affairs could be more unambiguously answered.

This is not to say that intervention would have been folly under any conditions. The American motives were the least defensible because they were, on the one hand, futile and/or disproportionate (to protect military equipment), and, on the other hand, sentimental (to protect the Czechs). The British and the French sought larger and more sensible goals (the overthrow of the Bolsheviks and the reactivation of the eastern front), but the means that they brought to bear were wholly insufficient to achieve such goals. All mankind would be in their debt if they had crushed the Bolsheviks at the outset and had managed to give rise to a stable, Western-oriented regime in Russia. As it was, all concerned managed only to confirm Bolshevik suspicions and write a magnificent propaganda script for Communists everywhere. Half-hearted measures in foreign policy are often more damaging than inaction, as later American administrations were also to learn.

Postwar Developments

The peace conference terminating World War I was held in Paris beginning in December, 1918. The Soviet government was not represented. The victorious Western democracies were in no mood to deal soberly and thoughtfully—much less unitedly—with the strange aberration in Moscow. There were a few official and unofficial efforts made to establish some kind of communication and understanding between the Versailles peacemakers and the Russian revolutionaries, but they all came to naught. One reason for this, from the Western side, was the lingering hope that the Bolsheviks could be unseated after all. In the spring of 1919, there were many false and misleading reports about the alleged progress of the Whites in the civil war. These reports contributed to the confusion and ignorance that characterized Western attitudes toward Soviet Russia and also to the fact that the conference ended in late spring without arriving at any concerted policies about the matter. With the final victories of the Red armies in 1920, these Western illusions were exposed and the long, slow process of groping for more sensible policies got under way.

Soviet policies did not create much ground for optimism. There was still a strong belief among many Bolsheviks that revolutions in the major capitalistic countries of Europe were just around the corner and could be effectively encouraged and supported by Moscow. The Bolsheviks, moreover, were growing further and further away from other socialist movements in Europe. This is not the place to go into an accounting of the divergent developments and internecine warfare of European socialism. Suffice it to say that Lenin and his associates espoused the most radical, militant, and undemocratic brand of Marxian socialism, and their contempt for the democratic, or evolutionary, or moderate, socialism of most left-wing parties in the West was absolute. The Second International—the existing international organization of the national socialist parties—was led by moderate socialists, and the Bolsheviks boycotted and condemned their postwar conference, which began in February, 1919. Instead, Lenin organized the Third International—or Communist International, or Comintern—and its first meeting was held in Moscow in March, 1919. Only thirty five people attended—only a few from outside Russia—and the prospects must have appeared rather bleak to most people, but not to Lenin. He now had the beginnings of an international organization of the radical socialist parties under his ingenious control. In July, 1920, the Communist International held its Second Congress, and this time 200 delegates were in attendance. Unlike the First Congress, many of the delegates represented parties of some strength in their own countries. Lenin controlled the proceedings from the outset, and he was successful in generating enough attention and enthusiasm for his Comintern that it became the worldwide rallying point for radical socialists and Communists. The existence and activities of this frankly subversive and irretrievably hostile engine of international Communist revolution became a considerable source of friction between the Soviet Union and the West.

The Second Congress of the Comintern convened during the final days of another unsuccessful military adventure against the Bolsheviks in which the Western Allies became implicated. The government of the new Polish state, created at Versailles, was dissatisfied with its eastern border and decided to take advantage of the weakness of the Bolshevik grip on the Ukraine. The hastily assembled Poles began their attacks in 1919 and in May, 1920, they actually captured Kiev. The Red Army, being largely released from the civil war by then, counterattacked at this point and pushed the Poles all the way back to Warsaw. This development alarmed the Western governments, inducing nightmarish thoughts about a Bolshevik conquest of Poland and a subsequent Communist revolution in Germany under the benevolent auspices of the bordering Red Army. The Allies dispatched a high-level military mission to Warsaw and sent munitions as well. Not necessarily for these reasons, the Poles thereafter launched a counterattack, and in the autumn a settlement was negotiated that gave the Poles some satisfaction in the east.

From the standpoint of Soviet-Western relations, the significance of this minor war was the fact that the Poles were encouraged, advised, and supplied by the Western Allies. Like the Allied interventions of 1918–1919, these efforts were futile and bound to confirm and reinforce Soviet suspicions and hostility.

Western fears of a communization of Germany were by no means dispelled with the final Polish military successes and a cessation of hostilities. There was a real possibility that a Communist revolution might be successful in defeated and embittered Germany even without the indirect intervention of the Red Army. The Soviets were devoting more attention and resources to the revolutionary effort there than to any other, and the chances for success were rather good. This prospect contributed to the general abhorrence with which the West viewed the pretentious but skillful revolutionaries in Moscow.

By 1921, however, Soviet optimism about the prospects of revolutions elsewhere began to decline. Moreover, Russia was experiencing acute economic difficulties, and the advantages of "normalizing" relations with the West began to take precedence over the more intoxicating but apparently premature efforts to instigate Communist revolutions. The Bolsheviks wanted Western loans and credits, increased trade and diplomatic recognition. George F. Kennan, with his usual skill and perception, has summarized in the following imaginary statement the ambivalence of Soviet attitudes toward the West in this period:

We despise you. We consider that you should be swept from the earth as governments and physically destroyed as individuals. We reserve the right, in our private if not in our official capacities, to do what we can to bring this about: to revile you publicly, to do everything within our power to detach your own people from their loyalty to you and their confidence in you, to subvert your armed forces, and to work for your downfall in favor of a Communist dictatorship. But since we are not strong enough to destroy you today—since an interval must unfortunately elapse before we can give you the *coup de grace*—we want you during this interval to trade with us; we want you to finance us; we want you to give us the advantages of full-fledged diplomatic recognition, just as you accord these advantages to one another.

An outrageous demand? Perhaps. But you will accept it nevertheless. You will accept it because you are not free agents, because you are slaves to your own capitalistic appetites, because when profit is involved, you have no pride, no principles, no honor. In the blindness that characterizes declining and perishing classes, you will wink at our efforts to destroy you, you will compete with one another for our favor. Driven by this competition, which you cannot escape, you will do what we want you to do until such time as we are ready to make an end of you. It is, in fact, *you* who will, through your own cupidity, give *us* the means wherewith to destroy you.[6]

Just as the Bolshevik leaders had looked to Germany as the nation where they could most profitably instigate rebellion, so too did they regard Germany as the nation that was most likely to be willing to deal with them on a mutually accommodating basis. In the postwar period, the two nations had at least one thing in common: They were, for different reasons, excluded from respectable international relations. The moderate socialist government in Germany received scant sympathy or assistance from a triumphant and revengeful Western Europe. The Germans resented the harsh terms of the Versailles Treaty, which deprived them of their colonies, took territory from them, and imposed unreasonable demands upon them for reparations payments. The Soviets, of course, were also hostile to the victorious Allies and were themselves the object of fear and contempt. It was perhaps inevitable that these pariah states should begin to look furtively at each other as a means of escaping their isolation.

One aspect of this that appears more serious in retrospect than it did at the time is the secret contacts made between Soviet and German military officers. The collaboration began in the autumn of 1920, with the Soviets taking the initiative, and continued for over a decade. For the Soviets, it provided some valuable German technical military advice and training and some limited assistance in the manufacture of armaments. For the Germans, it afforded an opportunity to violate clandestinely the restrictions imposed on them by the Treaty of Versailles. They used Russia as a training ground for some military personnel and bought some Soviet ammunition.

Since this did not become known in the West for many years, its impact on Soviet-Western relations was delayed. It does, however, underline the fact that the Soviet Union and the West were pursuing wholly different policies, which would be most difficult to reconcile, either then or later.

Of much greater immediate importance, however, were the diplomatic relations that developed between the two outcast nations. The German government was insecure and desperately in need of outside economic contacts and assistance, and it looked hopefully to the West. Great Britain

---

[6] George F. Kennan, *Russia and the West under Lenin and Stalin,* Atlantic-Little, Brown and Company, Boston, 1960, pp. 184–105. This remarkable book has been relied on extensively in this chapter.

and France afforded the Germans little hope and instead insisted, with blind consistency, on German payment of huge reparations. By 1920, there had developed, naturally enough, a growing sentiment in some German governmental circles for a policy of conciliation with the Soviet Union. Although the temptations were great, and the Soviets were eager, no significant public steps were taken in this direction until the Genoa Conference of April, 1922. This conference was originally supposed to deal with the gigantic problems of economic reconstruction in Europe, including Germany and the Soviet Union. The French refused, however, to discuss the basic question of reparations, and so the conferees were forced to concern themselves primarily with economic relations between the Soviet Union and the West. The Bolsheviks were suspicious of this, of course, and proceeded at once to try to split the capitalist countries. Germany was the obvious target, and Soviet diplomats began to press the Germans for a separate accord.

The resulting Treaty of Rapallo—named after the small town near Genoa where it was signed—was in good measure the result of Soviet diplomatic skill and the ineptitude of the French and the British. The latter delegation did not include a single senior official of the Foreign Office. The Germans came reluctantly to the conclusion that the only alternatives available to them were increased reparations and economic isolation or a separate agreement with the Soviets. They chose the latter. The treaty restored formal diplomatic relations, removed the specter of Soviet reparations claims against Germany, forfeited debt claims that Germany might have pressed against the Soviets, and provided that the commercial relations between each nation should be on the "most favored nation basis."

These provisions were, by themselves, rather unexceptional. But the Western response was one of astonishment, anger, and concern. It was alleged that the treaty created a perfidious alliance and represented a dangerous and undeserved betrayal by the Germans. Although it was neither of these, it did represent an ominous setback for British and French policies, and, not surprisingly, it further embittered relations between the Soviet Union and the West.

Soviet attitudes toward the West at this time were rather pungently expressed in a Comintern statement on the Genoa Conference issued as that ill-starred gathering came to an end:

At Genoa, the bourgeoisie revealed their utter powerlessness, their complete impotence. . . .

Never has the decadence of bourgeois society been exposed so clearly as now. The decay and disintegration of the bourgeois State are proceeding at a gigantic pace. The outward glitter of bourgeois governments is like the hectic flush on the cheeks of a consumptive. A declining class! . . . The star of the bourgeoisie has set. That is the chief lesson of Genoa. . . . Alone in Genoa the Soviet delegation represented the future of humanity while all the bourgeois delegations represented the decaying past.[7]

This kind of rhetoric did not, of course, prevent the Bolsheviks from seeking simultaneously to establish economic and diplomatic relations with representatives of "the decaying past." For their part, the Western governments were not disposed to let ideological sensitivities, outstanding debt claims, or uncouth Bolshevik pronouncements stand in the way of commercial relations. Postwar unemployment was a serious problem in the West, and the prospect of trading with the Soviet Union was an enticing one. In March, 1921, after much haggling, the British signed a trade agreement with Russia. This accord, it should perhaps be noted, preceded the Rapallo agreement by over a year. Other European countries followed suit shortly thereafter.

In 1924, more than six years after the Bolshevik seizure of power, England, France, and Italy all formally recognized the Soviet regime. This occurred despite unresolved problems centering on Western debt claims and Soviet sponsorship of worldwide propaganda campaigns calling for the overthrow of these and all other "decadent, bourgeois" governments.

Although recognition was achieved despite these barriers, their presence did manage to prevent any large-scale increase in trade. Taking a short-range and orthodox view of such matters, Great Britain and France refused to extend credit to the Soviets until the Soviets agreed to pay off the debts of the Czar and the Provisional Government. Without such credit, the Soviets were unable to buy much in the West, and a typical stalemate ensued, partly economic, partly political.

Moreover, Soviet-German relations after Rapallo were also less than satisfactory from the Soviet standpoint. Germany, in fact, had continued to seek better relations with France and Great Britain and had finally had some success.

Meanwhile, Soviet relations with Great Britain went from bad to worse. Recognition had been extended by Britain's first Labor (Socialist) government, which soon thereafter was voted out of office. The Conservatives who assumed power were not inclined to settle the debt questions with the disreputable Bolsheviks, and ambassadors were not even exchanged. In May, 1927, the British government raided the offices of the Soviet trade delegation in London, found evidence—naturally enough—of Soviet subversive activities in England, and severed relations altogether. It was not until the Laborites resumed power in 1930 that normal diplomatic relations between the two nations were established and ambassadors exchanged.

[7] Jane Degras (ed.), *The Communist International 1919–1943, Documents*, vol. 1, *1919-1922*, Oxford University Press, on behalf of the Royal Institute of International Affairs, London, 1956, pp. 344–349, quoted in Kennan, *Soviet Foreign Policy, 1917–1941, op. cit.*, pp. 143–144.

Frustrated in its efforts to subvert and/or trade with the West, the leadership of post-Lenin Russia—he died on January 21, 1924—began to apply itself with audacity and cruelty to the task of basically changing the Russian economy and, with it, the entire society. In 1928, the first Five-Year Plan was announced. In 1929, the ambitious and merciless program to force the collectivization of agriculture was begun. These and other developments in the Soviet Union were viewed with alarm and disgust by most Western governments, although the emphasis in the Five-Year Plan on industrialization resulted in increased trade for a few years.

During these formative years, the ideological and practical orientations of the party and therefore of Soviet policy were being molded. The struggle for leadership in the Bolshevik hierarchy after Lenin's death was not finally resolved until about 1929, by which time Joseph Stalin had effectively secured a commanding position. The character and personality of this man were thereafter centrally important to the tone and direction of Soviet policy and merit special attention.

Lenin was a cosmopolitan, a man who spent much of his life outside Russia in the doctrinaire but nonetheless international and civilized atmosphere of European socialism. He was a ruthless revolutionary, to be sure, but it is plausible to believe that both his fanaticism and his political appeal were based in part on a perverted but nonetheless real devotion to an ideology that purported to point the way to a better society and a better world.

None of these things can be said of Stalin. He was a Russian provincial who knew very little of the outside world of the educated, sophisticated Socialists in the rest of Europe. His chief characteristics were his matchless instinct for the right timing and moves in the brutal world of Bolshevik party politics, his transcendent suspicion, and his total lack of regard for moral considerations of any kind.

Oddly enough, this assessment of Stalin is one of the few things about which the Soviet leaders and the West now agree. George Kennan delivers a typical Western judgment on Stalin when he writes that "this was a man of incredible criminality, of a criminality effectively without limits; a man apparently foreign to the very experience of love, without pity or mercy. . . ."[8] This is scarcely any more condemnatory, however, than Nikita Khrushchev's pronouncements in his famous posthumous attack on Stalin at a closed session of the Twentieth Party Congress in February, 1956. Excerpts follow:

Stalin . . . practiced brutal violence, not only toward everything which opposed him, but also toward that which seemed to his capricious and despotic character, contrary to his concepts. . . .

---

[8] Kennan, *Russia and the West under Lenin and Stalin, op. cit.*, p. 254.

Stalin originated the concept "enemy of the people." This term automatically rendered it unnecessary that the ideological errors of a man or men engaged in a controversy be proven; this term made possible the usage of the most cruel repression, violating all norms of revolutionary legality, against anyone who in any way disagreed with Stalin, against those who were only suspected of hostile intent, against those who had bad reputations. This concept, "enemy of the people," actually eliminated the possibility of any kind of ideological fight or the making of one's views known on this or that issue, even those of a practical character. In the main, and in actuality, the only proof of guilt used, against all norms of current legal science, was the "confession" of the accused himself; and, as subsequent probing proved, "confessions" were acquired through physical pressures against the accused. . . .

It was determined that of the 139 members and candidates of the Party's Central Committee who were elected at the XVIIth Congress, 98 persons, i.e., 70 percent, were arrested and shot (mostly in 1937-1938). (*Indignation in the hall*) . . . The same fate met not only the Central Committee members but also the majority of the delegates to the XVIIth Party Congress. Of 1966 delegates with either voting or advisory rights, 1,108 persons were arrested on charges of anti-revolutionary crimes, i.e., decidedly more than a majority. This very fact shows how absurd, wild and contrary to common sense were the charges of counterrevolutionary crimes made out, as we now see, against a majority of participants at the XVIIth Party Congress. (*Indignation in the hall*) . . .

Facts prove that many abuses were made on Stalin's orders without reckoning with any norms of party and Soviet legality. Stalin was a very distrustful man, sickly suspicious; we knew this from our work with him. He could look at a man and say: "Why are your eyes so shifty today?" or "Why are you turning so much today and avoiding to look me directly in the eyes?" The sickly suspicion created in him a general distrust even toward eminent party workers whom he had known for years. Everywhere and in everything he saw "enemies," "two-facers" and "spies."[9]

As Khrushchev went on to argue, these characteristics of Stalin were also apparent in his decisions relating to international affairs. Khrushchev, of course, did not concede that Stalin's personality had anything to do with Soviet troubles with the West; he talked instead about Stalin's share of the responsibility for the break between Soviet Russia and Communist Yugoslavia in 1948. But it is quite obvious that Stalin's "sickly suspicion," his immorality, and his intemperateness were bound to and did have a profound effect on Soviet-Western relations. This man controlled the strength and destiny of a great nation for over twenty four momentous, critical years, until his death on March 5, 1953.

In the United States, the "return to normalcy" after World War I did not include a return to the traditional practice of recognizing existing

[9] Robert V. Daniels (ed.), *A Documentary History of Communism*, Random House, New York, 1960, vol. II, pp. 225–228. Used by permission.

regimes. A Soviet trading corporation was established in New York in 1924, however, and a comparatively small amount of trade was carried on during the 1920s. In 1930, it reached a modest peak of slightly over $100 million and then went into a decline until World War II.

The 1930s

In attempting to trace the major roots of the cold war, it should be emphasized that there were no diplomatic relations between the United States and the Soviet Union for the first sixteen years of the Bolshevik regime. This fact by itself probably did not contribute significantly to subsequent tensions and hostility, but it is suggestive of the extent to which the two governments were alienated from each other from the very beginning.

The failure of Woodrow Wilson's administration to recognize the Soviet Union was based primarily on its revulsion against the stated principles of the Soviet leaders. Bolshevik denunciations of traditional morality and practices, and their worldwide revolutionary aspirations—with the United States government among the targets—were regarded by a moralist such as Wilson as being wholly outside the area of permissible behavior. Such a government was not worthy of recognition.

In the Republican isolationist administrations of the 1920s, the official arguments against recognition increased and, appropriately enough, developed a more economic flavor. There were three official reasons for the nonrecognition policy of the 1920s: (1) The Soviets had confiscated the private property of American citizens and refused to make restitution. (2) They had repudiated the debts of predecessor Russian governments. (3) Most important of all, they were brazenly disseminating Communist propaganda in the United States that advocated the violent overthrow of the government.

Two other factors contributed to this policy. It would have been politically risky for any American administration to recognize the Bolshevik regime; and there were no strong economic reasons for doing so.

Franklin D. Roosevelt was elected president in 1932 at a time when several internal and external developments were beginning to put a rather different light on the recognition question. The nation and the world were being racked by the Great Depression, and in 1931 and 1932 trade between the United States and the Soviet Union had decreased disappointingly. This latter fact was thought to be related to the recognition issue, and during the depression it was especially easy for economic lures to overcome political or ideological considerations. There arose in some business circles a rather substantial, albeit ironic, sentiment for recognition. Moreover, the Japanese had launched their aggressive adventures in Manchuria in 1931, and the United States and the Soviet Union both regarded this as a threat to their interests.

Another development which may or may not have contributed to Roosevelt's decision to recognize Soviet Russia was the accession to the chancellorship of Germany in January, 1933, of a noisy and fanatical totalitarian named Adolph Hitler.

The Soviets were anxious for recognition, and, in some preliminary correspondence with Roosevelt, both sides referred to "the international situation" and agreed that the absence of diplomatic relations between them encouraged forces that tended to disturb the peace. Foreign Commissar Maxim Litvinov was dispatched to Washington in November, 1933, and talks were carried on in a spirit of cordiality. The old problems of repayment of loans made to the Provisional Government and of compensation to American citizens for property confiscated by the Bolsheviks were not resolved, but Roosevelt and Litvinov entered into what both sides called a "gentleman's agreement" on these matters, and recognition was granted. In a rhapsodic public speech a few days later, Roosevelt declared:

> I believe sincerely that the most impelling motive that has lain behind the conversations . . . was the desire of both countries for peace and for the strengthening of the peaceful purpose of the civilized world.
>
> It will interest you to know that in the year 1809 . . . Thomas Jefferson wrote as follows to his Russian friend, Monsieur Dashkoff: "Russia and the United States being in character and practice essentially pacific, a common interest in the rights of peaceable nations gives us a common cause in their maintenance."
>
> And so in this spirit of Thomas Jefferson, Mr. Litvinov and I have believed that through the resumption of normal relations the prospects of peace all over the world are greatly strengthened.[10]

No doubt the President was attempting to put the best face on his controversial move, but the statement fairly represents the official optimism that greeted recognition in both Washington and Moscow. The first American Ambassador to the Soviet Union, William Bullitt, reported that it would have been impossible to exaggerate the cordiality with which he was received. Stalin, who had not previously met with any foreign representatives, had Bullitt to dinner and told the impressionable ambassador that he would be glad to see him at any time, day or night. He said he had been following the New Deal with great interest and that he admired President Roosevelt, whom he described as one of the most popular men in the Soviet Union.

Whatever the reasons for this euphoric beginning, relations cooled off rather quickly. The "gentleman's agreement" did not lead to a debt settlement, United States credit was therefore not extended, and trade therefore did not develop. Nor were relations between the two potential giants in other spheres any more promising.

---

[10] Samuel J. Rosenman (ed.), *The Public Papers and Addresses of Franklin D. Roosevelt*, Random House, Inc., New York, 1938, vol. II, p. 492.

While the United States and Russia thus came together and drew apart, relations between the other major Western democracies and the Soviets were proceeding along a somewhat more promising path. The Soviets joined the League of Nations in 1934, and for a time they played a leading role in disarmament efforts and subsequently in efforts to create a "united front" between democrats and Communists against the rising menace of Nazi Germany and fascist Italy. In 1935, the Soviet Union concluded military treaties of alliance with France and Czechoslovakia, and the chances for genuine collaboration, at least in the short run, appeared rather good.

At the Seventh Congress of the Communist International in Moscow in July and August, 1935, Soviet spokesmen took a markedly less hostile line toward the West than previously. They stressed the fascist threat to peace, advocated "united fronts" against that threat, and even went so far as to call the Roosevelt administration a progressive, liberal regime.

But even at this Congress, the multifarious character of Soviet intentions was clear. The official resolution calling for united fronts in the struggle "against the offensive of capital, against the reactionary measures of the bourgeoisie, against fascism," was also quite explicit in declaring that such arrangements were only temporary expedients. Communists were instructed to enter into "short of long-term agreements" with "Social-Democratic parties, reformist trade unions and other organizations of the toilers against the class enemies of the proletariat." But such joint action "not only does not preclude, but on the contrary, renders still more necessary the serious and well-founded criticism of reformism, of Social-Democracy as the ideology and practice of class collaboration with the bourgeoisie, and the patient exposition of the principles and program of Communists to the Social-Democratic workers. . . ."[11] The irony of Soviet solicitude toward Social-Democrats—only yesterday they had been denounced as "Social Fascists" by a blind Stalin, who was thereby unintentionally facilitating Hitler's rise to power—was lost on very few non-Communists.

Moreover, this conciliatory Congress also provided the occasion for the first hostile official exchanges through the newly established diplomatic channels between Moscow and Washington. As part of the prerecognition accords, the Soviet government had pledged itself not to permit any activity on its territory by a group that had as an aim the overthrow of the social or political order of the United States. Yet, in attendance at the Seventh Congress were representatives of the American Communist Party, who duly reported on the alleged progress of the revolutionary movement in the United States. The United States filed a sharp protest and told the Soviets that "the strict fulfillment of the pledge of non-interference [is] an essential prerequisite to the maintenance of normal and friendly relations . . ."; that "the most serious consequences" would result from Soviet inability or

[11] *A Documentary History of Communism*, pp. 115–116.

unwillingness to prevent such violations in the future; and that it was regretful "in the present international situation" that friendly relations would be precluded by the continuance of such activities.[12] The Soviet government responded with the irrelevant and false claim that what happened at Congresses of the Communist International was not its responsibility.

From the Soviet standpoint, the duplicity and unreliability of Great Britain, France, and the United States were demonstrated by their responses to two indicative events in 1936. The Western powers stood by while German troops reoccupied the Rhineland in defiance of treaty obligations; and they refused to join the Soviet Union in coming to the aid of Republican forces in the Spanish Civil War, while Germany and Italy openly intervened on the side of General Franco's antidemocratic and anti-Communist forces.

In what may or may not have been in part a reaction to Hitler's success in the Rhineland, the increasingly worried and incessantly suspicious Stalin in the spring of 1936 ordered the beginning of the awesome purge trials, which continued into 1938. In these barbaric, almost incredible affairs, tens of thousands of Russians—party members, bureaucrats, military officers, and even members of the secret police and the prosecution—were tortured, forced into bogus confessions, convicted of plotting to kill Stalin or of treason, and shot. Although the extent of the horror was not fully known at that time, and although there was doubtless some substance to a few of the charges, a wave of revulsion swept over the West which was not easily forgotten. As Bolshevik turned on Bolshevik and comrade on comrade in an orgy of self-destruction, no serious efforts were attempted to bridge the chasm between antifascist democrats and antifascist Russians.

Developments in Europe, moreover, continued to confirm Stalin's darkest suspicions about the duplicity and cowardice of the capitalist states. Nazi Germany occupied Austria in March, 1938, with impunity. As Hitler's attentions turned toward Czechoslovakia, the Soviet Union was as much as ever, or perhaps more than ever, a pariah. Despite the fact that the Soviet Union was pledged by treaty to aid the Czechs if France did also, no Western nation sought the advice or support or participation of the Soviet government in those days; none trusted it. Moreover, there was a rather common and unfortunate tendency at that time to underrate Soviet strength. When the tragic Munich agreement was reached in September, 1938—Great Britain, France, and Germany agreed that Germany should be ceded the Sudeten areas of Czechoslovakia, in many parts of which the population was predominantly German-speaking—the uninvited Soviet government was isolated and embittered.

In March, 1939, Germany occupied most of the rest of Czechoslovakia.

---

[12] U.S. Department of State, *Foreign Relations . . ., The Soviet Union, 1933–1939*, p. 251.

The aroused British, now determining that it was futile to appease Hitler, pledged themselves to defend the territorial integrity of what appeared to be Hitler's next target, Poland. In addition, they and the French began negotiations with the Soviet Union in April, aimed at achieving a defensive alliance against Germany.

Stalin viewed all participants in the developing European crisis with equal contempt. Marxist ideology, the Soviet view of recent history, and his own acute tendency toward mistrust combined to convince him that there was little to choose between the Nazis and the capitalist democracies. Only one of them, however, posed a military threat to the Soviet Union, and hence the problem for Stalin was to try to ward off this threat. He had to choose between trying to reach an accord with Hitler—as Great Britain and France had tried to do—or siding for security reasons with Hitler's potential enemies. Sometime during the spring and summer of 1939, that fateful decision was made, and on August 23, the Nazi-Soviet Nonaggression Pact was signed. Nine days later, on September 1, Germany invaded Poland; on September 3, Great Britain honored its pledge by declaring war on Germany, and France followed suit. World War II was under way.

The nonaggression pact ranks among the most cynical accords of all time. Communism and Nazism, the two great totalitarian movements of the twentieth century, had long identified each other as the mortal foe. Hitler had decimated the Communist movement in Germany, and the Soviet Union had sought, however tardily or opportunistically, to create "united fronts" against Nazism and fascism in Europe. Now, they agreed not to engage in aggression against each other and to remain neutral if either party should be attacked by a third party. In a secret protocol, they divided up Eastern Europe between themselves.

Although the published version of the pact was not especially menacing on its face, Western governments assumed that its real significance went much further, and they drew the appropriate conclusions. The pact was an accurate measure of the abysmal state of Western-Soviet relations in the late 1930s. Great Britain and France, whose fates were directly and immediately involved, were alarmed and angry, but not completely surprised. This was what could be expected of the Bolsheviks. The United States government in early August had warned Stalin against taking such a step, predicting that Hitler would only use it as insurance for an invasion of France, after which he would attack the Soviet Union. Roosevelt had urged Stalin instead to reach an accord with Great Britain and France. He was, needless to say, not optimistic about the fate of this advice, but some hopes had remained up to the last minute, and the news of Stalin's decision was a grave disappointment.

During the next two years, before the Nazi invasion of Russia, Western-Soviet relations ranged from poor to rancorous. In the middle of September, Soviet troops absorbed the eastern half of Poland in accordance with the secret provisions of the pact. Later that autumn, when the Soviet government began making demands on Finland, Roosevelt reminded the Soviets of United States–Finnish friendship and said that he hoped that no unreasonable demands would be made. Foreign Minister Molotov said he was not surprised by this "American sentimental interest in Finland," and subsequently made a speech declaring that the Soviet Union had long ago granted independence to Finland, whereas Cuba and the Philippines were not independent of the United States. In the same speech, he ridiculed the British and the French and lauded the Germans. On November 30, 1939, the Soviet Union invaded Finland, and Roosevelt complained bitterly, in private, about "this dreadful rape of Finland," and said that the whole nation was "not only horrified but thoroughly angry." Upon learning of the Soviet bombing of Helsinki, he denounced the Soviets publicly and invoked a "moral embargo"[13] against them, which effectively cut off export of matériel relating to aircraft.

It would be difficult to exaggerate the suspicion, disapproval, and hostility that characterized the relations between the Western democracies and Hitler's newest ally during this tense period. But even these conditions were overshadowed by the fact of the war and the mutual fear of Nazi Germany. The realization that Hitler might attack either side at any moment gave the Soviets and the West something in common that was more immediately important than the ideological chasm or policy conflicts. Hence, neither side broke off relations or took other actions that might seriously compromise the possibility of future cooperation.

When Hitler conquered Norway, Denmark, Belgium, Holland, Luxembourg, and France in the spring of 1940, he struck fear into Soviet hearts as well as British and American. A few tentative moves toward cooperation ensued, including a relaxation and then a lifting of the moral embargo by the United States. Nothing very substantial resulted from Anglo-Russian or United States–Russian talks, however, despite a growing apprehension in late 1940 and early 1941 about Germany's next move. Stalin clung stubbornly to his policy of appeasing Germany and Japan, and apparently believed until the very end that this was practicable. On June 22, 1941, Nazi Germany invaded the Soviet Union. This historic event achieved what nothing else before it had: a rapprochement between Soviet Russia and the great capitalist, democratic powers of the West, Great Britain and the United States.

---

[13] The "moral embargo" was an extralegal device whereby the President issued a statement declaring that it was contrary to government policy to sell certain named products to countries engaged in opprobious activities, and asking that private companies voluntarily respect that policy. Moral embargoes were highly effective during this period.

The Strange Alliance

The response of Britain's peerless wartime Prime Minister, Winston Churchill, to the Nazi invasion of Russia demonstrates succinctly the attitudes of Western leaders toward the Soviet Union at that time. Churchill's private secretary questioned him about the propriety and wisdom of supporting Communist Russia. Churchill replied: "I have only one purpose, the destruction of Hitler, and my life is much simplified thereby. If Hitler invaded Hell, I would make at least a favourable reference to the Devil in the House of Commons."[14] When he went on radio the evening of the attack to address the British people, he spoke, in part, as follows:

No one has been a more consistent opponent of Communism than I have for the last twenty-five years. I will unsay no word that I have spoken about it. But all this fades away before the spectacle which is now unfolding. . . . I see the Russian soldiers standing on the threshold of their native land, guarding the fields which their fathers have tilled from time immemorial. I see them guarding their homes where mothers and wives pray—ah, yes, for there are times when all pray—for the safety of their loved ones. . . . I see advancing upon all this in hideous onslaught the Nazi war machine, with its clanking, heel-clicking, dandified Prussian officers, its crafty expert agents fresh from the cowing and tying-down of a dozen countries. I see also the dull, drilled, docile, brutish masses of the Hun soldiery plodding on like a swarm of crawling locusts. . . .

We have but one aim and one single, irrevocable purpose. We are resolved to destroy Hitler and every vestige of the Nazi regime. From this nothing will turn us—nothing. . . . Any man or state who fights on against Nazidom will have our aid.[15]

Here were all the ingredients of the wartime relationship: expediency, a pervasive sense of the monstrous evil that was Nazi Germany, and a hopeful representation of Soviet Russia against a historical background of political mistrust and ideological alienation. As the war lengthened, all of these elements played a part, with first one and then another gaining a temporary ascendancy.

Churchill and Roosevelt, who was then in his third term, had agreed in early June that, in the event of a German attack on Russia, Great Britain should welcome Russia as an ally and attempt to assist its resistance efforts. There was, however, a widespread opinion in the West, especially among military experts, that the Soviet Union could not last longer than a few months. For this and other reasons, Great Britain and the United States

---

[14] Winston S. Churchill, *The Grand Alliance*, Houghton Mifflin Company, Boston, 1950, p. 370.
[15] *Ibid.*, pp. 371–372.

moved cautiously at first in providing the Soviets with assistance. Nonetheless, although the Red Army was in retreat all along the front, it became clear during the summer and fall that the Soviets would not capitulate. Roosevelt facilitated Soviet military purchases in the United States during this period, and in November, he officially declared the Soviet Union eligible for assistance under the Lend-Lease program, which had passed earlier in 1941. In order to do this, he had to declare—in the face of substantial congressional and public opposition—that he had "found that the defense of the Union of Soviet Socialist Republics is vital to the defense of the United States." The first billion of what was to become an $11 billion assistance program was made available simultaneously.[16]

On December 7, 1941, the Japanese attack on Pearl Harbor, Hawaii, provided additional incentives for viewing the Soviet Union in a comparatively favorable light. Moreover, Germany then declared war on the United States, and the last major participant entered World War II.

During the war, Soviet-Western relations reached heights of great cordiality, perhaps even trust, but they also sank to ominous depths of acrimony and suspicion. The substantial amount of cooperation and coordination gave rise to legitimate and understandable hopes for peaceful and relatively harmonious relations. The central fact of the postwar world is that these hopes have been shattered. In this brief overview of the origins of the cold war, emphasis will be placed on the areas of friction in the wartime alliance, because they proved to be of greater importance than the areas of cooperation. It should be borne in mind, however, that what follows is not a balanced account but rather one that concentrates on the historic roots of the contemporary situation.

Perhaps the most troublesome problem between the Allies was Poland. For the West—the United States and Great Britain—Poland became the great testing ground of Soviet intentions. The Soviets failed that test by Western standards, and the resultant bitterness severely handicapped all other attempts at conciliation after the war.

The British had drawn the line at Poland in 1939; and when Hitler in-

---

[16] The irony of the new relationship with the Soviet Union and the deeply felt bitterness that it provoked in large sections of the American public can perhaps be summed up in a few remarks of Congressman Hamilton Fish, a Republican isolationist who represented Roosevelt's home district and was one of the President's chief antagonists. In September, the President had become embroiled in an unnecessary and embarrassing episode by saying to newspapermen that "freedom of religion" was then being observed in embattled Russia; and, moreover, that it was protected by the Soviet Constitution of 1936. The outrage that this provoked in religious and other circles in the United States reached a sarcastic peak when Congressman Fish suggested that Roosevelt invite Stalin to Washington where he "might be baptized in the swimming pool at the White House," after which everyone present could enroll in the "Stalin Sunday School." *New York Times*, Oct. 5, 1941, p. 17, quoted in Raymond H. Dawson, *The Decision to Aid Russia, 1941*, The University of North Carolina Press, Chapel Hill, 1959, p. 260.

vaded, Great Britain declared war. They therefore had a special sentimental investment in the future of Poland that went beyond a general
commitment to postwar solutions based on democratic principles and
practices. The United States had no such special interest in postwar Poland,
but it did have the same general commitment, and, in addition, it had a
large Polish-American population.

The Soviet Union, for its part, certainly had no commitment to a West-
ern-style democratic government in Poland. On the contrary, it wanted
and intended to install in postwar Poland a Communist regime. Twice in
this century, German armies had marched across Polish territory into
Russia. When the Soviets agreed with their Western allies that postwar
Poland should have a "democratic government, friendly to the Soviet
Union," its interpretation of these words was considerably different from
that of the West.

There were two basic questions about Poland: What were its postwar
boundaries to be? And, who was to govern? This first question proved to
be largely resolvable to the satisfaction of the major Allies, if not to the
Poles themselves. A substantial portion of prewar Poland's eastern territory was ceded to the Soviet Union. It had been Russian prior to World
War I, and was largely wrested from the Soviets by the new Polish state
by force of arms in 1920. Moreover, the population in the area was ethnically and culturally mixed, consisting of Lithuanians, Ukranians, and White
Russians, as well as Poles. Soviet claims were at least respectable. Poland
was compensated with substantial portions of eastern Germany, including
much of eastern Prussia.[17]

However, the second question about Poland—Who was to govern?—
played a major role in setting the tone of postwar diplomacy. When
Poland disappeared from the map in 1939, its government managed to
escape to London and establish a Polish-government-in-exile. These "London Poles" were recognized by the Western Allies as the legitimate
government of Poland; and after the Soviet Union was attacked, it also
extended them recognition.

Polish-Soviet relations were, however, strained from the very outset. As
previously noted, the Soviets had in 1939 joined with Germany in eliminat-

[17] The Western frontier of Poland—and hence the eastern frontier of defeated Germany—
has never been officially settled and is today a potential source of trouble. At issue is
the territory lying between the Western and Eastern Neisse Rivers, south of the Oder
River, which is now governed by the Poles and regarded by them as part of Poland.
The Yalta conferees had been unable to agree on the disposition of this particular
area. At the Potsdam Conference in July, 1945, the Western powers had reluctantly
acquiesced in Polish administration of the area pending a final peace settlement. No
peace settlement was ever reached, of course, and the West German government has
been particularly unwilling to concede the finality of this arrangement. Other Western
governments have shown conspicuously less interest in the matter, and, in any event,
it did not emerge as a serious source of friction between wartime allies after the war.

ing the Polish state. Moreover, they gave every indication of wanting to reclaim after the war the territory that they had occupied in 1939, while compensating Poland with parts of eastern Germany. As noted above, this territory was ethnically mixed and had been Russian prior to World War I. But the clash of interest was, of course, unavoidable and insoluble.

Other matters also divided the Western-supported Polish government from the Soviet Union. Many hundreds of thousands of Poles had been forcibly and cruelly shipped into the Soviet Union after 1939 for work in Soviet labor camps. Under the new conditions, some of these unfortunate people were to be released to join a reconstituted Polish army for action against Germany. But their release was slow and cumbersome, and, more ominously, thousands of Polish officers were unaccountably missing.

This last development ultimately provided the occasion for a break in diplomatic relations between the London Poles and the Soviet Union. In April, 1943, the Germans announced the discovery of mass graves for several thousand Polish officers in the Katyn Forest, an area near Smolensk, Russia. Germany declared that the Soviets must have murdered them sometime between September, 1939, and their retreat in the summer of 1941. The London Poles thereupon asked the International Red Cross to investigate. The Soviets, of course, were protesting their innocence and alleging that the Germans had performed the massacre. When they learned of the Polish request, which implied some doubts about Soviet veracity, they severed relations with the London Poles. They had never trusted the exiled government, arguing with some truth that it was a clique of aristocrats, whose prewar policies were proof of their hostility to the Soviet Union. They went so far as to charge the London Poles with being Nazi collaborators.

At about the same time, a group of Polish Communists living in Russia formed a group called "The Union of Polish Patriots." With some modifications, this group—later known as the Lublin Poles—became the Soviet candidate for the legitimate government of postwar Poland.

The Western governments were distressed by these developments but were not in a position to change them. Churchill and Roosevelt made repeated efforts to reestablish relations between the London Poles and the Soviet Union, without success. The potential divisiveness of the Polish issue was dramatically and tragically underlined during the summer and fall of 1944. With the advancing Red Army virtually in the outskirts of Warsaw, the Polish underground, directed by the London Poles, began an uprising against the Germans on August 1. The Soviet offensive suddenly stalled, however, and the uprising turned into an extended and grisly disaster.

The suspicion was widespread that the Soviets were not halting their advance for military reasons, as claimed, but for the political purpose of permitting the Germans to wipe out the core of the underground army. When Churchill requested that the Red Army help the insurrectionists,

Stalin reported that he had probed into the "Warsaw affair" and had come to the conclusion that it was "a reckless and fearful gamble, taking a heavy toll of the population," and he disassociated himself from it entirely. He later refused to permit American planes to drop supplies to the Poles and then land on Soviet-controlled air bases. He attacked the "handful of power-seeking criminals who launched the Warsaw adventure."[18] The tragic rebellion finally expired on October 2, and Soviet-Western relations had been badly shaken.

In January, 1945, Stalin rejected Churchill's and Roosevelt's pleas and recognized the Lublin Poles and put them in nominal charge of administering Polish civil affairs. It was an inauspicious prelude to the February Yalta Conference between Roosevelt, Churchill, and Stalin.

Poland was discussed at seven of the eight plenary meetings at Yalta and also in the private talks that the principals had with one another. The controlling fact was that the Red Army was already occupying most of prewar Poland, and the Western leaders were therefore necessarily in the position of supplicants. Stalin wanted the Lublin Poles to constitute the core of the Provisional Government. Roosevelt and Churchill wanted a coalition government drawn from the leadership of the five major Polish political parties. A compromise was reached, which called for subsequent negotiations aimed at a reorganization "on a broader democratic basis" of the already functioning government that had been installed by the Red Army. This arrangement left a lot to be desired from the Western standpoint, but it gave at least some promise of a Soviet willingness to tolerate non-Communist elements in the interim Polish government. Moreover, the real test was yet to come: Free elections were promised, to be held as soon as possible. The Provisional Government would then step down, and a democratic Poland would be launched in accordance with Polish wishes, not Western or Soviet.

These expectations were not realized, and, as we shall see, the resulting Western anger and bitterness were major contributants to the origins of the cold war.

Another problem that agitated the alliance during the war was the delay in establishing a western front in Europe. From June, 1941, until June, 1944, the Red Army and the Russian population absorbed the brunt of the destructiveness of the Nazi war machine. Estimates of the number of Russians who died in the war range as high as 20 million. Whatever the precise figure may be, there is no doubt that no other Allied nation suf-

---

[18] Ministry of Foreign Affairs of the U.S.S.R., *Correspondence between The Chairman of the Council of Ministers of the U.S.S.R. and the Presidents of the U.S.A. and the Prime Ministers of Great Britain during the Great Patriotic War of 1941–1945,* Foreign Languages Publishing House, Moscow, 1957, vol. I, pp. 252, 254, and vol. II, pp. 155–156. Hereinafter cited as "Ministry of Foreign Affairs of the U.S.S.R., *Correspondence.*"

fered as grievously as Russia did in terms of human and material losses. The eagerness of the Soviets to have their Western allies assume a larger share of the burden was wholly legitimate and understandable.

Stalin made his first request—or demand—for a second front immediately after the Nazi invasion. The British, of course, could not possibly have successfully launched an invasion of Europe at that time. Churchill has described the Soviet attitude in the summer of 1941 as "surly, snarly, grasping and so lately indifferent to our survival."[19]

When the United States entered the war, Stalin's hopes for a second front naturally were vastly increased. Soviet Foreign Minister Molotov came to the United States in late May, 1942, and his main concern was to press for a second front in 1942. Germany's spring offensive was underway, and Soviet anxieties were appreciated on all sides. Roosevelt authorized Molotov to tell Stalin that the United States expected the formation of a second front in 1942. Over his Chief of Staff's objections, Roosevelt authorized a public statement, which contained the following sentence: "In the course of the conversations, full understanding was reached with regard to the urgent tasks of creating a second front in Europe in 1942."[20] Nobody knew exactly what this sentence meant, and it subsequently yielded bitter fruit.

Churchill was, as usual, considerably less expansive and more circumspect than Roosevelt. He had talked in a noncommittal fashion with Molotov before the latter's trip to Washington, and when Molotov returned to London en route home, Churchill presented him with a carefully drawn *aide mémoire*, which succinctly stated the problem. It read, in part, as follows:

> We are making preparations for a landing on the Continent in August or September, 1942. As already explained, the main limiting factor to the size of the landing-force is the availability of special landing craft. Clearly however it would not further either the Russian cause or that of the Allies as a whole, if, for the sake of action at any price, we embarked on some operation which ended in disaster. . . . It is impossible to say in advance whether the situation will be such as to make this operation feasible when the time comes. We can therefore give no promise in the matter, but provided that it appears sound and sensible we shall not hesitate to put our plans into effect.[21]

In late July, 1942, Churchill and Roosevelt agreed that a European invasion in 1942 was not feasible. Churchill decided to try to explain this painful decision to Stalin in person. Their talks reached levels of consider-

[19] Churchill, *The Grand Alliance, op. cit.*, p. 452.
[20] As quoted in Herbert Feis, *Churchill, Roosevelt, Stalin*, Princeton University Press, Princeton, N.J., 1957, p. 67.
[21] As quoted in Winston S. Churchill, *The Hinge of Fate*, Houghton Mifflin Company, Boston, 1950, p. 342.

able cordiality and depths of bitter Soviet resentment. Stalin was alternately contemptuous and understanding about the decision not to invade Europe in 1942, and he showed the same ambivalence about the importance of the forthcoming North African landings.

The Western leaders understood and sympathized with the grounds for Stalin's anger and abusiveness, and demonstrated great patience with him. The trend of the war in 1942 was still eastward. The turning point in the war on the eastern front—if it makes sense to talk about turning points in a struggle so immense and complex—was the epic battle of Stalingrad. This did not begin until September, 1942, and it dragged on until February, 1943. When it was over, the tide of the war became favorable for the first time. In the meantime, the Russian government, army, and people had created an enormous reservoir of good will in the West, and their exploits and suffering had induced a profound sense of responsibility, even of guilt, among Western leaders. Moral, psychological, political, and military considerations combined, therefore, to emphasize the desirability of a Western invasion of Europe at the earliest possible moment.

In May, 1943, however, the two Western leaders again reluctantly postponed the landing in Europe for another year. On July 11, Stalin sent his reply and touched off one of the bitterest exchanges of the war. He recounted Western messages that had detailed plans for an invasion of France in 1943, and he strongly implied bad faith. He said that the postponement created great difficulties for the Soviet Union "and leaves the Soviet Army, which is fighting not only for its country, but also for its allies, to do the job alone, almost single-handed, against an enemy that is still very strong and formidable."

On June 19, Churchill sent a lengthy and restrained answer, defending the postponement as "the only thing that is physically possible in the circumstances."

Stalin's June 24 rejoinder quoted extensively from earlier Churchill cables, which had given the Soviets considerable cause for believing that an invasion across the Channel would be launched in 1943. He argued that conditions for such an invasion had greatly improved. The latter half of this message became increasingly acrid and concluded as follows:

> You say that you "quite understand" my disappointment. I must tell you that the point here is not just the disappointment of the Soviet Government, but the preservation of its confidence in its Allies, a confidence which is being subjected to severe stress. One should not forget that it is a question of saving millions of lives in the occupied areas of Western Europe and Russia and of reducing the enormous sacrifices of the Soviet armies, compared with which the sacrifices of the Anglo-American armies are insignificant.

Without consulting the President as he usually did, Churchill shot back an angry retort, dated June 27. Besides defending the postponement, he gave in to the temptation of reminding Stalin that "until June 22, 1941, we British were left alone to face the worst that Nazi Germany could do to us." He affirmed that he had done "everything in human power to help you. Therefore the reproaches which you now cast upon your Western Allies leave me unmoved."[22]

This exchange provides a glimpse beneath the congenial or businesslike surface that usually characterized Soviet-Western relations during the war. This is not to say that this Hitler-induced surface was not real or even that it had no chance of surviving after the war. But side by side with it was this ominous capacity for suspicion, bitterness, and recrimination, which ultimately proved to be more lasting.

On two occasions during the war, Soviet suspicions that the Western allies might negotiate Axis surrenders to the disadvantage of the Soviets prompted harsh exchanges and threatened Allied unity.

In the summer of 1943, the Western Allies entered into complicated surrender negotiations with the Italian government, which had just succeeded Mussolini's fascist regime. On August 19, Churchill and Roosevelt sent a lengthy message to Stalin explaining in detail what had transpired in the negotiations and what course was being pursued. As delivered to the Soviets, however, the message contained one garbled sentence and lacked the final paragraph. Stalin's suspicions were aroused, and he sent back a sharp message alleging that he was not being kept fully informed as promised. Moreover, he did not any longer want to be merely "a third party looking passively on," and he proposed the establishment of a military-political commission to consider surrenders.

Both Roosevelt and Churchill were angered by this display of bad temper that followed closely upon the chilling exchanges between Churchill and Stalin about the second postponement of the second front. Churchill foresaw "bloody consequences in the future"[23] and notified his cabinet that

> ... the black spot at the present time is the increasing bearishness of Soviet Russia. You will have seen the telegram received from Stalin about the Italian overtures. He has absolutely no ground for complaint. . . .
>
> The President was very much offended at the tone of this message. He gave directions to the effect that the new Soviet Chargé d'Affaires was to be told he was away in the country and would not be back for some days.[24]

This episode can be viewed as a prologue to a much more acrid and portentous controversy, which began in late February, 1945. To understand the full import of this latter crisis, it should be borne in mind that it

[22] Ministry of Foreign Affairs of the U.S.S.R., *Correspondence*, vol. I, pp. 132–138, 140–141.
[23] As quoted in Feis, *op. cit.*, p. 172.
[24] As quoted in Winston S. Churchill, *Closing the Ring*, Houghton Mifflin Company, Boston, 1951, pp. 93–94.

occurred after the auspicious Yalta Conference of February, 1945, and in the waning days of the European war.

An Italian industrialist told the Allied command in Italy that certain high-ranking German officers were interested in negotiating a surrender in northern Italy. Allied efforts were then made to facilitate contact with these officers, and the Soviets were notified of the potential negotiations. The Soviets immediately asked to be included in the initiating talks, which were to take place in Berne, Switzerland. These talks were to be merely preliminary and procedural, with the substantive negotiations to take place later in Italy. Allied military leaders feared that Soviet representatives might delay matters in the Berne talks, and they suggested that the Soviets attend only the substantive negotiations, and then only as observers and consultants. The military command in the area was deemed to be the proper authority to make the decision to accept or reject any surrender offer.

In mid-March, Molotov rejected the entire procedure. He said that the refusal to permit Soviet representatives at the Berne negotiations came as a complete surprise and that it was inexplicable in terms of the alliance. He insisted that the talks be discontinued at once. The United States Ambassador to the Soviet Union, W. Averill Harriman, replied that Molotov misunderstood the purpose of the proposed contact at Berne. Molotov then advised Harriman that something far worse than a misunderstanding was occurring. He charged that for two weeks negotiations had been going on at Berne "behind the back of the Soviet Union which is bearing the brunt of the war against Germany."[25]

This prompted Roosevelt to enter the controversy with a personal message to Stalin. He said that no preliminary meetings had even taken place as yet,[26] that the Soviets would unquestionably be in on any actual surrender negotiations, and declared that Molotov's objections were incomprehensible. Stalin was not moved. He told the President that he could not understand why Soviet officers should be excluded from any talks, that the Berne talks were indeed going on, and that the Germans had already taken advantage of the talks to move three divisions to the Soviet front. He added, somewhat unnecessarily, that the episode was engendering mistrust. When Roosevelt tried again to refute these charges, Stalin replied that the President was apparently not fully informed. He said his colleagues assured him that negotiations had taken place and had resulted in an agreement whereby the British and American troops were to be permitted to move east without opposition in exchange for eased armistice

[25] Ministry of Foreign Affairs of the U.S.S.R., *Correspondence*, vol. II, p. 297.

[26] According to Churchill's account, two preliminary meetings were actually held, March 8 and March 19, between a German officer and representatives of the United States and Great Britain. See Winston S. Churchill, *Triumph and Tragedy*, Houghton Mifflin Company, Boston, 1953, p. 441.

terms for the Germans. The last three paragraphs of this harsh cable merit quotation in full:

> And so what we have at the moment is that the Germans on the Western Front have in fact ceased the war against Britain and America. At the same time they continue the war against Russia, the Ally of Britain and the U.S.A.
>
> Clearly this situation cannot help preserve and promote trust between our countries.
>
> I have already written in a previous message, and I think I must repeat, that I and my colleagues would never in any circumstances have taken such a hazardous step, for we realize that a momentary advantage, no matter how great, is overshadowed by the fundamental advantage of preserving and promoting trust between Allies.[27]

Roosevelt was deeply offended and angered. His reply of April 5, one week before his death, reveals the agonizing shock and sorrow that was enveloping the tired President. He expressed astonishment at the Soviet allegation and repeated his earlier assurances. He concluded as follows:

> Finally, I would say this, it would be one of the great tragedies of history if at the very moment of the victory, now within our grasp, such distrust, such lack of faith should prejudice the entire undertaking after the colossal loss of life, material and treasure involved.
>
> Frankly, I cannot avoid a feeling of bitter resentment toward your informers, whoever they are, for such vile misrepresentations of my actions or those of my trusted subordinates.[28]

There was a final exchange on the matter in which Stalin took a less offensive line, but the meaning of this acrimonious affair could not be erased.

Indeed, the three months between the end of the promising Yalta Conference and the end of the European war were crammed full of ominous signs. Basic disagreements about the composition of the Polish government remained unresolved. This led to Stalin's refusal to send Foreign Minister Molotov to the forthcoming opening conference of the United Nations, despite Roosevelt's urgent pleas that the new organization not be slighted and its importance diminished. Finally, the treatment of liberated prisoners of war produced an angry blast from Moscow that came close to rivalling the Berne incident as a display of Soviet suspicion and surliness. As the Allied armies converged on Germany, the Red Army was liberating some Western prisoners of war, and Western armies were freeing Russians. Roosevelt was anxious to evacuate these Americans and in March asked Stalin for permission to operate an airlift out of Poland for this purpose.

[27] Ministry of Foreign Affairs of the U.S.S.R., *Correspondence*, vol. II, p. 206.
[28] *Ibid.*, pp. 207–208.

Stalin refused, saying their transference to American control was being handled expeditiously by the Soviets. Roosevelt pressed the issue, saying he did not understand Stalin's position. Stalin replied that the problem was virtually resolved and that he did not want United States officers milling around behind the lines in Poland. He then added:

> I must also say that U.S. ex-prisoners of war liberated by the Red Army have been treated to good conditions in Soviet camps—better conditions than those afforded Soviet ex-prisoners of war in U.S. camps, where some of them were lodged with German war prisoners and were subjected to unfair treatment and unlawful persecutions, including beating, as has been communicated to the U.S. Government on more than one occasion.[29]

The "Yalta honeymoon" did not last long.

There were other difficulties in Soviet-Western relations during the war. For example, when German submarine activity twice induced Western decisions to interrupt the northern supply convoys to the Soviet Union, Stalin reacted with scorn and charges of bad faith. And there was the steady and unappreciated Soviet pressure for Western acceptance of Russia's absorption of the Baltic states, substantial sections of northern Rumania, and a slice of prewar Finland, as well as the aforementioned area of prewar Poland.

As emphasized above, however, this narrative has stressed these difficulties at the expense of the many hopeful episodes and messages that grew out of the alliance. When the European war ended on May 8, 1945, most Western officials probably believed that postwar cooperation could be achieved. At the very least, it can be said with certainty that the British and American governments were determined to seek amicable relations with the Soviets.

Selected Bibliography

Browder, Robert Paul: *The Origins of Soviet-American Diplomacy*, Princeton University Press, Princeton, N. J., 1953. A sound treatment of the decision to recognize Soviet Russia.

Churchill, Winston S.: *Triumph and Tragedy*, Houghton Mifflin Company, Boston, 1953. The great British statesman relates, in this last volume of his monumental history of World War II, how the war ended and the cold war began. This is one of the most important books published since the war.

[29] *Ibid.*, pp. 196–197.

Dawson, Raymond H.: *The Decision to Aid Russia, 1941,* The University of North Carolina Press, Chapel Hill, 1959. A detailed analysis of a critical turning point in American history.

Feis, Herbert: *Churchill, Roosevelt, Stalin,* Princeton University Press, Princeton, N. J., 1957. The definitive account of the wartime leadership of the Big Three.

Kennan, George F.: *Russia and the West under Lenin and Stalin,* Little, Brown and Company, Boston, 1960. A superb account of the often stormy relations up to World War II between the emergent revolutionary giant and the antagonistic Western powers, by a man who experienced much of it and studied most of the rest. This, like Churchill's *Triumph and Tragedy,* is among the most important books of this era.

————: *Soviet Foreign Policy, 1917–1941,* D. Van Nostrand Company, Inc., Princeton, N. J., 1960. A brief treatment of Soviet policy, with significant documents appended.

McNeill, William Hardy: *America, Britain, and Russia, 1941–1946,* Oxford University Press, London, 1953. A solid historical treatment of the diplomacy of the Big Three during and just after World War II.

Ministry of Foreign Affairs of the U.S.S.R.: *Correspondence between the Chairman of the Council of Ministers of the U.S.S.R. and the Presidents of the U.S.A. and the Prime Ministers of Great Britain during the Great Patriotic War of 1941–1945,* Foreign Languages Publishing House, Moscow, 1957 (two volumes). These documents have not all been published in the West, but apparently this Soviet version is accurate. It is unquestionably fascinating.

U.S. Department of State: *Foreign Relations of the United States: The Soviet Union, 1933–1939,* Washington, D. C., 1952. An unusually instructive and interesting set of documents.

chapter 5 Winston Churchill entitled the last volume of his classic history of World War II *Triumph and Tragedy*. A great military triumph over the malignant and powerful Nazi regime was quickly followed by the tragedy of a reopening and a deepening of the chasm that had, in prewar days, divided the Soviet Union and the Western democracies.

Who or what was responsible for this melancholy and dangerous development? Some would argue that something impersonal called "the nation-state system" was responsible and that it is fatuous to attempt to allocate responsibility among nations or societies or leaders. In this view, the cold war was inevitable, a mere extension of the unavoidable conflicts that have divided states from each other throughout history. To talk as if it might have been avoided is to betray one's naïveté and failure to grasp the ineluctable pattern of international politics.

For Soviet leaders, historians, and publicists, however, the question is a meaningful one. Their answer to it, of course, is that the bourgeois, capitalist West, in attempting to arrest its inevitable decline, pursued provocative, imperialist policies designed to undermine and destroy the peace-loving Soviet Union.

For most Westerners, too, the question is a meaningful one, but there is considerable diversity in their answers. For free Western scholars, historical truth is difficult to establish, and the attempt to fix responsibility for the onset of the cold war has been and will continue to be a source of contention. A few offer interpretations that bear a marked resemblance to those of the Soviets, but theirs is a lonely and unpersuasive dissent. The amount of evidence available for all sides in the dispute is sufficient for "conventional," "revisionist" and other kinds of interpretations.

What follows is a rather "conventional" Western outline of the postwar origins of the cold war. It assumes and implies that the cold war was not an inevitable outgrowth of "the international system," that responsibility for it must be shared by both sides, but that by far the greater burden of culpability lies with the Soviet Union. It also assumes that the question of responsibility is an important one.

The cold war became manifest in the contentions over specific issues. A mere recital of these issues, however, would be a superficial account of the problem. It is necessary to look briefly behind the specifics at some of the major factors that contributed to the developing alienation. These factors were, of course, intertwined and reinforcing.

Communist ideology surely lies somewhere near the root of the matter, if indeed it is not the root itself. In undiluted form, it is so uncompromisingly, militantly, and eternally hostile to Western democratic governments, economies, and societies that if its disciples were wholly under its spell, no rapprochement would be remotely possible in the long run. How seriously the Soviets took—and take—their ideology is, of course, a matter in endless dispute among themselves and Westerners alike. As mentioned above, this book is based on the conviction that ideology is an important contributant to Soviet thought and action, not merely an intellectual façade or rationalization for the personal power of Soviet leaders. At the very least, it is a prism through which the Soviets see the world and their role in it. It is not a blueprint or a specific guide to action, but it does instill in its followers a badly distorted view of the world and a dangerous arrogance about historical developments—past, present, and future—and their own role therein. If anything made the cold war inevitable, it was the existence and apparent influence of this divisive and presumptuous creed, which created suspicion where none was justified and magnified nearly all policy differences, otherwise negotiable or manageable, into clashes over basic principles. Limited disagreements among rational men and nations induce attempts at compromise; among ideologues, they bring on crusades, pitting the True Believers, Truth, and Goodness against Nonbelievers, Falsehood, and Evil.

Another factor of incalculable importance was the personality of Stalin. This has already been alluded to above. It remains only to emphasize that by all accounts, Soviet and Western, in the last years of his life, he suffered "from suspiciousness and a persecution mania."[1] Any attempt to understand postwar developments must take this into account.

Another background factor that merits attention is recent Russian history and its effects on Russian—even non-Communist—thought. World War I dealt harshly with Russia and World War II was a colossal disaster. It was natural for the Russian government to exhibit a lively, even exaggerated, concern for future Russian security. Roosevelt and Churchill enthusiastically supported Stalin's demands, for example, for "friendly" governments in Poland and elsewhere in Eastern Europe. However, when this understandable anxiety was translated into a policy of imposing Communist regimes throughout the area, Western sympathy and agreement were transformed into Western fear, recriminations, and, ultimately, rearmament.

What follows is largely a summary of the major developments in the two seminal years after the Japanese surrender. By the autumn of 1947, the basic outlines of the cold war were rather well established.

Eastern Europe

Poland, which figured so prominently in wartime policy divergencies within the alliance, continued to plague relations after the war. Pursuant to the Yalta agreements, negotiations were held in an effort to reach agreement

---

[1] The quoted section is from a speech by Premier Khrushchev in March, 1963, to Soviet writers and artists, as reported by Victor Zorza in the *Los Angeles Times*, Mar. 11, 1963, p. 18.

on the composition of the Polish Provisional Government. These talks were deadlocked from the outset, neither the West nor the Soviets agreeing to the other side's proposed list of officials. Churchill and Roosevelt appealed to Stalin in the name of the Yalta agreements, and he replied that it was the West that was obstructing their implementation.

Foreign Minister Molotov stopped off in Washington on April 22 en route to the San Francisco conference inaugurating the United Nations Organization. He and the new President, Harry S Truman, had two meetings, and both of them dealt almost exclusively with the Polish question. After both officials assured the other that their government sought to maintain friendly relations with the other and after they both endorsed the Yalta accords, they quickly demonstrated the increasingly familiar inability to agree on anything specific about the Polish Provisional Government. The second conversation, on April 23, apparently took an unpleasant turn. As later recorded by Truman, he repeatedly and sharply insisted that the Soviets were not carrying out the Yalta agreements. When he told Molotov that the United States wanted to be friendly with Russia but not on "the basis of a one-way street," the foreign minister and former premier of the Soviet Union replied: "I have never been talked to like that in my life." Truman replied: "Carry out your agreements and you won't get talked to like that."[2]

On hearing of these conversations and after having received a lengthy communiqué on April 18 from Truman and Churchill on the Polish question, Stalin on April 24 made a spirited reply. He reiterated his claim that it was the Western powers that were not fulfilling the Yalta agreements and emphasized again the importance to the Soviet Union of having a friendly government in Poland. He added:

> One cannot but recognize as unusual a situation in which two Governments—those of the United States and Great Britain—reach agreement beforehand on Poland, a country in which the U. S. S. R. is interested first of all and most of all, and place its representatives in an intolerable position, trying to dictate to it. . . . You are asking too much. To put it plainly, you want me to renounce the interests of the security of the Soviet Union; but I cannot proceed against the interests of my country.[3]

[2] Harry S Truman, *Memoirs*, vol. I, *Year of Decisions*, Doubleday & Company, Inc., Garden City, N.Y., 1955, p. 82. Mr. Truman published this volume of his memoirs in 1955. It may be that these quotations are not altogether accurate. There is little doubt, however, that they accurately reflect the tone and temper of the new President at the time of his first confrontation with a high Soviet official. See, for example, Walter Millis (ed.), *The Forrestal Diaries*, The Viking Press, Inc., New York, 1951, p. 50.

One hardy Washington anecdote alleges that this second discussion terminated abruptly with the President in effect dismissing Molotov. The whole episode is sometimes lightly referred to as "the day the cold war began."

[3] Ministry of Foreign Affairs of the U.S.S.R., *Correspondence*, vol. II, p. 220. The quoted cable was sent to Truman. The one sent to Churchill differed slightly but not significantly; it appears in *ibid.*, vol. I, pp. 330–331.

The receipt of this cable moved Churchill on April 28 to a long and conciliatory, but frank, reply. He reviewed a broad range of emerging difficulties among the nearly victorious allies and then concluded with this eloquent and poignant paragraph:

> There is not much comfort in looking into a future where you and the countries you dominate, plus the Communist parties in many other States, are all drawn up on one side, and those who rally to the English-speaking nations and their Associates or Dominions are on the other. It is quite obvious that their quarrel would tear the world to pieces and that all of us leading men on either side who had anything to do with that would be shamed before history. . . . Do not, I beg you, my friend Stalin, underrate the divergencies which are opening about matters which you may think are small to us but which are symbolic of the way the English-speaking democracies look at life.[4]

Because of the mounting difficulties in Soviet-Western relations that victorious spring, the new President decided to send Harry Hopkins to Moscow on a mission of inquiry and conciliation. Hopkins had been Roosevelt's most trusted adviser and companion and, in addition, had developed a personal rapport with Stalin that for a Westerner may have been unparalleled in warmth and cordiality. Stalin welcomed the suggestion for a visit by Hopkins, and the frail, ill emissary arrived in Moscow on May 25. He told Stalin that of all the frictions developing between the two governments, the most troublesome problem was Poland. The Moscow-installed government and the Soviet Army were arresting and imprisoning the remnants of the valiant Polish underground and other non-Communist leaders. The negotiations aimed at expanding the Provisional Government were deadlocked. And the prospects for free elections were dim. Like the Yalta conferees, Hopkins and Stalin spent more time talking about Poland than any other matter.

There were the usual agreements "in principle." Stalin agreed to the desirability of a "democratic" Polish government and repeated his commitment to the principle of "free and unfettered elections" in Poland. Hopkins agreed that the Polish government should be "friendly" to the Soviet Union. And the two men actually reached an agreement on a list of Poles who would be invited to preliminary discussions in Moscow designed to form a coalition Provisional Government.

These discussions were then held in Moscow in June and resulted in the formation of a coalition Provisional Government slightly more representative of democratic elements but still dominated by Moscow-supported "Warsaw Poles," formerly called the Lublin Poles. The crucial issue then became whether free elections would actually be carried out by this supposedly interim Provisional Government. There were vague reassurances to this effect during and after these June consultations. Despite growing

[4] *Ibid.*, vol. I, pp. 343–344.

pessimism, the United States and Great Britain finally extended formal recognition to the expanded Provisional Government on July 5.

The Big Three, with Truman representing the United States for the first time, met at Potsdam, a suburb of Berlin, in July. Poland was, of course, still a major topic. The Western leaders pushed for more assurances that elections would in fact be held and that they would be free. This time, Stalin resisted any firm declarations, arguing that the Provisional Government was committed to free elections and should not be hectored or insulted by Allied meddling in Polish affairs. Stalin, of course, did not mention that he effectively controlled "Polish affairs" and intended to continue doing so. The Western Allies understood this well enough, but were still hopeful that the "free and unfettered elections" agreed upon at Yalta would be held.

They never were, and the ensuing arguments and bitterness were major elements in the alienation of the West from the Soviet Union. As the West clung stubbornly to its abstract principles about democratic governments—in an area, by the way, where democratic institutions and processes would have been largely unprecedented—the Soviet Union just as stubbornly proceeded to impose Communist regimes throughout almost all of Eastern and Central Europe where its troops were in control.[5] Its obsession with security combined with its desire to spread communism dictated a policy that violated the Yalta agreements and helped to poison relations with the West.[6]

The methods and timing of the communization of Eastern Europe varied, as did the character of the installed regimes. The Soviets did not rely exclusively on the crude methods of terror and force, but their goal and determination became quite clear as the weeks and months passed by. By early 1948, their satellite empire was an established fact.

At Potsdam, the United States had managed to gain approval of the creation of a Council of Foreign Ministers representing the Big Three, France, and China. The Council's assigned task was to do the preparatory work for the peace settlements.[7]

[5] The single exception was Czechoslovakia, from which Soviet occupation troops withdrew in December, 1945, and where democratic institutions and elections were actually tolerated for several years.

[6] The "Declaration on Liberated Europe" adopted at Yalta committed the wartime Allies to a set of high-sounding principles that were much easier to proclaim than to respect. The Big Three agreed, for example, to assist the newly liberated and former Axis satellite countries "to form interim governmental authorities broadly representative of all democratic elements in the population and pledged to the earliest possible establishment through free elections of governments responsive to the will of the people."

[7] The roles of France and China were sharply restricted by a provision that for each task "the Council will be composed of the members representing those states which were signatory to the terms of surrender imposed upon the enemy state concerned." This meant that the Big Three alone would work on the terms for Bulgaria, Rumania, and Hungary, with France joining in on the Italian Pact.

Its creation was a product of the strong American conviction that the Versailles Peace Conferences had been held too soon after World War I and that the resultant treaty and League of Nations Covenant had been imprudent and a major cause of the subsequent destruction of the peace.

The Council held its first meeting in London in September, 1945, and it quickly revealed the growing differences of policy. Among the major items on the agenda was the preparation of peace treaties for the former German satellites in Eastern Europe: Rumania, Bulgaria, and Hungary. Molotov made it clear that the Soviet government expected the Western governments to acquiesce in the enforced communization of these countries and to recognize the installed governments. There is some evidence that the Soviets were genuinely surprised when the West refused to accept this particular version of a Soviet "sphere of influence" in Eastern Europe. Stalin viewed the Western attitude as evidence that the West did not really want to protect Soviet security.

Secretary of State James F. Byrnes and Foreign Minister Bevin went to Moscow in December, 1945, in an effort to work out a solution to these and other important problems that were emerging. Some compromises were worked out, including some minor concessions by the Soviets regarding Eastern Europe and a reciprocal expression by Byrnes that the United States would recognize the rest of the satellite governments.[8]

The Council of Foreign Ministers met three times between September, 1945, and December, 1946, and managed to reach agreement on peace settlements regarding four defeated nations: Italy, Hungary, Bulgaria, and Rumania. United States approval of these treaties, coupled with recognition of the Soviet-imposed regimes in these countries, evidenced the Truman administration's reluctant acquiescence in the Sovietization of Eastern Europe. It was understood that Soviet policy was in clear violation of the Yalta Declaration on Liberated Europe, but it was also understood that there was nothing the United States, short of war, could do about it.

It was, nonetheless, a reluctant acquiescence, and the experience was an important element in the reconsiderations of basic policy that were going on all over the West in those postwar months and years. A January 5, 1946, memorandum from Truman to Secretary of State Byrnes shows the extent to which the spirit of the wartime alliance had already dissolved. In it, Truman labeled Rumania and Bulgaria "police states," referred bitterly to

---

[8] The United States had recognized the Hungarian government on September 29, 1945. This government was a coalition of several parties, including non-Communist parties. A semblance of democracy was retained in Hungary until 1947, when a thorough purge of non-Communist elements in the government was carried out by Soviet police. The United States recognized the Rumanian government on February 4, 1946. This government had been Communist-dominated since February, 1945, when the Soviet Union intervened and ousted a genuine coalition of democratic and Communist parties. The United States recognized the Bulgarian government on October 1, 1947. Its communization had been effectuated by the summer of 1945.

"the high-handed and arbitrary manner in which Russia acted in Poland," called this a "high-handed outrage," and said that the Russians had been "a headache" ever since their entry into the Japanese War. The final four paragraphs merit quotation in full:

> There isn't a doubt in my mind that Russia intends an invasion of Turkey and the seizure of the Black Sea Straits to the Mediterranean. Unless Russia is faced with an iron fist and strong language another war is in the making. Only one language do they understand—"how many divisions have you?"
>
> I do not think we should play compromise any longer. We should refuse to recognize Rumania and Bulgaria until they comply with our requirements; we should let our position on Iran be known in no uncertain terms and we should continue to insist on the internationalization of the Kiel Canal, the Rhine-Danube waterway and the Black Sea Straits and we should maintain complete control of Japan and the Pacific. We should rehabilitate China and create a strong central government there. We should do the same for Korea.
>
> Then we should insist on the return of our ships from Russia and force a settlement of the Lend-Lease debt of Russia.
>
> I'm tired of babying the Soviets.[9]

The West conceivably could have turned its back on these unpleasant developments and avoided making them sources of friction and hostility among the victorious Allies. There was, after all, nothing much the West could do about them unless it was willing to go to war with the Soviet Union. Instead, the American and British governments chose to make the fate of Eastern Europe a central issue in Soviet-Western relations. The results were as frustrating as they were predictable. In the face of determined and forceful opposition, Western principles could not be extended beyond those areas wherein Western power was controlling.

The Western response was not, however, wholly based on the sense of outrage that Soviet policy induced. The problem went deeper than that. There was a growing fear in the West that the Soviets were not only unpleasant and uncooperative, but that they were downright expansionist. There is a rather fine line between believing that a nation's disagreeable policies are essentially defensive in character—no matter how heavy-handed and inconsiderate of the wishes and interests of others—and believing that those policies are really aggressive and expansionist. There was a strong tendency in the United States during and right after the war to believe that Soviet policies were essentially defensive even when rather brutal. What happened in 1945, 1946, and 1947 was that this attitude was gradually replaced by one that ascribed quite different and much less palatable motives to Soviet leaders. The Sovietization of Eastern Europe, especially Poland, laid the groundwork for this shifting perception of

[9] Truman, *op. cit.*, pp. 551–552.

Soviet intention. By itself, however, it probably would not have caused the complete breakup of the wartime alliance. There were other potent factors working in the same direction.

Germany

A strong case can be made for the proposition that it was conflicting policies regarding postwar Germany that contributed more than anything else to the rupture. With Hitler and his debauched regime and its power gone, Germany ceased to be the cement of the alliance and became instead one of the chief causes of its dissolution. Between 1941 and 1945, Germany had been the common enemy, feared and hated. After May, 1945, Germany became increasingly the object of contention, the grand prize, partly reflecting, partly causing, and sorely exacerbating, the developing cold war.

At Yalta, the Big Three had confirmed earlier agreements on their respective zones of occupation in Germany and had agreed in principle that uniform policies would be pursued in the conquered country. An Allied Control Council—consisting of the commanding officers of the armies of occupation—was to be established to administer these policies. Earlier special arrangements for the joint occupation of "Greater Berlin" (Berlin and suburbs) were also confirmed, with each of the three powers being assigned clearly specified sectors of occupation of that area portentously deep inside the Soviet zone of occupation. An "Inter-Allied Governing Authority," or "Komendatura," was established for the special responsibility of governing this symbolically important capital city. These broad agreements were one thing, but when it came down specifically to what these "uniform policies" should be, divergent interests, intentions, and policies began to emerge. It would have been difficult for any coalition of governments to work out common policies toward a nation with the great potential strength and the amply demonstrated capacity for misusing that strength that characterized Germany. For the victorious Allies, it proved to be impossible.

Soon after the war ended, the Soviet press began to reflect official Soviet suspicion about the policies being pursued by the United States and Great Britain in their zones of occupation. On the Western side, reports began to filter back from the largely inaccessible Soviet zone about tactics that bore an unpromising resemblance to those being employed in the rest of Russian-occupied Europe. By the time Truman, Churchill, and Stalin met at Potsdam in mid-July, these anxieties had become quite lively.

The question of reparations was the most troublesome one. It was especially important to the Soviets: Reparations were to serve the dual purpose of helping to restore the Soviet economy while simultaneously punishing the Germans and delaying or rendering unlikely their revival as a major power. The Soviets understandably hated and feared the Ger-

mans and were anxious to exploit them and, if possible, to crush them once
and for all. For a time, the French inclined toward similar attitudes.
Among the Americans and British, however, somewhat different motives
were operative. Although there surely was a lively spirit of revenge among
the Western Allies—and those countries newly liberated from Nazi rule—
there was increasingly less willingness to base long-range policy on such
sentiments. Moreover, there was less need for economic retribution. The
United States emerged from the war with its economy intact and prosperous, and wanted no reparations for itself. Although Great Britain was
having serious economic difficulties and did want some reparations, it was
not in as great need as were the Russians, and its demands were much
smaller.

The United States in particular was resistant to a punitive and economically crippling reparations policy in Germany. Truman was determined that the experience of the 1920s should not be repeated, with
the United States in effect subsidizing the reparations payments of a
prostrate and dependent Germany. In the weeks following Germany's defeat, American policy makers moved increasingly away from their harsher
wartime conceptions in the direction of more practical considerations, such
as who was going to sustain the Germans—and, to some extent, the Western
European nations as well—even at subsistence levels if reparations with-
drawals and payments were to render Germany economically dependent.

But the real importance of the reparations question was neither its aspect
of revenge nor its economic dimension. Rather, it came to signify and
represent the diverging attitudes of Russia and the West regarding the
political future of Germany.

By the time of Potsdam, the Soviets were becoming increasingly impatient and suspicious about Western policy. There was no agreement in
sight on the total amount of reparations due or on the proportionate contribution of each zone. The Soviets were insisting on an overall figure of
$20 billion, with their share to be $10 billion. The United States was unwilling to set a specific figure, arguing that no one knew what industrial
machinery and factories could be taken at once or what later deliveries of
finished products or raw materials could be expected without turning
Germany into a vast dependency. The Soviets were not impressed by these
considerations. They knew little and cared less about the problems of
feeding and sustaining Germany. Increasingly, their omnipresent suspicions
were quickened: Why were their capitalistic Allies so protective of Germany and Germans and so heedless of Russia's needs? Were they reverting
to the old attitude of looking upon Germany as a bulwark against Communist Russia?

The Potsdam conferees finally reached an accord on reparations, based
on an American proposal that each power take its reparations primarily
from its own zone. In addition, 15 per cent of the "excess" industrial

equipment in the western zones—i.e., equipment that was not absolutely necessary for a peaceful German economy—would be made available to the Soviet Union in return for compensating deliveries from the eastern zone of food, coal, petroleum, and other products; and an additional 10 per cent of this "excess" equipment would be given over to the Soviets without compensation. Obviously, this compromise agreement carried within it the seeds of endless controversy. How and by whom, for example, was the word "excess" to be defined in practice? Any definition would imply a policy about the level and status to be accorded occupied Germany.

Further, this American proposal that most reparations come from the recipient's own zone was a tacit recognition of the controlling fact that, despite agreements to treat Germany as an economic unit and generally to pursue "unified" and "joint" occupation policies in Germany, different and unilateral policies were in fact emerging, economically and politically. The proposal was, in fact, accepted by the Soviets as part of a broader compromise arrangement whereby Great Britain and the United States agreed to acquiesce, pending a final settlement at a peace conference, in Polish administration of a portion of the Soviet zone of occupation. This acquiescence was itself another tacit recognition that the Soviets could do what they wanted to do in their own areas of occupation and were already doing so. The division of Germany had begun, and the bases of still greater division had been established.

The elemental task of keeping the German population alive became a difficult one in the winter of 1945–1946. As noted above, the reparations accord provided for deliveries from the Soviet zone of food and raw material in exchange for industrial equipment. These deliveries were not faithfully made, and the Soviet representative on the Allied Control Council began to hinder other ordinary economic exchanges among the zones. In March, 1946, the Soviets cut off delivery of supplies to the western zones entirely and, in general, continued to make difficult or impossible the treatment of Germany as an economic unit. On May 3, the United States suspended reparations deliveries to the Soviet Union. They were never renewed.

These developments, of course, took place within the larger context of a general deterioration of Western-Soviet relations. The Soviets were proving to be uncooperative on a whole range of relatively minor administrative issues such as the treatment and disposition of millions of refugees and displaced persons, and the creation of an occupation currency. More importantly, the differing conceptions of what political system should be installed in postwar Germany—or, to put it another way, what the mutually accepted goal of "democracy" meant in practice—were taking visible shape. In the summer of 1945, the United States began to restore German city and county government in its zone and to encourage the formation of local political parties. By early 1946, local elections were being held, and preparations were under way for the drafting—by Germans—of state constitutions. In the Soviet zone, of course, no such developments were taking place. On the contrary, steps were being taken to install a Communist dictatorship. The direction of Soviet policy became unmistakably clear in April, 1946, when the Social Democrats were forced—when necessary by terror and blackmail—to fuse with the Communists into a single, Communist-controlled, and dominant political party.

Economic problems are never far from the political arena, and this truism was especially pertinent in postwar Germany. The divisive effect of the reparations disputes has already been shown. In addition, there was a growing desire to ease the burden of sustaining the destitute Germans wherever and however possible. For what were largely or exclusively economic reasons, the United States and Great Britain decided in early 1946 to fuse their two zones economically. The French joined the Soviets in protesting this decision, arguing—quite reasonably—that such a move would undermine four-power unity. But fusion was carried out, and its administration naturally created problems requiring interzonal discussion and cooperation by the responsible German officials installed by the respective occupying power. Thus, the first threads of political union were constituted and sanctioned.

The Soviets, while proceeding unilaterally in their own zone, vigorously protested these developments. The French view of Germany at this time was not unlike the Soviet, and they often joined with the Soviets in expressing their distaste for this gradual Anglo-American abandonment of punitive policies. A major milestone in the disputes about Germany was a speech delivered in Stuttgart, Germany, on September 6, 1946, by Secretary of State Byrnes. He denounced the Soviet breach of the reparations agreement, called for the economic unification of Germany, and stated that the Germans themselves should, under proper safeguards, assume responsibility for conducting their own affairs. He added that American troops would remain in Germany as long as any other occupation troops did.

Meanwhile, contention between the Soviets and the West was growing on other fronts. Most notably, in the spring of 1947, the United States solemnly accepted the responsibility of providing substantial economic and military assistance to Greece and Turkey in their struggles against internal and external Communist threats.

Nonetheless, efforts were going forward to heal the growing breach. In March and April, 1947, the Council of Foreign Ministers met in Moscow. Four main topics were discussed: the reparations stalemate, the possibilities of concerting occupation policy, the future government of a reconstituted Germany, and the new Germany's eastern borders. No significant agreements were reached. Another Council meeting in November and December produced the same results. Neither side was willing to abandon or even to compromise its favored position in its zone or zones. Charges that demilitarization or denazification were not being vigorously pursued were freely exchanged, and proposals and communiqués began to look more and more like appeals to public opinion—in Germany and elsewhere—and less and less like serious suggestions.

The division of Germany was substantially completed during 1948. In January, the Department of State began to take over the administration of the American zone of occupation from the Army. This was generally and correctly interpreted as an indication of an American desire to terminate the occupation and proceed at once toward the formation of a German state consisting of the western zones of occupation. In February, the United States, Great Britain, France, Belgium, the Netherlands, and Luxembourg met in London to consider, among other things, the future of Germany.

While this meeting was under way, the Soviet Union engineered the Communist coup in Czechoslovakia. The shock that this event occasioned in the West can scarcely be exaggerated, and it reinforced the already clear direction of Western policy toward Germany and, indeed, the rest of non-Communist Europe.

In early March, the London conferees announced agreement in principle to the establishment of a federal government for the three western zones in Germany, and the future participation of this federal government in the emerging European Recovery Program. The last pretenses of Allied cooperation and even consultation were being abandoned.

Another important Western initiative in these early months of 1948 was the creation of the first Western military alliance. In January, the British foreign secretary proposed such an alliance; and in March, the Brussels Pact was signed by Great Britain, France, Belgium, the Netherlands, and Luxembourg. It provided that if any of the signatories should be attacked in Europe, the others would "afford the party so attacked all the military and other aid and assistance in their power." Unlike a similar treaty signed between Great Britain and France in 1947, the Brussels Pact was not concerned solely with defense against Germany. The reason for this broadened concern was clear.

The Soviets, of course, viewed these developments in the West with sharp disapproval. They walked out of the deadlocked Allied Control Council in March, and in April they began to inspect Western passengers and goods being transported into the western sectors of Berlin.

On June 24, the Soviet Union cut off all Western access to Berlin by road, rail, and canal. The ostensible reason for this was a dispute about currency regulation in Berlin, but the blockading of Berlin was clearly a Soviet reaction to the broader development of Western policy regarding Germany. It was an effort to force the Western powers out of Berlin and end the anomaly of a Western presence in the heart of the Soviet zone of occupation. It constituted a flagrant and forceful violation of the letter and the spirit of the wartime accords on the occupation of Germany. The

Soviets maintained that Western policies in Germany had effectively nulli-
fied those agreements and that in taking matters into their own hands in
their own zone they were merely duplicating Western performance.

The West responded to this ominous challenge by instituting a spectacular airlift, which managed to keep the Western troops in Berlin and the
West Berliners themselves supplied with fuel, food, and other necessary
supplies for eleven difficult months. By the time the Soviets lifted the
blockade the following May, the always slender chances for achieving
common policies for Germany were virtually eliminated. The Council of
Foreign Ministers met during May and June but were unable to resolve
their differences over the character and form that a united German government should adopt. No feat of diplomacy could any longer heal the breach.
On September 21, 1949, the Federal Republic of Germany (West Germany)
was launched, with Konrad Adenauer as the first chancellor. Western
occupation authorities were replaced by an Allied High Commission, which
retained control of the Federal Republic's foreign relations and assumed
responsibility for ensuring that Germany remained disarmed. Paralleling
this semisovereign creation—which graduated to full sovereignty in May,
1955—was the establishment by the Soviet Union on October 7 of the
German Democratic Republic (East Germany).

The division of Germany, like all the major postwar developments, was
both a cause and an effect. In one sense, it was responsible in considerable
measure for the beginning and much of the protraction and rigidities of the
cold war. In another, it merely reflected the preexisting unsatisfactory state
of Western-Soviet relations. The problems posed by the division of Germany and the international status and policies of the two Germanies are
to this day at the very core of the cold war.

Other Developments: 1945

The communization of Eastern Europe and the bitter division of Germany
were central dramas in the opening of the postwar chasm. There were many
other elements in the picture, however, and some of the more important
of them are discussed in the following paragraphs.

The Soviet Union had never been enthusiastic about the projected postwar international organization, but neither had they ignored or seriously
obstructed its development. Western observers were watching Soviet policy
in this area carefully; and when it became known that Foreign Minister
Molotov would not be attending the organizing conference of the United
Nations Organization in San Francisco, this was interpreted as a calculated
Soviet effort to diminish its significance. When Roosevelt died, only two
weeks before the scheduled opening of the conference, Stalin relented and
made the symbolic gesture of dispatching Molotov to San Francisco. As
noted above, the dour diplomat stopped off in Washington to meet the

new President, and their confrontation was rather abrasive. Taking note of the possibility that the Soviets might boycott the meetings because of the Western refusal to recognize the Soviet-installed Polish Provisional Government, Truman told a group of his top advisers that he intended "to go on with the plans for San Francisco and if the Russians did not wish to join us they could go to hell. . . ."[10]

This characteristic abruptness of Truman's reflected what Secretary of War Henry L. Stimson later described as an "attitude of general impatience which came over the administration in the last weeks of President Roosevelt's life and in the early days of the Truman administration."[11]

In a rather symbolic episode, the very day of the German surrender provided the occasion for a substantial straining of the already endangered bonds of the alliance. President Truman incautiously initialed an order that abruptly cut off all Lend-Lease assistance to both Russia and Great Britain except that which was for use against Japan. The order was based on a plausible but rigid interpretation of the requirements of the Lend-Lease Act and was not regarded by Truman as having any political significance. The Soviet Union, however, protested vigorously against the action and later advised the United States that if the action had been designed to pressure the Soviets in any way, it was unwise and doomed to failure from the outset.

The British response was merely to inquire into the reasons for the action and its relation to earlier agreements that seemed to commit the United States to a continuing program of assistance after the European war was over. The differences in response were good indicators of the fundamentally different character of United States–British relations and United States–Soviet relations. The former were based on mutual trust and confidence, whereas the latter were plagued by doubt and suspicion.

Three days after its untimely issuance, the order was rescinded, and a more agreeable policy was announced. But the damage, though perhaps rather slight, was already done.

In mid-June, the United States and Great Britain requested Soviet permission to send some representatives to Berlin to prepare for the forthcoming conference of the Big Three in suburban Potsdam and for the July 1 arrival of Western occupying troops in Berlin. The Soviets said this would have to wait until late June. The Soviet motive for this was not clear, but many in the West suspected that the Soviets wanted more time to settle accounts with Berliners and to extract reparations without West-

---

[10] *The Forrestal Diaries, op. cit.,* p. 50. The quotation is from notes of the meeting taken by Charles E. Bohlen, a Special Assistant to the Secretary of State.

[11] Henry L. Stimson and McGeorge Bundy, *On Active Service in Peace and War,* Harper & Brothers, New York, 1947, pp. 608–609. Incidentally, Stimson, a distinguished public servant and a Republican, did not at that time share this "attitude of general impatience." *Ibid.,* p. 608.

ern surveillance. The Soviets were notified that the delay was unacceptable, that the conference—scheduled to begin July 16—would have to be postponed if the Soviets continued to deny the requested permission, and that the reason for the postponement would be made public. The Soviets then acquiesced, but in Assistant Foreign Commissar Vishinsky's letter to Ambassador Harriman on this matter the following premonitory note was struck:

> . . . The threat contained in your letter . . . [to make public the reason for any postponement] is ill-advised. The Soviet Government has no intentions to limit the freedom of the American press, but it considers it necessary to draw the attention of the American government to the fact that there is a press in the Soviet Union which will be able to give a proper reply to such a type of statement in the American press.[12]

Meanwhile, similar difficulties were being experienced regarding Vienna. As in the case of Germany, Austria was to be divided into four occupational sectors. The Soviets controlled most of the country, however, and they refused to permit Western representatives into Vienna. This minor irritant persisted until the July Potsdam Conference when acceptable accords were finally worked out.

Some of the other issues taken up at the Potsdam Conference were not so amicably disposed of. The Soviets leveled some bitter charges at the British about their conduct in Greece where a civil war between Communist and non-Communist elements was under way. When it was alleged that the British were supporting the use of terror against "democratic elements" in the population, the British response was quick and angry. All efforts at including a statement about Greece in the protocol of the conference were abandoned.

1946

If 1945 was a year of blunted hopes and cautious reappraisals, 1946 was a year of increasing frustration and bitterness. The wartime spirit of camaraderie, compromised and limited though it was, was obviously dissipated. What the new relationship would be was still a matter of conjecture in the West. As the new year dawned, Truman was, as noted above, expressing heavily pessimistic attitudes to Byrnes about Soviet intentions and declaring his determination to meet their challenge. At about the same time, there was circulating among the highest levels of government a lengthy document analyzing Soviet motives and policies, which was written by

---

[12] As quoted in Herbert Feis, *Between War and Peace: The Potsdam Conference*, Princeton University Press, Princeton, N.J., 1960, p. 145

George F. Kennan, chargé d'affaires at the United States embassy in Moscow and the government's leading specialist on Soviet affairs. This document, which in revised form appeared anonymously in the influential journal *Foreign Affairs* in July, 1947, has been widely credited with having had a profound impact on American official thought.

Kennan argued that the Soviets had a "neurotic view of world affairs," deeply rooted in Russian history and reinforced by legitimate fears of the more industrialized European countries. Marxism found a fertile soil in this climate of opinion and added its own peculiar emphasis and concerns. It served as a rationale for traditional fears and justified great cruelties and sacrifice. It made Russia uniquely dangerous. He went on to predict— with awesome accuracy—the pattern of Soviet diplomacy and declared that

we have here a political force committed fanatically to the belief that with the U. S. there can be no permanent *modus vivendi*, that it is desirable and necessary that the internal harmony of our society be disrupted, our traditional way of life be destroyed, the international authority of our state be broken, if Soviet power is to be secure. . . . The problem of how to cope with this force is undoubtedly the greatest task our diplomacy has ever faced and probably the greatest it will ever have to face.[13]

On February 9, Stalin delivered a public address that was not calculated to allay Western fear and suspicion. He said that it

would be wrong to think that the Second World War was a casual occurrence or the result of mistakes of any particular statesmen, though mistakes undoubtedly were made. Actually the war was the inevitable result of the development of world economic and political forces on the basis of modern monopoly capitalism. Marxists have declared more than once that the capitalist system of world economy harbors elements of general crises and conflicts and that, hence, the development of world capitalism in our time proceeds not in the form of smooth and even progress but through crises and military catastrophes.

The fact is, that the unevenness of development of the capitalist countries usually leads in time to violent disturbance of equilibrium in the world system of capitalism, that group of capitalist countries which considers itself worse provided than others with raw materials and markets usually making attempts to alter the situation and repartition the "spheres of influence" in its favor by armed force. The result is a splitting of the capitalist world into two hostile camps and war between them.[14]

The response in the West to this sharply ideological speech was one of alarm. Supreme Court Justice William O. Douglas reflected the mood of

---

[13] *The Forrestal Diaries, op. cit.*, pp. 136–140.
[14] House Committee on Foreign Affairs, *The Strategy and Tactics of World Communism*, Report, Subcommittee No. 5, Supplement I, "One Hundred Years of Communism, 1848–1948," 80th Cong., 2d Sess., 1948, H.R. Doc. No. 619, pp. 168–169.

pessimism that it fostered when he privately labeled the speech "The Declaration of World War III."[15]

A month later, the other living member of the wartime Big Three delivered an equally important address. Winston Churchill had been out of office for about seven months when he visited the United States, but his voice was a distinguished and respected one. On March 5, at Fulton, Missouri, in a speech in which he publicly referred for the first time to the "iron curtain" that had descended across Europe, he called for a "fraternal association of the English-speaking peoples," which would entail "the continuance of the intimate relationships between our military advisers, leading to common study of potential dangers, similarity of weapons and manuals of instruction and inter-change of officers and cadets at colleges." In effect, he was proposing an unprecedented peacetime alliance between the United States and Great Britain. "Nobody knows," he declared ominously, "what Soviet Russia and its Communist international organization intends to do in the future, or what are the limits, if any, to their expansive and proselytizing tendencies."

He went on to express his "strong admiration and regard for the valiant Russian people and for my war-time comrade, Marshal Stalin," and he emphasized once again his understanding of the legitimate Russian need to be secured against German aggression.

He said that he did not believe the Soviet Union desired war, but rather that they desired "the fruits of war and the indefinite expansion of their power and doctrines."

> From what I have seen of our Russian friends and allies during the war, I am convinced that there is nothing they admire so much as strength, and there is nothing for which they have less respect than for military weakness. . . .
>
> If the population of the English-speaking commonwealth be added to that of the United States, with all that such cooperation implies in the air, on the sea and in science and industry, there will be no quivering, precarious balance of power to offer its temptation to ambition or adventure. On the contrary, there will be an overwhelming assurance of security.

Churchill's specific proposals were ahead of their time, and the response to his message was mixed. Truman, who heard the speech in person, refused either to endorse or repudiate it. But the British statesman had given expression to a point of view that was rapidly gaining ascendance in the West and that would be accepted in large measure within the following two years.

---

[15] *The Forrestal Diaries, op. cit.,* p. 134. Justice Douglas's interpretation is cited here not because it is an accurate assessment of the speech or of Stalin's intentions but rather to demonstrate the jarring effect that the speech in fact did have. Justice Douglas was not—and is not—the kind of person likely to prefer the harshest interpretation of Soviet behavior.

The pessimistic analyses and gloomy speeches were, of course, more the products of events than their creators. As Eastern Europe and the Soviet zone in Germany became Soviet satellites, Stalin's ambitions turned in other directions, with mixed results.

During the war, there was grave concern about the possibility of a German occupation of oil-rich Iran (Persia). This would not only have deprived the Allies of necessary oil but also would have severed a major supply line to the Soviet Union through the Persian Gulf. To guard against this eventuality, and with Iran's consent, the Soviet Union and Great Britain assumed defensive responsibilities in Iran. The 1942 agreement provided for Soviet occupation in the north, British occupation in the south, and withdrawal six months after the end of the war. Some American troops were also in the area performing supply functions.

In May, 1945, the Iranian government began to ask about Soviet and British evacuation plans. The matter was discussed inconclusively at Potsdam. Thereafter, there were growing fears that the Soviet Army did not intend to leave at all, or at least not until a puppet regime was installed in the occupied Azerbaidzhan region. In September, a group of Communists announced the formation of an autonomous Republic in the Azerbaidzhan region, thereby giving rise to the fear that this area would be annexed by the Soviet Union and attached to neighboring Soviet Azerbaidzhan.

The Iranian government, supported by the United States and Great Britain, appealed to the United Nations in January, 1946, and again in March. It denounced the formation of the dissident government and demanded the withdrawal of Soviet troops in accordance with the wartime accord. After some sharp words between the Western democracies and the Soviet Union, and some temporary concessions by the Iranian government, the Soviet troops withdrew in May. The experience deepened Western suspicions of Soviet intentions.

A similar and perhaps more ominous showdown occurred over Turkey. This nation controls the Straits of the Bosporus and the Dardanelles, which stand between the Black Sea and the Mediterranean. It has naturally been an historic Russian objective to secure this outlet to the sea. In the fall of 1940, for example, the Soviets advised their German associates that they would like to establish Soviet bases in the straits. At the Yalta conference, Stalin mentioned Turkey's "hand on Russia's throat" and suggested that the 1936 Montreux Convention, which regulated Turkey's responsibilities, should be revised. There was much sympathy expressed for this Soviet concern.

In the spring of 1945, the Soviets made several proposals, which, if accepted by the Turkish government, would have gone a long way toward turning Turkey into a satellite of the Soviet Union. They asked that Turkey cede certain territories to the Soviet Union because these territories had been Russian prior to World War I. Second, they suggested that the Soviets be permitted to establish bases in the straits in order to protect themselves and the Turks from the possibility of a hostile third power gaining control of this vital life line. Finally, they asked that the international control of the straits provided by the Montreux Convention be replaced by a joint Turkish-Soviet administration.

The Turks flatly refused all three proposals and, at great cost, maintained a large standing army to back up their policy. The question was taken up at the Potsdam Conference, and some lively exchanges between Stalin and Churchill resulted. But nothing was decided or accomplished except a general agreement that the Montreux Convention should be revised.

Soviet pressure continued; and in early 1946, the United States added to its diplomatic support of Turkey by dispatching the battleship *U.S.S. Missouri* on a symbolic mission to Turkey. This gesture reflected Truman's growing suspicions about Soviet intentions, as noted, and his willingness to take defensive measures. The following year, Turkey became one of the two recipients of the first overtly anti-Soviet foreign aid program.

Meanwhile, the United Nations Organization was holding its first meetings and quickly demonstrating that it was bound to be more a reflection of international politics than an instrument of a new kind of politics. The first meeting of the Security Council, in January, 1946, was confronted with the Iranian complaint about Soviet activities in northern Iran. The Western democracies supported Iran and the Soviet Union was embittered. During its first year, the Security Council considered eight charges, seven of which bore the imprint of the developing chasm between the founding nations. Outnumbered and increasingly isolated, the Soviets initiated their policies of dramatic departures from Council meetings and a liberal use of their veto power.

Another straw in the wind in those early postwar months was the foreboding, albeit natural, failure to reach any agreement on the management of that awesome new fact, nuclear power. In June, 1946, in the newly created United Nations Atomic Energy Commission, the United States put forward the so-called "Baruch Plan." This plan called for the creation of an International Atomic Development Authority, which would have exclusive control over "all phases of the development and use of atomic energy," from the mining of raw materials to the production and use of fissionable materials. The Authority would be empowered to own or otherwise control "all atomic-energy activities potentially dangerous to world security" and "to control, inspect, and license all other atomic activities." The Authority would be created by a treaty, which would spell out in detail its powers and responsibilities. The treaty would provide for an effective system of inspection to ensure compliance by all nations and for suitable punishments for any violators. When an adequate system of control was established, the United States would dispose of its atomic bombs in accordance with the treaty and would make available to the Authority "the further information essential to that organization for the performance of its function."[16] The Authority and its control activities were to be free of any veto power.

From the Soviet standpoint, the Baruch Plan had several serious short-comings and one fatal flaw. The flaw was the simple fact that under the terms of the proposed treaty, the United States would remain the only nation with the knowledge of how to build atomic weapons. Lacking confidence in the capacity of any international organism to enforce its regulations and being suspicious of American motives, the Soviets regarded this prospect as incompatible with their own security. They wanted the knowledge also, and they intended to obtain it. In addition, the Soviet Union was unenthusiastic about having international inspectors on Soviet soil, and it was even less inclined to agree to sacrificing its veto rights in this most sensitive area. Finally, it declared that the United States should destroy all of its atomic weapons in advance of any negotiations, not as part of an agreement. Needless to say, neither the Baruch Plan nor any other proposal for international control of nuclear power was agreed upon, then or later.

The steady veering away from a policy that attempted to establish or maintain amicable relations with the Soviets based on shared interests toward one of actively resisting Soviet policies and encroachments was not universally accepted in the United States or in the government. While some clamored for a harder, more militant policy, others criticized Truman for being too firm with the Russians. The most important spokesman for the latter point of view was Secretary of Commerce Henry Wallace. He had been Vice President from 1941 to 1945 and, like Byrnes, undoubtedly viewed with frustration the fact that he might very well have become President in April, 1945, instead of the rather obscure Truman. He felt quite qualified to challenge the very foundations of the administration's policies.

In July, 1946, he wrote the President a long private letter. He counseled patience and said that

> we should be prepared, even at the expense of risking epithets of appeasement, to agree to reasonable Russian guarantees of security. . . . We should make an effort to counteract the irrational fear of Russia which is being systematically built up in the American people by certain individuals and publications.

He also suggested that if the United States would revise its disarmament proposals in specified ways, "I believe the Russians will also negotiate seriously. . . ."[17]

---

[16] The text of the plan is printed in U.S. Department of State, *Bulletin*, vol. 14, No. 364, pp. 1057–1062, June 23, 1946.

[17] *The New York Times*, Sept. 18, 1946, p. 2, cols. 4-6.

On September 12, Wallace returned to these themes in a public address to a large Democratic rally in Madison Square Garden. He denounced a "get tough with Russia" policy and said "we should recognize that we have no more business in the political affairs of Eastern Europe than Russia has in the political affairs of Latin America, Western Europe, and the United States. . . ."[18]

There was, of course, a furor over this speech, and a week later, the President asked for and received Wallace's resignation. Wallace's point of view was in eclipse, and when he ran for the Presidency as a candidate of the Progressive Party in 1948, he managed to garner only 2.4 per cent of the popular vote. This is certainly not a statistically precise reflection of public sentiment on Wallace's prescription for United States policy toward the Soviet Union, but it surely indicates an overwhelming public repudiation of that prescription.

1947

Official attitudes in the United States regarding the Soviet government were changing rapidly, but specific policy manifestations of that change were not very obvious until 1947. The first dramatic event of this kind was the enunciation and implementation of what came to be known as the Truman Doctrine.

As noted above, a civil war had been raging in Greece ever since the departure of the Germans in 1944. Great Britain had shouldered the burden of ensuring that the Communist-led faction in the struggle did not gain the ascendancy. In addition, Great Britain was supporting the Turkish government in its expensive policy of resisting Soviet encroachments. These British operations were manifestations of Britain's traditional role in world affairs and its special historic concern with restraining the expansion of Russia. But they were costly burdens, and postwar Britain was experiencing severe economic difficulties while trying to adjust itself to the impending loss of its vast empire. On February 21, 1947, it solemnly advised the United States that it could no longer support its operations in Greece and Turkey.

The United States was not conditioned to assume such responsibilities. The traditional isolationism had not returned as after World War I, but there was a considerable hesitancy to become heavily involved in European affairs, and the superb war machine had been dismantled with customary haste. Nor was the domestic political situation auspicious. The 1946 elections had brought to Washington the first Republican Congress since 1931. The Republicans sensed a Presidential victory in 1948, and they were not looking for ways to make Harry S Truman look like a statesman.

Yet the President and the Congress responded with remarkable vigor,

[18] *The New York Times*, Sept. 13, 1946, p. 1, col. 1; p. 4, col. 5.

foresight, and cooperation. On March 12, President Truman appeared before a specially convened joint session of Congress. He told Congress of the urgent need for assistance to Greece and Turkey and stated that the aid could be forthcoming only from the United States. He then proceeded to spell out the rationale for this proposed assistance. Because of its historic significance, this original statement of the Truman Doctrine is quoted extensively below.

> I am fully aware of the broad implications involved if the United States extends assistance to Greece and Turkey. . . .
>
> We shall not realize our objectives . . . unless we are willing to help free peoples to maintain their national integrity against aggressive movements that seek to impose upon them totalitarian regimes. This is no more than a frank recognition that totalitarian regimes imposed upon free peoples, by direct or indirect aggression, undermine the foundations of international peace and hence the security of the United States.
>
> The peoples of a number of countries of the world have recently had totalitarian regimes forced upon them against their will. The Government of the United States has made frequent protests against coercion and intimidation, in violation of the Yalta Agreement, in Poland, Rumania, and Bulgaria. I must also state that in a number of other countries there have been similar developments.
>
> At the present moment in world history nearly every nation must choose between alternative ways of life. The choice is too often not a free one.
>
> One way of life is based upon the will of the majority, and is distinguished by free institutions, representative government, free elections, guarantees of individual liberty, freedom of speech and religion, and freedom from political oppression.
>
> The second way of life is based upon the will of a minority forcibly imposed upon the majority. It relies upon terror and oppression, a controlled press and radio, fixed elections, and the suppression of personal freedoms.
>
> I believe that it must be the policy of the United States to support free peoples who are resisting attempted subjugation by armed minorities or by outside pressures. . . .

No doubt this sweeping declaration of intent was too ambitious and would have to be applied with some selectivity in the years to come. Nonetheless, it reflected a view of the world and the United States role therein that was radically different from traditional American attitudes and equally distant from any that the war-weary country was anxious to adopt for the future. The great isolationist power of the peaceful 1930s was to become a great interventionist power in the peaceful second half of the 1940s and thereafter. The most powerful nation in the world was reluctantly assuming its responsibilities.

Truman asked for $400 million for military and economic assistance to Greece and Turkey, and for authorization to send civilian and military personnel to those countries to help administer the assistance. Many observers were not as confident as the President "that the Congress will face these responsibilities squarely," but it did, and quickly. The Senate version of the bill was approved April 22 by a decisive 67 to 23; the House acted on its version May 9 by an equally impressive vote of 287 to 108. The conference committee's report was accepted by both chambers (by voice vote) on May 15 and signed into law by the President on May 22.[19]

The speed—Congress ordinarily takes months to act on major pieces of legislation, especially those representing new policy directions—and the size of the majorities reflected the extent to which the postwar period of relaxation and optimism had already been undermined by events.

The meaning of this historic turn in American policy was not lost on Soviet leaders. The official government newspaper denounced the new policy as expansionist.

> Hitler used to refer to the Bolsheviks when he wanted to open the road for his own conquests. Now they want to take Greece and Turkey under control, they raise a din about "totalitarian states.". . . American claims to leadership in international affairs grow parallel with the growing appetite of the American quarters concerned. But the American leaders, in the new historical circumstances, fail to reckon with the fact that the old methods of the colonisers and diehard politicians have outlived their time and are doomed to failure.[20]

Aid to Greece and Turkey was just the beginning. Implementation of the doctrine that the United States must support free peoples resisting Communist subjugation was bound to be expensive as well as novel. The major arena of the struggle was Europe. Two calamitous wars within thirty years had left this ancient center of power and Western civilization drained and exhausted, militarily, economically, and psychologically. By contrast, the war had left the United States economically vibrant and, as a nation, generally untouched by the ravages of war.

As the face of the postwar world emerged more clearly amidst the disintegration of the wartime alliance, the central facts that emerged were that Europe needed assistance in her recovery efforts and that the absence of such assistance would create a revolutionary situation. By 1947, this definition of the challenge was widely accepted in informed circles, and on June 5, Secretary of State George C. Marshall publicly proclaimed the audacious proposals that became known as the Marshall Plan.

> It is logical that the United States should do whatever it is able to do to assist in the return of normal economic health in the world, without which there can be no political stability and no assured peace. Our policy is directed not against any coun-

---

[19] The appropriations bill, which actually provided the money, passed July 26. The entire $400 million requested was provided.

[20] *Izvestia*, Mar. 13, 1947, as quoted in William Appleman Willlams (ed.), *The Shaping of American Diplomacy*, Rand McNally & Company, Chicago, 1956, vol. II, p. 1005.

try or doctrine but against hunger, poverty, desperation and chaos. . . . Any assistance which this government may render in the future should provide a cure rather than a mere palliative. Any government that is willing to assist in the task of recovery will find full cooperation, I am sure, on the part of the United States Government. . . . It would be neither fitting nor efficacious for this Government to undertake to draw up unilaterally a program designed to place Europe on its feet economically. This is the business of Europeans. The initiative, I think, must come from Europe. . . . The program should be a joint one, agreed to by a number, if not all, European nations.

This speech had a less explicitly anti-Soviet tone than Truman's earlier message to Congress. Indeed, the Soviet Union was at least theoretically eligible to become a recipient of United States economic assistance under the proposal. But the doctrine espoused was nonetheless based upon the same basic objective as the plea for aid to Greece and Turkey: to stop the threatened spread of communism in Europe. It was generally assumed, moreover, that the Soviet Union would refuse to participate in the program, and it was even more apparent that Congress would almost certainly not provide any appropriations for aid to the Soviets if asked to do so.

The Soviets provided a momentary scare by showing up at the first conference held in Europe in late June to begin drawing up requisite joint proposals. In what may have been a major Soviet error, however, Molotov scorned the American insistence upon the provision of certain economic facts by the recipient nations as a prerequisite to aid and denounced the whole scheme as an attempt to meddle in the internal affairs of other nations, especially the Soviet Union. A more imaginative Soviet leadership —one that was, to requote Lenin, willing "to crawl on your belly through the mud"—might have moved to cooperate, at least temporarily. As it was, the United States was able to move ahead along the intended lines with the Soviet Union's bearing the onus of having turned the "magnanimous and nonpolitical" Marshall Plan into an instrument in the emerging conflict.

During the next few months, representatives of the Truman administration and the Republican Congress studied the situation, and the European nations moved swiftly to create the joint plans required by the United States. Equally important, the Soviet Union continued inadvertently to spur these developments on with its own policies. It forbade all six of the nations within its orbit to participate in the Marshall Plan. Czechoslovakia, however, was at that time still not controlled by Communists, and its reaction was watched with great interest. Czechoslovakia's prewar relations with the Soviet Union had been more satisfactory than, for example, Poland's, and during the war its exiled leaders had sought successfully to maintain amicable relations with the giant to the east. Near the end of 1945, the occupying Red Army withdrew. In May, 1946, free elections were actually held; and, although the Communists received 38 per cent of the popular vote, there was considerable hope that Czechoslovakia would be able to maintain its independence. Shortly after Marshall's speech, Czechoslovakia expressed an interest in participating in the Marshall Plan. When the Soviet Union was able to force Czechoslovakia to retract this expression and to spurn participation, the prospects of Czechoslovakia's remaining an independent nation suddenly became very bleak. And the incentives in the West to make the Marshall Plan work were multiplied.

They continued to multiply. During the war, the Soviet government had dissolved the Cominterm as a gesture of solidarity with its Western allies. In September, 1947, it created a new Communist international organization, the Communist Information Bureau, or Cominform. Its special purpose was to link the large Communist parties in France and Italy with the Soviet bloc parties, and therefore its formation at that particular time was especially significant to the nations then working out plans for the Marshall Plan. Speaking at the founding conference of the Cominform, Andrei Zhdanov, a leading Soviet theoretician and probable successor to Stalin, laid down a very hard anti-Western line. Excerpts are quoted below:

... America's aspirations to world supremacy encounter an obstacle in the U.S.S.R., the stronghold of anti-imperialist and anti-fascist policy, and its growing international influence, in the new democracies, which have escaped from the control of Britain and American imperialism, and in the workers of all countries, including America itself, who do not want a new war for the supremacy of their oppressors. Accordingly, the new expansionist and reactionary policy of the United States envisages a struggle against the U.S.S.R., against the labour movement in all countries, including the United States, and against the emancipationist, anti-imperialist forces in all countries.

Alarmed by the achievements of Socialism in the U.S.S.R., and by the achievements of the new democracies, and by the postwar growth of the labour and democratic movement in all countries, the American reactionaries are disposed to take upon themselves the mission of "saviors" of the capitalist system from Communism.

The rank expansionist program of the United States is therefore highly reminiscent of the reckless program, which failed so ignominiously, of the fascist aggressors, who, as we know, also made a bid for world supremacy.

Just as the Hitlerites, when they were making their preparations for piratical aggression, adopted the camouflage of anti-Communism in order to make it possible to oppress and enslave all peoples and primarily and chiefly their own people, America's present-day ruling circles mask their expansionist policy, and even their offensive against the vital interests of their weaker imperialist rival, Great Britain, by fictitious considerations of defense against Communism. The feverish piling up of armaments, the construction of new military bases and the creation of bridgeheads for the American armed forces in all parts of the world is justified on the false and pharisaical grounds of "defence" against an imaginary threat of war on the part of the U.S.S.R. ...

The Truman Doctrine, which provides for the rendering of American assistance to all reactionary regimes which actively opposed the democratic peoples, bears a frankly aggressive character. ...

The vague and deliberately guarded formulations of the Marshall Plan amount in essence to a scheme to create a bloc of states bound by obligations to the United States, and to grant American credits to European countries as a recompense for their renunciation of economic, and then of political, independence. Moreover, the cornerstone of the Marshall Plan is the restoration of the industrial areas of Western Germany controlled by the American monopolies.[21]

With the quotation of these remarks, we have entered into the language and the spirit of the cold war. To use Churchill's apt nouns again, the wartime alliance had moved from triumph to tragedy. Some partial explanations for this disaster have been offered above, along with a summary of the specific events that reflected and exacerbated it. It needs to be emphasized, in conclusion, that the antagonism, once begun, had a momentum of its own. Each maneuver and countermaneuver took on the aspect of a self-fulfilling prophecy. Soviet policy provoked a Western response, which in turn alarmed the Soviets, and so on. Even if there had been a mutual will to break out of this pattern and pursue conciliatory policies, it would have been very difficult to do it.

There is no further need to trace the developments that brought about the international political climate in which we live today. Many grave and momentous events, of course, occurred between 1947 and the present— some of them have already been touched upon in the section on postwar policies toward Germany—but none of them changed the basic character of American-Soviet relations.

The preceding remarks—and, indeed, the very presence of Chapters 4 and 5 in this book—should not be construed as meaning that the author believes "the basic character of American-Soviet relations" is unalterable; he believes the reverse of this. In fact, a strong case can be made for the proposition that the cold war has already undergone a basic transformation and that the "thaw" that followed the scare of the Cuban missile crisis in October, 1962, represents a qualitative change in United States–Soviet relations. That *may be* true, and is surely a development to be soberly sought and welcomed. But the cold war persists, even *if* it has been made more civil and is more and more likely to have nonmilitary manifestations. In addition to those ideologues who all along have insisted that the cold war is permanent—or, alternatively, that it can easily be eliminated if only the West would pursue more conciliatory policies—there are those who have been too eager to declare every relaxation in tension a dangerous illusion—or, alternatively, have been too eager to embrace every evidence of Soviet civility and to announce, thereupon, the end of the cold war. This book is based on the conviction that it is safer to err on the side of caution than on the side of hope—or, worse yet, faith.

This is not the posture of a cold warrior. It is the studied conviction

[21] Robert V. Daniels (ed.), *A Documentary History of Communism*, Random House, New York, 1960, vol. II, pp. 157–160.

of one who believes that until such root issues, for example, as Berlin, Germany, Cuba, and the continuing Soviet attempt at infiltration and subversion on a global scale are resolved, the cold war will persist.[22]

At this point the chronological method of accounting for international politics and, more particularly, American foreign policy, is put aside. The succeeding chapters deal with specific contemporary diplomatic problems of the United States. Each of them is placed in its historical context, and therefore much of the history from 1947 to the present is at least sketchily recounted. But no effort is made to cover all significant postwar history, and the reader in search of a systematic history of the cold war will have to look elsewhere.[23]

Selected Bibliography

Feis, Herbert: *Between War and Peace: The Potsdam Conference,* Princeton University Press, Princeton, N. J., 1960. A careful, objective treatment of a seminal event.

Graebner, Norman A.: *Cold War Diplomacy, 1945–1960,* D. Van Nostrand Company, Inc., Princeton, N. J., 1962. Despite the author's apparent conviction that the United States response to the Sovietization of Eastern Europe was somehow a major cause of the cold war, this is a useful summary and documentation of the postwar period.

Millis, Walter (ed.): *The Forrestal Diaries,* The Viking Press, Inc., New York, 1951. A revealing account of, among other things, the American government's response to Soviet policy during and after the war.

Spanier, John W.: *American Foreign Policy since World War II* (rev. ed.), Frederick A. Praeger, Inc., New York, 1962. A superficial but useful history.

Truman, Harry S: *Memoirs,* Doubleday & Company, Inc., Garden City, N. Y., 1955 (two volumes). These volumes should not be mistaken for detached history, but they do reveal the state of mind of their author, a man of some importance.

U.S. Department of State: *Foreign Relations of the United States: The Conferences at Malta and Yalta, 1945,* Washington, D. C., 1955. A valuable collection of documents about some crucial events.

————: *Foreign Relations of the United States: The Conference of Berlin (The Potsdam Conference),* Washington, D. C., 1960 (two volumes). Another valuable set of documents.

---

[22] This and related questions are reverted to in the final chapter. The reader is referred to it and the Selected Bibliography attached thereto.

[23] Unfortunately, no exhaustive and authoritative history of the cold war has been written. There are several brief accounts of major developments, including John W. Spanier, *American Foreign Policy since World War II* (rev. ed.), Frederick A. Praeger, Inc., New York, 1962, and Norman A. Graebner, *Cold War Diplomacy, 1945–1960,* D. Van Nostrand Company, Inc., Princeton, N.J., 1962. For an ambitious but fatally distorted account, see D. F. Fleming, *The Cold War and Its Origins, 1917–1960,* Doubleday & Company, Inc., Garden City, N.Y., 1961 (two volumes).

Part Two

chapter 6   In order to understand American policy in and regarding the United Nations, it is necessary to understand something of the character (nature) and functions of that international body. The United Nations is subjected to an unseemly amount of misrepresentation and misunderstanding. There is something about the very notion of an international organization that elicits the most fatuous kind of sentimentality and the most reactionary kind of narrow nationalism from different elements in the United States. In a way, those who place most of their hopes for the future in the United Nations and those who fear it make the same mistake: They overrate its impact on international affairs.[1]

But it is possible to underrate the United Nations, too. It does have *some* impact, and the United States government is properly concerned about its relationship to the institution.

Background

The United Nations was created in the latter days of World War II. The three major Allies took the initiative in its founding, but the United States was largely responsible for bringing it into being and giving it its formal structure. President Franklin D. Roosevelt and most Americans were convinced that the failure of the United States to join the League of Nations was a major factor in that body's impotence and in the concomitant and related collapse of the post–World War I peace. There is perhaps no better proof of the decline of isolationism in this country than the Senate's 89 to 2 vote in favor of ratifying the treaty of adherence to the Charter of the United Nations.

It is sometimes suggested that the United States government substituted a naïve utopianism for isolationism in those heady days near the end of the war, that it looked to the new international organization as a panacea, a mechanism that would somehow effectuate the age-old dream of peace on earth. And some of the speeches made then do lend themselves to this kind of interpretation.

But the fact is that, for the most part, a more sober set of expectations prevailed. One need look no further than the Charter itself to see that behind the idealistic rhetoric and the high hopes there were some competing and more cautious expectations and concerns at work. The three pri-

[1] This discussion will deal exclusively with the political role and impact of the United Nations. This is not to deny the importance or even the long-range political significance of the many other United Nations activities in such fields as economic assistance, education, health, and so forth. But it does imply that the most important and the most controversial United Nations activities are political. Moreover, this book is primarily about America's role in international *politics*, not the entire spectrum of international *relations*.

mary elements or organs of the United Nations Organization established by the Charter were the General Assembly, the Security Council, and the Secretariat. The Charter set forth in some detail, but not unambiguously, their respective responsibilities and powers. An attempt to define and explain these responsibilities and powers would be beyond the scope of this book,[2] but a brief account of those pertaining to the Assembly and the Council will substantiate the view that the Charter did not represent an attempt to revolutionize international politics with one stroke.

In briefest summary, the Charter provided as follows: The General Assembly, consisting of all members of the United Nations, "may discuss any questions or any matters within the scope of the present Charter" and may, with certain unimportant exceptions, "make recommendations to the Members of the United Nations or to the Security Council or to both on any such questions or matters" (Article 10). In other words, the General Assembly was empowered to debate, to pass resolutions, and to make recommendations on virtually all matters. It was, quite obviously, designed to be a grand "talking shop" and huge conference arena, and its power was limited to mere "recommendations."

The Security Council, consisting of eleven members, five of them permanent members of the Council—the United States, Great Britain, the Soviet Union, France, and China—was designed to be the most significant and powerful decision-making unit in the United Nations. It was assigned "primary responsibility for the maintenance of international peace and security . . ." (Article 24). In the event of a dispute, "the continuance of which is likely to endanger the maintenance of international peace and security," the Security Council was empowered to "call upon the parties to settle their dispute by [peaceful] means" (Article 33), and to "recommend appropriate procedures or methods of adjustment" (Article 36). These "powers," such as they are, were aimed at the "Pacific Settlement of Disputes" (Chapter VI, which encompasses Articles 33 through 38).

But by far the most significant allocation of power to the Security Council had to do with "Action with Respect to Threats to the Peace, Breaches of the Peace, and Acts of Aggression" (Chapter VII, encompassing Articles 39 through 51). Herein, the Security Council was empowered, as a last resort, to "take such action by air, sea, or land forces as may be necessary to maintain or restore international peace and security" (Article 42). As subsequent articles made clear, such war-making decisions were to be implemented by the armed forces of member nations, and all members were charged with the responsibility of making such forces available to the Security Council for use at the Council's discretion. (The fact that the

---

[2] There are many excellent books about the United Nations. See the Selected Bibliography at the end of this chapter.

letter of the Charter in these matters has never been carried out is, at this point, not relevant.)

The Security Council, therefore, was empowered to order action, whereas the General Assembly was merely empowered to make certain recommendations. If this were all that needed to be said about the Charter, there would be grounds for believing that those governments which drafted and ratified it were indeed headed by dreamers and utopians; and perhaps dangerous fools as well, being willing to make commitments to and grant such powers to an international organization whose decisions might sooner or later run seriously counter to the best interests of their nations. But the major governments involved were, of course, not really so unguarded: *They armed themselves with the power to veto any such Security Council decision.* Decisions of the Security Council on "procedural" matters were to be made by an affirmative vote of any seven members, but decision "on all other matters shall be made by an affirmative vote of seven members including the concurring votes of the permanent members . . ." (Article 27).[3] In other words, the Security Council would not be able to initiate military action if any of the Big Five disapproved.

The presence of the veto power in the Charter is clearly not evidence for the proposition that the victorious Allies assumed that their alliance would certainly survive the war and that they would assuredly cooperate in the maintenance of peace after the war. It is, in fact, evidence for something very nearly the opposite, namely, an assumption that the alliance might *not* survive the war, that unanimity might *not* prevail. The United Nations, far from being a panacea, could be an efficient, peacekeeping instrument of the Allies only if cooperation continued. If it did not, none of them was willing to permit the others to use the new institution against the interests of its own nation. The insistence on the veto is evidence of a lively concern by the major powers for the traditional prerogatives of sovereignty in the very possible event that postwar cooperation should prove unattainable.

The Soviet Union has used the veto so often since 1945 that many Americans have come to regard it as a Communist invention serving exclusively Communist ends. The fact is, however, that the United States was just as insistent upon the veto power as anyone else and, more importantly, would almost certainly not be willing to abandon it today. It has often been used to frustrate our objectives in the United Nations, but it continues to be

---

[3] The article goes on to provide that in decisions under Chapter VI, the Pacific Settlement of Disputes, and in one other (and insignificant) instance "a party to a dispute shall abstain from voting." This applies to permanent members as well, and was strenuously objected to for a time by the Soviet Union. But this suspension of the veto does not, of course, apply to the basic matter of the Security Council's warmaking power, and is not, therefore, of any significance to the argument being made in the text.

a highly regarded safeguard against Security Council decisions that might adversely affect our interests.[4]

The reason for the less-than-certain language in the next to the last sentence is that the United States has from time to time demonstrated a rather surprising willingness to turn over to United Nations majorities (two-thirds of the General Assembly) the right to make decisions of considerable consequence; therefore one cannot be absolutely certain that the United States would not at some future time even be willing to abandon the veto in the Security Council. Any such formal move, however, would require a revision of the Charter and would therefore involve the United States Senate. Whatever may be the controlling sentiment in some future American administration, it goes beyond the imagination of this writer to conceive of a Senate that would approve of such a proposal. However that may be, the aforementioned willingness of the earlier United States administrations to grant substantial powers to United Nations majorities without an applicable veto is itself an important matter and will be discussed next.

The Uniting for Peace Resolution

As related above in another context, the United Nations became involved in the Korean War from the very beginning. The Security Council passed resolutions condemning the North Korean invasion and calling on member nations to contribute armed forces to the defense of South Korea. This vigorous response, initiated and largely supported by the United States, was made possible by the absence of the Soviet Union from the Security Council. The Soviets were boycotting the Council in protest against the nonadmission of Communist China, and were not there to veto the United States-sponsored resolutions.[5] But it was recognized that their absence was

---

[4] By 1964, the Soviet Union had cast 101 vetoes; 52 of these had to do with membership applications, and the remainder were scattered among a wide range of issues. France had cast 4 vetoes, Great Britain 3, China 1, and the United States none. These figures are among the most striking pieces of evidence that the United Nations, especially in its earlier days, has been much more favorably disposed toward Western than Soviet interests.

[5] There is scarcely any better evidence than this episode for the proposition that governments, like interested persons, interpret legal documents to suit what they believe to be their own best interests. The Charter never uses the word "veto." As noted above, the relevant section provides that nonprocedural decisions of the Security Council "shall be made by an affirmative vote of seven members including the concurring votes of the permanent members. . . ." After returning to the Security Council in August, 1950, the Soviets quite naturally—and, if one merely reads the Charter, quite reasonably—argued that the United Nations operation in Korea was illegal because the Soviet Union had not cast one of the "concurring votes." The United States, of course, was hardly interested in such fine points when they did not suit its interests, and blandly replied that there was ample precedent for not regarding a failure to vote as sufficient to invalidate a Security Council resolution. And, in fact, we did have some precedents to cite. This was, of course, neither the first nor the last time that the United States government—like all governments—has stood the apparently plain meaning of a document on its head.

wholly fortuitous, and there developed a growing feeling that there was a need for creating some means of getting around the veto. During the late summer and early fall of 1950, the gratifying successes of the United Nations armies—largely United States and South Korean—contributed to a general feeling of elation and confidence at the United Nations head-quarters. The clear intent of the Charter to prevent United Nations–sponsored military action if one of the permanent members disapproved was alternately denied, ignored, or regarded as an anachronism. These were not only the days of rousing United Nations military successes; they were also the days when the United States could easily get a two-thirds majority vote in the General Assembly for its own resolutions. So it was that the United States took the lead in creating the means for getting around the veto.

On November 3, 1950, by the lopsided vote of 52 to 5—the five being the Soviet bloc—with 2 abstentions, the "Uniting for Peace Resolution" was adopted by the General Assembly. It was—and is—*potentially* a very great extension of the role of the General Assembly. It provided that if a veto has blocked Security Council action "in any case where there appears to be a threat to the peace, breach of the peace, or act of aggression," "the General Assembly shall consider the matter immediately with a view to making appropriate recommendations to Members for collective meas-ures, including in the case of a breach of the peace or act of aggression the use of armed force when necessary. . . ." It further provided that if the General Assembly was not in session at such a time, it could be convened in emergency special session within twenty-four hours after a request for such a meeting. The request could be made by any seven members of the Security Council or by a majority of the General Assembly. Finally, it authorized the creation of a Peace Observation Committee to go to the scene of the difficulty and report back to the Assembly.

The General Assembly did not arrogate to itself the Security Council's exclusive right actually to "take such action by air, sea, or land forces as may be necessary. . . ." It stayed within its Charter-formulated boundary of merely *recommending* action to member nations. And representatives of the United States and other nations made learned speeches to the effect that the resolution was quite a legitimate, "constitutional" extension of the responsibilities of the General Assembly. In plain fact, however, this resolution altered rather basically the potential role of the General Assem-bly, extending that potential role well beyond anything contained in the Charter itself. It created the new possibility of United Nations–endorsed military activity that was not endorsed by the Security Council and was veto-proof.

It goes without saying that the Soviets opposed it from the outset as an illegal usurpation of the responsibilities given by the Charter to the Secu-rity Council. It should also be obvious by now that the Soviet position on this matter was not simply a manifestation of their generally negative and uncooperative international behavior. It was, rather, the natural response of a nation that was being decisively outvoted on virtually all important matters coming before the General Assembly. It therefore disapproved of any expansion of that body's role and favored a retention of the original arrangements by which it had a veto over the most important United Nations actions.

This suggests an interesting and rather important question for American policy today. At the time the Uniting for Peace Resolution was adopted, the United Nations was still a comparatively small (fifty-eight members) Western-dominated institution. It wasn't until roughly a decade later that the massive influx of nonaligned, newly independent nations undermined Western—and especially American—control of the organization. It was easier in 1950, therefore, to believe that an activist General Assembly would always function on behalf of Western interests (or, as the public rhetoric would have it, would always "support the principles of the Charter"). But what of today, when nearly half of the General Assembly consists of non-Western nations that have received their independence since World War II? Can this unwieldy and sometimes antagonistic body be relied upon to implement the Uniting for Peace Resolution with wisdom and prudence?

These questions, needless to say, elicit many different responses. Although the worst fears of what the United Nations would become with a majority made up of nonaligned and underdeveloped nations have not been realized, neither is it accurate to suggest that there is no cause for concern. The potential for mischief making through the Uniting for Peace Resolution does exist, and it may one day be used. It would not be the first time that an institutional "reform" came back to haunt the original reformers.[6]

Some observers have argued that there is no cause for concern because no significant United Nations action against vital American interests is feasible. There are usually two elements to this argument. One is that although the United States may no longer control the General Assembly, it can still muster enough votes—even in the face of a hostile and organized majority—to deprive any resolution of the necessary two-thirds support. This is probably true, but caution about such prognostications is obviously required.

Another and related line of argument is that such a "hostile and organ-

A casual acquaintance with the writings of Dean Acheson over the last decade or so strongly suggests that he, a prime mover as Secretary of State for the Uniting for Peace Resolution in 1950, would not support such an innovation today. This would not make him inconsistent: At both times he would support what he believed best for American interests at the time. What it would say about his capacity to anticipate change is another matter.

ized majority" is simply unimaginable. Although anything is hypothetically possible, it is argued, this prospect goes well beyond the realm of the plausible. Those who stress this argument take the position that the character of American interests, values, and policies is such that they are bound to find a sympathetic audience among substantial numbers of governments at all times.

This position is quite likely to be borne out by events. But again, some caution is necessary. Suppose, for example, that the United States should determine that an invasion of a small neighboring country was a distasteful but necessary expedient. Suppose further that the Soviet Union led an attempt to implement the Uniting for Peace Resolution by calling for a United Nations–sponsored counterintervention in another part of the invaded country. It is conceivable, though admittedly it is highly improbable, that a two-thirds majority of the United Nations might endorse such an action. Such an action might very well involve Soviet troops, a sort of Korea-in-reverse. Such action in the 1960s seems to belong exclusively to the realm of fantasy; however, whether it always will is an open question.

With these meager causes for concern and with its potential for providing a United Nations sanction for desirable actions otherwise blocked by a veto, what is and what should be the American attitude toward the Uniting for Peace Resolution? The official position has never changed, although, as suggested above, there is reason to doubt whether there is anywhere near as much enthusiasm for it today as there was in 1950. As for what the official position *should be*, the answer depends in good measure on what the specific issue under consideration is. It would surely not be a wise diplomatic move simply to denounce the Uniting for Peace Resolution in the abstract as a dangerous or illegal development. What will have to be done is to judge each proposed use on its merits, without being blinded either by an abstract commitment or an abstract rejection of the instrument contained therein.

Meanwhile, the Uniting for Peace Resolution remains as a potential legitimizer of General Assembly—endorsed action. And if it ever is used, the likelihood is very high that it would be a means of overcoming a Soviet, not a Western, veto.[7]

---

[7] The Uniting for Peace Resolution has been employed only once as a method of creating a United Nations military force. This occurred during the Suez crisis in 1956, and the force created was strictly a passive, buffer force installed between the Israeli and Egyptian troops. All of the other major United Nations peace-keeping operations (in Korea, the Congo, and Cyprus) were created through the Security Council. The Uniting for Peace Resolution was invoked during both the Suez and Hungarian crises of 1956, but only to *condemn* the "aggressive" powers,—and, in the Suez instance, to authorize the buffer force—not to recommend military action against them. For two expert opinions to the effect that there is a strong and decisive bias *against* implementing the military aspects of the resolution, see H. G. Nicholas, *The United Nations As a Political Institution*, 2d ed., Oxford University Press, London, 1962, p. 110, and Inis L. Claude, Jr., *Swords into Plowshares, The Problems and Progress of International Organization*, 3d ed., Random House, Inc., New York, 1964, pp. 245–248.

The Most Valuable United Nations Role

The preceding discussion of the potentialities of United Nations–sponsored action initiated by the General Assembly leads to a more basic question: From the standpoint of United States interest and objectives, of what value is the United Nations? Some of its less significant impacts, positive and negative, on United States interests will be discussed later in the chapter. At this point, its most valuable role will be analyzed.

Among the most important, if not the most important, American interests in the world today is the avoidance of thermonuclear war. The United Nations is obviously not able to ensure that such a war will be avoided. It does not control the decisions of sovereign states, especially those great powers that will determine for the foreseeable future whether such a war occurs. But the United Nations has had and may again have a very substantial impact on certain affairs that, however insignificant they may be intrinsically, conceivably might play some role in bringing on such a war. By far the most ambitious United Nations experience of this kind was the organization's involvement in the Congo, especially in the period from July, 1960, through January, 1963. It constituted the most expensive and probably the most important United Nations peace-keeping venture, and it was made possible by one of the most crucial, controversial, and difficult American postwar foreign policy decisions. As such, it will be described and analyzed extensively below. It says a good deal about both the United Nations and United States foreign policy.

The Congo

In 1945, there were only two "black African" members of the United Nations: Ethiopia and Liberia. In 1956, Sudan became a member, and Ghana and Guinea followed in 1957 and 1958, respectively. In 1960, the decolonization of Africa reached its numerical peak as sixteen new African nations joined the United Nations, swelling the total of African members from south of the Sahara to twenty-one. (This figure excludes South Africa.) Most of them were former French colonies and were at least minimally prepared to assume responsibility for their own affairs in an orderly and peaceful manner. One notable and tragic exception to this was the former Belgian Congo. Up until the late 1950s, the Belgians had shown no inclination whatever to respond to the growing Congolese demands for independence. In the 1950s, they did begin to talk in terms of a "Belgian-Congolese Community," which purportedly would involve a permanent association of the two peoples on the basis of equality. This objective was largely rhetorical, and was so understood by both groups, and the Belgians gave little or no serious attention to the possibility that the Congo would or should one day be free. As it became increasingly clear that organized Congolese movements were not willing to accept continued Belgian rule indefinitely, the Belgians abandoned their illusions and announced—in

January, 1959—a policy of decolonization. In January, 1960, they astonished themselves, the Congolese, and nearly everyone else by announcing
that the Congo would be given its independence on June 30, 1960.[8] Unlike
the British and French, the Belgians had not taken even the most elemen-
tary steps in the direction of preparing their colonial subjects for this
momentous day. There were fewer than twenty Congolese university gradu-
ates and only one doctor and one lawyer; this from a population of approximately 13 million. Of equal or greater importance, political activity
had been prohibited during most of the colonial period, thereby effectively
ruling out the development of the necessary political institutions and skills
that any population requires for self-government.

Following national elections in May, 1960, the loosely organized, diverse,
and sharply competitive Congolese political factions—"parties" would be
too strong a term—did manage to form a government for installation on
June 30. The Premier-designate was Patrice Lumumba, a thirty-five-year-
old former postal worker, brewery director, and newspaper correspondent,
who had managed to develop the closest thing to a nationwide political
party. It may have been the case that no person could have been skillful
enough and politically strong enough to provide effective leadership in the
Congo at that critical moment. The Congo, like most former colonies, was
not a nation in any strict sense of the word. Its massive territory—one-
fourth the size of the United States—was a wholly arbitrary consequence
of the nineteenth-century European colonization process, and its population
consisted of a myriad of often primitive tribes, many of them hostile to
each other, with a very slightly developed sense of unity. It quickly became
clear that Lumumba was not able to control the centrifugal forces un-
leashed by independence, and the Congo descended into anarchy and
bloodshed.

The decisive blow to stability and order was delivered by the very group
whose existence was thought to be the main bulwark of the new nation:
The *Force Publique*, a combination army and internal security force. This
well-trained gendarmery had long been a disciplined and efficient instrument of Belgian rule. But the heady wine of freedom shattered its discipline, and the Congolese troops mutinied in protest against the fact that
their officers were still Belgian. In the ensuing chaos, with Belgium flying
in troops to protect its citizens, the Congolese cabinet appealed to the
United States for help in restoring order. President Eisenhower declined
to accept this awesome responsibility and urged Lumumba to appeal to
the United Nations for assistance. On July 12, he did.

Moving with great speed at the end of a stormy session the night of

---

[8] There are two Congo Republics, and both became independent in 1960. One is a former
French colony and its capital is Brazzaville; the capital of the former Belgian Congo
is Leopoldville. The two countries, which adjoin each other, are usually distinguished
by reference to their capitals.

July 13–14, the Security Council passed by a vote of 8 to 0 a resolution
that authorized the Secretary-General "to take the necessary steps, in consultation with the Government of the Republic of the Congo, to provide
the Government with such military assistance as may be necessary until . . .
the national security forces are able to meet fully their tasks." The United
States enthusiastically supported this resolution, and the Soviet Union
acquiesced, but American officials were concerned about the fact that the
United Kingdom and France, as well as Nationalist China, abstained. The
resolution appeared to be in line with our traditional conception of the
United Nations as an institution capable of pacifying dangerous situations,
especially those that might eventually draw in the United States and the
Soviet Union on opposite sides. It was this last consideration that loomed
so ominously on the horizon in the summer of 1960. The Soviet Union,
always anxious to exploit dissident factions for their own ends and especially anxious to secure a base in decolonizing Africa, was viewed sympathetically by certain important elements in the infinitely complex Congolese
political picture. The United States, therefore, had its usual two motives
in supporting a United Nations presence: It was interested in securing
stability simply for its own sake, and it was anxious to keep the Soviet
Union out of the heart of Africa.

It would be well to pause at this point and underline that last proposition. The United States is interested in the United Nations for a variety
of reasons, but in this era of the cold war, it is inescapable that we—like
the Soviets—tend to view everything at least partially in terms of its effects
on our competitive position with our chief adversary. In this case, the
United States looked on the United Nations as an appropriate instrument
of our own policy of containing Soviet influence. It may be a bit crude to
refer to the United Nations as an instrument of American policy, but that
is the unvarnished truth, and it suggests a basic fact about the United
Nations: Whatever may be its other values and contributions, the United
Nations is primarily an instrumentality that all sovereign states seek to
use for their own ends. In other words, it is pious and false propaganda
to charge that the Soviet Union seeks to use the United Nations for its
own ends while the United States supports the United Nations as a matter
of principle. The United States supports the United Nations when it believes such support serves its own interests. What distinguishes the Soviet
and American attitudes toward the United Nations is not their shared
desire to serve their own ends but the nature of those ends.

It should perhaps be emphasized that the two superpowers are not alone
in this matter. *All* nations seek to use the United Nations for their own
purposes. A proper understanding of this fact can go a long way toward
dispelling many of the illusions and undermining much of the sentimentality that surround the United Nations.

As the summer of 1960 wore on, it became increasingly clear that the

United Nations had assumed a staggering responsibility. The disintegration of the Congo was nearly complete. Among the most important developments was the reckless secession of mineral-rich and Belgian-influenced Katanga province. Katanga was the chief source of income for the Congo, and for this as well as symbolic reasons its secession was regarded as intolerable by Lumumba. He demanded that the United Nations troops forcibly end the secession. Secretary-General Dag Hammarskjöld did not believe that the Security Council resolution could be interpreted as authorizing such a bold maneuver against the well-armed, white-led Katanga Army, and he rejected the demand. Lumumba, who was in a desperate position, was embittered by this and turned to the Soviet Union for support. Grasping their unexpected opportunity, the Soviets fully endorsed Lumumba's demands and then began to call for the resignation of Dag Hammarskjöld.[9]

Meanwhile, a struggle for power was under way in the Congo, and Lumumba was imprisoned by his political foes and reconstituted elements of the Congolese Army under Congolese leadership. In February, 1961, Lumumba was murdered by his captors.

But the United Nations–sponsored troops—about 20,000, drawn from African and neutral nations—were accomplishing little beyond maintaining a modicum of law and order. Katanga, under its stubborn leader, Moise Tshombe, continued its secession, and central government leaders continued to demand its reincorporation into the Congo, by force if necessary. Sensing the need for a new mandate, Hammarskjöld induced the Security Council in February, 1961, to pass a resolution that urged "that the United Nations take immediately all appropriate measures to prevent the occurrence of civil war in the Congo, including arrangements for cease-fires, the halting of all military operations, the prevention of clashes, and the use of force, if necessary, in the last resort." It was this authorization of the use of force, even for very limited purposes, that fundamentally altered the character of the United Nations operation in the Congo.

The vote on this resolution was 9 to 0, with abstentions by France and the Soviet Union. The Soviet abstention reflected two things: its disillusionment with the United Nations operation that had tolerated the elimination of Lumumba and had effectively and sharply reduced Soviet influence in the Congo, and its unwillingness to veto a resolution that had the nearly unanimous support of the African states. Support of the resolution by the new Kennedy administration reflected its endorsement of its predecessor's policy of working through the United Nations on this matter and, more significantly, its willingness to broaden the mandate.

[9] Premier Khrushchev showed up at the General Assembly sessions in September of 1960 to press these demands. It was during a subsequent discussion on colonial matters that he set a new diplomatic standard by taking off one of his shoes and pounding it on the desk.

The matter dragged on inconclusively for many months. The United Nations command on the scene became impatient and in September, 1961, became involved in some rather serious fighting with the Katanga Army. It was inconclusive, and Hammarskjöld lost his life in a plane crash while attempting to arrange a cease-fire. In November, a new Secretary-General was selected—U Thant of Burma—despite the fact that many observers thought the Soviet Union would never permit another individual to head the Secretariat, which was demonstrating its capacity to pursue policies that were contrary to those of the Soviet Union.[10]

Shortly thereafter, the Security Council passed still another resolution, which authorized "the Secretary-General to take vigorous action, including the use of requisite measure of force, if necessary, for the immediate apprehension" of all foreign military personnel, mercenaries, and political advisers. This still did not authorize the use of force directly for the purpose of ending the secession, but it came very close to it, because the secession was being made possible by foreign (white) military personnel, mercenaries, and political advisers. Apprehending them would almost necessarily involve ending the secession. The new Secretary-General promised to carry out his new mandate with "determination and vigor."

Fighting broke out again in December, and this time the United Nations forces improved their position, but the secession was still not ended. Finally, in December, 1962, and January, 1963, renewed combat resulted in a routing of the Katanga forces and a reabsorption of the province into the Congo. During all of these skirmishes, the Kennedy administration stood squarely behind the United Nations forces; in fact, American financial and airlift support were essential to the United Nations operation.

The above is a very brief résumé of a most complicated situation, one which might degenerate into chaos again at any moment. As suggested earlier, the United Nations operation in the Congo through January, 1963, illustrated two centrally important points. First of all, it showed the capacity of the United Nations, if supported by enough member states, to play a truly significant political role in the world, including the management of armed force. Second, it demonstrated the willingness of an American administration to use the United Nations in new and creative ways *despite* substantial opposition both at home and among our closest allies. This second point merits emphasis.

[10] The Soviets at that time were demanding the reorganization of the Secretariat into an executive establishment with three top officials, each one capable of vetoing policies. This was their famous "troika" proposal. The three officials would represent the democratic West, the Soviet Union and its bloc, and the nonaligned nations. The proposal was one of the Soviet responses to what they regarded as the anti-Soviet policies being pursued by Dag Hammarskjöld. The Soviets quietly buried their troika demands after it became clear that the nonaligned nations were not the least bit interested in installing a veto in the Secretariat, which they regarded as an instrumentality capable of creative statesmanship on the international scene.

In the summary description of the Congo operation above, the American role might appear to be quite natural and even inevitable. Actually, as briefly noted, the administration's policies were the subject of a stormy debate in the United States and the source of considerable friction with our allies. The support of the United Nations in the Congo was a policy decision of courage and vision, but the dissenters were—and are—able to make a powerful case against that support.

The arguments of the domestic opposition were directed more at the wisdom of this specific use of the United Nations. The arguments of our European allies were directed more at the very idea of using the United Nations for such purposes, anywhere and at any time. The latter, therefore, raise more basic issues, but the former also suggest some matters of long-range importance.

France opposed the United Nations action from start to finish as a matter of principle. General de Gaulle took the position that the United Nations has no right to go around meddling in the internal affairs of sovereign nations. He disliked the precedent that was being established. What were to be the logical limits of the idea that the United Nations has a worldwide responsibility to settle all disputes, internal as well as between nations? France was especially sensitive to the United Nations tendency to take a broad view of its rights and responsibilities because the French had not yet resolved the agonizing problem of Algeria, and the General Assembly had the habit of conducting debates and passing resolutions on the matter. This was an inexcusable invasion of France's internal affairs in de Gaulle's view, and it reinforced his inclination not to back adventures such as the one in the Congo. France was unwilling to veto the Security Council resolutions, which probably would only have induced the General Assembly to take the matter over, an even less desirable prospect. So, she abstained and refused to make any contribution to the financing of the operation.

The British position was similar but less dogmatic. They favored the United Nations presence but disapproved of the use of force to end the secession. The Belgians, still reeling from the loss of their colony and shocked by the ensuing nightmare, were also opposed. Ultimately, however, these two powers accepted their share of the responsibility for the operation, but the British opposed to the very end the use of force as a means of ending the secession.

On the domestic front, the Kennedy administration was faced with an angry and disapproving Republican sentiment and division in the ranks of its own Democratic party. In December, 1961, Vice President Nixon, for example, called American policy in the Congo "the worst foreign policy blunder since . . . the Cuba invasion," and the Republican National Chairman echoed the sentiments of many when he asked, "What in the name of sanity are we trying to do in the Congo?" Some Democrats were taking a similar line.

Some critics were simply reactionaries who favored some kind of reimposition of colonial rule and looked on the Katangan secession as the means for creating such chaos that the Belgians would be obliged to come back in force. Most critics, however, took a much more reasonable line. In substance they argued that Kantaga was the only orderly, stable area in all of the Congo, that its leader, Tshombe, was pro-Western—Nixon called him "the educated, Christian, anti-Communist head of Katanga"—that the central government was hopelessly inefficient, corrupt, and infiltrated by Communists, and that the principle of self-determination applied to Katanga. Far from being persecuted and singled out for blame and attack, Katanga should be encouraged to maintain a separate identity, perhaps within a loose federation, and the United Nations should busy itself with cleaning up the mess in the rest of the Congo.

The Kennedy administration was, of course, itself divided over United States policy in the Congo. The sentiment that prevailed demonstrated that administration's willingness to take unprecedented action on behalf of a cause that might very well end in failure, to do this despite sizable opposition at home and abroad, in the belief that no better alternative was available. The rationale of the administration's policy was something like this:

Whatever the merits of Katanga's secession, it is doomed to failure. It is opposed by all African governments who believe, rightly or wrongly, that Tshombe is being used by European interests who have heavy investments in mining in Katanga, who do not want to share the tax burdens of the Congo as a whole, and/or who fear expropriation by a leftist central government. This kind of neocolonialism, or alleged neocolonialism, cannot last in the new, independent Africa that is emerging. If the United Nations does not end the secession, somebody else will, and that somebody else might very well be a Moscow-oriented Congolese government, which, in frustration or by desire, turns to the Soviets for help. In sum, the only viable anti-Communist policy in the Congo is to end the secession, if necessary by force. The United States is fortunate that the United Nations forces are there and can do the job if properly supported. If they were not, the awful possibility of United States and Soviet competitive interventions might become a reality. As it is, the United States can assist the United Nations in an operation that serves the interests of the Congolese as a whole, of world peace, and therefore of the United States. Far from being a dangerous extension of United Nations responsibilities, it is a creative and promising one, giving hope that the United Nations can be an effective instrument in the avoidance of direct confrontation and war.

Whatever ultimately happens in that unhappy land and whatever one may think about the arguments summarized above, it is clear that the Congo episode raised the most basic questions about the United Nations and United States policy relating to it.

Preventive Diplomacy

At the beginning of this section it was suggested that the United Nations has had and may again have a very substantial impact on certain affairs that, however insignificant they may be intrinsically, conceivably might play some role in bringing on a thermonuclear war. The United Nations role in the Congo was probably the most significant example of this kind of impact, but it was by no means the only one. Leaving aside the Korean War, which is really in a class by itself, the United Nations has played or is playing significant "peace-keeping" roles in Kashmir, Lebanon, the Arab-Israeli disputes, and Cyprus. Only in the Congo (and Korea) was armed force actively employed under United Nations auspices; these other missions were or are of a pacific, noncoercive nature. United Nations-sponsored troops in such circumstances provide a buffer between hostile forces, patrolling "neutral zones" and monitoring tenuous cease-fires.

But whatever the specific form that United Nations intervention in a crisis may take—and no one can predict what it may be in the future—it is a matter of some significance that such an institution exists on the international scene. It is absolutely certain that nations will continue to quarrel, and it is quite likely that they will continue to fight wars. As decolonization continues and for many years after it is over, it seems likely that some new nations will disintegrate and invite competing interventions. In this kind of world, modern technology being what it is, it is a matter of grave interest to all concerned that such wars and civil strife be localized and that the clashing interests of the superpowers be kept apart where possible.

The United Nations is at best an imperfect instrument for playing this role of international fireman, damping down the flames of war as they occur. But it is often the best one available.[11] It has an aura of impartiality about it, despite the fact that any intervener, whether a sovereign state or an international organization, inevitably serves some interests more than others. It has a certain legitimacy about it, as well. Even the Soviets hesitate to attack the United Nations directly or to scuttle its operations too flagrantly.[12]

The Politics of Finance

These coercive and noncoercive peace-keeping activities are not the only functions performed by the United Nations, but they are probably the most significant ones. Provided they continue to serve the interests of the

---

[11] It goes without saying, of course, that it is not *always* the best instrumentality at hand. The United States has, for example, consistently preferred action by the Organization of American States (OAS) to action by the United Nations in delicate situations in Latin America. See Inis L. Claude, Jr., "The OAS, the UN, and the United States," *International Conciliation*, no. 547, March, 1964.

[12] For a brilliant analysis of "preventive diplomacy"—as Dag Hammarskjöld called the role described above—see Claude, *Swords into Plowshares*, pp. 285–303.

United States, broadly conceived, a strong case can be made for the proposition that the continued existence and vitality of the United Nations should be a high priority objective of American foreign policy. It has become painfully clear in recent years, however, that not all nations share this appraisal of the United Nations' utility, and the result has been that its very existence has been endangered. This has posed and undoubtedly will continue to pose serious questions for American policy makers. It therefore merits some attention.

Peace-keeping operations, coercive or noncoercive, can be quite expensive. The force in the Congo cost approximately $10 million a month for several years. This money had to be raised in addition to all the assessed, or "nonvoluntary," payments and all the other "voluntary" contributions that together comprise the financial support for "the United Nations system."[13] Needless to say, there were many nations that refused to pay their assessed share for the Congo operation because they disapproved of it.

The two major withholders of support were the Soviet Union and France. This position of France was a source of embarrassment and concern to the

[13] The terms "voluntary" and "nonvoluntary" are somewhat misleading. *All* contributions to the United Nations are "voluntary" in the sense that there is no means of enforcing payment; they are not like taxes. The payments on the regular United Nations budget are called "nonvoluntary" because they are assessed by the General Assembly, and a nation which does not pay them may lose its vote in the General Assembly. The Specialized Agencies [such as, for example, the World Health Organization (WHO) and the United Nations Educational, Scientific and Cultural Organization (UNESCO)] also assess their members, and nonpayment theoretically results in expulsion.

The "voluntary" payments to special programs of "the United Nations system" are not assessed; nations contribute as much or as little as they wish, and there are no sanctions involved. ["Special programs" include such things as the United Nations Children's Fund (UNICEF), the United Nations technical assistance program, and specialized WHO projects such as the malaria eradication program.] The overall budget of "the United Nations system" is considerably higher than the regular budget. The following figures, for example, represent the calendar 1961 expenditures of "the United Nations system" (in thousands of dollars):

Regular budget	72,696
Specialized agencies	64,858
U.N. Emergency Force	19,000
Congo operation	135,000
Special programs	159,032
Total	450,586

The United States share of these budgets varies. Our assessed share of the regular budget is 32.02 per cent; we often contribute a higher proportion to the voluntary programs. In fiscal year 1961, the United States contributed just over $226 million to "the United Nations system." Since that figure is for *fiscal* 1961 and the earlier figures are for *calendar* 1961, no precise percentage figure can be calculated. A comparison of the two figures is roughly accurate, however, meaning that the overall United States share was—and usually is—approximately 50 per cent.

Sources: Senate Foreign Relations Committee and House Foreign Affairs Committee, *Information on the Operations and Financing of the United Nations*, 87th Cong., 2d Sess., (Feb. 6, 1962), pp. 69–70 (Comm. Print); and *Review of United States Participation in the United Nations, Hearings before the Senate Committee on Foreign Relations*, 88th Cong., 1st Sess., March 13, 1963, p. 17.

United States, but it did not raise as serious a question as the Soviet refusal to pay. The debate over the matter was conducted, as one might expect, in highly legalistic terms. The Soviets took the position that such peace-keeping operations could only be sanctioned by the Security Council and concluded from this that only the Security Council—where their veto would apply—could assess member states for the costs of such efforts. The regular procedure of General Assembly assessments did not apply, they argued, and they therefore refused to contribute the monetary support levied by the General Assembly.

The United States argued that peace-keeping operations were an integral part of the United Nations operation, that member states were required to support them, and that the ordinary assessment organ (the General Assembly) was the proper agency for allocating this financial burden. To buttress its case, the United States supported a General Assembly resolution that asked the International Court of Justice (World Court) to render an advisory opinion on the matter. In 1962, the Court handed down the expected judgment: The General Assembly was responsible for such assessments, they should be regarded as mandatory just as regular-budget assessments, and a failure to pay could result in the denial of voting rights to the delinquent states.

None of this skirmishing has affected, or is likely to affect, the Soviets, the French, or any of the other resisters. Hazy legal debates seldom obscure a government's perception of its own interests as it defines them, and this episode was no exception. The Soviets stopped approving of the Congo operation when it developed that the United Nations forces, far from facilitating Soviet interests and penetration, were a positive barrier to Soviet ambitions in the Congo. Is it reasonable to expect them to help pay for the United Nations forces under these conditions?

As for the United States, all the legal briefs and appeals to the Charter could not hide the fact that the United Nations Congo operation was, in the opinion of the administration, serving the interests of the United States. Support, financial and otherwise, was therefore quite understandable.

It does not clarify the matter any to argue that if the Soviets understood their long-range interests better, they, too, would support such enterprises. The fact is that they do not regard them in this light, and until they do, American administrations will be confronted with difficult policy problems. There will always be those who argue that if the Soviets refuse to pay their "fair share," we should refuse to underwrite such operations. But for a responsible American administration, the problems raised by Soviet nonpayment are not so simple. The preceding argument can be stood on its head with equal plausibility. That is, it can be argued that since the Soviets refuse to pay, therefore we should. Soviet nonpayment, in this view, is strong evidence that the operation is not conducive to Soviet interests; therefore, we should see to it that the operation succeeds.

Although the second of these two positions is more intelligent than the first, both of them suffer from the same basic error: They prescribe American policy exclusively in terms of a reaction to Soviet policy. This, in effect, turns over to the Soviet Union the ability to determine United States policy on such matters. The folly of painting ourselves into such a corner is nearly self-evident.

The fact is that the Soviet Union and the United States have both divergent and common interests. Each development must be judged on its own merits. If it appears to further American interests, broadly conceived, it should be supported; if not, it should not be. The question of whether the Soviets support it is like the question of whether a majority of the United Nations members support it: such matters should be taken into account, but they should not by themselves be decisive.

This means that it is quite possible that in future crises, the United States will once again find itself paying a disproportionate amount for the support of a United Nations peace-keeping operation. Whether this burden should be borne will probably be debated in terms of legalities, and this debate will undoubtedly reflect a frustration about nonpayment by adversaries and/or allies. It will be a measure of any administration's wisdom and, perhaps more importantly, its courage whether it bases its policy on such largely irrelevant matters or whether it calculates the overall advantages and disadvantages and then makes its policy accordingly.

A related question for American policy makers is what to do about the voting rights of those nations that refuse to pay some of their assessments. The Charter provides (Article 19) that a member "which is in arrears in the payments of its financial contributions to the Organization shall have no vote in the General Assembly if the amount of its arrears equals or exceeds the amount of the contributions due from it for the preceding two full years."[14]

If the only nonpayers were Communist nations and there were a general predisposition within the General Assembly to enforce Article 19, the United States might find little difficulty in supporting a strict interpretation of the proviso. Moreover, as noted above, the World Court has rendered an opinion to the effect that assessments for peace-keeping operations are just as binding as regular assessments. But neither of the two conditions mentioned above does in fact obtain. Among those nations refusing to pay for certain peace-keeping missions, for example, are the Arab states. They have refused to pay their assessments for the United Nations Emergency Force (UNEF) that was installed as a buffer between Egypt and Israel after the 1956 war and Israeli pullback. They have argued that the "ag-

---

[14] The article goes on to state that the "General Assembly may, nevertheless, permit such a Member to vote if it is satisfied that the failure to pay is due to conditions beyond the control of the Member." This exception is not, of course, relevant to the matter of Soviet or French nonpayment.

gressors"—Israel, Great Britain, and France—caused the problem and they should be solely responsible for its effects. In 1964, there were sixteen nations, including the Soviet Union, in arrears on their United Nations payments because of a refusal to pay for one or more of the peace-keeping operations.

This figure suggests why there has been something less than widespread enthusiasm for invoking Article 19. What position should the United States take on the issue? The matter has dragged on for years, and as this is written the United Nations is still deadlocked on it. The entire 19th Session of the General Assembly (1964–1965) was conducted without taking any formal votes in order to avoid meeting the issue head on.[15]

There are some signs that the United States is beginning to soften its position. There apparently is a growing awareness in government circles that a dogmatic insistence on payment for peace-keeping functions may be unwise. Not only is this rigid position endangering the possibility of such actions in the future, but it also raises the possibility that the United States may some day be "required" to pay for an operation that it does not favor. The legalistic United States position nearly amounts to giving the General Assembly the power to tax member states, and a realization of this appears to be dawning in the State Department.[16] A government that becomes the victim of either its own legalisms or its own propaganda is not likely to be able to perceive its nation's interests with a clear eye.

Other Problems Relating to United States Participation in the United Nations

American critics of the United Nations and our involvement therein are often concerned about many things besides its cost and the appropriateness or legitimacy of its peace-keeping functions. There is a rather widespread sense of uneasiness about the overall impact of United Nations proceedings on the interests of the United States. These legitimate concerns will be discussed presently, but first some crude and uninformed attacks must be confronted.

Some people regard the United Nations as a threat to United States sovereignty. In this view, the United Nations is an incipient world government, which will inevitably grow in strength until it displaces national governments as the source of basic political decisions in the world. Ironi-

[15] Actually, one vote was taken, near the end of the session. An Albanian motion to force the Assembly to abandon its no-voting procedure—designed to embarrass both the Soviet Union and the United States—was overwhelmingly defeated with both of the superpowers voting with the majority. The United States justified its willingness to let the Soviet Union vote on the motion by disingenuously arguing that it was merely a "procedural" vote.

[16] For an excellent review and discussion of this whole affair, see Meg Greenfield, "The Lost Session at the U.N.," *The Reporter*, vol. 32, no. 9, pp. 14–20, May 6, 1965.

cally, many of the United Nations most enthusiastic supporters have the same vision, only for them it is a dream, not a nightmare.

These people misunderstand the nature and potential of the United Nations. It is possible, of course, that in some distant future, nations will disappear and a world government will assume their responsibilities. It is also possible that the United Nations might serve as the framework for such a universal body. But if this day should ever come, it would not be because the United Nations had become so powerful that it absorbed the sovereignties of member states. Rather, it would be because sovereign nations had decided to yield their sovereignties to a world organization, and the presence or nonpresence of the United Nations would have had only a marginal effect, if any, on such decisions.

In other words, the basic political decision-making unit in the world today remains the sovereign state. For better or worse, the existence of the United Nations does not seriously alter the fundamentally decentralized character of the international arena. Whatever powers are granted to the United Nations are granted by the member states and can be withdrawn by them. If the United Nations should ever attempt to constitute itself as a supranational decision-making organization—and it is difficult if not impossible to imagine how any such attempt could be made—it would surely be rebuffed by all, or nearly all, sovereign entities. The United Nations is derivative; it is and can be only what its members want it to be; and any member can opt out at any time.[17]

It is a sign of the growing maturity in this country regarding the United Nations that contemporary debates on the subject for the most part do not get bogged down in such illusory matters. The controversy over the Congo operation and peace-keeping generally, discussed above, was at its base a reasonable and legitimate one. Neither side misconstrued the character of the organization; they only disagreed about the wisdom of some of its operations and related United States policy.

United Nations Influence on United States Policy

There are, of course, sensible questions which can be and are being raised about the institution. Senator Henry Jackson (D-Wash.) raised many of them in an address on March 20, 1962, before the National Press Club,

[17] It might be objected that these remarks leave out of consideration the considerable and perhaps growing capacity of the Secretariat to make and implement policy decisions, some of which are quite important. Does this not constitute a supranational function? It is true that the United Nations is not *merely* a reflection of majority sentiment in the General Assembly or Security Council and that the Secretariat does exercise discretionary judgment during, for example, peace-keeping operations. But whatever independence the Secretariat may achieve in such matters—and the deliberate vagueness of many resolutions suggests that it may be substantial in certain matters—it is finally dependent upon the members for its support, financial and otherwise. This is not said in order to belittle the importance of the Secretariat's role, but only to place it in perspective.

and some quotations from that speech will serve as focal points in the following paragraphs. The general tenor of his remarks, which touched off a considerable amount of controversy and had a special news value because of the Senator's earlier close political and personal ties with then President Kennedy, can be sensed from the following excerpt from his introductory remarks:

> The United Nations is not, and was never intended to be, a substitute for our own leaders as makers and movers of American policy. The shoulders of the Secretary-General were never expected to carry the burdens of the President or the Secretary of State. But do we sometimes act as though we could somehow subcontract to the U. N. the responsibility for national decision-making?[18]

This question is a much more intelligent and appropriate version of the concern that prompts the absurd allegation, discussed above, that the United States has turned its sovereignty over to the United Nations. But even the Senator's version cannot be supported. It was United States support for the Congo operation that reactivated this concern about who is in charge of American policy, but common sense and a close inspection of events show how unfounded such concerns are. The American government did not support that operation simply because it was a United Nations operation. It supported it because it believed that the operation was enhancing the interests of the United States.

It would be misleading to suggest that the Kennedy administration was not sensitive to and influenced by majority sentiment in the United Nations. And it may be that if there had been a slightly different United Nations policy, we would have supported that one instead. But this is a long way from saying that United Nations policy *controlled* United States policy or that we "subcontract[ed] to the U. N. the responsibility for national decision-making."

There may in fact be some instances in the past or in the future when an American administration did or will simply support United Nations policy without making an independent judgment on the matter. Such behavior would, however, be wholly untypical for this or any other government and without any doubt could not involve any matter of great importance. Those who fear, for example, that American disarmament or space policy is likely to be subject to the whims of United Nations majorities are almost certainly worrying about the wrong things.

Senator Jackson then went on to ask if we are "taking an exaggerated view of the U. N.'s role." Whether the United States was taking, or is likely to take, "an exaggerated view of the U. N.'s role" is an open question. There

[18] The speech was reproduced in the *Congressional Record*, March 21, 1962, pp. 4277–4278 (daily ed.). All quotations are taken from that source.

can be no doubt that many persons in this country, including a few prominent political figures, do take such a view. And nearly all American Presidents express patently utopian ideas about the institution, especially when formally addressing it. But actual United States policy is another matter. Perhaps the most convincing evidence for this last proposition is the unilateral action taken by the United States at the time of the missile crisis in Cuba in October, 1962. It never entered any ranking policy maker's mind to appeal to the United Nations for substantive action. Although the Administration did make the appropriate gestures toward the United Nations, all of the decisions and most of the action were unilateral.

The United Nations as a Goad
Senator Jackson then raised another issue that troubles many observers:

> . . . There has been too great a tendency to bring every issue to a vote. Indeed there are too many votes on too many issues in the U. N.—and too much of the time and energy of every delegation is spent in lobbying for votes.
>
> A vote requires a division of the house, a sharpening and even an exaggeration of points at issue, and it emphasizes the division of opinion rather than the area of agreement. . . .
>
> Voting has a way of raising the temperature of any body, and I think we should be doing what we can to keep the temperature of the United Nations near normal.

It is undeniable that the existence of the United Nations forces the United States to take a public stand on many issues that it would prefer to deal with more privately or perhaps not at all. Moreover, these issues and resolutions regarding them recur again and again, compounding the problem. The most delicate votes of this nature in recent years have had to do with the decolonization process in Africa. The United Nations has taken a lively interest in this process. The newly independent states have seized on the United Nations as a forum for airing their own grievances and those of the still-subject peoples of southern Africa. Voting on such matters nearly always poses a painful dilemma for the United States. On the one hand, there is our general commitment to anticolonial principles; on the other, there is our felt need not to alienate our European allies, who view our anticolonial attitudes with suspicion and sometimes even with distrust. This dilemma lingers long after most colonies in Africa—and nearly all colonies elsewhere—have become independent. The best way to illustrate this problem is to deal with a concrete policy issue, such as the Portuguese colony of Angola.

Angola   Portugal is a small country, which contributes little or nothing to the defense of Western Europe. Moreover, it is a dictatorship, having been ruled since the early 1930s by Antonio de Oliveira Salazar. It is, therefore, intrinsically not very important as a concern of American foreign policy, and it constitutes something of an embarrassment to its friends and allies because of its policies at home and abroad. It insists that Angola —as well as its other African holdings, Mozambique and Portuguese Guinea—is an integral part of Portugal. Unlike Britain, France, and Belgium, it has not changed its African policy in response to the persistent demands of black Africans for self-government. It has a substantial psychological and material investment in Angola, and approximately 170,000 white Portuguese live there, ruling about 5 million black Africans. It shows no sign of yielding despite the fact that a nationalist rebellion has been going on sporadically in Angola since 1961 and will presumably succeed one day in gaining independence.

Many factors conspire to suggest that the United States should pursue a straightforward, unambiguous policy of supporting the nationalists. Their cause is in accord with our principles, their ultimate success seems assured regardless of our policy, and Portugal is not a major ally.

Unfortunately, it is not that simple. The primary reason, apparently, for American sensitivity to Portuguese sentiments is a military one. Portugal owns the Azores, a small group of islands in the Eastern Atlantic. The United States uses these islands for military bases, which the government claims are vital to our defense posture in Europe. Without access to classified information, it is impossible to make a judgment regarding their cruciality to American defense needs. Suffice it to say that every recent administration has regarded them as vital; and the result has been that Portugal has a certain amount of leverage on United States policy regarding her territories. This leverage has been applied and is reflected in our votes and policies at the United Nations.

Another factor that has dulled the natural American tendency to support independence movements has been the Congo experience. The idea that certain areas could be granted independence too soon had long been an element of American official thought, but the tragedy of the Congo gave it new meaning and new supporters. Would an independent Angola also plunge into anarchy and bloodshed, requiring—or at least raising the possibility of—another delicate and expensive United Nations involvement? The mere thought of it introduces a strong element of caution into American policy.

Finally, despite her size and undemocratic government, Portugal is a European member of NATO. For reasons that will be examined in Chapter 7, European governments today are deeply concerned about the reliability of American policy. Any desertion of an ally, for whatever reasons, would be regarded by many Europeans as evidence of American inconstancy and susceptibility to sentimentality and non-European pressure.

Even if there were no United Nations, a great power such as the United States would be confronted with a policy dilemma in this matter. But as

Senator Jackson suggested, proceedings in the United Nations spotlight our dilemma and, of equal importance, force us with some regularity to take a public position.[19] A few examples will illustrate the problem.

In December, 1962, the General Assembly passed two condemnatory resolutions regarding Portuguese policy in Angola and/or other territories controlled by Portugal. The first one condemned the Portuguese attitude as being inconsistent with the United Nations Charter, urged Portugal to recognize immediately the right of the peoples of the territories to self-determination and independence, called on all member nations to use their influence to induce Portugal to meet its obligations under the Charter and earlier Assembly resolutions, and requested all states to refrain from offering Portugal assistance enabling it to continue repressing peoples of the territories and for this purpose "to prevent the sale and supply of arms and military equipment to the Portuguese Government."

This resolution passed 82 to 7, with 13 abstentions. The United States voted against it. The United States delegation explained that its chief objection was to the prohibition on the supply of arms to Portugal. It insisted that it had assurances that none of the military assistance being given to Portugal by the United States was being diverted for use in Africa. It therefore construed this aspect of the resolution as an interference in the programs of NATO for the defense of Western Europe. It also objected to the resolution's implication that self-determination necessarily meant immediate independence. It was stated that although the United States has always favored self-determination for these territories, it did not want to prejudge the results of that self-determination.

The second difficult vote came a few days later, when the General Assembly, in a mood of frustration and with some redundancy, supported "immediate independence" for the peoples of Angola, condemned Portugal's "colonial war" there, requested that Portugal be denied any assistance that might be used for the suppression of Angola, particularly the supply of any arms, and requested the Security Council to take "appropriate measures, including sanctions," to secure Portugal's compliance with previous Assembly and Council resolutions. Again the majority was overwhelming—57 to 14, with 18 abstentions—and again the United States voted negatively. Again, the primary stated reason for United States objection was the request for an arms embargo, and it also objected to the call for sanctions.

In July, 1963, the Security Council took up the same issue with similar

[19] As mentioned in Chap. 3, the United States must do more than vote on these matters, though voting poses enough problems just by itself. It also must participate in the preliminary and postdecisional discussions and negotiations designed to determine the precise character of the resolutions and the manner of their implementation, if any. These diplomatic challenges are often as fraught with dangers and embarrassment as the votes themselves.

results. It affirmed that "the policies of Portugal in claiming the Territories under its administration as 'overseas' territories and as integral parts of metropolitan Portugal are contrary to the principles of the Charter and the relevant resolutions of the General Assembly and the Security Council." It held that the situation was seriously disturbing peace and security in Africa, called again on Portugal to take the requisite steps leading toward early independence for the territories, and repeated the request that all states withhold any assistance that would enable Portugal "to continue its repression."

The resolution passed 8 to 0, with the United States (and France and Great Britain) abstaining. This abstention reflected the unwillingness of the United States either to veto or to approve the resolution.

Ambassador Adlai Stevenson took a line even less critical of Portugal than the one taken by the United States during the earlier General Assembly debates. He chose to emphasize the alleged legal problems involved in the resolution. Article 2, paragraph 7, of the Charter states that with the exception of enforcement measures under Chapter VII ("Action with Respect to Threats to the Peace, Breaches of the Peace, and Acts of Aggression"), "Nothing in the present charter shall authorize the United Nations to intervene in matters which are essentially within the domestic jurisdiction of any state. . . ." Stevenson argued that there was no threat to the peace, and that therefore the United States could not support the resolution. He also contended that the real problem was the absence of a dialogue between the various contending factions.

Needless to say, Article 2, paragraph 7, is taken with varying degrees of seriousness by members of the United Nations. The more conservative powers cite it with great regularity in attempting to restrict the tendency of more revisionist states to involve the United Nations in more and more ambitious resolutions and endeavors. They call such efforts "meddling," whereas their adversaries refer to them as "implementations of the Charter." For the most part, these legalisms are merely a façade for more political concerns. That is, the more conservative powers fear and resent United Nations efforts to influence their internal and external policies, whereas the more revisionist states, having less to lose and more to gain, want to use the United Nations as a weapon against the *status quo.*

The immediate point, however, is that these and other votes tend to exacerbate the already delicate position of the United States in these contentious matters. The example of the Portuguese territories has been used herein, but there are many others that might be cited contemporaneously.

South Africa   Among the most troublesome is the situation in South Africa. In that tragic land, a minority of approximately 3 million whites ruthlessly controls a nonwhite majority of about 13 million, and the frustrations of the latter are being increasingly aired at the United Nations. From the standpoint of American foreign policy, the situation there has points of similarity and dissimilarity with the patently colonial situation in the Portuguese territories. There are no strategic islands like the Azores involved, and the white government is European only by race. But the United States is deeply worried about the prospect of a war in South Africa that might, as any war these days, drag in outside forces. South Africa, in other words, poses a threat to the peace and stability of Africa and therefore of the world. In addition, and less nobly, American investments in and exports to that wealthy and economically highly developed nation are substantial. Moreover, South Africa provides over one-half of the world's gold production. Finally, there is the remnant of a "European angle" involved because South Africa was once a member of the British Commonwealth and she has economic and ethnic ties with Continental powers as well.

What, then, should our policy be on the recurring and increasingly harsh proposals coming before the United Nations? In actual fact, our policy has been, in this as in many other matters, especially of this type, somewhat imprecise. We have consistently condemned South Africa's racial policies, have joined in urging her to abolish them, and we have stopped selling arms to South Africa.

But what about proposed boycotts of South Africa products or, more desperately, an embargo on all trade? We have resisted such proposals, arguing that they would only make matters worse in South Africa. What our position will be in the future as the situation deteriorates, only time will tell. The central point of this discussion, however, is not to analyze exhaustively the policy problem posed by South Africa but rather to underline the fact once again that the mere existence of the United Nations imposes on the United States—and all other members, of course—with frequency and in the midst of great publicity and institutional pressures the necessity of choice. Now and for years to come, the United States will be forced to take positions on such matters in the United Nations—and outside as well, of course—and it will constitute a formidable challenge to our diplomacy. The existence of the United Nations accelerates and multiplies the challenge.

Red China Another contemporary example is Red China. The United States government is increasingly isolated in its policy of nonrecognition and nontrade. Whatever may be the merits of the United States position, it is not aided by the fact that every year we are forced to go through the tedious and embarrassing effort of keeping Red China out of the United Nations. As with these other matters, the United Nations is not responsible for creating or even for perpetuating the basic problem. It does, however, spotlight our position, and it makes additional demands upon the diplo-

matic skills and resources of an already harassed and burdened great
power.

An Appraisal   In each of the problems discussed above, and in many
others, the Soviet Union voted affirmatively. Unlike the United States, she
is in a position to do this at virtually no cost and with considerable propaganda profit. The Soviets thereby appear to demonstrate their fidelity to
the principles of the charter, associate themselves wholeheartedly and
stridently with the newly independent nations, and help to embarrass the
United States. It is easy to exaggerate the significance of such rhetorical
and symbolic triumphs for the Soviets, but it is also easy to underrate or
overlook them. The beguiling misconception, not uncommon in the underdeveloped nations, that the West is incurably hostile if not downright
colonialist and that the Soviet Union is the champion of national self-
determination and development is powerfully and emotionally underscored
by these votes and the diplomatic skirmishing associated with them.

The character of such problems will change over time, but the fact that
participation in the United Nations requires frequent policy decisions and
intricate diplomatic maneuvering will not.

The broad implication of the above discussion has been that this additional element of decision and maneuver has been and is likely to be rather
difficult and sometimes clearly disadvantageous for the United States. It is
possible, of course, and quite reasonable, to argue the reverse of this, to
contend that this necessity of frequently taking public positions and persistently being required to engage in diplomatic bargaining over resolutions
is a positive good. The position one takes on this depends, as might be
expected, on whether one believes our policy-making process tends to
promote stagnation or to be responsive to changing needs. Those who
worry about the extra demands that United Nations participation makes
on our diplomacy are by and large either satisfied with the traditional
policy process or disapprove of it because it is *too* responsive to the kinds
of influences that are predominant at the United Nations. Those who are
not concerned about, but who in fact welcome, these United Nations–
inspired demands tend to be those who believe our policy process is too
prone to inertia and to the blind pursuit of established policies whether
they retain their appropriateness or not.

So it is that the anxieties expressed above generally originate from
sources whose primary concerns are such traditional areas of American
interest as Europe and the Far East, whereas those who welcome the United
Nations' pressing role tend to be those whose focus is on the newly independent, underdeveloped, and numerous countries of Africa and South
Asia. This overview of the problems posed by United Nations votes and
United Nations diplomacy should not be construed as implying that the
traditional concerns are necessarily or always the more significant ones.

Each case must be decided on its own merits within the context of the existing conditions.

The "Parliament of Man" Myth

Another problem associated with the passage of resolutions in the United Nations is the tendency in some quarters, at home and abroad, to attach excessive moral and legal weight to them. As a leading authority on the United Nations has written,

> . . . The beginning of wisdom for the student of international organization . . . is to learn to avoid the illusion that decisions made by many states, whether they be small or great powers, are, simply because of their collective origin, almost automatically superior in wisdom and righteousness to decisions made by individual states.[20]

The notion that the United Nations—in this case, usually the General Assembly—is a "Parliament of Man," imbued with a special legal and/or moral stature, holds a great fascination for some unsophisticated minds and serves as a useful propaganda gimmick for others. It is usually tied up, at least unconsciously, with the notion that the General Assembly is a democratic legislature that faithfully mirrors "world public opinion."

There are several difficulties with this set of assumptions. Perhaps the basic problem centers in the concept of a "world public opinion." This phrase has a grand ring to it, but it is largely devoid of content. It is difficult enough to discern what "public opinion" in one country is—if indeed it exists at all in any meaningful sense on any given issue—but any attempt to find out what everyone, or nearly everyone, in the world believes about some matter is doomed to failure from the outset. There is a myriad of differing interests, levels of information, and value systems in the world; in short, there are a great many "publics" with equally as many opinions.

But even if one were to set these objections aside as being either irrelevant or pedantic, there would still be the problem of the extent to which General Assembly decisions are in any sense "democratic." Many of the governments whose representatives speak and vote in the General Assembly are anything but popularly elected governments. But this is the least of the problems. A much more serious objection relates to the way populations are represented in the General Assembly. To cite merely one example, the continent of Africa now has well over thirty votes in the General Assembly and a population of somewhat under 250 million. China, with about 700 million people, has no vote at all and upon admission would have only one; and India, with over 400 million people, has only one vote. These kinds of arrangements can scarcely be called democratic in any ordinary sense of that term.

[20] Claude, *Swords into Plowshares*, p. 24.

But even if these disparities between voting strength and population statistics could be eliminated—and they almost certainly cannot—and even if a broad consensus does exist on some issue or other, Assembly resolutions would still not constitute anything like supranational mandates and would still not merit acceptance as legally or morally binding documents. Until that unlikely day when nations turn over their sovereignty to some supranational body, the source of legitimacy is still the nation itself. The source of morality may not be so altogether restricted; that is, it is quite reasonable to regard moral principles as being applicable everywhere and at all times, regardless of whether any particular government or nation accepts or practices them. But even from this natural-law perspective, it requires considerable faith and even greater innocence to believe that Assembly resolutions will of necessity reflect such universal moral principles.

As one descends from these idealistic heights to the more mundane realities of the world, the "Parliament of Man" notion becomes no more appropriate. Real parliaments reflect, albeit usually imperfectly, the existing power configurations in any society. In the international arena, power attaches to such things as military strength, economic productivity, diplomatic skill, and so forth. These factors are not inconsequential in the General Assembly—a single great power usually wields much more influence than a single small power—but neither are they controlling.

So, whether one ascribes to the "Parliament of Man" notion an idealistic or a more realistic content, the General Assembly fails to measure up to the requirements. Assembly resolutions are political documents that, because of their source, merit careful and prudent treatment by sovereign nations. But to invest them with anything approaching a binding or even an especially solemn quality is to misconstrue their intrinsic significance as well as their likely impact.

United Nations Rhetoric

The concept of a parliament serves as a convenient bridge to the next type of criticism often leveled at the United Nations. As in real parliaments, there is an inordinate amount of speech making at the United Nations. To quote Senator Jackson's remarks again:

> Everyone talks too much. It is a world-wide disease. Sometimes it seems that the appropriate legend to place above the portals of the U. N. might be: "Through these doors pass the most articulate men and women in the world."

General de Gaulle is reported to have publicly delivered the following judgment regarding the United Nations:

> [It is] a permanent scandal marked by intemperate speeches, by warlike threats and by absurd efforts on the part of different blocs to outbid each other.[21]

[21] As quoted in Edmond Taylor, "Why de Gaulle Stayed Home," *The Reporter*, vol. 23, no. 7, p. 29, Oct. 27, 1960.

There is surely some truth, as well as gross exaggeration, to this type of observation. The United Nations is a major platform for many smaller and newly independent nations. It is a natural forum for the airing of their just grievances and their petty recriminations alike, and their language is often intemperate. As Ernst Haas has written, "Revolutionary style thrives on apocalyptic language, immoderate threats, and manufactured international crises." But, as he also commented, ". . . shoe-thumping, name-calling, unbearably long harangues by bearded heroes dressed in green fatigues, uncompromising language, appeals to some universal brotherhood—whether of the black, the downtrodden, or the victims of various conspiracies, *are aspects of style rather than of policy.*"[22]

The last eight words are the crucial ones, and their import is that United Nations speech making should not be taken too seriously. Because the United Nations is in New York City and because the press coverage is extensive, it is quite easy to get a distorted picture of the importance of such exercises, and it is especially easy to ascribe too great an influence on United States policy makers to this sometimes bizarre talking-shop. The fact is that the interminable rhetoric flowing out of the various United Nations institutions should not and does not weigh heavily on Washington officials. A high discount factor is applied and should be. The irritation implicit in Senator Jackson's and others' remarks about this incurable tendency is understandable, but it is not suggestive of the actual relationship between the forum in New York and the decision makers in Washington or anywhere else.

Moreover, it should be noted that this excessive, often immoderate, and sometimes vicious stream of verbiage is not without its positive aspects. There is a therapeutic value to all this letting off of steam. In part because the intrinsic significance of United Nations speech making tends to be overrated by many inexperienced new nations, these exercises can be useful substitutes for other and less desirable manifestations of frustration and resentment. Even if the United Nations were nothing more than a grand talking-shop—and it is, of course, more than that—it would be worth preserving. All that is required of the American government and public in this connection is that they maintain some perspective about the real meaning of much of the rhetoric reverberating in the chambers and corridors of the United Nations.

Moreover, it should be borne in mind, especially by a free society, that open forums can be used by all sides in a controversy. The United States has used and will continue to use the United Nations for the propagation of its own views. We are not a helpless recipient of all manner of advice, special pleading, and denunciation. We are an active participant in the

---

[22] "Dynamic Environment and Static System: Revolutionary Regimes in the United Nations," in Morton A. Kaplan (ed.), *The Revolution in World Politics*, John Wiley & Sons, Inc., New York, 1962, pp. 274, 273. Italics added.

rhetorical exercises. The skill with which we do this is a matter of some consequence.

Finally, much can be learned about the attitudes, fears, suspicions, hopes, and, therefore, the policies of member nations by listening to the grand debates with a trained and sensitive ear. The United Nations does indeed provide a window to the world that ordinary diplomacy does not if only a nation can develop the skill and the patience required to see through it.

Red China

There are other problems associated with United States participation in the United Nations. Among the most discussed, if not the most significant, of these is the possibility of Communist China's becoming a member. There are many legal and political problems involved in this matter, and it is far from clear that she would accept membership in the manner in which it is most likely to be offered. Among the many legal problems are whether she should be regarded as a new member or merely as a successor government to the Nationalist Chinese. If the former, presumably Nationalist China (or the United States) could veto her application for membership, and that would be the end of it, at least technically. If the latter, the veto may not apply, at least regarding membership in the General Assembly. But what, then, would become of the Chinese permanent seat on the Security Council? Would that continue to be occupied by the Taiwan government? To put it another way, how might the Taiwan government be removed from this seat legally?

There are nearly as many answers to these questions as there are legal and political experts disposed to answer them. How or whether they will be resolved in practice are imponderable questions at this writing. As mentioned above, the United States resistance to Red Chinese entry into the United Nations is becoming increasingly difficult to sustain in the face of such major defections as France. Great Britain has long favored Red Chinese admission into the United Nations, and it seems likely that the United States will not be able to block it many more years.

The question of whether the United States should continue to resist it is an interesting but largely impractical one. It is impractical for two reasons: The United States probably cannot stop it indefinitely (because, as mentioned above, the question of where and whether the veto applies is not altogether clear); and it seems unlikely that any American administration in the foreseeable future would dare to soften our opposition, whatever its private attitudes might be. It is—or at least it is thought to be—one of the sacred cows of American politics; to favor Red China's admission into the United Nations, or even to consider the matter, is allegedly regarded by a substantial portion of the population as nearly treasonous. Whether most of the public really does hold this view or whether it still would in the aftermath of a Presidential "educational campaign" on the facts of international life and on the desirability of having contacts with one's adversaries are open questions.

The major question for the future, then, is what China's admission will mean to the United Nations and United States relations thereto. To put it another way, what difference will it make when China joins the organization? Much depends, of course, on whether she gains the permanent seat on the Security Council with the attendant veto or whether she simply gains a seat in the General Assembly. Assuming that it is the former, what impact would this have on the utility of the United Nations from the standpoint of American interests? Some have suggested that it would destroy the usefulness of the United Nations and that it should prompt our withdrawal. Why this should be the case is not made clear, however, and the opinion usually comes from those elements in American life that misunderstand and fear the United Nations. The assumptions are almost certainly false. The Red Chinese would have no more luck in trying to control the United Nations than the Soviets have had. And even if they did exercise an influence inimical to our interests, there is very little that they could do with the United Nations that would seriously harm Western interests.

But even if one assumes that they could in fact instigate much mischief from the inside, that does not mean that the appropriate response in terms of American interests is to withdraw. The Soviets have been shrewd and patient enough to stay with the institution during all the trying years when it has been effectively controlled by forces unfriendly to their interests as they see them. We could profit from that example. Even if the admission of Red China meant the crippling of the United Nations' positive functions in international affairs—and this seems unlikely—the United States should remain in the institution. There are at least two compelling reasons for this. First of all, we could act as a check on any pernicious designs for the organization advocated by the Chinese (or, for that matter, anyone else). To withdraw would be to increase the stature and influence within the organization of the very forces we are determined to resist in the international arena. It would be foolhardy to hand them such an easy victory and such a useful tool. Withdrawal would serve no purpose whatever, save the cheap thrill of snubbing our noses at the Chinese and all other foreign governments whose policies we found distasteful. Secondly, the gesture would be widely resented and would diminish rather than refurbish our stature and our reputation for intelligence, maturity, and prudence in foreign affairs. The inevitable consequence would be a decline in American influence outside as well as inside the United Nations.

If Red China comes into the Security Council and has a veto, the positive role of the United Nations will surely decline and perhaps disappear altogether. Moreover, the level of irritation stemming from proceedings at the United Nations will increase perceptibly. It will, once again, be a time for a cool calculation of what policies will best serve the national interest and not an occasion for indulging ourselves in the expensive luxuries of petulance and withdrawal.

The Politics of the Secretary-General

The final concern to be discussed herein relates to the nature and policy orientation of the Secretariat, especially the Secretary-General himself. It has been noted above that the Secretariat is playing an expanding and somewhat independent role in United Nations affairs. It is therefore a matter of legitimate concern that that body be motivated by intentions that are, at the very least, not in conflict with Western interests. The first Secretary-General (1946–1953) was Trygve Lie, a Norwegian, and the second was Dag Hammarskjöld (1953–1961), a Swede. Both of these statesmen made genuine and admirable efforts to behave in accordance with the model of a wholly impartial international civil servant, and both were moderately successful, at least for a time. Both, however, ultimately became anathema to the Soviet Union, which came to regard each of them as pro-Western. There can be no doubt, moreover, that in their private attitudes, both of them were pro-Western. Whether this private set of preferences influenced their performance in office to anything like the extent that the Soviets claimed is an open question. But there can be little doubt that the personal political attitudes of any Secretary-General are bound to influence his performance to some extent, however subtly and even unconsciously.

Therefore, the assumption of that office by U Thant of Burma disturbed many Americans. His selection in 1961 after the death of Hammarskjöld was clearly a reflection of the growing numerical strength of the non-aligned, non-European, underdeveloped, largely newly independent, and largely nonwhite members of the United Nations. (This strength, by the way, is also reflected in the increasing number of persons from nonaligned nations who are assuming positions of prominence in the entire Secretariat.) The United States government strongly supported his selection, but many wondered whether this was out of political expediency rather than real conviction.

In office, U Thant has provided a good deal of ammunition for those who mistrust him and for those who approve of him. He is more outspoken than either of his predecessors and has not resisted the temptation to lecture both of the superpowers on matters vitally important to them. He has gone to Moscow and publicly chastised the Soviet government for its secrecy, its unwillingness to pay for peace-keeping expenses, and its unwillingness to provide the Russian people with accurate information about the United Nations. He has urged compromise on both sides in the disarmament negotiations. He has publicly told the United States government, among other things, that it does not understand the "fact" that the cold war has radically changed its character and that it is therefore unnecessarily perpetuating old divisions and animosities. He has also declared flatly that our Southeast Asian policies are doomed to failure and that China should be admitted to the United Nations.

Many people resent these excursions into national policy by U Thant. And some go so far as to charge him with overt favoritism toward the Soviets. But it seems abundantly clear that U Thant is nothing more or less than a classic representative of the nonaligned nations. From our perspective, he may be a bit naïve regarding the Soviets and the Chinese, and too outspoken for a person in his position. But it is very difficult to believe, for example, that the author of the following remarks, spoken to the General Assembly on November 26, 1963, at a unique session honoring assassinated President Kennedy, is in any important sense anti-American:

> All of us at the United Nations felt that we had lost a friend—not only a friend of the Organization, not only a friend of peace, but a friend of man. . . . When a young and dynamic leader of a great country, with his brilliant promise only half fulfilled, is felled in the prime of life by an utterly incomprehensible and senseless act, the loss is not only a loss to the bereaved family, whose head he was, nor even the country over whose destinies he presided with rare ability and distinction as Head of State. It is a loss suffered by the entire world, by all humanity, for the late President embodied a rare and quite remarkable combination of intellect and courage, of vigor and compassion, of devotion to the arts and sciences—all focused on serving his basic concern for the well-being of mankind.

U Thant will not always be Secretary-General, of course, and the hypothetical possibility of an anti-American in that position is understandably a matter of concern. But that possibility is extremely remote due to the great influence of the Western world within the United Nations and to the simple fact that it would serve hardly any nation's interests to create such a condition. For the foreseeable future, this prospect is very dim indeed.

A Conclusion

This chapter has attempted to set forth the chief opportunities and the major problems for American foreign policy occasioned by the existence of the United Nations and United States participation therein. It has also attempted, in the light of this analysis, to suggest what attitudes and policies are most appropriate for the leader of the Western world, upon whom unique responsibilities devolve.

This analysis and these prescriptions are necessarily time-bound. The United Nations, like all other human institutions, is changing all the time It is not today what it was ten years ago, and it will not be ten years from now what it is today. What it will be like even in the near future is difficult to surmise. It certainly will not be a world government; it may even collapse. There is no inevitable pattern of evolution for the institution. It may serve United States interests better or it may serve them less well;

only time will tell. It is therefore the responsibility of American administrations constantly to reassess the precise nature of American policy in and attitudes toward the United Nations. In this, as in other matters, the guide should be neither starry-eyed idealism nor selfish cynicism, but rather a sober assessment of what serves the enlightened self-interest of this strong, proud, free, and humane nation.

Selected Bibliography

Bloomfield, Lincoln P., et al.: *International Military Forces,* Little, Brown and Company, Boston, 1964. A sophisticated set of essays about an important subject.

————: *The United Nations and U.S. Foreign Policy,* Little, Brown and Company, Boston, 1960. A generally sensible overview of a widely misunderstood topic.

Claude, Inis L., Jr.: *Swords into Plowshares, The Problems and Progress of International Organization,* 3d ed., Random House, New York, 1964. Probably the best book on the United Nations and related institutions.

Gardner, Richard N.: *In Pursuit of World Order, U.S. Foreign Policy and International Organizations,* Frederick A. Praeger, Inc., New York, 1964. An informed book by a high-ranking government official.

Lefever, Ernest W.: *Crisis in the Congo, A U.N. Force in Action,* The Brookings Institution, Washington, D. C., 1965. The emphasis is on the meaning of this important operation for United States foreign policy.

Nicholas, H. G.: *The United Nations as a Political Institution,* 2d ed., Oxford University Press, Fairlawn, N. J., 1962. A wise book by a British scholar.

Stoessinger, John, et al.: *Financing the United Nations System,* The Brookings Institution, Washington, D. C., 1964. An intelligent discussion of a pressing issue.

U.S. Department of State: *U.S. Participation in the UN., Report by the President to the Congress for the Year 19–,* Washington, D. C. (an annual publication).

Justice without might is gainsaid,
because there are always offenders;
might without justice is condemned.
We must then combine justice and might,
and for this end make what is just
strong, or what is strong, just.

Pascal

chapter 7

Introduction

Military policies, like all other policies, are rational to the extent to which they are realistically related to some desired objective or objectives. These objectives may be modest and respectful of the rights and interests of others, or they may be ambitious and contemptuous of the rights and interests of others.

The basic *military* objective of the United States is to contain the spread of Communist or other hostile regimes and thereby to protect the security of the United States. It is hoped that this can be achieved by convincing them in advance that any military adventures they might engage in would be resisted and defeated. That is, the United States hopes to *deter* Communist military aggression by making its likely consequences unattractive to its perpetrators. In order to do this, the United States—along with its allies—maintains large and expensive military forces. And if these *deterrents* are not successful—that is, if aggression occurs anyway—the armed forces will (presumably) be employed to throw back and perhaps punish the aggressors.

The military policy of the United States, therefore, is designed to serve essentially *defensive* objectives, or purposes. For this reason, the term "defense policy" is a more precise characterization than "military policy," and will be employed herein.[1] The United States has no territorial ambitions as such and has no strong desire to impose policies on other nations, except insofar as another nation's policies affect America's vital interests. It is conceivable, of course, that someday the United States may initiate military action, but almost certainly this would be for essentially defensive purposes. If, for example, the United States should ever invade Cuba, the objective would be more to eliminate a threat to the security of the United States than it would be to satisfy an expansionist urge or to impose a certain set of policies unrelated to defensive considerations.

Admittedly, these distinctions are difficult to make. They involve an assessment of the *motives* of official policy, and that is always a risky enterprise. Moreover, these distinctions may appear to carry an implicit moral judgment, "offensive" intentions being bad and "defensive" intentions being good. This is not altogether an unwarranted inference, but neither is it a necessary or crucial one. It is simply a fact that the United States today is essentially a "satisfied," *status quo*–oriented power. This has not

---

[1] The term "defense policy" is meant to cover both the question of what types and amounts of military force are desirable *and* the question of how and when they should be used. Both of these questions are policy questions that bear directly on whether a defense establishment is realistically related to the objectives of the government.

always been the case, of course, as anyone familiar with the origins of our present boundaries and overseas possessions can testify. But it is true today, and it follows, therefore, that we are a defensive power in the international arena, even if we should in the future initiate military action abroad.

In a world of satisfied and/or nonbelligerent nations, there would be no need for the implementation of or even the existence of defense policies. If, for example, international policies were typified by the relations between the United States and Canada or the United States and Great Britain, there would be no real need either for armed forces or for doctrines regarding their use. But unfortunately these examples are exceptional rather than typical, and hence the maintenance of armed forces is a normal aspect of the policies of nearly all nations. It is, of course, possible to abandon military strength even in the kind of world in which we live, and pacifists recommend doing so. But pacifists have seldom, if ever, controlled the policies of any nation and will almost certainly never control the policies of the United States. Therefore, the rest of this chapter will assume that the possession of a military capability is appropriate for the United States, and the discussion will center on *what kind* of military capability has been, is being, and should be maintained by the United States and *how* it has been, is being, and should be used.[2]

There is no "natural" or permanently appropriate defense policy for the United States. A wise government will change its policies, perhaps radically, as it adjusts to such variable factors as modern technology, the nation's economic capacity to sustain its defense efforts, the adversary's capabilities, and the adversary's intentions. It is a complex and difficult job to try to adjust to technological change, and the question of how much defense expenditure the economy can or should bear is endlessly debatable. Moreover, in attempting to ascertain the adversary's capabilities, a government is always dealing to some extent in the unknown; and the attempt to establish with any certitude the adversary's intentions necessarily approaches, if it does not enter, the realm of the unknowable. Therefore, a government's defense policy is always and unavoidably based not only on expertise but also on estimates, guesses, and even hunches. *This is true even when the government is making a conscious and intelligent effort to relate its defense policy to its objectives and the challenges confronting the nation.* The fact that this effort is not always made—and that sometimes the need for it is not even perceived—merely means that defense policies, like all other policies, can run the gamut from brilliant and suited to the objectives to absurd and irrelevant. American defense policies in the postwar world have ordinarily been somewhere in between these poles.

What follows is a description and analysis of some of the major events affecting and some of the important changes in American defense policy

---

[2] Pacifism will be discussed in Chap. 9.

since the end of World War II, after which there will be a more detailed analysis of selected contemporary defense problems.

Background

As American expectations about Soviet intentions underwent their somber changes in the postwar years, so did American defense policy. But the latter changed much more slowly. In 1945 and 1946, as United States–Soviet relations were seriously deteriorating, the United States was rushing to dismantle its superb military establishment.

The war having been won and the urge to "bring the boys back home" being controlling, the United States demobilized with great haste. There were some high-ranking government officials who viewed this spectacle with grave apprehension, and who perceived the relationship between this "unilateral disarmament" and the American capacity to back up its foreign policies in Europe and elsewhere. For the most part, however, there was not much resistance to demobilization even from those persons who were most apprehensive about Soviet intentions. In peacetime, it had long been an American tradition to divorce one's thoughts about defense and foreign policies. The fact that the two were intimately related was not as obvious to most Americans then as it is today. It was, therefore, one thing to reach a consensus on the need to contain the Soviet Union; it was quite another to devise and effectuate a defense policy calculated to achieve the objective of containment.

The June, 1947, speech that launched the Marshall Plan had an exclusively economic theme and prescription. By 1948 the emphasis was shifting, as the United States began to push for the creation of a peacetime alliance that would commit her to the defense of Europe. The result was the North Atlantic Treaty of April, 1949, which created the North Atlantic Treaty Organization (NATO), whose membership consisted of the United States, Canada, Great Britain, France, Italy, the Netherlands, Belgium, Luxembourg, Portugal, Denmark, Norway, and Iceland. (Greece, Turkey, and West Germany joined later on.) NATO will be discussed at some length later in this chapter. At this point it needs to be understood solely as a manifestation of America's emerging recognition of the need for confronting what was deemed to be a Soviet military threat with countervailing military power. In addition, as the first peacetime military alliance in American history, it marked a recognition on the part of the United States that our fate is intimately bound up with the fate of Western Europe and Britain.

Even so, defense expenditures—and therefore defense capabilities—lagged far behind the verbalization of cold-war needs. In fiscal 1948 defense expenditures reached a postwar low of $11.8 billion. In fiscal 1949 they climbed slightly to $12.9 billion, thus beginning the gradual rise of the late 1940s, which reflected belatedly the sobered view then being taken about the character of postwar Soviet policy. But in fiscal 1950, which ended just as the Korean War began, defense expenditures were still only $13 billion. Despite the deepening cold war, despite the fact that the Soviet Union had exploded its first atomic weapon in 1949, and despite the gaping disparity between NATO and Soviet military force levels,[3] there was little disposition here or in Europe to invest vast sums of money in a defense structure that would bear some realistic relationship to the alleged Soviet threat. Obligations and objectives far outstripped the capacity to support them; practice had not caught up with doctrine.

The North Korean invasion of South Korea accomplished what abstract thought and exhortation from various sources had not: The United States began to rearm in earnest. After 1950 the major questions about American defense policy were less questions about *whether* the United States should have a large peacetime military establishment, and were more questions about *what kind* of large military establishment we should have, and *under what kinds of circumstances it, or part of it, should be used.* The Korean War raised these questions in very stark terms and touched off debates about defense policy that in one form or another persist to this day and promise to continue for as long as military forces are retained. For this and other reasons, the Korean War merits some detailed analysis.

The Korean War

Four Phases

The Korean War can be divided into four phases. In the first phase, lasting for approximately two months after the outbreak of hostilities in late June, 1950, the North Korean Army nearly conquered the entire peninsula. The remaining South Korean defenders and a hastily brought together, ill-prepared, and ill-equipped American force—brought over from rather more pleasant duties in Japan—were holding on grimly to a small perimeter around the city of Pusan; the rest of Korea was in the hands of the "Korean People's Army."

The second phase began spectacularly on September 15, when American Marines staged a successful amphibious landing at Inchon, a port city near the capital city of Seoul, far behind the North Korean front lines. Faced with a two-front war and vastly strengthened South Korean and American forces, increasingly supplemented by token contributions from other

---

[3] In the late 1940s there were approximately twelve understrength Western divisions in Europe compared to approximately twenty-five full-strength Soviet divisions in Central Europe, backed up by at least 140 other Soviet divisions. See Robert E. Osgood, *NATO: The Entangling Alliance*, The University of Chicago Press, Chicago, 1962, p. 29.

United Nations members,[4] the North Korean Army began to dissolve. A portentous decision then faced the United States government: Should the scattered and largely beaten North Korean Army be pursued into North Korea and the country reunited by force, or should the object of the war be merely to reinstate the conditions prevailing before the war began? The major risk in pushing on was the possibility of Chinese intervention. It was decided that this risk should be taken, and on October 1, the 38th parallel—the dividing line between North and South Korea, which had been established as the "temporary" demarcation line between the Soviet and American zones of occupation in 1945—was crossed by South Korean troops. On the same day, General Douglas MacArthur, the commander of United Nations forces in Korea, broadcast a demand for the immediate surrender of the North Korean Army.

In mid-October, General MacArthur and President Harry S Truman met on Wake Island in the mid-Pacific in an atmosphere of impending victory and issued a statement, which, among other things, was designed to demonstrate that they had no policy differences regarding either the objectives or the conduct of the war. On November 24, MacArthur launched an offensive designed to wipe out the last resistance in North Korea and end the war.

The third phase of the war began the following day, November 25, when American troops encountered the army of Communist China. The first intelligence to the effect that the Red Chinese were about to intervene was received in early November. It had caused grave concern in Washington, but MacArthur was unruffled. Suddenly the nightmare became a reality, and the overextended, divided, outnumbered, and therefore highly vulnerable United Nations forces were confronted with a new enemy, a new war. With great heroism and skill, and an appalling number of casualties, the United Nations forces managed to retreat in some order. But they were two-thirds of the way back down the peninsula before they were able to halt the Chinese in January, 1951. By April, they had pushed the Chinese back across the 38th parallel on the central and eastern fronts, while stopping south of the parallel in the west. In April and May, the Chinese launched two major offensives and managed to push the United Nations forces back into South Korea, but their objective of winning the war was effectively denied them. By July, the United Nations forces had moved back into North Korea, improving slightly on their position as of

[4] Throughout the first year of the war, the United States forces always constituted more than half of the United Nations force, and, in the early stages, much more than half. By 1963, the last year of the war, United Nations forces numbered over 750,000, with the South Koreans providing about 400,000 of them. Other United Nations member contributions totaled about 44,000, which was numerically small but not insignificant; and, of course, these contributions had some symbolic importance. From beginning to end, the United Nations military operation in Korea was controlled by the United States government.

early April. By this time, there were indications on both sides that a truce would be acceptable along lines roughly equivalent to the 38th parallel.

The fourth phase of the war was the stalemate that lasted until the truce in July, 1953. Despite some serious and costly battles, only minor rearrangements of the front lines occurred, and the truce line was essentially the same as the front lines had been for two years.

The Debate about Objectives

It should be clear from even this sketchy outline of the course of the war that it raised fundamental questions about the nature of American defense policy. The Korean War was among the most frustrating and divisive experiences in American history. The total casualties among American military personnel numbered 142,091, and 33,629 lost their lives. Yet there was no "victory" in the traditional sense; and equally important, after the Chinese intervention, there was no attempt to achieve it. Needless to say, there was an immense and acrimonious controversy about this in the United States, inside and outside the government.

The root question was: What is (are) the purpose(s) of our participation in this war? The Truman administration answered this question one way, and General MacArthur and a host of other Americans answered it in quite another. The debate divided sharply along partisan lines, thus adding that especially divisive element to the already highly charged atmosphere. Truman's original decision to commit American troops in Korea appears to have been based primarily on the notion that aggression must be opposed or it will become attractive to too many governments and the security of the United States will sooner or later be endangered thereby. This leaves open the question of whether the aggressor shall merely be checked or whether he shall be punished, or even defeated, as well. After Inchon, this question broke rather suddenly on the President and his advisers. Urged on by MacArthur and the heady successes then being experienced, the President decided to go beyond merely reinstating the prewar boundaries and instead to defeat the aggressor and reunite Korea. This was an expansive view of the objective of the war.

But Truman did not regard this objective as a necessary one, to be achieved at all costs. He was willing to run some risks—for example, Chinese intervention—and to incur some costs—for example, increased loss of life. After the intervention of the Chinese, however, he regarded the risks and costs of this objective as too high. He therefore abandoned the objective and replaced it with a more limited one: the restoration of the prewar boundaries. The aggression would have been resisted and a lesson would perhaps have been taught thereby.

General MacArthur and his supporters regarded this view as unworthy of an American administration. In attacking it, the General made two kinds of arguments, one purportedly based on abstract principle and the other of a more pragmatic character. These two kinds of arguments are not always compatible, but in public debates such niceties are often obscured or overlooked altogether.

General MacArthur made the first kind of argument in a letter to Joseph Martin, the Republican (Minority) Leader in the House of Representatives, written on March 20, 1951. Martin had recently made a flamboyant speech, in which he had called for a Nationalist Chinese invasion of China and had said, among other things, "If we are not in Korea to win, then this administration should be indicted for the murder of thousands of American boys." Martin had then written a letter to MacArthur, enclosing a copy of his speech and asking if the General would comment on the suggestion that Nationalist Chinese be permitted to invade China. MacArthur replied that Martin's views ". . . follow the conventional pattern of meeting force with maximum counterforce, as we have never failed to do in the past. . . . There is no substitute for victory."[5]

This last sentence has become something of a battle cry in certain political circles in the United States. (See Chapter 1 for a discussion of the related slogan of "total victory over communism.") General MacArthur reinforced it in his dramatic speech to a joint session of Congress after being relieved of his command by President Truman for insubordination: "In war, indeed, there can be no substitute for victory."[6] And in his own testimony before the Senate Committees investigating his dismissal, he commented as follows:

> I do unquestionably state that when men become locked in battle . . . there should be no artifice under the name of politics, which should handicap your own men, decrease their chances for winning, and increase their losses.[7]

According to this line of argument, a negotiated settlement of a war is wrong in principle. There should be no calculation about the comparative advantages and disadvantages of seeking victory or seeking a truce. The former is *always* the appropriate objective; the latter is *never* so.

This position has a simplicity and emotional flavor to it that appeal to many people. But it is ultimately indefensible. Only an adventurer or a madman would engage in modern warfare simply for the sake of winning

---

[5] *Hearings on the Military Situation in the Far East of the Senate Committee on Armed Services and the Committee on Foreign Relations.* 82d Cong., 1st Sess., 1950, pt. 5. The quotation from Martin's speech appears on p. 3178, his letter to MacArthur and the latter's reply on p. 3182. These momentous hearings were instituted "to conduct an inquiry into the military situation in the Far East and the facts surrounding the relief of General of the Army Douglas MacArthur from his assignments in that area." Their five volumes report one of the most exhaustive and important congressional investigations ever held. Hereinafter, they shall be referred to as *MacArthur Hearings.*

[6] *Ibid.,* pt. 5, p. 3557.

[7] *Ibid.,* pt. 1, p. 45.

a war. Wars, if they are to be at all rational, must be fought in pursuit of some objective(s) other than simply victory. If that objective (or those objectives) can be achieved by something short of victory, victory is not a reasonable objective. It is a reasonable objective only if it is necessary as a step toward some broader, political objectives.[8]

General MacArthur's usage of such phrases probably reflected more his temperament and skill as an orator than they did his considered opinion. A man of his brilliance and erudition could hardly have been unaware of and unimpressed by Clausewitz's famous dictum that "war is only a continuation of state policy by other means." And, as a matter of fact, General MacArthur did base his opposition to administration policy on something more substantial than these misleading and untenable slogans. The reason he disagreed with administration policy was that he did not regard the liberation of North Korea as involving too many risks and costs. He came back to the more ambitious objective in Korea after the Chinese intervention had been turned back because he still regarded that objective as practical and reasonable. Thus, the General's real argument was a pragmatic one, and the slogan about there being no substitute for victory was probably merely a sop to his less intelligent supporters or a verbal flourish, or both.

---

[8] The word "political" is, of course, among the most ambiguous in the English language. The meaning of such related words as "economic" and "military" is nearly self-evident, but what does it mean to refer to "political objectives"? No attempt will be made herein to resolve a problem that has engaged the attention of scholars for years, but it is necessary to suggest something of what is meant by the term in this book. At its base, an objective is "political" if it relates to who governs whom, where, and how. In the Korean War, for example, the immediate political objective of the United States was to prevent the communization of South Korea. The objective dictated our immediate military objective. When the question arose as to whether we should expand our objectives to include the liberation of North Korea as well, that was a political question. So, later on, was the question of whether a truce should be entered into.

Of course, in answering such questions, military considerations were of fundamental importance. Political objectives, if they are to be at all rational, must be realistically related to the means available for achieving them, and those means may be military— or economic or psychological, or some combination of these. But not all objectives that are feasible are appropriate, and the question of whether they should be pursued is a political question.

In making judgments about what political objectives should be pursued, a government should—and usually does—take a multitude of factors into consideration. In the Korean case, the Truman administration was gravely worried about Western vulnerability in Europe, and this affected its view of how much of our power should be concentrated in the Far East. MacArthur and his supporters had a different set of priorities and a different angle of vision. They wanted to pursue different and more ambitious objectives in Korea. This was a dispute over high policy; it was political in character.

It should perhaps be emphasized that, as used herein, the term "political" should not be construed as having anything to do with partisan considerations. The word is often used that way, but herein it is not. When partisan considerations are at work they will be labeled "partisan," not "political."

The central point of this analysis thus far has been that armed conflict does not carry within it its own rationale or imply what its objectives are. Armed conflict is a process that can have many consequences, and can serve a variety of purposes. The responsibility of a government is to determine what those objectives should be in the light of the circumstances prevailing. The achievement of these objectives may require military victory or it may not, but the fact of war does not automatically answer the question of whether the appropriate objectives include victory on the battlefield.

Many of those who take the position just criticized do not really mean to say or imply that warfare by its very nature implies its own objective, namely "victory." What they mean, rather, is that victory is an intermediate objective on the way toward another and more important objective. This latter can be summarized as the elimination of the evil that brought on the war in the first place. Americans have traditionally had a moralistic attitude toward war. We have usually tried to avoid it, but once involved we have treated war as a grand crusade. We have tended to look upon each war as having something of the character of Armageddon. And when the forces of good confront the forces of evil, it is the responsibility of the former to crush and eliminate the latter. In crusades, there are no uncertainties and no moral ambiguities, and the necessary and obvious objective is victory.

But crusades, at least in the secular world, are notoriously ineffectual or self-deluding or fraudulent or dangerous, or even all of these things. Evil is never going to be extirpated from human affairs, and this will be so even if it is true in a given clash that one cause is largely virtuous and the other debased. It follows, therefore, that even victory is no guarantee that desirable objectives can be achieved; they may or they may not be. And since victory is no panacea, it must take its place alongside other possible objectives in time of war, to be sought or not on the basis of a detached assessment of what intermediate objective(s) will best serve the interests of the United States. Note that, therefore, it is not a matter of "principle" whether victory is an appropriate objective; it is, instead— and much less dramatically—merely a matter of calculating the advantages and disadvantages of various objectives, comparing them, and making a prudential choice.

The question of whether Truman's or MacArthur's objective was the more appropriate one is a separate matter and one that is destined to be in endless dispute. No attempt will be made here to resolve it. But because of the intrinsic significance of the Korean War experience in American history and because a discussion of their policy differences affords a richer background for both the preceding and the following analysis, they will be further discussed in the following paragraphs.

The Korean War began less than one full year after Mao Tse-tung's Communist Chinese had achieved control of mainland China, forcing Chiang Kai-shek's Nationalist Chinese to flee to Taiwan, the Pescadores Islands, and a few small islands close to the mainland. The shock of that great tragedy was still fresh in the United States, and the hope that it could be undone was still lively. But no one had any clear idea of what could or should be done to support that hope. When the Chinese entered the Korean War, there were many who believed this misfortune could be turned into an opportunity, an opportunity to weaken and perhaps even destroy the Red Chinese regime.

General MacArthur shared this view. He had spent many years in the Far East before, during, and after World War II. The communization of China was something akin to a personal affront to this distinguished general who had so recently commanded the forces that liberated the Far East from its Japanese rulers. He did not regard the Chinese civil war as a finished chapter. Moreover, he was not distracted much by events in Europe or anywhere else. His focus was on the Far East, and he firmly believed that the decisive struggles between Communist and anti-Communist forces would take place there.

President Truman and his advisers, both military and civilian, had rather different perspectives. For them, the main arena was Europe, and they were therefore not anxious to become embroiled in large-scale activities in the Far East. They were less disturbed about the dismal fact that the Chinese civil war had been won by the Communists than they were about the dismal prospect that something similar might happen in Europe. Hence, while they were willing to enter the Korean War and would not tolerate a Communist victory there, they were not willing to attach the high priority to it that MacArthur did.

These differences began to manifest themselves early in the Korean War. On June 27 President Truman declared that the attack on South Korea made it plain that the Communists were going beyond subversion and were now using war as a means of conquering independent nations.

In these circumstances the occupation of Formosa by communist forces would be a direct threat to the security of the Pacific area and to the United States forces performing their lawful and necessary functions in that area.

Accordingly, I have ordered the Seventh Fleet to prevent any attack on Formosa. As a corollary of this action I am calling upon the Chinese Government of Formosa to cease all air and sea operations against the mainland. The Seventh Fleet will see that this is done. The determination of the future status of Formosa must await the restoration of security in the Pacific, a peace settlement with Japan, or consideration by the United Nations.

General MacArthur approved of Washington's decision to reverse its earlier policy of not being willing to protect Formosa, but he strongly disapproved of the rest of the message. He did not want to see Chiang's forces "neutralized," and he did not approve of the apparent willingness ultimately to consider the disposition of Formosa in some manner other than as a bastion of Nationalist and American power.

He and many prominent members of Congress who had dissented for many years from our "hands off" policy regarding the Chinese civil war, wanted a much stronger commitment to Chiang. This sentiment was reinforced when Chiang quickly offered Nationalist troops for use in Korea. The administration declined this offer; the last thing it wanted to do was to drag the Korean conflict into the Chinese civil war. MacArthur assured the administration that he would follow official policy, but there was much concern about this in Washington. When he flew to Formosa on July 31 for a conference with Chiang, and the latter then issued a ringing communiqué which asserted, among other things, that "the foundation . . . for Sino-American military cooperation has thus been laid,"[9] these apprehensions increased.

A more powerful and explicit challenge to official policy came from General MacArthur in late August. He sent a long message to the annual convention of the Veterans of Foreign Wars, excerpts of which follow:

In view of misconceptions currently being voiced concerning the relationship of Formosa to our strategic potential in the Pacific, I believe it in the public interest to avail myself of this opportunity to state my views thereon to you. . . .

[The Pacific Ocean] acts as a protective shield to all of the Americas and all free lands of the Pacific Ocean area we control to the shores of Asia by a chain of islands extending in an arc from the Aleutians to the Marianas held by us and our free Allies. From this island chain we can dominate with air power every Asiatic port from Vladivostok to Singapore and prevent any hostile movement into the Pacific.

If we hold this line we may have peace—lose it, and war is inevitable.

Nothing could be more fallacious than the threadbare argument by those who advocate appeasement and defeatism in the Pacific that if we defend Formosa we alienate continental Asia.

Those who speak thus do not understand the Orient. They do not grant that it is the pattern of Oriental psychology to respect and follow aggressive, resolute and dynamic leadership. . . .[10]

In this and the subsequent difficulties between the President and the

---

[9] *MacArthur Hearings*, pt. 5, p. 3383.
[10] *Ibid.*, pp. 3477–3480.

general, policy divergencies were only part of the problem. An even more pressing matter was whether the general was permitting his policy disagreements to lead him into outright insubordination. President Truman has written that he "gave serious thought" to relieving General MacArthur of his command because of this message,[11] and it is easy to see why. The whole tone of MacArthur's message was arrogant and condescending. Truman had only recently come around to the view that Formosa should be defended. Therefore, until June 27, only two months earlier, he presumably was among those who had "misconceptions . . . concerning the relationship of Formosa to our strategic potential in the Pacific." And he, presumably, had also been oblivious to the dictum that "if we hold this line we may have peace—lose it and war is inevitable." The most patronizing line of all was the one that outlined the type of leadership that, according to the general, "Oriental psychology" respects. Had the President been less than "aggressive, resolute and dynamic" prior to June 27? The implication was clear.

Beyond these matters of respect and decorum was, of course, the policy dispute about Formosa. MacArthur's message implied quite clearly that the island must become either an American military bastion, or an American-supported center of anti-Communist activity from "Vladivostok to Singapore." The Truman administration had embraced no such conception. The neutralization announcement of June 27 had explicitly stated that Nationalist Chinese would not be permitted to pursue either sea or air operations against the mainland. The President had just sent a letter to the American Ambassador to the United Nations in which he had outlined the United States position regarding Formosa. It had a very different tone and substance from the general's message. It declared that the neutralization was necessary as a safeguard to the security of the United Nations forces in Korea, but that the United States had "no designs on Formosa, and our action was not inspired by any desire to acquire a special position for the United States." It went on to say the legal status of Formosa was still undetermined and that "international action" would be required to determine its future. Finally, the President said that the United States "would welcome United Nations consideration of the case of Formosa."[12]

This letter of Truman's was designed to counter Communist allegations that the United States had decided to take over Formosa. It was part of a broader effort to conciliate allies and neutrals in an effort to gain support for the effort in Korea. Upon learning of MacArthur's message to the VFW, Truman ordered the general to withdraw it "because various features with respect to Formosa are in conflict with the policy of the United States and

---

[11] See Harry S Truman, *Memoirs*, vol. 2, *Years of Trial and Hope*, Doubleday & Company, Inc., Garden City, N.Y., 1956, p. 355.
[12] *MacArthur Hearings*, pt. 5, pp. 3476–3477.

its position in the United Nations."[13] The message had already leaked to the press, however, and the split was public knowledge.

As related above, the Inchon landings on September 15 changed the entire direction of the war. Within a short period, the North Korean forces were completely routed and the end of the war appeared near. The President and the general met at Wake Island and proclaimed their harmony.

The entrance of the Chinese into the war in November abruptly shattered all this, and the underlying differences of perspective and policy began to reappear with even greater clarity and meaning. As noted above, General MacArthur's differences with the administration after the Chinese intervention were not really, or at least not solely, based on anything so naïve or doctrinaire as the notion that "there is no substitute for victory." In more practical and reasonable terms, he arrived at different policy conclusions because he appraised the policy options differently, which led him to different and more ambitious objectives. In short, he believed the war could still be won, that it could be won at a tolerable cost, that the risks were not prohibitive, and that the failure to do so would be disastrous. The administration rejected this entire argument.

General MacArthur's specific proposals can be summarized as follows: (1) He wanted permission to bomb the "privileged sanctuary" of Manchuria from which Chinese air and ground strength crossed the Yalu River into Korea. (2) He wanted to blockade the coast of China. (3) He wanted to use Nationalist Chinese troops in Korea and perhaps in South China as well as a diversionary tactic. In sum, he wanted to bring the war home to the Chinese with the expectation that this would militarily and psychologically undermine the Chinese efforts in Korea, thereby facilitating a victory there for United Nations forces. He was powerfully supported in the United States by a resurgent Republican party, which had come close to capturing the Senate in the fall of 1950 and had reduced the Democratic majority in the House to a mere 36.

The war in Korea following the Chinese entry had become a major war with all the attendant costs, particularly in human lives. After their initial retreat of approximately 275 miles—the longest retreat in American military history—the United Nations forces had begun to counterattack in late January. From then until the truce talks began in July—and sporadically for two years thereafter—the war was a bitter, closely contested war of attrition. The urge to resolve it and end the slaughter was perfectly natural, especially for the commanding officer in the area.

Moreover, MacArthur was unimpressed by the reasons for caution that lay behind the administration's restrictive policy. He did not believe the Russians would enter the fray regardless of what actions the United States might take. He was equally unimpressed by the fact that the Europeans—

[13] *Ibid.*, p. 3480.

and the United Nations as a whole—were anxious to limit the war in Korea to that ravaged peninsula.

In short, he believed that the Chinese could be routed and Korea re-unified and that the attendant costs and risks were quite tolerable. This view, his temperament, the fact that his immense reputation as a man of decisive and heroic action was involved, and his occasional obsession with a perfectionist view of the purpose of warfare combine to explain his nearly total lack of sympathy with administration policy.

President Truman and his advisers had differing problems, purposes, and perspectives. Their primary concern had always been Europe, and after the Korean War broke out, they had taken the lead in attempting to strengthen NATO.

Dwight D. Eisenhower had been called out of military retirement to become the Supreme Allied Commander in Europe, and in early 1951 the administration provoked a storm of controversy by announcing that it intended to send four American divisions to Europe to join the two that were there.[14]

Soon after the United Nations forces had demonstrated their capacity to withstand and then to reverse the Chinese onslaught, the administration began to show an interest in a negotiated settlement. Having no abstract commitment to "victory" and being urged by the British and other members of the United Nations not to expand the war, the President and his advisers considered the various alternatives and the accompanying advantages and disadvantages, and decided that although they would not accept defeat in Korea, neither would they seek victory. They wanted to *limit* the war; it remained to be seen whether the Chinese would also come around to this position.

There were self-imposed limitations being observed on both sides. While United Nations aircraft attacked North Korea constantly and with some effect, Chinese planes seldom attacked South Korea. The Chinese air force was markedly inferior to the United Nations force, but this is not a sufficient explanation for their restraint. It seems likely that the Chinese feared reprisals, perhaps of a nuclear character. Nor did the Chinese bother the American Navy much. Again, any large-scale Chinese attacks would have been costly and probably would have induced reprisals, but the fact remains that they could have inflicted serious damage on the Navy and did not do so.

---

[14] This Soviet-focused, Europe-centered policy was forcefully underlined by General Omar N. Bradley, who told the Senators conducting the hearings on MacArthur's release that "enlargement of the war in Korea to include Red China would probably delight the Kremlin more than anything else we could do. It would necessarily tie down additional forces, especially our sea power and our air power, while the Soviet Union would not be obliged to put a single man into the conflict. . . .

"This strategy would involve us in the wrong war, at the wrong place, at the wrong time, and with the wrong enemy." *Ibid.,* pt. 2, pp. 731–732.

A mutual limitation was the restriction of the war to Korea itself. Mac-Arthur's call for attacks on Manchuria raised the possibility of retaliatory action such as Chinese attacks on the American "privileged sanctuary," Japan.

On its side, the United States did not commit anything like its full strength to the conflict and, significantly, refrained from using nuclear weapons. When the Korean War broke out, the United States no longer had a monopoly on nuclear weapons. It was assumed that the Soviet arsenal of nuclear weapons was small and that its means of delivery was comparatively unimpressive. But the Soviets did have the bomb, and this fact alone acted to restrain the United States. For this and other reasons related to the disadvantageous propaganda impact of their use, their dubious military utility in Korea, and, presumably, the element of caution that surrounds everything nuclear, the Truman administration decided not to use nuclear weapons in Korea.[15]

This delicate balance of limitations would have been seriously challenged and perhaps undermined by the acceptance of MacArthur's proposals to expand the action to include Manchuria. There was, of course, nothing formal or negotiated about these limitations that developed in the Korean War, but there was a widespread presumption that abandoning one would result in a rapid and dangerous expansion of the entire war.

As for blockading China, MacArthur's second suggestion, this was regarded as having few advantages and many disadvantages. A blockade necessarily involves the blockading nation in the threat or use of force against all those nations that desire to trade with the blockaded nation. If a blockade had been deemed very useful, it might have been employed. But the main source of supply for China was the neighboring Soviet Union, and a naval blockade would scarcely have affected their intercourse.

As for the use of Nationalist troops, the administration differed on two grounds. It had a much lower opinion of the utility of these troops than did MacArthur, and it was unwilling to involve itself once again in the Chinese civil war.

Finally, and especially after the miscalculations regarding the likely Chinese response to American involvement north of the 38th parallel, the administration was concerned about the Soviet response to any expansion of the war.

Behind all these technical and judgmental factors, however, lay an even more fundamental difference, one with contemporary significance. The administration looked on the Communist challenge as formidable and long-range. It wanted to *contain* that challenge, but it was reconciled to

---

[15] MacArthur, by the way, never proposed the use of nuclear weapons, but his pronouncements about the need for victory may have implied that it was being considered. At any rate, many of his supporters endorsed the idea.

living with it. It looked with suspicion on any crusade to "solve" the problem; for the foreseeable future it regarded the problem as unresolvable.

The general and his supporters regarded the Communist challenge as formidable but vulnerable. Most of them were not so foolish as to believe that it could be eliminated easily or soon, but they were not prepared to accept it as a fact of life. Any such inclination was labeled as "appeasement," one of the harshest words in the English language since Munich in 1938. Therefore, when the United States becomes involved militarily with one manifestation or another of this despicable phenomenon, there should be no temporizing, no "artifice under the name of politics" restraining the use of force. There should be victory.

It will not be difficult for the reader to identify these patterns or styles of thought in the 1960s. Their differences are only partially subject to rational debate. Presumably, there is something of the calculator in every man, and presumably therefore a person can be moved toward or away from one of these sets of attitudes by argumentation that shows, or appears to show, that one or the other of them is more likely to yield long-range advantages to the nation, or the West, or whatever standard is being appealed to. But ultimately, these styles cannot be reconciled. They reflect fundamentally different personality types and value systems; such matters are beyond proof and disproof.

The most unique aspect of the Truman-MacArthur controversy was the general's public challenge to official policy. It was related above how this issue flared in the summer of 1950 and was then swept aside by the expectation of a quick victory after Inchon. With the "new war" upon him and the administration imposing restrictions upon him that he found intolerable, MacArthur displayed once again his extraordinary willingness to make his disagreements public. It should be emphasized that all the examples cited below took place *after* a December 6, 1950, message from the Joint Chiefs of Staff to MacArthur, which, among other things, transmitted a Presidential order that "No speech, press release, or other statement concerning military policy should be released until it has received clearance from the Department of Defense."[16]

On February 13 he issued a public statement in which he said, among other things, that the "concept advanced by some that we should establish a line across Korea and enter into positional warfare is wholly unrealistic and illusory. . . . The attempt to engage in such strategy would insure the destruction of our forces piecemeal."[17] He knew, of course, that something very like this was in fact the emerging objective of the Administration.

On March 7 he issued another statement in which he outlined the situation then prevailing. He referred to the "abnormal military inhibitions"

---

[16] *MacArthur Hearings*, pt. 5, p. 3180.
[17] *Ibid.*, p. 3539.

under which he was operating and "the existing limitation upon our freedom of counter-offensive action." He concluded with this sentence:

> Vital decisions have yet to be made—decisions far beyond the scope of the authority vested in me as the military commander, decisions which are neither solely political nor solely military, but which must provide on the highest international levels an answer to the obscurities which now becloud the unsolved problems raised by Red China's undeclared war in Korea.[18]

He could scarcely have challenged the administration any more directly without being completely explicit.

On March 20 General MacArthur was notified by the Joint Chiefs of Staff that there would soon be a Presidential announcement that with South Korea now largely free of aggressor forces, the United Nations was now prepared "to discuss conditions of settlement in Korea" with the Chinese. Here was final proof that the administration was not anxious to pursue the traditional objective of victory.

The general's response was his most defiant. On March 24 he issued a statement describing China's military weaknesses and declaring that the Chinese could not conquer Korea "even under inhibitions which now restrict activity of the United Nations forces and the corresponding military advantages which accrue to Red China." He continued,

> The enemy therefore must by now be painfully aware that a decision of the United Nations to depart from its tolerant effort to contain the war to the area of Korea through expansion of our military operations to his coastal areas and interior bases would doom Red China to the risk of imminent military collapse.
>
> Within the area of my authority as military commander . . . it should be needless to say I stand ready at any time to confer in the field with the commander in chief of the enemy forces in an earnest effort to find any military means whereby the realization of the political objectives of the United Nations in Korea, to which no nation may justly take exceptions, might be accomplished without further bloodshed.[19]

If this statement had only anticipated the President's announcement of a willingness to negotiate, it would nonetheless have been an act of rare arrogation, probably unprecedented in American history. But it went beyond even this. In issuing this statement, the general proclaimed himself as the source of the offer to negotiate, and took upon himself the responsibility for setting the terms of that negotiation. In addition he referred to "the political objectives of the United Nations." The precise character

[18] *Ibid.*, pp. 3540–3541.
[19] *Ibid.*, p. 3542.

of these objectives was not altogether clear, but everyone knew how the general defined them: the removal of Communist forces from all of Korea. This was clearly no longer the objective of the administration.

Moreover, the general's statement was a clear and flagrant violation of the December 6 order that no statements concerning military policy should be released until cleared by the Department of Defense.

President Truman has written that he decided that with this statement, his recalcitrant commander had gone too far and would have to be relieved of his command.[20] But still he delayed taking this difficult step. With the release by Congressman Martin on April 5 of the famous MacArthur letter referred to above, the President summoned his courage and acted. His action had the unanimous support of the Joint Chiefs of Staff and his highest civilian advisers, but it goes without saying that it provoked one of the most emotional and acrimonious controversies in American history. General MacArthur, a military hero of nearly matchless dimensions, returned to the United States for the first time since the 1930s. He was received by tumultuous crowds in several major cities—his ticker-tape parade in New York was by far the largest reception in that city's history, dwarfing even the one given Charles Lindbergh in 1927—and his eloquent address to a joint session of Congress induced a most dramatic and emotional response from the legislators and the country at large.

The Meaning and the Lessons of the Korean War

The Korean War was a unique and consequential experience for the United States. Scholars and others will be probing its meaning and significance for years to come. In a discussion of defense policy, three aspects of it stand out: (1) Aggression was challenged, and the aggressors were denied their objectives. (2) The United States fought a "limited war," and the resultant controversy promises to last indefinitely. (3) The American tradition of civilian supremacy was challenged, partially undermined for a time, and then reasserted. Each of these will be discussed briefly because of their contemporary relevance to American defense policy.

Resisting Aggression   History is supposed to be a great teacher, but its "lessons" are by no means clear and unambiguous. World War II has left a deep imprint on most Americans, and one of the most widely held generalizations growing out of that experience has been that unopposed aggression whets the appetites of the aggressors. Therefore, if powerful nations launch or sponsor aggression, it is both morally correct and strategically sound to oppose them from the very beginning. To acquiesce will only make the ultimate challenge more formidable.

---

[20] Truman, *op. cit.,* p. 442.

Not everyone, of course, would agree that World War II teaches such a lesson. A few would argue that Germany could really have been appeased if only the assumptions underlying the Munich Pact had remained operational in the West for a longer period. Many more would argue that the appeasement at Munich neither added to nor detracted from Hitler's will to conquer. Finally, the whole notion that history can provide such all-encompassing generalizations as "unopposed aggression whets the appetites of the aggressors" is open to serious doubt. Any situation will always be more complex than such a simple remark suggests. What constitutes "aggression"? Has it occurred? Who are the aggressors? Are their aims limited or unlimited? Is resistance at the outset likely to involve military or political hazards that will not be present if resistance is postponed? These and other questions will always be relevant, and the answers to them may very well suggest that resistance should not be forthcoming in a particular instance.

Nonetheless, although the generalization under discussion probably does not apply to all aggressors at all times, it does seem to have a rather widespread applicability. In the case of the North Korean invasion of South Korea, it is generally agreed that the Soviet Union supported the attack, that the Communists hoped to achieve a quick and easy victory, that South Korea was surely not the only object of Soviet ambitions, and that the Soviets were surprised and sobered by the American intervention. There seems to be little reason to doubt that the American intervention had a dramatic impact on Soviet leaders and that the general import of that impact was to introduce an increased element of caution in future Soviet calculations. The Americans were, after all, willing to fight, and even in remote places like Korea.

At the very least, it should be noted that the intervention itself was based on such assumptions, and subsequent American interpretations of its significance have generally followed this line. The fact that finally the United States settled merely for the *status quo ante* does not alter that. The Korean experience manifested and reinforced the widely held view that aggression —at least Communist aggression—should be resisted from the outset. This view retains its powerful grip on the minds of most Americans, and the result is that the United States is committed by treaty and less formally to resisting Communist expansion nearly all over the globe.[21]

---

[21] Two kinds of problems are especially associated with this posture. The first centers on the question of whether the United States is not overcommitted; even the power and resources of the world's strongest nation are, after all, limited. The second has to do with the difficulties of defining and then resisting "aggression." There are more ways of expanding than simply launching traditional military attacks across frontiers, and the Communists are using them. The challenge in Southeast Asia, for example, has little in common with the one that was confronted in Korea. These matters will be discussed later in this chapter.

Limited War   For the United States, the Korean War was unlike any-thing previously experienced. American troops went abroad, fought against an enemy, and did not win. It has already been discussed above how this unique experience affected the major public officials and how it frustrated so many Americans. It remains to assay the long-range significance of it.

Korea was a "limited war." A limited war is one in which the objectives sought by both sides are relatively limited—as compared, for example, with the unconditional surrender of one's foes—and the means employed to achieve them are similarly restricted.[22] It might have been the case that even in the absence of nuclear and thermonuclear weapons, the United States and the Soviet Union would have evolved policies after World War II that sought to avoid a direct confrontation at nearly all costs. But the presence of these fantastic instruments of destruction has provided a com-pelling reason for doing so. A hitherto unknown circumspection has en-tered into American thinking about problems of defense and the conduct of wars. Objectives are defined with greater care, even—in fact, *especially*—after the shooting begins.

In sum, the military challenge confronting the United States is only partially the awesome and terrible possibility of a Soviet attack on the United States. Indeed, in most informed observers' view, that is the least likely prospect. Much more likely are encounters such as the ones in Korea or South Vietnam. Unless the United States is to treat each aggression or outbreak of guerrilla activity as a sufficient grounds for the initiation of total war, it must face the prospect of some—perhaps many—less apocalyp-tic struggles. In these more limited engagements, it is presumably not in the interests of the United States to do either of two things: yield, or pre-cipitate a direct clash of arms with the Soviet Union. These desiderata require, therefore, a substantial military capability—and many allies or like-minded associates—coupled with a prudent definition of what is worth trying to achieve and what is not in any given set of circumstances.

It should be emphasized that limited wars are not necessarily stale-mated wars. They can be won, and victory over enemy forces in a limited war may very well be an appropriate intermediate objective. In the case of Korea, for example, if the Chinese had not finally agreed to a cease-fire, it might have been necessary even for the purpose of achieving our limited objectives there to expand the war and rout the Chinese Army. Even so, it would not have ceased to be a limited war until and unless the United States had determined to destroy the Chinese Communist regime or had decided to use means that could scarcely be called restricted, or limited.

Moreover, the use or nonuse of nuclear weapons does not by itself de-termine whether a war is limited. World War II was not a limited war

---

[22] The self-imposed limitations operating on both sides in the Korean War were set forth *above*, pp. 217–218.

either in terms of objectives or means employed, and yet no nuclear weapons were used until the closing days, and none were employed against Germany. Conversely, nuclear weapons might have been employed in Korea without changing the basically limited character of the war.

It is, however, admittedly difficult to draw a neat line between limited and unlimited wars. As far as objectives are concerned, the line is rather easier to draw. But regarding means, what constitutes limited means and what not are very difficult to determine. Some, including this author, would argue that the use of nuclear weapons is itself such a momentous act that their employment could not ever be regarded as a limited means.

These problems of definition and categorization are ultimately unresolvable. But the basic point remains that Korea was the first time in at least modern American history that the United States had fought for something less than the total destruction of the enemy's will to resist and the first time that the United States had not used anything like the full force of its military capabilities.

Many different kinds of limited-war challenges may face the United States in the future. Unless the United States is willing to convert all such encounters into the more traditional total conflict, it will presumably be living with the frustrations, costs, and risks of limited war for many years to come.

Civilian Supremacy   Most Americans take for granted the fact that our military officers take orders from civilian superiors. This is not only traditional; it is embedded in the Constitution. The fact that in as democratic and mature a country as France, Charles de Gaulle came to power in 1958 on the strength of what was in effect a military *coup d'état* is not regarded by most Americans as having much relevance to this country. And this confidence would seem to be well justified regarding the possibility of an actual coup.

But the threat to civilian supremacy in this country is more subtle. General MacArthur apparently never gave a moment's thought to the possibility of a coup, and presumably neither did any but his most fanatical and disreputable supporters. But his challenge to civilian supremacy was nonetheless real and substantial, and it suggests how that supremacy would probably be circumvented if it ever is.

When General MacArthur returned to this country, there could be no mistaking his enormous popularity. Moreover, his adversary was a President whose popular support was at an all-time low, due in large part to the frustrations of the Korean War. What if the general, while still in military command, had been less open and unmistakable in his efforts to undermine official policy? Suppose he had released fewer argumentative press releases and had instead confined himself to misinterpreting deliberately his official orders and to marshaling more quietly the support of his civilian supporters in the United States. Given their respective popularity indexes and the great receptivity to the general's policy prescriptions, it is not absolutely certain that the President would have either sensed the magnitude of the challenge or been willing to deal with it if he had. Truman had, after all, displayed a remarkable forebearance regarding the general's statements for a very long time. If MacArthur had not thus alerted him, or if Truman had ultimately been a less resolute man, MacArthur might have succeeded in keeping his post and undermining official policy at the same time.

This is, of course, all conjectural regarding what might have happened had MacArthur and Truman played their hands somewhat differently. But it does suggest that military *coups d'état* are not the only and are not even the most likely way in which civilian supremacy might be endangered in this country.

The Korean War has been analyzed from a variety of perspectives. It had many interesting and important facets. In conclusion, it should be emphasized once again that one matter that has *not* been carefully examined is the substantive policy issues raised in the Truman-MacArthur controversy. The absurdity of absolutist views on war, the challenge to civilian supremacy, the theoretical significance of the resistance, and the rationale of limited war have all been touched on. But no attempt has been made to determine which side in the controversy was proposing the sounder policy.

The reason for this abstention is that any such attempt would necessitate the marshaling of a gigantic amount of information and then the combining of that information with hypotheses and hunches to form a final judgment. Such questions as the following regarding the adoption of MacArthur's proposals would have to be answered or at least speculated about: What would the Soviets have done? What retaliatory measures might the Chinese have employed, and how effective would they have been? How would the participating United Nations have responded, and how would this have affected such matters as the war effort in Korea and the building of NATO? What effect would the Chinese Nationalist troops have had in Korea or South China? Would the blockade or the bombing in Manchuria have seriously affected the Chinese effort in Korea? In sum, what would have been the overall political and military consequences of adopting these proposals?

It may be that had the general's prescriptions been followed, the outcome would have been more satisfactory from the standpoint of the long-term interests of the United States, or it may not. If the reader senses that this writer believes the administration had the better policy, he is correct. But one cannot be certain about such complex and conjectural matters. We know what did happen; we can only guess about what might have happened.

The Eisenhower Years

General Dwight D. Eisenhower left his NATO position in the spring of 1952 and came home to capture the Republican nomination in a close contest with Senator Robert A. Taft of Ohio. Senator Taft had long been associated with the defense policies symbolized by General MacArthur in Korea, and had he been elected President, the American objectives *might* have been expanded to include "victory."[23] General Eisenhower, on the other hand, was willing to accept a truce; and about five months after he assumed office, a cease-fire was arranged. The manner in which this occurred left a deep impression on the Eisenhower administration's defense policies.

The Chinese were almost certainly weary of the war. It was a severe strain on their economic resources in addition to extracting a heavy toll in human life. On March 5, 1953, Stalin died, and this may also have affected Soviet attitudes toward the war. But from the administration's point of view, a third factor appeared to outweigh any other in Chinese calculations: an American threat in late May that it would expand the war, including the use of atomic bombs against bases in China. Whether by coincidence or as a consequence, the elusive truce was reached shortly thereafter. And from this the Eisenhower administration drew what may or may not have been a correct inference, namely, that their willingness to threaten nuclear war against the source of aggression had effectively deterred further aggression. This technique was later labeled "brinkmanship"—the willingness to go to the brink of war in an effort to deter aggression—and became one of the most distinctive and controversial aspects of the Eisenhower defense policy.

Defense policy, like other aspects of foreign policy, is the product of a large number of factors. Abstract theory and idealized projections are influenced by such things as congressional attitudes, public opinion, partisan considerations, campaign oratory, the condition of the economy, and the administration's economic policy. Although postwar American foreign policy has exhibited a remarkable continuity regardless of which political party and individuals have been in control, there have been distinct differences in emphasis and style; and sometimes these differences have been sufficiently consequential so as to constitute a meaningful difference in

---

[23] Senator Taft's 1951 book on American foreign policy does not provide a definite answer as to what his policy in Korea would have been had he been elected President. See Robert A. Taft, *A Foreign Policy for Americans*, Doubleday & Company, Inc., Garden City, N.Y., 1951, pp. 103–113.

substance. This is perhaps most evident in defense policy, where the Republican Eisenhower administration pursued significantly different policies from either its predecessor or successor Democratic administration. The reasons for this were, of course, many and diverse, and include such things as the changing external environment and the personality and temperament of the top officials dealing with defense policy. But the three primary reasons probably were the differing domestic policy priorities, the circumstances surrounding General Eisenhower's election, and the manner in which the truce was achieved in Korea in the early and formative days of the Eisenhower administration.

The Republicans have traditionally feared the expansion and costs of the Federal government more than the Democrats have. They were determined to reduce expenses wherever possible, and since defense expenditures then constituted two-thirds of the Federal expenditures, it was an obvious target for close scrutiny. The Republicans wanted to cut taxes and balance the budget. They genuinely feared that the economy was in danger of either breaking down or experiencing runaway inflation if the heavy governmental expenditures and high taxes were not cut back and the budget balanced. Moreover, they disapproved in principle of the expanding economic role played by the Federal government. Their whole set of opinions about what was economically sound induced them to look with suspicion on national defense costs, which had risen from $13 billion in fiscal 1950 to $50.4 in fiscal 1953, even though they shared the Democrat's view that a large peacetime military establishment was a necessity after Korea. Such differences in emphasis can have profound implications for defense policy in practice.

The Republicans assumed office at a time of great weariness with the Korean War. The stalemate had dragged on for over a year and a half, and the casualties and costs continued to mount. Whatever the resolution of that dilemma was to be, there was a strong sentiment against becoming similarly involved anywhere else. "Containment" and "limited war" were unpopular words and concepts.

During the 1952 presidential campaign, the Republicans had denounced containment and had announced a new objective: liberation of the captive peoples living under communism. Taken at its face value, this might have implied an increase rather than a decrease in military expenditures. But "liberation" was always little more than a slogan with deliberately imprecise implications regarding means, and consequently it did not stand in the way of the other and more powerful impulses such as ending the Korean War, cutting costs, and thereafter avoiding such imbroglios.

Finally, as suggested above, the alleged relationship between the United States threat of nuclear expansion of the war and the Chinese acceptance of a truce had a powerful impact on the new administration. It concluded that if it only had enough courage to go along with its powerful strategic capability,[24] the mere threat of using that capability would deter any and all Communist aggression.

Thus it was that the Eisenhower administration announced its "New Look" defense policy, featuring cutbacks in spending and increased reliance on nuclear weapons, both strategic and tactical. By fiscal 1955, defense spending was down to $40.7 billion, and the number of Army and Marine divisions capable of fighting "limited war" had been cut back sharply.

Massive Retaliation and Its Critics

Secretary of State John Foster Dulles gave the definitive exposition of this doctrine in a speech on January 11, 1954, less than one year after the new administration had assumed office. Excerpts follow:

> It is not sound military strategy permanently to commit United States land forces to Asia to a degree that gives us no strategic reserves.
>
> It is not sound to become permanently committed to expenditures so vast that they lead to what Lenin called "practical bankruptcy."
>
> Local defense will always be important. But there is no local defense which alone will contain the mighty land power of the communist world. Local defense must be reinforced by the further deterrent of massive retaliatory power.
>
> A potential aggressor must know that he cannot always prescribe the battle conditions that suit him. Otherwise, for example, a potential aggressor who is glutted with manpower might be tempted to attack in confidence that resistance would be confined to manpower. He might be tempted to attack in places where his superiority was decisive.
>
> The way to deter aggression is for the community [the United States and its allies] to be willing and able to respond vigorously at places and with means of its own choosing.

The substance of these ideas had been expounded by Dulles for several years; with this speech it became known as the policy of "massive retaliation." His meaning was not altogether clear, however, and this contributed

---

[24] The terms "strategic" and "tactical" are among the most imprecise in the whole lexicon of defense jargon. The definitions supplied below accord with typical usage; the fact that they lack precision is also typical. "Strategic" refers to weapons and plans that are designed for all-out war between major powers. Long-range bombers and missiles are "strategic" weapons. The Strategic Air Command (SAC) of the United States consists of our instruments of mass destruction. "Tactical" refers to weapons and plans that affect a more limited area and have more restricted purposes. Nuclear cannon designed for battlefield use that shoot low-yield nuclear warheads are "tactical" weapons, as, of course, are the nonnuclear tanks and guns that might be used in a conventional battle. The line between "strategic" and "tactical" weapons is, of course, sometimes difficult to draw. But it is meaningful to distinguish between those weapons that are designed for long-range, massive destruction and those designed for more limited purposes.

to the considerable controversy that ensued. The quoted passages were the most noted ones, and they seemed to imply that the United States would respond to any aggression with "massive retaliatory power." But he did make a reference to "local defense," saying it would always be important. Moreover, in another part of the speech, he quoted President Eisenhower's recent statement that United States forces in the Far East would feature "highly mobile naval, air and amphibious units," and that in this way the United States would have a capacity to oppose aggression "with even greater effect than heretofore."

Democrats and others began to raise many questions. Did the "new" policy rule out the use of land forces? Would we respond massively to any aggression anywhere? If not, how did the policy differ from that of the Truman administration, whose nuclear arsenal had presumably been a major deterrent against Soviet aggression since World War II? Did the mention of "highly mobile naval, air and amphibious units" mean that "massive retaliation" might take the form of "not-so-massive," selective attacks on something other than the aggressor's forces and cities? If so, what and with what effect? Could the Soviet Union and China be expected to understand this? Since Dulles's relatively short speech made frequent references to the need for controlling defense expenditures, was the "new" policy really a risky and ineffectual one dictated by budgetary considerations rather than a sound appraisal of defense needs? In sum, would the threat of massive retaliation effectively deter Communist aggression, and if not, what choice would we have other than total war or acquiescence?

The chief difficulty with the policy of "massive retaliation" was that it came at a time when such threats, especially against the homeland of the aggressor, were becoming increasingly less credible. In order to be effective as a deterrent, a threat must be believed, or it must be at least believable enough to raise serious questions in the mind of the entity being threatened. By 1954, such conditions probably did not exist. In 1949, several years ahead of American expectations, the Soviet Union had exploded a nuclear (fission) device. In 1953, less than a year after the United States, the Soviets exploded a thermonuclear (fusion) device. The day was fast approaching when the Soviet Union would be able to launch a devastating attack on the United States. Under these new conditions, would the Soviets —or anyone else—believe that we would respond to a local aggression with an assault on the Soviet Union or with any other kind of "massive retaliation"?

When the Soviets astonished the world with the first man-made earth satellite in October, 1957, the credibility of massive retaliation was further undermined. The sputnik demonstrated a long-range missile capability that was not only far superior to anything then possessed by the United States, but that was, more importantly, usable as a means of raining thermonuclear bombs on the United States. The demands for an increased limited-war capability to deter—and if necessary defeat—Communist aggression grew in volume but not much in influence.

Tactical Nuclear Weapons: Pro and Con

The Eisenhower administration did not rely entirely upon the threat of massive retaliation. In accordance with Dulles's vague reference to "highly mobile . . . units" and similar comments made in an attempt to clarify the "massive retaliation" speech, the United States did maintain a reduced Army and Marine Corps, including five divisions in Europe. But the critics were unhappy about these tactical forces, on the grounds that they were not large enough and that they were becoming too dependent on tactical nuclear weapons. As for the problem of size, it was generally agreed on all sides that the Soviets had a marked superiority in ground forces in Europe during the 1950s and that NATO forces, whatever their deterrent value, would not be able to defend Europe against a major Soviet assault. These propositions were generally accepted despite the absence of precise agreement on the comparative sizes, equipment, states of readiness, etc., of the Soviet and NATO forces.[25]

The problem of overdependence on nuclear weapons was underlined in late 1954, when NATO officially and publicly adopted a policy of primary reliance on tactical nuclear weapons for the local defense of Europe. The reasoning behind this endorsement of the use of nuclear weapons in response to any Soviet aggression was comparable to the even more fundamental policy of massive retaliation. It was believed, first and foremost, that this reliance would be an appropriate and effective supporting deterrent, less awesome than strategic retaliation but nonetheless quite fearsome just by itself. Secondly, it was believed that if deterrence should fail, tactical nuclear weapons would compensate in battle for the planned reductions in manpower and would, in fact, give the West battlefield superiority. Finally, it was believed that reliance on nuclear weapons would permit substantial cuts in defense expenditures.

The critics were unimpressed by each of these arguments. While granting that the threat of using tactical nuclear weapons *might* deter a Soviet attack better than a nonnuclear (conventional) defense force, they raised again the question of credibility. If we became largely dependent on a nuclear response, might the Soviets not be emboldened to nibble at Western territory in the belief that the West would not dare use nuclear weapons against anything but an all-out assault? The vulnerable position of Berlin raised this question with special force. If our only response to a Soviet take-over there could be nuclear, would we in fact respond? More importantly, would the Soviets believe our threat to do so?

---

[25] For example, see Osgood, *op. cit.*, pp. 29, 87–88, 118, 163–164, 374–375.

If the credibility of an American nuclear response to Soviet aggression in Europe was in doubt, it was even more in doubt in less vital areas. Would the United States use nuclear weapons against Communist aggression in such "peripheral" areas as the Middle East or Southeast Asia? To the extent to which the answer to that question was in doubt, so was the credibility of America's willingness to resist aggression there if our tactical forces were incapable of fighting with conventional weapons.

As for the argument that, should deterrence fail, nuclear weapons would compensate in battle for the planned force reductions, this also was disputed. The basic objection was that these claims were apparently based on the unstated assumption that the Soviets were not also developing tactical nuclear weapons. It might be true that if the Soviets used only conventional weapons and the West employed nuclear weapons, the West would be able to get by with many fewer troops. But the Soviets were hardly likely to confront the West with an aggressive assault wherein their conventional forces were met by Western tactical forces equipped with nuclear weapons. If, on the other hand, it should be assumed that the Soviets were also developing tactical nuclear weapons—and they were—would the United States really want to initiate their use in any developing struggle? Since the answer would quite likely be in the negative, the alleged battlefield advantages resulting from total or nearly total dependence on these weapons was deemed to be nonexistent or at least highly conjectural.[26]

Even if it seemed likely in any given circumstance that the West would gain a certain advantage from initiating the use of tactical nuclear weapons, there would be powerful arguments against their use. Most importantly, nobody knows what the Soviet response would be, and the possibility that the use of even very low-yield tactical nuclear weapons might trigger an all-out war is a potent restraint. The writings of Soviet military specialists have never made any sharp distinction between tactical and strategic nuclear weapons. The use of the former might very well be taken by them to mean the first step down a road leading inevitably to total war. If they do reason this way, they might very well launch a preemptive strategic strike against the United States.[27]

---

[26] "The question of who would gain from the use of tactical nuclear weapons can only be answered by saying that it depends on a host of variables including who uses them first, the geographic area, the terrain, the sympathies of the indigenous population, and the state of technology and production at the time." Morton H. Halperin, *Limited War in the Nuclear Age*, John Wiley & Sons, Inc., New York, 1963, pp. 68–69.

[27] The term "preemptive" in military jargon refers to an action that is taken because of a certainty or at least a conviction that the other side is about to do the same thing. In the cold war today, each side believes that it must display sufficient strength to deter and, if necessary, resist an enemy attack; but each side also wants to avoid actions that might lead the other to believe it was about to attack, that thereby might encourage a preemptive strike.

Another argument made against the use of tactical nuclear weapons even where it might appear that a battlefield advantage would accrue was that there are bound to be heavy political costs involved.

The Europeans acquiesced, with varying degrees of enthusiasm, in our plans to make NATO's tactical forces largely nuclear. Their primary motivation, apparently, was to go along with whatever the United States wanted to do in order to assure continued American participation in the defense of Europe. But it was bound to become impressed upon them sooner or later that the actual use of such weapons would probably devastate Europe. The exchange of low-yield nuclear attacks in Europe might be a "limited" war from the standpoint of the Soviet Union or the United States, but it would be disastrous for Europe. As more and more Europeans begin to realize this—and they did—the European governments might seek to ensure that the weapons would never be used. The ensuing intra-NATO struggles might either reduce the deterrent value of the existing NATO forces or actually dissolve the alliance. At the very least, this realization was bound to increase neutralist sentiment in Western Europe, a perennial fear of Western governments and a perennial objective of Communists.

An additional political cost is the anticipated reaction of nonallied, neutralist nations around the world. There is a great fear of nuclear weapons all over the world, and any nation initiating their use is bound to suffer politically. This would, of course, be especially true if the provocation were generally deemed to be slight.

Finally, it should not be overlooked that a substantial proportion of the American public shares this antipathy to the use of nuclear weapons, at least under conditions short of total war. One of the handicaps of a democracy in the international arena is the fact that popular opinion has to be taken into account over the long run. America's overall posture and effectiveness in the world depend in some measure on the extent to which the government can rally the energies and support of its own people. Initiating the use of nuclear weapons in response to anything short of an all-out Soviet attack would be deeply divisive.

As for the expected savings, these were variously denounced as illusory and as irrelevant. Especially those who assumed a Soviet tactical nuclear capability was also forthcoming were convinced that a nuclear army would be every bit as costly as a conventional one. And those who suspected that the whole "New Look" policy was dictated not by considered defense policy needs but rather by budgetary and partisan considerations were especially caustic in their strictures.

The Persistence of Policy

The Eisenhower administration became increasingly harassed by partisan, academic, and press criticisms of its defense policies during the late 1950s. But it was protected against an even greater clamor by two very powerful facts. The first was that the President was a man of unrivaled military prestige. Needless to say, there were conflicting appraisals inside and outside the military regarding General Eisenhower's abilities as a military strategist; the same is true for every prominent figure. But the public at large knows little and cares less about such esoteric matters. Dwight Eisenhower's superb military record spoke for itself in the minds of most Americans. Defense policy was, ironically, the policy area in which he was least vulnerable to criticism and in which he was perhaps the most deserving of criticism.

The second fact that protected the Eisenhower administration from politically damaging criticism of its defense policies was its considerable success. The Korean War was terminated, and during the remaining seven and one-half years of the administration, the Soviets and the Chinese were largely contained, and, more conspicuously, the United States did not become involved in any wars. There were, of course, some uneasy moments—especially during the Suez and Hungarian crises in 1956, in the Formosa Straits in 1955 and 1958, in Lebanon in 1958, in Berlin after November, 1958—but deterrence had worked, and the peace had been preserved. The only areas wherein it might be argued that containment had not been achieved were Cuba and Indochina. In the former, the accession to power in January of 1959 of Fidel Castro installed what became the first Communist government in the Western Hemisphere. But this event could scarcely be laid at the door of the Eisenhower defense policy. It was indubitably a misfortune for the United States, and it became a serious problem, but it did not happen because of American reliance on nuclear weapons or any other aspect of our overall defense policy. As for Communist gains in Laos and Vietnam, these did raise some serious questions about the wisdom and utility of the Eisenhower policies. The challenges there were unorthodox ones, not likely to yield to military solutions in any event, and surely not likely to yield to the threat or use of nuclear weapons. But this constituted what at that time was at best a minor exception to the general success of Eisenhower defense policy.

The experience during the Eisenhower years underlines the fact that the final determinant of whether a defense policy is successful or not is the action of one's adversaries. And since one cannot forecast this action with any degree of certitude, it is never clear in the abstract which policy is the most appropriate one. As suggested above, the wisdom of the Eisenhower-Dulles policies was open to some very serious doubts on several scores, *but they worked.* This does not prove that the critics were wrong or that grave and unnecessary risks were not run or that better policies were not available. More importantly, it surely does not prove that such policies could have gone on being successful indefinitely.

Why did they work? The final answer to that question remains locked in the minds of the Soviet and Chinese leadership. It may have been the case, of course, that no Communist government was interested in aggression in the first place, even if it had appeared attractive and rewarding. This seems highly unlikely, but it cannot be ruled out. A much more likely hypothesis is that the Communist leadership is exceedingly cautious when it comes to matters that might involve it in a shooting war with the West, especially the United States. If this is true, it could be argued that much of the complicated and sophisticated analysis of defense policy that is carried on today is largely beside the point. Talk of "credibility" and "conventional-war capability" has very limited or no practical significance. All that really needs to be done is to maintain a menacing strategic (and tactical?) nuclear capability and to talk as if it might really be employed if aggression were to take place. This by itself will be so sobering to the Communist leadership that even if it believes the employment of such weapons is highly unlikely in most situations, it will not be willing to test the West. A miscalculation would be fatal, and no potential object of aggression is worth such a risk even if the risk is minor.

Something like this kind of rationale seems to have informed the defense policy of the Eisenhower years. And it should be emphasized again that whatever the shortcomings of such a view, it did work during that period.[28]

Nonetheless, for all the reasons cited above and for others, many knowledgeable people in and out of government were dissatisfied with defense policy during the Eisenhower years. Whichever party is out of power searches carefully for issues to use against the incumbent party in the next election, and the Democrats therefore were much more receptive to the criticisms of the established policy than they were to its defense. So it was that a persistent theme in the Democratic attacks during the 1960 elections was the defense policy of the outgoing Republican administration.

Ironically, however, the Democrats spent most of their energies denouncing an alleged "missile gap" between the United States and the Soviet Union. It was charged that the Eisenhower administration had not learned the lesson of the sputniks and that if current policies were continued, we would soon be far behind the Soviets in missile technology and would be at a serious military disadvantage. This, in turn, would enable the Soviets if not to blackmail us at least to intimidate us and pursue whatever reckless policies they might have in mind. The first irony along this line was that it had little to do with the defense debates that had raged for years. The

---

[28] It should also be noted that American defense policy during this period was considerably less doctrinaire and clear-cut than parts of the preceding analysis might indicate. Talk of massive retaliation and the official nuclearization of NATO must be considered alongside the facts that nuclear weapons were never used and conventional forces were never wholly discarded. Top officials did occasionally hint that official policy was not as thoroughly wedded to nuclear weapons as was widely believed. President Eisenhower, for example, repeatedly deprecated the utility of nuclear weapons as a means of defending Berlin.

Republican "massive retaliation" policy presumably depended as much or more than other defense policies on the existence and utility of strategic weapons. If they were slighting these for budgetary reasons, they were twice wrong because the major criticisms heretofore had to do with our *conventional* inferiority and the allegedly dangerous implications of that. The second irony—and this says more about the nature of intelligence information and partisan debates than it does about defense policy as such —was the fact that the "missile gap" turned out to be a myth. If there was a missile gap, it was the other way around, with the United States having a large numerical superiority over the Soviet Union.

Nonetheless, beneath the campaign rhetoric lay a real concern with the state of our defenses, and the advent of the Kennedy administration resulted in some rather important changes. These will be sketched briefly, and then some of the most pressing contemporary defense problems will be analyzed.

Democratic Changes

With the election of John F. Kennedy, a different group of men with different views on defense policy assumed control of the executive branch of government. It is the function of the opposition party to find fault with the incumbents, and the Democrats had begun to perform this function regarding defense policy with greater zeal as the popular President's days in office shortened. Among their allies in this were the intellectuals, who have a natural affinity both for criticizing the established order and for the Democratic party. Prominent among the intellectuals was a rather new breed, the "defense intellectuals." These individuals—some with academic backgrounds, some from industry, others coming out of the armed forces— represented a great diversity of thought and opinion, but in the postwar period they constituted an unprecedented and apparently inexhaustible reservoir of ideas and arguments. They and the triumphant Democrats descended on Washington en masse after November, 1960.

In his first defense budget message to Congress, March 28, 1961, the new President emphasized his conviction that our conventional forces were inadequate. An excerpt from that message follows:

> Non-nuclear wars and . . . guerrilla warfare have since 1945 constituted the most active and constant threat to Free World security. . . . In the event of a major aggression that could not be repulsed by conventional forces, we must be prepared to take whatever action with whatever weapons are appropriate. But our objective now is to increase our ability to confine our response to non-nuclear weapons, and to lessen the incentive for any limited aggression by making clear what our response will accomplish.

The new Secretary of Defense, Robert S. McNamara, was even more blunt, as the following statement to a congressional committee suggests:

There has been a tendency since the end of the Korean War to emphasize the nuclear capabilities of [our limited-war] forces. These capabilities are, of course, essential to our overall national strategy since all of our forces have a role in general nuclear war. Even in limited war situations, we should not preclude the use of tactical nuclear weapons, for no one can foresee how such situations might develop. But the decision to employ tactical nuclear weapons should not be forced upon us simply because we have no other means to cope with them. There are many possible situations in which it would not be advisable or feasible to use such weapons. What is being proposed at this time is not a reversal of our existing national policy, but an increase in our non-nuclear capabilities to provide a greater degree of versatility to our limited war forces.[29]

Some action was undertaken at once to implement this new policy, but it took the shock of a new Soviet threat against West Berlin in the summer of 1961 before really extensive steps were taken. Essentially, three elements of a conventional war capability were affected: airlift capacity, modernization of conventional weapons, and increased numbers of troops. The first of these was a matter that had been receiving increasing attention from defense critics. It was alleged that our conventional forces were not only too small, but that they were also lacking in mobility. The increased orders for aircraft designed to move men and equipment around quickly were the result. The meaning and purpose of the other two elements are self-evident.

Something of the dimensions of these changes can be sensed from the following data. When the Kennedy administration assumed office, the active-duty strength of the Army was about 850,000 troops, making up eleven combat-ready divisions. Three years later, the figures had stabilized at about 970,000 troops and sixteen combat-ready divisions. These divisions, moreover, were reorganized and reequipped for the primary purpose of increasing their conventional firepower. In 1961 President Kennedy made three separate requests for extra money to modernize the Army's conventional capability, and Congress appropriated an additional three-quarters of a billion dollars on the basis of these requests.

Also in 1961, President Kennedy induced Congress to appropriate more than two and a half times as much for airlift expansion and modernization as his predecessor had asked for. Fifty-three additional planes were ordered, including the first jets for this purpose. In 1964, Secretary Mc-

---

[29] *Hearings on Military Procurement Authorization, Fiscal Year 1962, of the Senate Committee on Armed Services,* 87th Cong., 1st Sess., 1961, p. 17.

Namara said that by 1968 airlift capacity would be about four times that of 1961. In addition, the Marine Corps—the archetype limited-war instrument—was increased from 175,000 to 190,000 men.

In line with their campaign talk, the Democrats also moved to bolster the nation's missile capabilities. One of Kennedy's first acts as President was to allocate funds to accelerate the construction of missile-firing Polaris submarines, so that nineteen of them would be available by early 1964, instead of a year later. He also asked for and received additional funds for the regular intercontinental ballistic missile (ICBM) program, especially the Minuteman missile. After they had been in office a few months, the Democrats conceded that revised intelligence reports about Soviet missile strength had effectively abolished the alleged "missile gap," but increased budget allocations continued to be made for these strategic programs. The widespread concern over the comparative missile strengths of the two major powers had diminished somewhat, but such spectacular Soviet achievements as the successful completion of two manned space flights in 1961 demonstrated a continuing and substantial Soviet superiority in rocketry.

Finally, the new administration began to grapple with the baffling problems of "sublimited," or "guerrilla" warfare. If atomic forces were often an inappropriate response to a challenge, so were conventional forces in many areas. This issue had begun to assume serious proportions in the last couple years of the Eisenhower administration, and they descended with great force on the new one. President Kennedy made his interest in this matter very clear to Congress and the Army, and the result was that the Army's "Special Forces" were substantially expanded, and throughout the rest of the Army new emphasis was given to counterguerrilla training.

These actions made it quite clear that the new administration was not going to be nearly as concerned about balancing the budget as the preceding one had been. Despite chronically unbalanced budgets, defense expenditures rose sharply after 1961. By fiscal 1961, defense expenditures had crept up to $47.5 billion. In fiscal 1962 they jumped to $51.1 billion, and in fiscal 1963 they climbed to $53.0 billion. President Johnson was apparently determined to arrest that trend, and for fiscal 1965 he submitted a budget of $54.0 billion, a reduction of $1.3 billion from the preceding year. But whatever the future may hold, it is clear that the Democrats brought into office a quite different set of ideas about defense policy, and proceeded to implement them.

Needless to say, new policies—especially when they involve higher expenditures—bring new criticisms and controversies. In the following sections, some specific and some more general contemporary problems will be discussed. In the process, many of the more important areas of contemporary controversy about defense policy will be examined.

Contemporary Defense Problems

What follows is an examination of *selected* contemporary problems of American defense policy. It, like the rest of this book, is not designed to be an exhaustive review. The problems of defense policy are nearly unlimited and have prompted an avalanche of learned books and articles in recent years alone.

Nor does the following purport to be definitive regarding the topics that are discussed; only *selected* aspects of each will be dealt with. Aside from the fact that knowledgeable opinion about virtually all such questions is always divided, defense problems undergo nearly constant change due to altered political conditions and technological advances. The purpose, therefore, of the rest of this chapter is to illustrate by examples what some of the major contemporary defense problems are, how they are being dealt with, what alternative policies are available, and, more generally, how to think intelligently about such matters.

NATO and the Defense of Western Europe

The origins of this extraordinary peacetime alliance have been outlined above. It was originally simply a guaranty pact, and the operational sentence was contained in Article 5 of the treaty:

> The Parties agree that an armed attack against one or more of them in Europe or North America shall be considered an attack against them all and consequently they agree that, if such an armed attack occurs, each of them . . . will assist the Party or Parties so attacked by taking forthwith, individually and in concert with the other Parties, such action as it deems necessary including the use of armed force, to restore and maintain the security of the North Atlantic area.

The primary significance of the pact, in both European and American eyes, was that it committed the United States to the defense of Western Europe. It was, of course, recognized that the language was loosely drawn and permitted a reluctant signator to do nothing at all in the event of an attack. But there is little reason to doubt that each signator regarded it as a serious commitment which it intended to keep.

In the fall of 1950, after the shock of Korea, the member nations agreed to the establishment of an integrated military force, commanded by a Supreme Commander. General Dwight D. Eisenhower was named the first Supreme Commander in December, and by early 1951 a NATO military organization was in the making. Two years later, the institutionalizing of the alliance was extended by making the North Atlantic Council a permanent body with regular diplomatic representatives from the member states and a secretary-general. By these and other steps, the guaranty pact was made the foundation for an international organization.

Measured against its basic objective—the preservation of a non-Communist Western Europe—NATO has been a complete success. Measured against certain other criteria, it has been less successful. It has never achieved its stated manpower or equipment goals, and its member nations have never really agreed on what its basic military strategy should be. In recent years, these problems and the many policy divergencies among the member nations have become ever more conspicuous, and references to "the disarray of the alliance" have become commonplace. Some have suggested that the alliance will be dissolved, and the maneuvering to fix the blame for this eventuality has begun in earnest in the United States. The most frequent nominees for culprit are the other political party and General de Gaulle. Others have suggested that the alliance *should* be dissolved, arguing either that its basic purpose—the defense of Western Europe—is no longer a pressing problem, or that the resurgence of Europe permits the withdrawal of the American protective guarantees.

Alliances cannot avoid certain potent centrifugal forces. Chief among these is the cardinal fact of international affairs, sovereignty. As long as the participants in an alliance view each issue first from the standpoint of the interests of their own nation and only secondly from the standpoint of "the alliance as a whole," there are bound to be differing policy preferences among them. The fact that each member will probably be able to convince itself that its own interests are happily identical to the interests of the alliance as a whole compounds the problem. Divergencies tend to be regarded as violations either of good faith or of sound judgment, and either way the cohesion of the alliance is bound to suffer.

These remarks apply with special force to peacetime alliances. In time of war, the incentives to cooperate are bountiful, but they fluctuate inversely with the danger posed by the common enemy. During World War II, for example, the tenuous character of the Grand Alliance became clearer as the Nazi menace receded. In peacetime, the identity, intentions, and strength of the enemy are subject to many diverse interpretations, calling forth many diverse prescriptions for dealing with them. It should come as no surprise to anyone, for example, that many Europeans have different perspectives on contemporary affairs from those of most Americans and that this affects the cohesion of NATO.

The reason for being and the cement of the alliance has been the threat of Soviet aggression. In the opinion of many people on both sides of the Atlantic, that threat is now miniscule, at least if defined as a massive attempt to conquer Western Europe militarily. Indeed, there are some who always regarded it as most implausible. But even those who continue to believe that a strong deterrent against Soviet military adventures should be maintained—and most observers on both sides of the Atlantic do so believe—are sharply divided over such matters as what the deterrent should consist of and who should control it.

In sum, the NATO alliance *is* in disarray, but to some extent it always has been, and it almost surely always will be. The pertinent questions do not have to do with how to eliminate this endemic condition. Rather they have to do with how to manage and, if possible, rise above it.

As suggested several times in the preceding sections and chapters, the basic problem confronting NATO today is how to adjust to the revolutionary fact that the United States, the core of the alliance and its primary source of strength, is now as vulnerable to a devastating nuclear attack as any other nation in the world. Is it reasonable under these conditions to believe that the United States would actually go to war with the Soviet Union over something less than a direct attack on the United States? Would we, in other words, seriously endanger the survival of our own nation in order to help defend another one? Despite repeated American assurances that we continue to regard the security of Western Europe as inseparable from our own and will fight in its defense, despite the fact that we retain over five divisions in Europe and a token, "hostage" force in West Berlin, many Europeans have quite naturally become less sure of what we would do in an actual showdown. Since the NATO nations are heavily dependent on the United States for the military strength to deter and, if necessary, to defend against any Soviet adventures in Europe, this uncertainty about America's responses in the ICBM era has led many Europeans to believe that they must develop their own means of deterrence and defense. The resultant policies, especially but not exclusively of France, have conflicted with United States policies, and the always fragile cohesion of the alliance has been jeopardized.

Many different but related controversies and problems have been engendered by the situation described above. The following discussion takes up only two for illustrative purposes; but they are crucial ones.

Control of the Nuclear Deterrent

There have been nearly as many official responses to this situation as there have been member governments in NATO. The British had decided after the war to develop their own atomic bomb; in 1952, they were successful. In the mid-1950s they began to make a determined effort to build an "independent nuclear deterrent." Their efforts have been far from a notable success.[30] And the Labor party, which assumed power in 1964 for the first time since 1951, is deeply divided over the issue. For years it had ridiculed

---

[30] For a review of the British program, see H. A. DeWeerd, "The British Effort to Secure an Independent Deterrent," in R. N. Rosecrance (ed.), *The Dispersion of Nuclear Weapons: Strategy and Politics*, Columbia University Press, New York, 1964, pp. 87–100. DeWeerd concludes that the British effort "is the story of a losing struggle against the rapid obsolescence of first line military equipment, against the spiraling costs of such equipment, against the mounting requirements for penetrating the air defenses of a Great Power with certainty, and against the difficulty of maintaining a secure second-strike force in the face of a Great Power threat" (p. 87).

its predecessor's nuclear pretensions—saying that Britain's strategic forces were neither independent nor a deterrent—but once in office it did not drastically revise Britain's nuclear policies. Whatever may develop in this regard, the United States never objected seriously to the British nuclear program, despite the fact that it was widely regarded as superfluous, ineffectual, and a drain on other, more desirable British defense programs. (The "special relationship" between the United States and Great Britain is not simply a dead relic of World War II; it is a vital reality.) The United States has not looked favorably upon any additional national efforts to create an independent nuclear deterrent; and this position has brought us into divisive and sometimes angry conflict with the French.[31] Especially since the return to power of General Charles de Gaulle in 1958, the French have been playing an increasingly independent role in Western affairs. The essential military motive for their position has been their apprehension about the long-range reliability of the American deterrent in Europe, but this merely coincides with other French and Gaullist impulses that also tend in the direction of greater self-reliance. In the first place, nuclear weapons are not only military instruments in today's world; they are also symbols of great power status, and the grandeur that de Gaulle envisages for France demands nothing less than that. The French position cannot be understood in full until an appreciation of prestige factors is added to the more tangible element of military strength. The General is offended by the fact that since World War II, Europe has been something of an American protectorate. He is determined to use the economic resurgence of France—and, if possible, of Europe as a whole—as a means of ending this dependence.

Moreover, the problem of dealing with this imperious personality is compounded by his strongly negative feelings about the United States. These feelings are apparently deep-seated and probably can be accounted for in part by his unsatisfactory relationships with President Franklin Roosevelt and British Prime Minister Winston Churchill during World War II. As leader of the Free French forces that fled France and fought on against Hitler after 1940, he was not accorded either the respect or the authority that he thought was his due. But whatever the origins of his attitudes, he and many of his supporters are known to believe that the United States is essentially an immature and uncultured nation whose influence in Europe is unfortunate regardless of defense considerations. When de Gaulle refers to "the Anglo-Saxons," meaning the United States and Great Britain, there is a kind of lofty contempt implied. He is not unmindful of American and British contributions to Western life and culture, but they are not *Europeans*, with all that implies in terms of culture, tradition,

[31] For a review of the French program, see Ciro Zoppo, "France as a Nuclear Power," in *ibid.*, pp. 113–156.

and style of life. Although this view is especially noticeable in France, it is by no means restricted to that nation.

Nonetheless, the root issue is control of a nuclear deterrent force, and this de Gaulle intends to have in French—or, perhaps, some day, "European"—hands. No amount of assurance from any American government has shaken or, presumably, will shake his conviction that sooner or later, if not now, the United States will either withdraw altogether from Europe or be an unreliable defender even if it stays.

The American response to this sentiment has not been altogether unsympathetic. After all, the French concern is shared by many Europeans and is quite easy to understand. But there are many reasons beyond simply a desire to maintain an exclusive—except for Great Britain's small contribution—control of nuclear weapons in the alliance that account for the fact that the United States has opposed French policy. Two of the most important ones cannot easily be publicly discussed. There is, for one, a fear that the French might use their capability irresponsibly. This is the basic argument against the proliferation of nuclear weapons: the more nations that have them, the greater the possibility that someone will misuse them. This is so dangerous that it should be resisted wherever possible, even if the immediate issue involves an old and trusted ally.[32]

The second usually unspoken reason why we disapprove of the French program is because it may whet the appetites of the Germans for their own independent nuclear deterrent. The United States is, of course, opposed to *any* proliferation of nuclear weapons, but there are special reasons why German possession would be undesirable. Not only would the Soviets be deeply alarmed by such a development—with unpredictable consequences —but so would most European nations; the last two world wars have not been altogether forgotten in the cold-war era. It has therefore been an urgent necessity for the United States to treat the entire issue raised by the French with the utmost gravity and respect and to attempt to devise arguments and programs to deal with it.

These American efforts have been mainly in three directions. First of all, top government officials have made repeated and probably genuine public declarations of America's determination to defend Western Europe at all costs. President Kennedy made a special trip to Europe in 1963, for example, with no apparent purpose except to "show the flag" and reassure

---

[32] A less friendly subtheme is that the French may want this capability merely as an available means of deliberately triggering the American nuclear arsenal. The idea is that since the Soviet Union would not know where the attack (presumably a counterattack) was coming from, they would have to assume it was American. Thus, in our own interests, we would have to finish what the French began. This bizarre nightmare has prompted the equally bizarre—but perhaps sensible—suggestion that the United States and the Soviet Union should devise some means of distinguishing each other's explosions from those of any other nation.

the Europeans. There have been countless efforts through regular diplomatic channels to convey the same message and to counter the assiduous efforts of the French to cast doubt on our reliability over the long haul. These protestations have apparently had some effect, but not on General de Gaulle. He continues to argue, quite plausibly even if inaccurately, that someday the Americans will go home and the Europeans had therefore better prepare for that day.

The second line we've taken is that an independent nuclear deterrent in Europe is not only unnecessary, it is bound to be ineffectual. The United States and the Soviet Union have invested fantastic amounts of money and effort in the development of their strategic capabilities. We argue that the late-starting, meagerly financed—by United States–U.S.S.R. standards—French program is doomed to failure as a deterrent. It will either possess too small a nuclear striking force or that force will not survive an original Soviet attack or, even if it does, will be unable to get through Soviet defenses, or both.

The technical aspects of this are obviously beyond the scope of this book,[33] but it goes without saying that the French deny the validity of the American argument. And when it is suggested that the British experience demonstrates the futility of any but a great power attempting to develop and maintain such a capability, the French aver that their determination is greater.[34]

Lastly, we have gone beyond argumentation and proposed an alternative nuclear deterrent program, the so-called "multi-lateral force" (MLF). Al-

---

[33] For a brief discussion of this and related matters, see *ibid.*, pp. 126–138. Perhaps the most authoritative, nonclassified discussion of the utility of independent nuclear deterrents by nations other than the two superpowers is Albert Wohlstetter's "Nuclear Sharing: NATO and the N + 1 Country," which originally appeared in *Foreign Affairs*, vol. 39, no. 3, pp. 355–387, April, 1961. He sums up his argument against such forces as follows: ". . . [F]rom the national standpoint of a responsible power, they are costly and of dubious military value. Their political value has been exaggerated, for, as the English have learned, it encourages emulation and is therefore transient. From the standpoint of world stability, wide nuclear diffusion would be gravely disruptive. It would increase the likelihood of the use of nuclear weapons both by accident and by deliberation" (p. 371).

[34] It should perhaps be emphasized that there is a vast difference between building a nuclear bomb and building an independent nuclear deterrent vis-à-vis a great power. The former is relatively easy and inexpensive; the latter is much more difficult, exorbitantly expensive, and subject to rapid obsolescence. To achieve a meaningful deterrent force, a nation must develop, in addition to the bomb, a means of delivering it and a method of protecting this means of delivery against the adversary's initial assault. To achieve a responsible deterrent force, a nation must, in addition, develop complex means of ensuring that it is used only and authorized by the highest governmental authority. All these ingredients require enormous expenditures, far exceeding the cost of the bomb itself. See the Wohlstetter article cited in the preceding footnote and also R. N. Rosecrance's concluding chapter, "International Stability and Nuclear Diffusion," in Rosecrance, *op. cit.*, pp. 293–314.

though the Johnson administration apparently pulled back in 1964 from its earlier enthusiastic sponsorship of this scheme, the MLF was—and may again be—a major American foreign policy proposal and is therefore worthy of careful analysis. The idea of a NATO nuclear force began to be seriously discussed in the latter days of the Eisenhower administration and was actually publicly endorsed by outgoing Secretary of State Christian Herter. The incoming administration hesitated for a time, but then embraced the idea enthusiastically, and began to try to sell the idea to the Europeans. Essentially, the MLF would be a fleet of surface ships manned by mixed crews from several NATO nations and armed with missiles capable of delivering nuclear weapons to the Soviet Union. All participating nations would be empowered to veto the use of the missiles.

As a proposed substitute for independent national nuclear deterrents, the MLF has been criticized on several grounds, some technical and some political. There were many doubts about the practicability of a fleet of ships, each of which was to be manned by crews from several different countries. What language would be used? What codes of discipline would be enforced? (Would American sailors, for example, be permitted to share their shipmates' whisky?) Was it reasonable to assume that all participating governments would be able to communicate their orders to the ships— or some central control post—during an emergency? Would MLF add anything militarily to the existing strategic deterrent? If not, would the fact that other nations could veto its use seriously compromise the existing American deterrent force?

But these technical difficulties pale into insignificance alongside the basic political problem: The United States would still have a veto. If the original motive was to provide Europeans with a deterrent that was not dependent upon American willingness to use it, the MLF clearly would fail to accomplish the objective. The proponents of the MLF concede this, but say that the MLF is a step in the direction of the "nuclear sharing" desired by the Europeans and that, moreover, it would have political significance even if it lacked military significance.

It is by no means clear what these arguments mean in concrete terms. If "nuclear sharing" only means that the allies should consult with each other at the highest levels and regularly about nuclear policy, that the Europeans should be given more information about United States nuclear capabilities, that they should participate in such matters as the selection of targets, and that their counsel should be considered seriously by the United States, MLF might be a meaningful gesture. Supporters of MLF suggest that this is the case and that at this point most Europeans do not have nuclear ambitions that reach Gaullist proportions.

Dogmatism is especially unwarranted in matters as complex as this, but it seems highly unlikely that this is a valid argument. The concern engendered in Europe about the credibility of the American deterrent occasioned by the vulnerability of the United States to Soviet attack is not likely to be much diminished by schemes that merely increase European "participation" in decisions that would remain finally American. Indeed, if this is all that "nuclear sharing" means to non-Gaullist Europeans, one wonders what all the talk and anguish is about and why, moreover, we even went so far as to propose MLF; lesser accommodations would have sufficed.

Proponents of MLF say that this is a crude view and that the value of MLF is that it moves in the direction of meeting current demands and can be used to meet future ones as well. Here the argument becomes quite murky. One argument that is sometimes put forward is that MLF would *evolve* into a genuine European deterrent. Suppose, for example, that a directorship of five nations (Great Britain, France, West Germany, Italy and the United States) were to control MLF, with decisions requiring unanimity. Later on, decisions could be made by a majority vote, provided the United States was among the majority. (In other words, at this stage, the United States would still retain a veto.) Finally, a simple majority would suffice, with the United States relinquishing its veto. Thus, proponents argue, the creation of MLF would be a substantial step toward a genuine European deterrent.[35]

This argument appears no more convincing than the preceding one. The Europeans have no assurances or even any substantial reasons for believing that such an evolution would take place. In the first place, no American President is likely to favor relinquishing our veto over nuclear weapons supplied by us. Secondly, such a proposal would require congressional action because current law prohibits such a practice; and it is unlikely in the extreme that Congress would ever agree to such a proposal.[36]

In the meantime, moreover, the Europeans would still be without an independent (of the United States) nuclear deterrent, so that even if this evolution were feasible, the interim period would not be covered.

MLF would appear to be more of a gimmick than a serious proposal designed to quiet European fears about America's reliability. And, as a

---

[35] This particular example of how MLF might evolve into a genuine European deterrent appears in Malcolm Hoag's "Nuclear Strategic Options and European Force Participation," in *ibid.*, pp. 222–258. This article, by the way, states a case *for* MLF.

[36] In the 1946 McMahon Act, Congress forbade the transmission of information regarding nuclear weapons to other nations. The act was amended in 1958 to permit such transmission to a nation that has made "substantial progress in the development of atomic weapons." The amendment was adopted to facilitate cooperation with Great Britain, but it has not been invoked to permit cooperation with France, much to the latter's annoyance. The fact that France has fulfilled the "substantial progress" criterion and yet has not been the recipient of any American nuclear assistance is, by the way, strong evidence of this government's great reluctance to foster the spread of nuclear capabilities.

matter of fact, it has been viewed in this light by most European governments. France, of course, has rejected it completely. Great Britain's position under the Conservative Government was uncertain but far from
enthusiastic. The Labor Government has put forward a complicated and
incompatible alternative proposal which, if anything, reflects even less
satisfaction with the MLF. West Germany, on the other hand, has welcomed it. The reasons for this are subject to various interpretations. It
may be that the German government is merely anxious to please the American government upon which it depends so heavily for its own security. Or
it may be that the Germans are genuinely interested in all steps which may
lead to greater European cooperation, however uncertain the prospects for
any particular step may be. Or it may be that they believe this could be
a way of blunting the general opposition to German nuclearization by
demonstrating their cooperative spirit on nuclear matters.[37] Or, finally,
it may be that they do anticipate some kind of evolution in MLF control
arrangements that would give them something of the substance as well as
the shadow of control over nuclear weapons. Whatever their motives, it is
the Germans to whom the proposal has been primarily directed, and it has
been the Germans who have been most responsive to it.

The Soviet response has been sharply negative; it might even be called
alarming. The Soviets appear to regard MLF as an elaborate façade behind
which the United States is preparing to transfer the control of some nuclear
weapons to West Germany. If this prospect frightens most of Western
Europe, it is easy to envisage the reaction in the Kremlin. Critics of MLF
regard this as the final absurdity; not only is MLF militarily unnecessary,
politically unsatisfactory, and potentially troublesome within the alliance,
it is also provocative.

If one believes—as this writer does—that the criticisms of MLF given
above are unanswerable and that the proposal is therefore unsound, and
perhaps even dangerously so, it becomes necessary to seek alternatives. This
attempt is likely to engender in anyone a greater sympathy for the effort
to make MLF look attractive. For the melancholy fact is that there is no
way, short of some kind of Atlantic Union, that would irrevocably tie the
United States to the defense of Western Europe and that would, therefore,
resolve the doubts induced by our new vulnerability. Modern technology
has partially undermined the complex set of calculations and reciprocal
benefits upon which the Atlantic Alliance was founded, and nothing is
likely to alter this new fact.

---

[37] Germany is under a solemn obligation not to *manufacture* on its territory any atomic
weapons, biological weapons, or chemical weapons. This obligation was undertaken
by the West German government in the fall of 1954; it was a precondition to Germany's entrance (in 1955) into NATO. Note that this does not prohibit the *possession*
of such weapons.

The second problem associated with American defense policy and NATO to be discussed was also chosen because, like the preceding one, it illustrates both the complexity of defense policy and the delicate character of alliance cohesion, even among nations with a preponderance of common values and common interests.

The Emphasis on Conventional Weapons

As described above, the incoming Democratic administration in 1961 was determined to reduce America's, and therefore NATO's, reliance on tactical nuclear weapons. It was widely believed that the President should have some choice in the event of a local skirmish, or even a larger-scale but conventional attack, besides resorting to nuclear weapons or doing nothing at all. So the United States reversed the trend and began emphasizing conventional capability and urging its NATO allies to bring their forces up to strength. From the American point of view, this was merely a prudent, albeit expensive, means of expanding the options available in time of crisis.

But many Europeans saw it differently. They were far from anxious to incur the costs of increased defense expenditures, but that was probably not the fundamental issue. They had originally been somewhat dubious about the wisdom of American insistence on the nuclearization of NATO in the mid-1950s. They then accepted it and, in fact, became quite comfortable with it. Insofar as they retained any real concern about Soviet military intentions in Europe, they were more interested in deterrence than in defense. For this purpose, nuclear reliance at the tactical level had worked splendidly. So why change? They had absorbed the military doctrines espoused by the Americans in the 1950s, and now they were suddenly being asked to accept a new and quite different set of doctrines. It was to be expected that they would wonder why.

Many, of course, took the new emphasis at face value. A case could be made for it, there was a new administration in Washington, and so forth. But others were more suspicious. Was this backing away from a nearly automatic reliance on nuclear weapons the first step toward a complete renunciation of their use in Europe? Were the Americans becoming so cautious as to be ineffectual? Was the deterrent being devalued too far, inviting Soviet adventures?

It was this last aspect that troubled many observers in Europe and the United States. Was the new administration, wittingly or unwittingly, giving the Soviets cause to believe that Western will and determination were cracking? Perhaps the new policy was theoretically better for an actual military encounter, but it might be dangerously less effective as a deterrent.

The Kennedy administration, of course, denied all of these interpretations. It was not renouncing the use of tactical nuclear weapons, it said; it was merely supplementing them.[38]

Who was right, the administration or its critics? It should be clear by now that there is no certain answer to that kind of question. The success of a defense policy depends on many unknowable factors, most particularly the responses it will induce in one's adversaries. If the Soviets were reading the new emphasis as a failure of nerve or sign of weakness, there was no convincing evidence of this. But only time will tell, and even then it will be impossible to determine whether the older policy would have been more or less effective.

This example shows how delicate relations are within the alliance and how ramifying are the defense policies of the United States in particular.[39]

The Future of the Alliance

The North Atlantic Treaty will be in force until 1969. Thereafter, any member may withdraw on one year's notice. This has given rise to some speculation about whether the organization that has grown up around the treaty will survive at all, whether it should, and what the alternatives are. From the standpoint of American foreign policy, it is difficult to imagine any circumstances—short of the effective termination of the cold war—

---

[38] In 1964, the administration began to take an unprecedentedly optimistic line about the relative strength of Soviet and NATO forces in Europe. For many years, it was widely believed that the Soviets had several times as many available troops in Europe as NATO did. These estimates had begun to be revised in a more hopeful direction in the late 1950s, but as late as 1963, Secretary McNamara told Congress that the combined forces of all NATO countries in Europe would not be able to contain an all-out conventional Soviet attack without resorting to nuclear weapons. In 1964, however, he made the following observations in his annual appearance in connection with the defense budget:

> An intensive study of the size and character of Communist ground forces has convinced us that our ability to deal with conventional attacks in Europe is greater than had previously been supposed. I have been convinced for some time, as have many Members of Congress, that we have been overestimating the size and capability of the Communist ground forces. These inflated estimates have led, in turn, to an unduly pessimistic view of our prospects in non-nuclear war. Actually, the problems we face in this area are related more to readiness, deployment capability, and certain shortages in equipment and stocks than they are to overall manpower levels or defense budgets. (*Source: Hearings on Military Posture and H.R. 9637, before the House Committee on Armed Services, Jan. 27, 1964, 88th Cong., 2d Sess., p. 7021.*)

The manpower gap has apparently vanished along with the missile gap.

[39] A related example was the gigantic airlift of an entire American division from Texas to Germany in the fall of 1963. This extraordinary feat, accomplished in sixty-four hours, was designed to show how quickly the United States, with its vastly increased airlift capacity, could reinforce the troops in Europe. Some, however, viewed it as still another step in the direction of the withdrawal of American troops from Europe. The success of this effort, it was argued, would be used as an excuse for reducing the American forces in Europe.

under which the demise of NATO would be welcome.[40] What its precise character will or should be is another matter.

The "good old days" of American hegemony and European complaisance are presumably gone forever. Whatever may be the realities of military power in the foreseeable future—and it seems quite likely that the United States will continue to provide the bulk of the Western deterrent strength—Europe has reacquired its prosperity and its self-confidence. France is not the only European nation willing and able to disregard American wishes regarding defense and other matters; she is merely the most conspicuous. But the United States is not interested in controlling Western Europe, so these developments are not in themselves undesirable. The basic problem for the future is how to ensure the defense of Europe under these changed conditions.

President Kennedy often spoke of closer United States–European ties, of "interdependence." The precise character of this interdependence was not clear, but the general outline was of an "Atlantic Community," whose common interests and values would draw the nations ever closer together on all fronts. Trade would be virtually free of tariffs, quotas, or other restrictions. Educational and cultural intermingling would be extensive and would help to blur national consciousness. Defense efforts would be cooperative and indivisible. Over the long haul, the more ambitious supporters of these trends envisaged common political institutions and ultimately a vast new nation embracing Western Europe, Great Britain, and North America.

Less ambitious schemes envisage the political unification of Europe and then a fruitful era of cooperation between the United States of Europe and the United States of America.

It seems more likely, however, that neither of these patterns will develop in the foreseeable future and that many independent national sovereignties will continue to seek their individual and common interests as best they can.[41]

Whether NATO itself can survive and, if so, in what form remain to be seen. Much will depend on the policies pursued by the major interested parties, of course. The traditional but unintended role of the Soviet Union has been to provoke an occasional crisis—such as a threat against the allied

---

[40] For a contrary opinion, see Ronald Steel, *The End of Alliance*, The Viking Press, Inc., New York, 1964. The author of this book believes that the Soviet military threat has disappeared. If one is willing to make that assumption, the rest of his argument is quite plausible.

[41] There are other possibilities, too, some of them rather bleak. Europe could, for example, unite and then turn its back on the United States, establishing a "Third Force." Or it could abandon the path toward integration, dissolve into warring factions again, and pose serious dangers to the peace of the world. The first of these could perhaps be deemed a real possibility, but the second is very remote.

presence in West Berlin—which would draw the allies together and remind everyone of NATO's reason for being. If a relaxation of East-West tensions should persist, NATO may fall on hard times. The alliance is not, after all, an end in itself.

Another variable of great consequence is French policy. If President de Gaulle stays in office for many more years, NATO may change entirely or even disintegrate. According to a news dispatch from Madrid in May, 1964, for example, French Foreign Minister Maurice Couve de Murville told a news conference that "France thinks that the North Atlantic Treaty Organization is old-fashioned because it does not leave enough room (to develop) the national responsibility of each state." He said that such alliances were designed for wartime.[42]

German policy will also affect NATO greatly. France and the United States seem to be engaged in an unfortunate competition for Germany's primary allegiance, and the result of that is bound to affect the character of European politics and therefore NATO for years to come.

Finally, American policies will, of course, have a considerable effect on European and NATO affairs. What can the United States profitably do to strengthen the alliance? Two kinds of proposals, in addition to those discussed above, are sometimes heard. The first is that we should arrange one or more Western summit conferences or, less spectacularly, arrange for increased consultations within the alliance. These kinds of proposals assume that current difficulties are primarily the product of poor communications and lack of understanding. It would be pleasant if this were the case, but it should be clear from the preceding discussion that NATO's current problems stem from genuine and apparently unavoidable conflicts of interest. They will not be eliminated by conversations, no matter how eminent or friendly the discussants may be.

The second kind of proposal sometimes put forward is that the United States should overcome the divisiveness of the nuclear issue by reversing its policy and assisting those nations, especially France, that are attempting to develop independent nuclear capabilities. The proponents of this idea suggest that since the development of these capabilities is inevitable in any event, we should not permit it to divide and weaken the alliance.

There are several difficulties with this proposal. Most importantly, it would be a virtual invitation to Germany to join the nuclear club. The ramifications of this were mentioned briefly above. It is hard to see what useful purpose this would serve. Secondly, it would result in precisely the kind of general dispersion of nuclear capability that we—and the Russians —so correctly fear. Thirdly, it would violate the spirit, though not the letter, of the partial nuclear test ban agreement reached in August, 1963, and might result in the destruction of that limited, but intrinsically and

[42] As quoted in *The Los Angeles Times*, May 31, 1964, section A, p. 24.

symbolically important, step toward the international control of nuclear weapons.[43]

What, in the face of these disintegrative tendencies and inadequate or undesirable prescriptions to halt them, should United States policies regarding NATO be? There do not appear to be any magical or even promising formulas available. But there are clearly some things that should *not* be done. The first is that we should not give in to the temptation of abandoning the annoying burden of helping to defend Europe. Even if common traditions, shared values, and solemn commitments were not involved, the defense of Europe would still be the top priority of American foreign policy. The six Common Market states—France, Italy, West Germany, Belgium, the Netherlands, and Luxembourg—plus Great Britain constitute a total population and gross national product well in excess of that of the Soviet Union. The communization of this area would obviously be a momentous and perhaps fatal blow to the security and well-being of the United States. Moreover, tradition, values, and commitments are involved, and do count.

Nor should we indulge ourselves in the satisfying practice of denouncing General de Gaulle and those who support his policies. Theirs is a perfectly legitimate point of view, and, more importantly, nothing will be accomplished by attacking them. We should try to hold the alliance together, even without France, but we should not be dogmatic about our prescriptions. The precise character of NATO at any given time is not as important as we sometimes pretend it is, and, moreover, our capacity to influence such matters is bound to be limited.

Above all, we must not lose sight of our basic objectives. NATO, to repeat, is not an end in itself. If it loses its cohesion or vitality, we must seek to supplement it with unilateral and multilateral arrangements designed to serve the same purpose it has served: the defense of Europe. With or without France—or even NATO itself—United States troops in Europe are a vital necessity for the security of the West. So are impressive

---

[43] The partial nuclear test ban treaty was negotiated by the United States, Great Britain, and the Soviet Union and has been signed by almost every nation in the world. It provides that "Each of the Parties to this Treaty undertakes to prohibit, to prevent, and not to carry out any nuclear weapon test explosion, or any other nuclear explosion, at any place under its jurisdiction or control: (a) in the atmosphere; beyond its limits, including outer space; or underwater, including territorial waters or high seas; or (b) in any other environment [i.e., underground] if such explosion causes radioactive debris to be present outside the territorial limits of the State under whose jurisdiction or control such explosion is conducted." It does not ban most underground tests or prohibit the transfer of nuclear information to other states. It obligates signators "to refrain from causing, encouraging, or in any way participating in, the carrying out of any nuclear weapon test explosion, or any other nuclear explosion . . ." in any of the aforementioned environments. This, of course, leaves open the rather remote possibility of assisting another power in underground tests.

The two most significant nonsigners are France and Communist China.

—to the Russians—Western European armed forces, integrated with or outside the formal NATO structure. And, of course, the American strategic arsenal must remain in the background as the ultimate deterrent.

The preceding section has emphasized the disagreements within and the shortcomings of NATO. But the impression should not be left that NATO is doomed or, even more absurdly, that Western Europe is gravely imperiled. Regarding the latter, it is partly because Western Europe is *not* gravely imperiled, but is, instead, ever more prosperous and self-confident and secure, that many of the difficulties discussed above have arisen. The success of our European policies is, to some extent, rendering those same policies obsolescent. Europe is not gravely imperiled; and if she and the United States manage to maintain a sensible combination of resistance and accommodation in dealing with the Soviet Union, she will not be.

As for NATO itself, insofar as the need for it continues, there are good grounds for expecting that it will persist and accomplish its purpose. Whether its organizational characteristics or its strategies always accord with what is most appropriate and prudent is another, and much less important, matter.

Berlin

Postwar contention over Berlin has almost certainly been the most dangerous aspect of the cold war. It may even be true that in the absence of this divisive, emotional, and mutually frustrating issue, some kind of accommodation, tacit or otherwise, regarding Europe would already have been worked out between East and West. However that may be, the problem of Berlin exists, and there is little reason not to believe that it will continue to provide the most tense and most dangerous episodes of the cold war.

Background

As related in Chapter 5, Berlin became this special problem because of decisions made in another era, when different assumptions and expectations prevailed within the wartime Grand Alliance. Berlin, like Paris, was much more than the capital of the nation. It was indisputably the economic, cultural, and political center of Germany. Each of the victorious allies wanted to occupy a section of this great city because of its political and symbolic significance; and each one was duly assigned a sector. Since Berlin lay well inside the area of Germany that was quite naturally assigned to the eastern member of the alliance, this arrangement contained within it the seeds of endless conflict.

As noted earlier, the Soviets tried to force the Western Allies out of West Berlin as early as 1948 by instituting a blockade of all road and canal traffic from the Western zones of occupation in Germany to West Berlin. The West's response was to launch a spectacular airlift, which lasted over ten months, involved over 275,000 flights, carried over 2.3 million tons of food, coal, and other supplies, and resulted in the loss of seventy-two lives.

The motivation behind the Soviet termination of the blockade in May, 1949, is not known and cannot easily be surmised. Their blockade had been rendered largely ineffective by the airlift, to be sure, and there were propaganda disadvantages in their stance, but even so they would seem to have gained little by terminating it, and the Western allies were much relieved. Whatever the cause of their backdown, it was not an irrevocable decision to accept as permanent the Western presence in Berlin. There was periodic harassment of Western traffic to and from Berlin in the years that followed.

Meanwhile, West Berlin—i.e., those portions of Greater Berlin occupied by the United States, Great Britain, and France—was becoming increasingly embarrassing to the Soviets and their puppet regime in East Germany (the "German Democratic Republic" or GDR). There were essentially three reasons why this city constituted what Khrushchev aptly called "a bone in our throats." Heavily subsidized by the Western allies and, more significantly and lavishly, by an economically booming West Germany (the "Federal Republic of Germany"), West Berlin became a glittering symbol of prosperity and political freedom right in the midst of the drab Communist empire. Communist propagandists railed about its decadence and superficiality, but their unhappy subjects in East Germany —and in Eastern Europe generally—looked on it through different and envious eyes.

A second factor in the Soviet discomfiture was West Berlin's function as an escape hatch for disenchanted East Germans who wanted to flee to the West. The population of East Germany is approximately 17 million compared with West Germany's approximately 70 million, and the Soviets did not look with favor upon "their" Germans' defecting to the West. Yet, between 1945 and August 1, 1961, an estimated 3,300,000 East Germans did defect, most of them through West Berlin.[44] The propaganda disadvantages of this massive exodus—in Lenin's phrase, the people were "voting with their feet"—was bad enough from the Soviet perspective. But in addition, it was a serious drain on East Germany's trained and potential manpower needs. The number of physicians defecting was especially alarming to the Communist regime, but there were many other professionals. Perhaps worst of all, about half of the defectors were under twenty-five years of age.

The third reason why the Soviets found West Berlin an intolerable

---

[44] Until 1953, it was relatively easy for Germans to cross the border between East and West Germany. But then the East Germans constructed an ominous and largely impenetrable border "death strip," complete with barbed wire, watchtowers, and guards. But until August 13, 1961, a refugee who got to East Berlin could get to West Berlin rather easily by foot or by subway provided he carried no luggage or other evidence of an intention to flee.

annoyance was the fact that it served to some extent as a center and source for anti-Communist activities. The extent to which West Berlin functioned —and functions—in this manner and with what effect are, of course, not easily knowable. Such activities are by their very nature secret or semi-secret. But the Soviets were vehement in their allegations that West Berlin was a hotbed of subversion, espionage, and sabotage directed against the GDR, and that it harbored "revengeful circles" bent on undoing the territorial and political consequences of World War II.

The Soviet Union did not, of course, publicly rest its case on the first two factors mentioned above; such matters hardly reflected favorably on the Soviet system. But the Soviets did emphasize publicly their allegations of subversive activities in West Berlin, and they coupled it with an argument designed to show that the Western presence in Berlin was illegal. They argued that the anomalous situation in Berlin depends for its legitimacy on wartime agreements. These agreements, they charged, have been repeatedly violated by the West, most significantly in the rearming of Germany. As a result, the wartime accords are null and void, and, consequently, the Western presence in Berlin is legally untenable as well as politically intolerable.

The Western response to these arguments has been, needless to say, almost entirely unsympathetic. The charges of subversion have been consistently denied. The argument that the Western presence is illegal has been emphatically rejected. The wartime agreements are not invalid, the West argues, and, moreover, even if they were, the Western presence would be legitimate by right of conquest until some new international accord were reached.

But these technicalities scarcely scratch the surface of what is really at stake in Berlin. The United States and its allies are not especially concerned about whether Berlin is a useful base for subversion within the Communist orbit or whether the Western presence there can be demonstrated to be legal or not. What they do care about, and care very profoundly about, is the political implications of their staying in Berlin or withdrawing under Soviet pressure. Berlin has become the great testing ground of Western will and courage. Whether it was done after due consideration or impulsively, wisely or imprudently, the West—and particularly the United States—has affirmed and reaffirmed its irrevocable determination to defend the freedom of West Berlin. A falling away from that pledge would reveal the determination and courage of the West to be frail and unreliable. The consequences of such a revelation would probably be disastrous. It might be, of course, that the Soviets would not interpret such a development as sufficient evidence of Western weakness to warrant their attempting to exploit it. But it seems much more likely that the Soviets—and/or the rest of the world—would try to take advantage of the alleged weakness of will, and this would be extremely dangerous, whether it resulted in further Western retreats or whether it elicited an angry and warlike Western response. In today's world, a failure of will on one side could very well result in a disaster for both sides.[45]

One other obvious fact should be noted. From the standpoint of partisan politics, any "softness" regarding Berlin would be quite risky. Whichever party was out of office would denounce the administration for not "standing up to the Russians." No matter how stale this allegation may be, there would probably be some partisan mileage left in it if an administration could be shown to have sacrificed something important in Berlin.

The 1958–1961 Crisis

The Soviet Union began its second serious assault on the Western position in Berlin—the first having been the 1948–1949 blockade—in 1958. On November 10, Premier Khrushchev told a Soviet-Polish rally in Moscow that it was time "to renounce the remnants of the occupation regime in Berlin" and to have the Western powers reach agreements with East Germany regarding Berlin. On November 27, the Soviets delivered an ultimatum to the three Western occupying powers. It demanded that the Western powers leave Berlin within six months and that West Berlin be converted into a "free city." If the Western powers refused to do this, the Soviet Union would unilaterally terminate its responsibilities in Berlin, and the West would have to reach agreements with East Germany about its status in Berlin. The wartime agreements would be null and void.

The Western powers rejected the Soviet demands entirely, and the six-month deadline date passed without incident. But for the next several years there were periodic crises over Berlin, some of them raising with stark urgency the possibility that one side or the other might begin to shoot. Western convoys were held up on the autobahn leading from West Germany to West Berlin. Western aircraft flying to West Berlin were threatened and endangered by Soviet military planes, and verbal fireworks emanated from the Kremlin. But nothing calamitous happened, and nothing was basically changed.

By 1961, Premier Khrushchev had been making menacing gestures and speeches for over two years, and the West had not budged. There had not always been agreement about how to respond to Khrushchev's challenge and what counterproposals, if any, to put forward, but the Western allies were united in their determination not to yield their basic position

---

[45] The preceding analysis does not imply that such things as the freedom of the 2.25 million West Berliners and the honoring of solemn commitments are not intrinsically important to Western statesmen; they are. But even such considerations are secondary in importance to the preservation of the West's reputation for strength and seriousness of purpose; and it is this consideration that is thrown onto the scales every time there is a Berlin crisis.

in Berlin. And the new American administration adopted the Eisenhower administration's position without hesitation or reservation.

By the summer of 1961, the Soviets were ready for another round in this dangerous game of showdown. The specific causes of the new Soviet thrust are, of course, not known, but they may very well have had something to do with the recent debacles of the new administration. The first international crisis handled by the Kennedy administration was the deteriorating situation in Laos, where pro-Communist rebel forces—the Pathet Lao —were advancing against the existing pro-Western regime. President Kennedy had called a dramatic press conference—carried live by the radio and television networks—on March 22, 1961, and had strongly implied that United States military intervention was imminent. Naval and troop movements in the Far East reinforced this impression. But then, despite continuing rebel successes, nothing was done.

In April, the incredibly inept Bay of Pigs invasion of Cuba by exiles reinforced the impression that the new Administration was long on talk and short on effective action.[46]

Premier Khrushchev may have come to such a conclusion. He had allegedly scoffed at the West as being "too liberal to fight."[47] and the new assortment of liberal politicians and liberal intellectuals in the White House may have seemed to him to fit this description exactly. In June, he and the new President met at Vienna for their first—and last—face-to-face confrontation. Near the end of their talks, he handed Kennedy an *aide mémoire* that touched off another—and perhaps the most dangerous— Berlin crisis. It urged the United States to sign a peace treaty with both German states and agree to a "demilitarized free city" status for Berlin, with all occupation rights being terminated. It assured the United States that the Soviet Union favored "the most reliable guarantees . . . against interference in the affairs of the free city on the part of any State." But if the United States would not agree to such arrangements, the Soviet Union would sign a peace treaty with the GDR, which

. . . would specifically define the status of West Berlin as a free city and the Soviet Union, just as the other parties to the treaty, would of course observe it strictly; measures would also be taken to ensure that this status be respected by other countries as well. At the same time, this would mean putting an end to the occupation regime in West Berlin with all its implications. In particular, questions of using the means of communication by land, water or air within the territory of the GDR would have to be settled solely by appropriate agreements with the GDR. That is

---

[46] For a brief résumé of the Bay of Pigs fiasco, see pp. 269–271.
[47] The poet Robert Frost told a news conference in New York on September 8, 1962, that Khrushchev had recently told him that the United States was "too liberal to fight." Frost may have misunderstood Khrushchev. See Franklin D. Reeve, *Robert Frost in Russia*, Little, Brown and Company, Boston, 1964, pp. 115, 120–123.

but natural, since control over such means of communication is an inalienable right of every sovereign State.[48]

President Kennedy reportedly remarked, on seeing this message, "Mr. Chairman, it's going to be a cold winter." The *aide mémoire* contained another six-month deadline, and in the ensuing weeks there were ominous additional statements by Khrushchev and other prominent Communist leaders. The familiar war of nerves was building up.

On July 25, President Kennedy addressed the nation on the renewed tension over Berlin and reasserted that the United States "cannot and will not permit the Communists to drive us out of Berlin, either gradually or by force." He declared that

we need the capability of placing in any critical area at the appropriate time a force which, combined with those of our allies, is large enough to make clear our determination and our ability to defend our rights at all costs and to meet all levels of aggressor pressure with whatever levels of force are required. We intend to have a wider choice than humiliation or all-out nuclear action.

He then announced the steps that he had taken in recent months and those he intended to take in the immediate future to achieve this "wider choice." The most dramatic maneuver was a request for congressional authorization—which was quickly granted and used—to call a substantial number of reservists to active duty "to give us the airlift capacity and protection that we need."

There ensued a typical Berlin crisis of threat and counterthreat, mutual military build-ups, and ultimately no decisive action. If Khrushchev had been testing the new President's will, he apparently became convinced that that will was at least strong enough to make any direct assault on Berlin unacceptably risky. Except for one new and significant development, the 1961 Berlin crisis would have had the same general history as earlier ones: Soviet threats, Western resistance, and no significant change.

The Wall

The new development in 1961 was the construction of the wall between East and West Berlin. During the night of August 12–13, less than three weeks after President Kennedy's address to the nation quoted above, the East Germans built the wall that, among other things, divided the city, terminated the employment of thousands of Berliners who lived in one sector and worked in another, and stopped the flood of refugees that had been streaming into West Berlin from East Germany in sharply in-

---

[48] Senate Committee on Foreign Relations, *Documents on Germany, 1944–1961*, 87th Cong., 1st Sess., 1961, pp. 644–645.

creased numbers since the new crisis began. For these and other reasons, the wall created new dangers. It provided new incentives for violence and new opportunities for tragic miscalculations or accidents on both sides, and it increased the possibility that the East Germans would one day rise up against their oppressive government and perhaps drag the West Germans into the resulting struggle. This nightmare has haunted both East and West for years, but the wall, by closing off the "safety valve" of West Berlin, increased the danger.

The construction of the wall and the Western response to it have been focal points of controversy in the United States and elsewhere ever since. The original Western response was to protest that the wall was illegal in that it violated the joint occupation status established by the wartime accords and also subsequent agreements regarding what the West called "free circulation" within the city. The Soviets, of course, replied that the West had forfeited its legal rights in Berlin and that the wall was a perfectly legitimate means of cutting off the flow of spies and subversives that the West was sending into the GDR. International law specialists on both sides of the Iron Curtain issued learned pronouncements that purported to show that the wall was, or was not, a violation of the West's rights. The Western powers organized groups of military personnel to make tours of East Berlin, thereby reasserting the rights of the military, at least, to "free circulation." And much angry rhetoric flowed back and forth about such momentous issues as whether East German guards should be permitted to check the passes of Western military personnel going into East Berlin or whether the Russians, as the occupying power, should do this. The reason that such essentially trivial matters were elevated to high matters of statecraft was that the West—and maybe the Soviet Union —tended to believe that if it permitted any alteration of previously established procedures, it would ultimately find itself stripped of all its rights in West Berlin, including the fundamental rights of being there and having free access thereto.

In the afterglow of those tense days, the main argument has been over whether the United States should have tolerated the construction of the infamous wall. Critics of the restraint shown in that critical period have argued that the West's rights—variously defined and understood—were indeed violated and that this should have provoked a forceful Western response, including the physical destruction of the wall.

It is not clear at this time whether the Kennedy administration ever seriously considered using physical force against the wall, but it is relatively easy to understand why it would have rejected this proposal if it had considered it. The wall was built on territory that had been controlled by the Soviet Union since 1945. Whatever the hazy legalities may have been, the hard fact was that since the late 1940s both sides in the cold war had proceeded unilaterally in those areas under their control. As noted earlier, for example, the Communists had built a "wall" all along the border between East and West Germany in 1953. Whatever the legitimacy of such an undertaking, very few people had ever taken seriously the possibility of using physical force to remove this frontier fence. As the cold war settled in, each side clung tenaciously to what it had, but neither side was willing to run the risks inherent in trying to force the other side to alter its policies or activities within its own bailiwick.

Knocking down the wall would have required the use of physical coercion against the Soviets or the puppet East German regime on territory heretofore controlled by the Soviet Union. The initiative in this showdown involving physical force would have been the West's. Was the protection of some rather uncertain "rights" in East Berlin worth this much? Granted that the use of force might very well be appropriate in some circumstances —such as, for example, to ensure continued access to West Berlin for the occupying powers—was this such a circumstance?

The wall has now become a familiar aspect of the cold war. A few argue that it should be knocked down, even today, but for the most part even the more militant cold warriors suggest merely that its destruction should be a precondition to further East-West accommodations, or that its demise should have the highest priority in any further discussions with the Soviets. From the standpoint of propaganda, the wall has probably benefited the West almost exclusively. The Soviet claim that the wall was necessary in order to curtail Western subversion has a rather feeble impact alongside the grim fact that the wall has converted East Germany into a prison, a totalitarian society from which there is no escape. The frightful meaning of this is presumably understood very widely. This may be of little consolation to the West and none at all for the Berliners and East Germans involved, but it is not inconsequential. If West Berlin is a showcase for economic and political freedom, the wall and its prisoners are a most distressing advertisement for the glories of communism and its contemporary practitioners.

The Persistent Problem

But the problem of Berlin persists. The Western position there continues to be exposed and extremely annoying to the Soviets. The Russians and their German satellite regime can create an emergency there any time it suits their purposes by threatening a blockade, instituting one, or simply engaging in harassing tactics. Moreover, West Berlin's vulnerability to a quick and irresistable Soviet takeover, especially as a counterstroke to some Western military move (in Cuba?), continues to pose one of the most worrisome problems for American policy makers.

The Soviets have issued ultimatums and threats, they have attempted to make more accommodating gestures, and they have built their "wall of shame"; yet, the West remains in West Berlin. It is not known, of course, how seriously the Soviets really do take the Western presence in Berlin; presumably their concern waxes and wanes. But what if they should ever become emboldened or reckless enough to "liberate" the city by armed force? What would the United States do? What should it do? What would France, Britain, and West Germany do? The questions about what the Western Allies *would* do are unanswerable questions. It is to be hoped that this uncertainty will suffice to cause the Soviets to continue to tolerate the Western presence there. But one can never be sure of such things, and the consequences of a Soviet seizure are not pleasant to think about. There are approximately 10,000 Western troops in West Berlin, and no one pretends that they could actually defend the city if the Soviet Union should decide to annex it. These troops are hostages, kept there to warn the Soviets that an attack on West Berlin would automatically result in serious retaliatory action by the Western powers.

But would it? Suppose, for example, that the Soviets marched in and, after some minor skirmishes, gained control of the city. Suppose that they rounded up the Western military personnel and flew them instantly to the border between East and West Germany and released them into West Germany. What would the West do?

There are many "contingency plans" locked up in Pentagon and NATO files that presumably set forth various responses to this and the many other hypothetical developments that could conceivably occur in or affecting Berlin. These plans undoubtedly entail many ingenious schemes for countering such a move, but in general terms the options are necessarily rather limited. Some of them will be outlined below.

One option would be to do nothing, except to file "vigorous protest notes," and denounce from every available platform, including the United Nations, "this unprovoked and dastardly aggression." This option would have the advantage of avoiding any military confrontation with the Soviets and hence preserving the peace. It would have all of the bleak disadvantages described above. The failure of the West to "defend Berlin" in some way or other would have enormous consequences for NATO, and the credibility and reputation of the West throughout the world. Nearly all these consequences, except perhaps for a fleeting propaganda benefit, would be disadvantageous for the West.

Another option would be to launch an attack on the Soviet Union, perhaps after having warned her that such an attack was imminent if she did not withdraw. The United States has sometimes implied that such a "massive retaliation" would be forthcoming, but the reasons why it would be unlikely are clear enough to all concerned, and have been discussed above.

Another option would be to launch an attack on East Germany. Such an attack could have any of several purposes and, therefore, characteristics. A limited excursion into East Germany could be designed to present the

Soviets with a countervailing *fait accompli.* Or a concentrated effort could be made to advance on Berlin with the intention of liberating the city. Or a selective air attack on one or more East German or Soviet military installations could be launched with the threat of more to follow unless the Soviets withdrew from Berlin.

Obviously, each of these schemes would entail very grave risks. It is not at all certain that the first two would be militarily feasible for the NATO forces, but even if they were, the risk of the military encounter exploding into the all-out thermonuclear war that neither side wants would be substantial. The same risk, of course, applies to the third scheme as well.

Another option would be to launch an attack against a Communist position somewhere else in the world, as a *quid pro quo.* An invasion of Cuba might commend itself to some policy makers. It, like West Berlin, is surrounded by hostile neighbors, and there is at least some justification for treating Berlin and Cuba analogously. One difficulty with the analogy is that Cuba would presumably be much more difficult to subdue than West Berlin, but this consideration is not centrally important. But would such a *quid pro quo* be acceptable, even as the best of a bad bargain? Would all or even most of the disadvantages flowing from the abandonment of West Berlin be compensated for by the liquidation of Castro's regime in Cuba?

This brief overview of some of the options before the United States and its allies in the unlikely event of a Soviet or East German seizure of West Berlin should make it clear that the West hopes fervently never to be confronted with such a situation. It could explode into a disaster for all concerned.

A more likely development than an outright seizure of Berlin is another blockade. In recent years, the Soviets have often held up Western traffic going to West Berlin for many hours or even days. Each time, the question arises as to what the West would do if the stalling and harassment should be converted into a full-scale blockade. Would another airlift be feasible? Some observes have suggested that it would not because an airlift would have to depend in part on radar-directed landings and takeoffs, and the Soviets now have equipment that can jam and render ineffective such techniques. Others have said that an airlift is no longer feasible because the West Berlin standard of living is so much higher than it was in 1948–1949 that mere subsistence rations would no longer suffice. The West Berliners would, according to this view, begin to flee West Berlin for West Germany in great numbers, and increasingly as the blockade dragged on.

Even if these and other technical and psychological problems could be overcome, the question remains as to whether an airlift would be an appropriate response to a new blockade. While most people look back on the 1948–1949 airlift as a great and stirring success, others view it as a cowardly alternative to breaking through the blockade by force. Whatever may have been the practicability of such an action then—and most military experts believe it was wholly impracticable[49]—it would appear to be more feasible today. As noted above in the section on NATO, Western military strength in Central Europe today is, whatever its deficiencies, much closer to parity with Soviet strength there than was the case in 1948–1949. Nonetheless, shooting one's way through a Communist blockade in East Germany would be no small matter, for obvious reasons.

Aside from another airlift or an attempt to end the blockade by force, what alternatives would the West have? It could let West Berlin "wither on the vine," with all the attendant disadvantages of that as discussed above. Or it could institute a temporary airlift to get the West Berliners out of the city and safely into West Germany. Or it could impose a counter-blockade against a vulnerable Communist outpost, perhaps Cuba. Or it could combine one or more of these courses of action.

One possibility that is sometimes discussed—and would also be applicable to the problem of an outright Soviet seizure of West Berlin—would be to issue an ultimatum to the Soviets to end the blockade or face some retaliatory action, perhaps specified, perhaps not. Ultimatums in the thermonuclear age can, however, be very dangerous instruments of policy. The recipient power might take the ultimatum seriously and yet be unwilling to back down. It might then conclude that there is no advantage to being hit first and decide, therefore, to initiate an attack. In a Berlin crisis, an ultimatum by the West *might* induce the Soviets to strike first.

It should be noted that the extent to which an ultimatum is likely to induce a violent response depends in good measure on the circumstances. The two six-month deadlines given the West by the Soviet Union were in some sense ultimatums. Yet their danger potential was of a lower order than would be a Western ultimatum to the Soviets, say, to end a blockade —or to evacuate a West Berlin that they had just seized. The difference has to do with timing and the differing domestic and international pressures that would be operative. The West has been in West Berlin ever since 1945; its presence there does not represent a recent and dramatic alteration

---

[49] See, for example, Osgood, *NATO, op. cit.,* p. 29:

At the time of the Berlin blockade, the United States, with total ground reserves of about 2½ divisions, was unable to send more than a division anywhere without resorting to partial mobilization. In the Department of Defense the West's position in Berlin was considered militarily untenable, and the government soon decided that American forces could not afford to try to break the blockade with an armed convoy. Although the United States enjoyed a monopoly of the atomic bomb and the capacity to deliver it, there were no plans or even inclinations to use the bomb in any contingency short of massive assault upon Europe, and, in that event, it was generally assumed that Europe (at least to the Pyrenees) would soon be overrun anyway. [Here he cites Walter Millis (ed.), *The Forrestal Diaries,* The Viking Press, Inc., New York, 1951, chap. 12.] Only the unexpected success of the airlift— by a very narrow margin, at that—saved the West from the consequences of its local military inferiority.

of the *status quo*. Moreover, the Soviet regime is under no great pressure either at home or abroad to liquidate the Western presence. The Chinese Communists have occasionally upbraided the Soviets for tolerating this nuisance, but the Soviets do not feel the same intensity of demands from their ideological associates as do the more democratic regimes of the West. The consequence of these two factors—the fact that the Western presence in West Berlin does not represent a change in the *status quo,* and the relatively unpressured condition of Soviet policy makers—is that both the West and the Soviets have every reason to believe that Soviet threats about Berlin will not be carried out. Such threats, in other words, involve relatively less risk.

A Western ultimatum to the Soviets to end a blockade—or to evacuate a West Berlin that they had just seized—would be much more dangerous because the circumstances would be very different. The Soviet blockade—or presence in West Berlin—*would* represent a recent and dramatic alteration of the *status quo*. And the Western governments—especially the United States—would be under very great pressure at home and abroad to "do something" about it. Domestic partisan politics alone would make it nearly imperative for an American administration to take some corrective or retaliatory action.

These factors, then, make a Western ultimatum to the Soviets under such hypothetical conditions a much more serious matter than the many Soviet ultimatums to the West, though the latter are serious enough. Ironically, however, it is precisely these same factors that also make a Western ultimatum a quite likely development under the described circumstances. Feeling greatly the need to act, the Western powers might very well try an ultimatum first. And since both sides would have every reason to believe that the West was deadly serious, the incentives for the Soviets to initiate some kind of further assault on the West would be clear; and very dangerous.

To repeat the core of this argument: Issuing ultimatums in the cold-war context is inherently risky, but some ultimatums are much riskier than others. Specifically, a Western ultimatum to the Soviets to end a blockade —or to get out of West Berlin—would be a much more dangerous undertaking than are the periodic Soviet demands that the West get out of West Berlin.

But it is impossible, of course, to predict with certainty what would happen. Suppose that in either of the hypothetical situations under consideration the West did issue an ultimatum and the Soviets neither initiated an attack in response nor agreed to end the blockade. What, then, would the West do? It would be right back where it started except that it would have run a very grave risk and accomplished nothing.

The arguments in favor of an ultimatum are that the Soviets might actually capitulate, or, alternatively, that they would not simply reject it but would, instead, find it prudent at least to open the whole matter up for negotiation. The prospects for capitulation are impossible to predict with any confidence and would presumably fluctuate drastically from context to context. As for negotiations, what could they reasonably be expected to accomplish in any such drastic situation? At best, they could provide a cooling-off period, which might contribute to the avoidance of a war triggered by the anger and passion of the moment. But they would almost certainly not, under the conditions, result in any accords favorable to the West. So, although negotiations might be desirable, they would probably have to be accompanied by some other action if the West were not going to be confronted with a major setback and the ultimate loss of West Berlin.

In practice, as distinguished from rhetorically, the Soviets have behaved with considerable circumspection regarding Berlin. They have harassed and threatened the West, but have never forced a final showdown. Nonetheless, the situation remains potentially explosive, and both sides have a common interest in resolving it. But how? The Western powers insist on remaining in Berlin, and the Soviets insist that they get out. Both sides have defined the issues and their interests in such a way as to leave very little room for compromise.

There would appear to be only two types of proposals that have even the slightest chance of being adopted. One would involve some kind of "internationalizing" of West Berlin and the access routes thereto, and the other would involve some kind of wider settlement in which the entire problem of a divided Germany would itself be resolved. Neither type of proposal seems to have much chance of adoption, but since they are often discussed and because they apparently are the only peaceful and honorable resolutions even remotely possible, they will be examined briefly below.

The internationalization idea has been advanced in various forms by both the United States and the Soviet Union. In Khrushchev's June, 1961, *aide mémoire* to Kennedy, for example, the Soviet Premier put forward the following proposal:

> The U.S.S.R. proposes that the most reliable guarantees be established against interference in the affairs of the free city [West Berlin] on the part of any State. Token troop contingents of the United States, the United Kingdom, France and the U.S.S.R. could be stationed in West Berlin as guarantors of the free city. The U.S.S.R. would have no objections, either, to the stationing in West Berlin, for the same purpose, of military contingents from neutral States under the aegis of the U.N. The status of free city could be duly registered by the United Nations and consolidated by the authority of that international organization. The Soviet side is prepared to discuss any other measures that would guarantee the freedom and independence of West Berlin as a free demilitarized city.[50]

---

[50] *Documents on Germany, op. cit., 1944–1961*, p. 644.

The Western powers rejected this idea for several reasons. Among them was the suggestion that Soviet troops should join Western troops in West Berlin. Aside from the fact that no reciprocal arrangement was being suggested for East Berlin, the mere presence of Soviet troops would ensure that the international authority controlling the city—whatever it might be—would in some important way be dependent upon Soviet cooperation. This was—and is—totally unacceptable. Moreover, what did it mean to say that "the status of free city could be . . . consolidated by the authority" of the United Nations? What guarantees could there be that the United Nations would be able to ensure free access to and freedom within West Berlin?

The United States has, on the other hand, also made some proposals that envisage some kind of internationalization. In March, 1962, for example, the United States suggested that an "International Access Authority" be established to govern access on the ground and in the air between West Germany and West Berlin. The precise character of this proposed Authority was never made public, but according to press reports, it was to consist of representatives of five Western governments, five Communist governments, and three neutral governments.

The Soviets rejected this idea because it envisaged the permanent presence in West Berlin of Western troops and the further legitimation of the whole setup. But many Americans and, very significantly, the West German government also opposed the idea. The basic criticisms were two. One of the Communist governments was to be the East German regime. The Western powers—and especially West Germany—do not recognize the East German regime and are unwilling to do anything that they construe as constituting *de facto* recognition. Sitting on an Authority with the East Germans was regarded by many as constituting such a *de facto* recognition.[51]

The second, and more important, objection to the American proposal was the uncertainty about what policies would be implemented by the Access Authority. Since the neutral members would have the decisive votes, their views would be of critical importance. Who would they be? How could the West be sure that they would always respect Western

---

[51] What constitutes *de facto* recognition and what does not are questions to which there are, needless to say, nearly as many answers as there are governments. The West German government, for example, is quite sensitive on this issue and tends to interpret nearly all diplomatic contact as bestowing some legitimacy on the East German regime and therefore as bad. And it looks with disfavor, for example, on the much more pliant attitude of the government of West Berlin when the latter seeks to reach agreements with the East Germans about such things as holiday visits in East Berlin by West Berliners. At the same time, however, the two Germanies carry on a flourishing trade, and its terms are worked out by high-level officials from both governments. This is not, of course, the only instance of a Western government's putting trade considerations ahead of ideologically based "principles," but it is an especially anomalous one.

access and occupation rights? This proposal never amounted to anything, and its fate says something about the delicacy of diplomacy on the Berlin issue. The four Western governments most directly concerned tend to emphasize different aspects of the problem and therefore tend to favor somewhat different kinds of responses to it. The West German government is inclined to take a very "hard line," sometimes disapproving even of discussing the matter with the Soviets. Since discussions may imply that some aspect of the matter is negotiable, it is better not be have any discussions at all. General de Gaulle takes the same general position. The British have usually been the "soft liners," emphasizing the need to preserve peace and expressing more candidly than others their great distaste at being put in the ironic position of risking their very survival in defense of Berlin, of all places. Even so, the British have never flatly repudiated the Western commitment to protect West Berlin. The United States, for its part, has usually stood somewhere between these two positions. It has been willing to talk, but not willing to sacrifice anything of importance.

The result of all this has been that Berlin divides as well as unites the alliance. Which impulse is dominant at any given moment depends upon the situation, but any assessment of the diplomatic significance of the Berlin problem must take into account its impact on interallied relations as well as East-West relations.

Germany

The cold truth of the matter is that there is no satisfactory solution to the Berlin problem short of the reunification of Germany; and that event is not likely to occur for a very long time. It should be clear from earlier sections and chapters that the future of Germany has been at the very core of the cold war from the beginning. The twentieth century provides ample evidence of why Germany deserves to be feared and respected. The direction of its policies for the future is quite naturally a matter of deep concern to the Soviets and the West alike.

Germany could be reunified in short order if the Soviets would permit the creation of an all-German government based on nationwide free elections. But the Soviets are not interested in reunification on those terms because they know that such a Germany would almost certainly ally itself with the West. The only kind of reunification that the Soviets favor is that which would eventuate in a Communist government. Until that unlikely day, the Soviets will hang on to what they have of Germany.

Western governments, like everyone else, pay extensive lip service to the idea of German reunification, but they show a conspicuous lack of interest in doing anything about it. It may be that nothing can be done, but surely the arming of West Germany and its integration into the NATO alliance were not calculated to facilitate reunification; they have made it infinitely more difficult. The fact is that both the Soviets and the Western powers will approve of reunification only on their own terms, and each side's terms are wholly unacceptable to the other. And neither side is terribly unhappy about the absence of reunification.

But the Germans—or at least a sizable number of them—are unhappy about the division and want badly to do something about it. Since the East German regime is presumably entirely under the control of the Soviet Union—which still retains about twenty divisions in East Germany—the only conceivable source of policy redirection is West Germany. If reunification were really the highest priority of most West Germans, they could have it—on Soviet terms. So far, reunification has not in fact been the highest priority of most West Germans, and it may never be. Their standard of living and their freedoms are exceedingly attractive, and at least the latter is dependent upon their continued affiliation with the West.

It is occasionally suggested that the solution of the problem is to provide for a *neutral* Germany. There are several difficulties with this idea from the Western standpoint. It would eliminate NATO's largest contributor of troops, and it would do this without simultaneously providing plausible guarantees against the communization of the new Germany either by subversion or outright Soviet aggression. It would, in effect, move the Western lines of defense far to the west, and not only would there be no compensatory gains, but there might be the catastrophic loss to communism of all of Germany. In sum, neutralization would have no apparent advantages for the West and might even prove to be a disaster.

So, "the German problem" persists and will continue to do so for the foreseeable future. A broad implication of the preceding discussion has been that, as compared to any realistic alternatives, the *status quo* should be preserved. It goes without saying that neither this nor any other *status quo* should be preserved merely for its own sake or at all costs. But regarding Berlin and Germany, no better alternative is or seems likely to be available.

Cuba

Berlin may have been the most dangerous and important foreign policy problem facing the United States in the postwar world, Southeast Asia may have been the most troublesome and costly, but Cuba has been the most emotional. The presence of a Communist or quasi-Communist regime on that island "only 90 miles away" has plagued American policy makers and agitated American domestic politics since 1959 and probably will continue to do so for years to come.

The question of whether Fidel Castro is really a Communist—or, as he has called himself, a "Marxist-Leninist"—is both unanswerable and misleading. Even if there were any general agreement on what it means to be a Communist—and there is not—and even if there were any general agreement about whether Castro fits the definition, it would still be more relevant and more helpful to know what the foreign policies and foreign objectives of his government are. With a few bizarre exceptions—such as Hitler's Germany and contemporary South Africa—the United States has ordinarily not concerned itself primarily with the ideology of foreign governments except insofar as that ideology has prompted foreign policies inimical to the interests of the United States.

How characteristic of American policy this tendency has been is debatable—especially regarding Communist regimes—but the general principle is sound. While we would prefer to have "democratic, peace-loving" governments in all nations, this is clearly impossible, and we must, therefore, face squarely the question of whether we propose to live with these facts of international life or whether we intend to launch a crusade against all nondemocratic regimes. It should be obvious that the only practicable policy is the former. Therefore, we cannot afford the luxury of opposing governments—even Communist governments—simply because they do not live up to our standards of what governments should do and not do internally. Our criterion must instead be the traditional one of whether a given government pursues policies inimical to our interests. If so, and if these policies pose really serious problems for the United States, the United States may have to oppose that government and its policies, perhaps even through the use of armed force.

As noted, this line of argument applies even to Communist regimes: We are primarily interested in their foreign policies, not their domestic policies. We gladly supported Yugoslavia after its break with Stalin in 1948, and we are increasing our trade and contacts with many Eastern European nations today. Most significantly, we are attempting—and have been all along—to reduce the areas of friction with the Soviet Union and seeking ways of living together in peace despite our radically different economic, social, and political systems. There are some romantics in this country who believe that this acceptance of "coexistence" is cowardly and immoral, but it has the support of most Americans and has been the objective of every postwar administration, Republican and Democratic alike.[52]

But the problem is more complex than the preceding paragraphs would suggest, because the foreign and domestic policies of any given regime are not that completely separable; and this brings us back abruptly to the problem of Cuba. When a foreign government abuses the rights—personal or property—of Americans abroad, this may seem to it to be a purely internal matter, but to some extent or other, it is bound to engage the attention of and will probably induce some response from the United States government. It was originally the domestic policies of the Castro regime that brought it into conflict with the United States, because these

---

[52] The presidential campaign of 1964 was the first one that seriously challenged this consensus. The Republican platform and candidates for President and Vice President did not look with favor on the acceptance of coexistence as a necessity in today's world. Their overwhelming defeat may have eliminated this spurious issue from future presidential campaigns.

policies infringed quite directly and spectacularly on the rights of American citizens.

This is not the place to go into an extended discussion of the deterioration of Cuban-American relations after Fidel Castro succeeded in overthrowing the despotic and corrupt regime of Fulgencio Batista in January, 1959.[53] Instead, the two significant military encounters of 1961 and 1962 will be discussed, and then the contemporary military-diplomatic problems posed by Castro's Cuba will be considered.

The Bay of Pigs

By the fall of 1960, Cuban-American relations had deteriorated to the point where President Eisenhower approved the formation of an army made up of Cuban exiles for the ultimate purpose of invading Cuba and overthrowing the Castro regime. The mass executions that followed Castro's assumption of power, the increasingly anti-American tone of Castro's speeches and the government-controlled press, and the extensive confiscation of American-owned property in Cuba combined with an inept and bewildered American diplomacy to create a situation of mutual distrust and animosity.

The Democratic candidate for President, John F. Kennedy, had attempted to capitalize on the widespread concern that this situation had provoked by taking a very "hard line" during the campaign on the issue of Cuba.[54] When he assumed office after his narrow electoral victory, he

---

[53] Among the best descriptive and analytical treatments of this matter are Theodore Draper, *Castro's Revolution, Myths and Realities*, Frederick A. Praeger, Inc., New York, 1962, and Tad Szulc and Karl E. Meyer, *The Cuban Invasion, The Chronicle of a Disaster*, Ballantine Books, Inc., New York, 1962. See also the following articles by Draper: "Castro, Khrushchev and Mao," *The Reporter*, vol. 29, no. 3, Aug. 15, 1963; "Five Years of Castro's Cuba," *Commentary*, vol. 37, no. 1, January, 1964; and "The Confused Martyr," *Encounter*, vol. 23, no. 2, August, 1964. See also Herbert L. Matthews, "Dissent over Cuba," *Encounter*, vol. 23, no. 1, July, 1964; and Arthur Schlesinger, Jr., "The Risks of Dissent," *Encounter*, vol. 23, no. 2, August, 1964.

[54] What happened regarding our policy toward Cuba during the 1960 presidential campaign was a classic demonstration of how difficult it is to have a sensible debate about foreign policy during a presidential campaign. Kennedy did not know that the Eisenhower administration was undertaking the training and support of an army of exiles, and yet he was fearful that the Eisenhower administration was going to take the issue of Cuba, on which it was vulnerable, out of the campaign by invading Cuba. Candidate Kennedy therefore moved to associate himself with the popular "hard-line" position by advocating that refugees be trained and supported for the purpose of invading Cuba and overthrowing Castro. His opponent, Vice President Richard M. Nixon, knew of the secret plans and felt constrained to mask them as best he could. He therefore took a much "softer line" than Kennedy, and he berated Kennedy for proposing something that would violate our international agreements.

All other considerations aside, Kennedy probably would have been less inclined to seek a military solution than Nixon would have been. But because of a combination of partisan fears, campaign rhetoric, and official concern about a secret project, the candidates wound up taking positions that were something close to the reverse of what they would probably have preferred to take. At least Kennedy had Nixon's position; whether Nixon had Kennedy's is an open question. Such are the ironies and pitfalls of presidential campaigns.

was anxious to accomplish something, and he inherited the project of preparing the exiles for an invasion of their homeland. If the exile forces had been strong enough and Castro's regime had been weak enough, it would have been a rousing success. Some persons, of course, would have objected to the use of force for such ends, and others would have questioned the suitability of some of the exile leaders. (A few of them were in some sense identifiable with the despicable and discredited regime of Castro's predecessor, Batista). And there was always the question of what line a new Cuban government would take once it assumed office. But almost anything would have been better from the American standpoint than Castro, and most Americans would have applauded a successful rebel invasion.

But the invasion was a dismal failure and ranks among the worst fiascos in American diplomatic history. On April 17, 1961, approximately 1,500 Cuban exiles landed on the southern coast of Cuba at Cochinos Bay (the Bay of Pigs). It was well known that they had been trained, supplied, and commanded—prior to the invasion—by the United States Central Intelligence Agency (CIA) in the United States, Guatemala, and Nicaragua. They were not given adequate air support, and Castro's air force quickly assumed control of the skies, raining destruction on the small, vulnerable rebel forces on the beach. There was no popular uprising in conjunction with the invasion, the Cuban armed forces remained loyal to Castro, and by the evening of April 19, the invasion had been crushed.

It would have been hard to concoct a more complete humiliation for the United States. We suffered all the opprobrium both of instigating aggression and then of proving militarily inept. We handed Castro—and all our other adversaries—a huge propaganda bonanza and had nothing to show for it.

Needless to say, the repercussions were extensive. Internally, the new administration was embarrassed and vulnerable. After a suitable pause on behalf of "national unity in time of crisis," the Republicans quite understandably and appropriately began to attack the administration for its flagrant blunder. The effect abroad was, if anything, much worse. Our allies wondered whether the new President, whose election they had by and large welcomed, was capable of leading the Western world with skill and prudence. In Asia and Africa, the widespread excitement and approval that had greeted the coming to power of "the new generation" and its attractive young leader turned to bewilderment or angry disapproval. And in Latin America, the ancient fear of and resentment against the "Colossus of the North" came alive, and the appeal of the "Fidelistas" was much enhanced.

In addition, the event brought the new administration and the Soviet government into sharp conflict for the first time. Khrushchev demanded a halt to the invasion and assured Kennedy that the Soviet Union would give Castro "all necessary assistance." Kennedy replied that "in the event of any military intervention by outside force, we will immediately honor our obligations under the inter-American system to protect this hemisphere against external aggression." But these exchanges were insignificant alongside the fact that the fiasco apparently led the Kremlin to believe that it was dealing with an administration that was not only young and inexperienced, but also incompetent.

In this connection, it should be noted that not the least of the repercussions was the impact that this humiliation had on the new President and his new administration. It was a brutal baptism into the realm of foreign policy, and it left a deep scar. The mood in Washington changed from untempered optimism to a more sober and wary view of the world *and* such things as omnicompetent intelligence agencies and military expertise. Although the cost was too high, this consequence was undeniably salubrious.

If there had been any doubt about the direction of Castro's foreign policies before the Bay of Pigs debacle, there was none afterward. Cuba moved closer and closer to the Communist orbit and became almost entirely dependent upon the Soviet Union economically. The stage was being set for the most direct and dramatic Soviet-American confrontation of the cold war. After April, 1961, and in line with the type of reasoning set forth at the beginning of this section on Cuba, the United States had begun, however uneasily, to become accustomed to living with Castro's Cuba. There were apparently no plans for a new and bigger invasion. The Kennedy administration continued to castigate the Castro regime and managed to have it expelled from the inter-American regional organization, the Organization of American States (OAS). And there were repeated declarations that Castro's regime was intolerable and that some day Cuba would be free. But on the practical level, no one seemed to have any idea of how this latter goal was to be achieved in a manner involving an acceptable level of costs and risks.

The Missile Crisis

Background. There were two matters that threatened to upset this uneasy and frustrating stalemate. One was Castro's boldness in exporting his revolution to Latin America. Not only was Cuba becoming a training center for Latin American revolutionaries, but there was increasing evidence that propaganda and arms were being smuggled into Latin America from Cuba. At some point, this policy was bound to goad other Latin American countries and the United States into some kind of reaction.

The other potentially explosive development was the buildup of Soviet armed forces in Cuba and the increased shipment of Soviet arms to the Castro regime in the late summer of 1962. Many Americans found this intolerable just in and of itself, but the administration remained outwardly calm over the issue, arguing that the Soviet military presence there posed no military threat to the United States. Protests were duly sent to Moscow, but the presence of Soviet troops and technicians was not regarded as a sufficient cause for any kind of aggressive action.

The administration drew the line at what it called "offensive" weapons.[55] On September 4, 1962, for example, the White House issued a statement in response to a growing concern about the Soviet buildup in Cuba. President Kennedy said that there was no evidence "of the presence of offensive ground-to-ground missiles; or of other significant offensive capability either in Cuban hands or under Soviet direction and guidance. Were it to be otherwise, the gravest issues would arise."

This statement was issued amidst a rising clamor at home and heightened tension abroad about the Soviet military buildup in Cuba and the American response to it. On September 7, the President asked Congress for authorization to call up 150,000 reserves for a limited period. While he maintained that he was more concerned about the situation in Berlin than the one in Cuba, his action aroused still graver concern at home and abroad. The Soviets denounced the action and repeated their pledge to "render assistance to any peace-loving state." During the next few weeks, some prominent Republicans, acting on information supplied by Cuban exile groups, began to insist that the Soviet arms buildup was not merely "defensive"; they demanded some kind of action, perhaps a blockade, to stop the flow of arms to Cuba.

October 14–October 28, 1962.   On Sunday, October 14, the crisis took a decisive turn for the worse. An American U-2 reconnaissance plane took pictures of Soviet medium-range ballistic missiles (MRBMs) already in-

---

[55] The term "offensive" is obviously ambiguous and has been the subject of much debate. As the administration used it with regard to weapons in the fall of 1962, it apparently had two essential components, one having to do with capability and the other with intent. First, the weapon had to be a ground-to-ground missile capable of hitting targets some distance outside the user's territory. Hence a missile that could be fired from Cuba to the United States could be an "offensive" weapon, whereas one that was merely capable of shooting down atttacking aircraft—a ground-to-air missile—would be a "defensive" weapon.

But the United States had, for example, ground-to-ground missiles in Turkey pointing at the Soviet Union. Moreover, these missiles were above ground and therefore highly vulnerable to a Soviet first strike. Since these missiles could probably not have been used in response to a Soviet attack—they would presumably all have been destroyed—were they "offensive" weapons? The United States said they were "defensive" because their purpose was entirely defensive.

Ground-to-ground missiles in Cuba, however, were defined as "offensive" because their purpose was regarded as offensive. By American standards, then, a weapon is an "offensive" weapon if it is capable of reaching another nation's territory and the intentions of those who control it are offensive. Hence, no American missiles are offensive missiles.

Regardless of how accurate this attribution of intent as between the United States and the Soviet Union may be, it goes without saying that not everyone either understood or agreed with this definition of "offensive."

stalled about 100 miles west of Havana. The awful truth came to official Washington the following afternoon after intelligence officers positively identified the missiles from the photographs. These missiles had a range of about 1,100 miles, and preparations for the installation of intermediate-range ballistic missiles (IRBMs) with double that range were discovered on subsequent photo-reconnaissance flights. As President Kennedy said in his speech to the nation on October 22, which initiated the public and most serious phase of the crisis, the already installed MRBMs were capable of carrying a nuclear warhead to such places as Washington, D.C., and Mexico City or any other city in the southeastern part of the United States, in Central America, or in the Carribbean area. The IRBMs, once installed, would have been capable of striking most of the major cities in the Western hemisphere.

The ensuing two weeks were among the most tense, dramatic, and important diplomatic encounters in history. Two uniquely powerful nations confronted each other in a situation that *may have* involved a greater potential for exploding into a major war than any other since World War II. The following is a brief account of that crucial event.[56]

After a week of decisions and preparations,[57] President Kennedy addressed the nation at 7 P.M., EST, on Monday, October 22. He described the findings of the U-2 photographs and said that the Soviet action "contradicts the repeated assurances of Soviet spokesmen, both publicly and privately delivered, that the arms buildup in Cuba would retain its original defensive character and that the Soviet Union had no need or desire to station strategic missiles on the territory of any other nation." He noted that the United States had already become accustomed to living under the threat of Soviet missiles, but he sought to make it clear why this new development was intolerable.

> . . . This secret, swift and extraordinary buildup of Communist missiles—in an area well known to have a special and historical relationship to the United States and the nations of the Western Hemisphere, in violation of Soviet assurances, and in defiance of American and hemispheric policy—this sudden, clandestine decision to station strategic weapons for the first time outside of Soviet soil—is a deliberately

---

[56] For an extensive collection of documents and readings relating to this episode, see David L. Larson (ed.), *The "Cuban Crisis" of 1962*, Houghton Mifflin Company, Boston, 1963. The account that follows is drawn largely from this collection, and especially from the reprint of the remarkable summary printed in *The New York Times*, Nov. 3, 1962. For a description and analysis "from the inside," see Roger Hilsman, "The Cuban Crisis: How Close We Were to War," *Look*, vol. 28, no. 17, pp. 17–21, Aug. 25, 1964. At the time of the crisis, Hilsman was Director of Intelligence and Research in the Department of State.

[57] During this entire period, President Kennedy met with a specially selected group of advisers. This group became known as the Executive Committee of the National Security Council; its composition and role are discussed in Chap. 3, pp. 68–72.

provocative and unjustified change in the status quo which cannot be accepted by this country if our courage and our commitments are ever to be trusted again by either friend or foe.

Accordingly, he announced seven "initial steps" being taken by the United States, and declared that "these actions may only be the beginning." First, a "quarantine" (blockade) on all offensive military equipment being shipped to Cuba was being initiated. Second, the close surveillance of Cuba was being continued and increased. Third, it was declared to be American policy "to regard any nuclear missile launched from Cuba against any nation in the Western hemisphere as an attack by the Soviet Union on the United States, requiring a full retaliatory response upon the Soviet Union." He then announced that the United States was taking military precautions for the defense of its naval base at Guantanamo, calling for a meeting of the Organization of American States (OAS), and requesting an emergency meeting of the Security Council of the United Nations. Finally, he called upon Khrushchev "to move the world back from the abyss of destruction" by withdrawing the offensive missiles.

The Soviet response the following day was in the form of a long and inconclusive statement. It denounced the President's announced policy and said that the United States was "playing with fire." Soviet assistance to Cuba was "exclusively designed to improve Cuba's defensive capacity." Despite its length and self-righteous tone, however, the note did not flatly declare that the missiles would not be withdrawn. The statement was interpreted in Washington as evidence that the Soviet government had been surprised by the President's action and had not yet decided what to do about it.

Meanwhile, the NATO allies were publicly declaring their support of the United States, and the OAS had acted with unusual dispatch and unanimity in passing, 19 to 0, a resolution authorizing the use of force to enforce the blockade and "to prevent the missiles in Cuba with an offensive capability from ever becoming an active threat to the peace and security of the Continent. . . ."

The usual bipartisan support that manifests itself in times of national crisis prevailed in the United States, and the expected charges and counter-charges were being hurled back and forth at emergency meetings of the Security Council in New York.

On Wednesday, October 24, Acting Secretary General U Thant proposed that both the arms shipments to Cuba and the blockade be suspended for two or three weeks. Premier Khrushchev accepted the proposal at once, but President Kennedy declined. Not only was he distrustful of such Soviet promises, but he was also anxious to resolve the problem promptly. Given the very high state of tension and even fear, this anxiousness was quite understandable. Moreover, any delay would permit the Soviets to put still more missiles into place. And work was continuing on the missile sites.

A tense world awaited the results of what was expected to be the first contact Wednesday evening between a Soviet convoy of ships and the American blockade. But late in the afternoon, the Pentagon announced that the Soviet ships had apparently altered course, and the confrontation was delayed. On Thursday morning, a Navy ship made contact with a Soviet oil tanker. Because it was obvious that the ship carried no offensive weapons, it was allowed to proceed without a search. But all through that day, concern was mounting as the Soviets continued to work on the missile sites and the American government grew more and more impatient. A massive American military concentration in the southeastern part of the United States had been underway for about ten days and it was widely— but apparently erroneously—believed to be only a matter of time before an invasion of Cuba or an air attack on the missile sites, or both, would take place.

Early Friday morning, October 26, a Soviet-chartered ship permitted a United States Navy search party to come aboard and conduct an inspection. The ship was cleared and proceeded on to Cuba. But work on the missile sites continued, and early in the evening the White House issued a statement that the activity "apparently is directed at achieving a full operational capability as soon as possible."

On Friday evening, the United States received a message from Khrushchev which has never been made public. It has been described by some —whose information was probably second-hand—as "hysterical" and "highly emotional." Whatever its precise contents, the fact that it was not —and never has been—made public does suggest that it was so unusual either in style or in content, or both, that the United States government decided it would not be prudent to embarrass the Soviet leader by releasing it. At any rate, and despite its apparently frantic character, the letter was taken as partial evidence that the Soviets had decided to negotiate a withdrawal of the missiles.

This letter arrived on the same day that an unofficial and unorthodox, but quite promising, contact had been initiated by a Soviet intelligence agent in Washington. The Soviet agent contacted John Scali, the State Department reporter for the American Broadcasting Company (ABC), and arranged a secret meeting.[58] He asked Scali what would be the likely response if the Soviets should offer to remove the missiles, agree to a

---

[58] The following references to the role played by the agent and Scali are based on the Hilsman article referred to on page 273. This remarkable aspect of the crisis emphasizes once again the sometimes significant role played by unofficial persons in politics, international as well as domestic.

United Nations verification of their removal, and pledge never to install missiles there again in return for an American public pledge not to invade Cuba. Scali took this auspicious proposal to a high-ranking official in the State Department and, after hurried consultations, was told to notify the agent that the United States was interested, but that time was growing short.

On Saturday morning, October 27, however, a second Khrushchev message arrived, and it contained a wholly different and unacceptable proposal. In the midst of a generally conciliatory letter, the Soviet Premier proposed that the Soviet missiles be removed from Cuba in exchange for the removal of American missiles from Turkey. The White House issued a statement saying that "several inconsistent and conflicting proposals" had been made by the Soviet government in the preceding twenty-four hours. The statement then rejected the Turkey-Cuban proposal, arguing that the current crisis involved only Cuba and the security of the Western hemisphere and that this would have to be resolved first. As for the proposals regarding Turkey, efforts at "properly inspected arms limitation" could go forward after the current crisis was resolved. That same morning, the situation became aggravated by Communist action. A U-2 plane was missing over Cuba and presumably had been shot down. Heretofore, the Cubans and the Soviets had tolerated American aerial reconnaissance, apparently out of fear that a refusal to do so would bring on something worse, such as an invasion or a bombing of the missile sites. Now, the unwritten ground rules of this historic confrontation were being changed. It was an ominous development.

Meanwhile, Secretary Rusk asked Scali to contact the Soviet agent again, and the two men met again on Saturday afternoon. Scali informed the agent in strong language that the second proposal was unacceptable and that the administration did not look favorably on the procedure of making proposals and then reneging on them. He stressed again the time factor. The agent seemed appropriately impressed and presumably relayed this reaction to Moscow at once.

President Kennedy was required to make some delicate decisions. An attack against the antiaircraft batteries that were responsible for shooting down the U-2 would almost certainly kill Russian technicians. What would the Soviet response to this be? Could he, on the other hand, afford to delay action on this front in the hope that some general settlement was imminent? And, perhaps most importantly, how should he respond to the several and conflicting proposals emanating officially and unofficially from the Kremlin?

He and his advisers decided virtually to ignore the second letter and to respond instead to the more hopeful suggestions contained in the first letter and in the Soviet agent's talk with Scali. This proved to be a shrewd gambit, but the uncertainty about what Khrushchev was really up to is reflected in the following excerpt from Kennedy's message, sent Saturday evening:

> As I read your letter [the first one], the key elements of your proposals—which seem generally acceptable as I understand them—are as follows:
>
> 1) You would agree to remove these weapons systems from Cuba under appropriate United Nations observation and supervision; and undertake, with suitable safeguards, to halt the further introduction of such weapons systems into Cuba.
>
> 2) We, on our part, would agree—upon the establishment of adequate arrangements through the United Nations to ensure the carrying out and continuation of these commitments—(a) to remove promptly the quarantine measures now in effect and (b) to give assurances against an invasion of Cuba. I am confident that other nations in the Western Hemisphere would be prepared to do likewise.

No one knew what to expect from the Soviets in response. Some hopes had been kindled by the first letter and by the agent's talk with Scali, but the mystery of the second letter remained, and the decision to shoot at American reconnaissance flights could be interpreted as portending a grave turn of events. And then suddenly, on Sunday morning, October 28, the Soviets accepted the proposal contained in the President's letter. Moreover, Khrushchev's reply, affectively terminating the most dangerous cold-war showdown, was strikingly conciliatory in tone as well as in substance. For example:

> I have received your message of 27 October. I express my satisfaction and thank you for the sense of proportion you have displayed and for realization of the responsibility which now devolves on you for the preservation of the peace of the world.
>
> I regard with great understanding your concern and the concern of the United States people in connection with the fact that the weapons you describe as offensive are formidable weapons indeed. Both you and we understand what kind of weapons these are.
>
> In order to eliminate as rapidly as possible the conflict which endangers the cause of peace, to give an assurance to all people who crave peace, and to reassure the American people, all of whom, I am certain, also want peace, as do the people of the Soviet Union, the Soviet Government, in addition to earlier instructions on the discontinuation of further work on weapons construction sites, has given a new order to dismantle the arms which you described as offensive, and to crate and return them to the Soviet Union. . . .

> I regard with respect and trust the statement you made in your message of 27 October 1962 that there would be no attack, no invasion of Cuba, and not only on the part of the United States, but also on the part of other nations of the Western hemisphere, as you said in your same message. Then the motives which induced us to render assistance of such a kind to Cuba disappear. . . . We are prepared to reach agreement to enable U. N. representatives to verify the dismantling of these means.
>
> . . . Vested with trust and great responsibility, we must not allow the situation

to become aggravated and must stamp out the centers where a dangerous situation fraught with grave consequences to the cause of peace has arisen. If we, together with you, and with the assistance of other people of good will, succeed in eliminating this tense atmosphere, we should also make certain that no other dangerous conflicts, which could lead to a world nuclear catastrophe, would arise.

This was in truth a most remarkable moment in East-West relations. The respectful tone of the Soviet Premier was reciprocated in a statement made by President Kennedy in swift response: "I welcome Chairman Khrushchev's statesmanlike decision. . . . This is an important and constructive contribution to peace." A few hours later, in a formal reply to Khrushchev, Kennedy took a similar laudatory and respectful line. He was clearly attempting to make Khrushchev's capitulation as painless as possible.

An Analysis and Some Appraisals.   The Cuban missile crisis, like all major historical events, has been interpreted in a variety of ways. Likewise, the performance of the Kennedy administration has been both praised and criticized, though there has been much more of the former than the latter. It is instructive to analyze the basic decisions that were made and some of the assumptions and attitudes that informed those decisions.

The Kennedy administration was surprised by the Soviet effort to put ground-to-ground missiles in Cuba. Despite all its verbal excesses and deep antagonism, the cold war has been conducted with a considerable amount of caution on both sides. The Red Army has not invaded any country— although the manner of its crushing of the Hungarian Revolution in 1956 could be regarded as an invasion—Berlin has not been permanently sealed off or seized, and provocations—such as the occasional shooting down of American aircraft that may or may not have strayed over Communist territory—have been met with diplomatic protests rather than military countermeasures. There have developed, in other words, some tacit "rules of the game," whereby neither side, reluctantly perhaps, does anything that leaves the opponent little choice but to fight back. In the minds of most prominent members of the administration, these tacit rules of the game made it very unlikely that the Soviets would do anything as provocative as placing ground-to-ground missiles in Cuba. Khrushchev, for all his bluster and guile, was regarded as essentially a prudent calculator who would know that such an action could have the most serious consequences. Because of this basic attitude, or assumption, the Kennedy administration discounted heavily all the Republican and exile reports that such weapons were indeed being sent to Cuba. Aerial reconnaissance was increased, just in case, but the idea still seemed too bizarre.[59]

[59] For an excellent analysis of Soviet motives, see Arnold L. Horelick, "The Cuban Missile Crisis: An Analysis of Soviet Calculations and Behavior," *World Politics*, vol. 16, no. 3, pp. 363–389, April, 1964.

Then came the jolt of the photographic evidence on October 15. President Kennedy was confronted with an unexpected and explosive challenge. What should the United States do about it? This was surely one of the most difficult and vital decisions any American President has ever faced.

There were a great many options. He could have done nothing about it. In support of inaction, he *might* have concluded and then argued that the presence of these missiles did not basically change the military picture. The Soviets already had Intercontinental Ballistic Missiles (ICBMs) on Soviet soil that were capable of reaching the United States. The MRBMs and IRBMs being installed in Cuba would merely supplement an already impressive strategic capability. Moreover, it was true that the United States had similar missiles in Britain, Italy, and Turkey, so Khrushchev's action could have been construed as merely reciprocating American actions already taken.

Some people outside the government did take this position, of course, and it was not an uncommon one among neutralist governments and others abroad whose primary concern was to avoid a holocaust and who were largely or totally uninterested in any other aspects of the crisis. President Kennedy and his advisers, however, apparently never seriously considered the possibility of accepting the presence of the missiles, and there were many potent factors militating against any such acceptance.

In the first place, the missiles almost certainly *did* alter the strategic relationship between the two superpowers. The Soviets had ICBMs, but not nearly as many as the United States, and they may have been fearful that their small ICBM force would not by itself be enough to impress or deter "the imperialists" in the United States. By supplementing them with a substantial array of MRBMs and IRBMs in Cuba, they may have believed that their strategic posture would be so radically improved as to justify the risk of trying to sneak them into Cuba. But regardless of what they believed or what motivated them, such an assessment of the strategic significance of the missiles in Cuba would have been quite natural—and probably accurate—for any American administration.[60]

Moreover, other strictly military disadvantages for the United States were involved. Missiles from Cuba would arrive virtually without warning even if the best radar network were available for monitoring that area; and no such radar network did exist for that area. Our radar facilities had been built in the north, to detect any ICBM or bomber attacks from the Soviet Union itself. Finally, missiles from Cuba would probably be more accurate than missiles from the U.S.S.R.

There were other reasons why action was virtually imperative. Congressional elections were coming up in November. No democratically elected government, however wise and noble, is likely to be utterly unmindful of the partisan implications of its actions under such circumstances.

[60] For an expert discussion of this, see *ibid.*, pp. 374–377.

The Republicans had apparently been profiting from the Cuba issue *before* the unmistakable evidence was uncovered; they could be expected to make further gains if nothing were done afterward. (It would, by the way, have been virtually impossible to keep such information secret for very long; and it would be hard to conceive of any American administration's attempting to do so, anyway.)

But even if there had been less powerful military and partisan reasons for taking action, it seems nearly certain that President Kennedy would have done so. At some point or other in politics, one reaches what might be called "the instinctive level." Whatever might be the facts about a given situation and whatever conclusions might be drawn from such facts standing alone, they yield before some kind of more powerful impulses. Khrushchev had violated the rules of the game in the minds of Kennedy and his advisers. He had insulted the United States by this act, and such reckless arrogance could not be countenanced. Something of the sense of this instinctive response can be discerned from a reading of that part of Kennedy's original public statement quoted below:

> . . . . This secret, swift, and extraordinary buildup of Communist missiles—in an area well-known to have a special and historical relationship to the United States and the nations of the Western Hemisphere, in violation of Soviet assurances, and in defiance of American and hemispheric policy—this sudden, clandestine decision to station strategic weapons for the first time outside of Soviet soil—is a deliberately provocative and unjustified change in the status quo which cannot be accepted by this country if our courage and our commitments are ever to be trusted again by either friend or foe.

There is, to be sure, a powerful element of cool calculation in this: Response was necessary to ensure credibility of courage in other matters. But beyond the calculation was sheer outrage and an elemental response to it, which went beyond and probably could not have been countermanded by any calculation. It is a risky business for either side to make the other side look weak or foolish, and most of the responsible officials on both sides have recognized this most of the time.

So some response was mandatory, and it would have to go beyond merely protesting to the United Nations and denouncing the Soviets. It would have to get rid of the missiles. Several possible methods were available. Perhaps the most obvious method—and the one that appealed to large numbers of observers abroad as well as some at home—was to arrange some mutual concessions. As noted above, this became something other than a hypothetical possibility when Khrushchev offered to withdraw his missiles from Cuba if the United States would take its missiles out of Turkey. The proposal came at a time when the administration was happily preparing to embrace the immediately preceding proposal, which appeared to offer a withdrawal of the missiles in exchange merely for an American pledge not to invade Cuba. Inauspicious timing was therefore added to the proposal's liabilities, and it was ignored.

A strong case could have been made for the Cuba-Turkey deal. The missiles in Turkey were due to be removed soon anyway (as they in fact were the following year) because they were going to be replaced by less vulnerable Polaris missiles on submarines in the Mediterranean and elsewhere. Moreover, the missiles in Turkey were directly comparable to the Soviet missiles in Cuba. They were highly vulnerable, above-ground missiles placed in an area immediately adjacent to the adversary's territory.

But the administration was unwilling to make the trade, and its reasoning was somewhat as follows: As noted above, the President issued a statement on the day the proposal was received in which he argued that the missiles in Turkey were not relevant to the immediate crisis and could be discussed at a later time. Whether he would have clung to this position if Khrushchev had insisted on the removal of the missiles in Turkey is an open question, but there are additional reasons for believing that he probably would have. Again, timing and prestige were major factors. The missiles had been in Turkey since 1959. They were, according to American perspectives, established elements of the East-West struggle. Their presence represented no jarring alteration of the *status quo*, whereas the missiles being put into Cuba did.

In addition, the United States did not want to appear to be yielding under pressure. It was demanding that the Soviets do precisely that, but the responsibility for such an unfortunate development was the Soviet Union's; it was the Soviets who had rocked the boat. This could easily— and perhaps accurately—be labeled a nationalistic view of the matter. However that may be, the Soviet Union ultimately accepted the solution that this view supported.

It should not be forgotten, of course, that the administration could not forget partisan politics altogether even at a moment of grave emergency. It is not being suggested here that partisan considerations determined policy; they almost certainly did not. But they did combine with other considerations to move the President in the direction of rejecting the Turkey-Cuba deal.

A final element was related to the administration's distinction between "offensive" weapons, as discussed above. The physical characteristics of the missiles in Cuba and Turkey were very similar. In Washington's view, the missiles in Cuba were offensive because the intentions of those who controlled them were offensive. The missiles in Turkey were defensive because American intentions were defensive. Hence, there was fundamentally no comparability between the two sets of missiles.

Whatever the reasons—and they doubtless included all of those mentioned above in some manner or other—the United States rejected the Khrushchev proposal. And got away with it.

There were four other prominent alternatives before the President and his advisers: a selective blockade coupled with an ultimatum to remove the missiles, a total blockade coupled with an ultimatum, bombing of the missile sites, and an invasion. Each one had advantages and disadvantages, and apparently each one was carefully weighed during the nearly two weeks of crisis deliberations.

Elaborate preparations for an invasion were made, and by the time the President made his original announcement there was no doubt that a large-scale invasion of Cuba could have been launched momentarily. Such an assault would not only have solved the problem of the missiles—though some of them might have been launched during the excitement—but would also have afforded the opportunity of getting rid of the Castro regime. This latter objective appealed to some Americans nearly as much as the former.

Apparently, an invasion was never seriously contemplated except possibly as a desperate last resort. The costs and risks would have been considerable. First and foremost, it was not known what the Soviet response would be. They did have thousands of Russian personnel on the island, and they did have a substantial rhetorical and emotional commitment to the defense of Cuba. In fact—and this was never far from anyone's mind during the entire crisis—Cuba had become to the Russians something very much like what Berlin had become to the United States. Whether this condition ever should have been permitted to develop and who was responsible for it were separate, though bitterly disputed, questions. The harsh fact was that it had developed, and it raised two interrelated but distinguishable possibilities. The first was that the Soviets might really carry out their threats about "defending Cuba" by attacking the "aggressor," the United States. This was a dim possibility, of course, but no one could be sure. It was comparable to the situation involving Berlin. What would we do if the Soviets took West Berlin? The Soviets must believe that it is quite unlikely that we would unleash the holocaust over such a matter, but a slight uncertainty about it has almost certainly helped to stay their hand.

The related possibility—and it was this one that was most thought about —was that instead of hitting the United States the Soviets would simply reciprocate an invasion of Cuba with an invasion of West Berlin. All of the constraints that ordinarily would operate on any Western response would be strengthened in such an instance by a realization that the Soviets were merely doing to their "bone in the throat" what we were doing to ours. The possibility—probability?—that the Soviets were indeed thinking along precisely such lines gave pause to American policy makers. In the age of mutual terror, one of the first rules of prudence is not to call the other fellow's bluff unless it is absolutely necessary; *it may not be a bluff.* If it is true that an invasion was threatened by troop movements and the like but never seriously contemplated, it is easy to see why.

An invasion had other liabilities. It would have been costly in terms of human life. The Cubans are well-armed and apparently determined to fight; it would not have been a picnic. Moreover, the propaganda costs in Latin America and elsewhere would have been heavy, especially if all other remedies had not been exhausted. The OAS backed the resolution authorizing the use of force, but many Latin American governments would have been quite unhappy about an invasion. And every anti-American in Latin America—which would make up a sizable proportion of the population—would have denounced the "Yankee imperialists" loudly and long and with damaging effects.

The next most drastic step would have been an aerial attack on the missile sites. This would have had fewer advantages and fewer disadvantages than an invasion. It would not have toppled Castro, and it would have been a less certain method of eliminating the missiles. On the other hand, it would have had a less obvious bearing on something the Soviets might like to do in Berlin, would have involved less loss of life, and would probably have afforded less of a propaganda opportunity for anti-American forces all over the world. But the Administration apparently never considered this alternative too seriously, either, preferring the more limited blockade action and hoping it would work and preclude the necessity of considering stronger measures.[61]

The selective blockade coupled with an ultimatum to remove the missiles was chosen, and it worked. This spectacular American success has not, however, been without its critics. Three criticisms have been most prominent. First of all, Castro was not eliminated. The administration considered making his demise a basic objective but decided against it. It determined that the prime immediate objective was the elimination of the missiles and that insisting on other objectives might be too costly. The critics said that the crisis afforded a golden opportunity of using American strength under cover of an imperative necessity and accomplishing secondary objectives at the same time.

Secondly, some observers objected to the American pledge not to invade Cuba. This pledge was tied to the requirement that the removal of the

---

[61] It is interesting to note in this connection that moral—or at least not exclusively self-interested—considerations apparently played some role in the rejection of aerial attack. Robert Kennedy apparently argued that an air strike would be comparable to the Japanese attack on Pearl Harbor and was unacceptable on moral grounds alone. This argument was apparently generally accepted. Whatever one may think of the analogy or of the question whether such an attack really would have been immoral under the circumstances—and this writer rejects both the analogy and the conclusion—the episode does suggest that allegedly moral issues are not necessarily ignored even in such pressing moments.

missiles be verified by the United Nations. Since such verification was never permitted by the Cuban government, the pledge is presumably not binding. But it was offered, and it does presumably have some lingering status as an obligation. It can be argued, therefore, that the situation is back to where it was in the summer of 1962 except that Castro now has an American pledge—or part of one—against invasion, leaving him free to pursue his nefarious activities all over Latin America.

The third criticism, now somewhat vitiated, was that there never was any guarantee that all of the missiles had in fact been removed. After the Cubans defied the Soviets and refused to permit inspectors on their soil, the Soviets cooperated elaborately with American efforts to witness the departure of the missiles on Soviet ships, and the Kennedy administration became convinced that the missiles were gone. This criticism declined as time wore on, but there are still occasional refugee and other reports that offensive missiles are still in, or are back in, Cuba.

None of these criticisms, nor all of them taken together, have made much of a dent on the general conviction that President Kennedy conducted American policy brilliantly and achieved a shining success. Nor should they. There is little reason to doubt that the missiles are gone. As for the no-invasion pledge, it is not even technically binding since inspection was not permitted; and it surely would not be binding in practice if, as seems most unlikely, some future administration should determine that such a drastic step were imperative. As for getting rid of the Castro regime, that was and is a question entirely separable from the challenge posed by the missiles. It may be that an invasion would not have caused a drastic Soviet response and would have been worth it on other grounds as well, but such matters are highly speculative, and *the fundamental challenge was met and overcome.* The problem of Castro's continued presence was available for handling after as well as during the crisis and at much less risk. And even this line of argument, of course, concedes that the elimination of Castro's regime is an appropriate and reasonable objective for American foreign policy. This by itself is debatable, and will be discussed below in the section entitled The Contemporary Problem.

At least one other question regarding the Cuban missile crisis deserves close scrutiny: How close were we to a thermonuclear war with the Soviet Union? There has been much loose talk to the effect that such a war was merely a short step away during the crisis, and there is no doubt that this possibility haunted the entire world for about a week. All appraisals of this kind must necessarily be at least partially based on estimates or guesses; no one—not even the leading participants—knows or knew with any certitude the answer to this question. Nonetheless, there are compelling—or at least strong—reasons for believing that the possibility of a thermonuclear war was increased only slightly if at all during this tense showdown.

There are essentially four ways in which total war might come about: a calculation (or miscalculation) that an attack would destroy the enemy and result in an acceptably low, or no, amount of damage to the attacker; a mistake or accident; escalation; and an irrational act by a government. It is very unlikely that either side in October, 1962, believed that it could strike first and get by largely unscathed; and the existence of the crisis reduced, if anything, such a possibility even more because both sides were alerted and ready. The other three possibilities may have been slightly increased and will be examined in the following paragraphs.

In the "mistake or accident" category should be included such things as a mistaken judgment by one side that it was being attacked or a technological failure that resulted in one or more bombers' or missiles' launching an attack not intended by the government. With nerves frayed and tension high, mistakes *may be* more likely. Khrushchev alluded to such a nightmarish possibility in his Sunday, October 28, message in which he announced that he was removing the missiles. He was complaining about earlier U-2 flights over the Soviet Union and then added:

> A still more dangerous case occurred on 28 October, when one of your reconnaissance planes intruded over Soviet borders . . . in the north and flew over our territory. The question is this, Mr. President: How should we regard this? What is this, a provocation? One of your planes violates our frontier during this anxious time we are both experiencing, when everything has been put into combat readiness. Is it not a fact that an intruding American plane could be easily taken for a nuclear bomber, which might push us to a fateful step; and all the more so since the U. S. Government and Pentagon long ago declared that you are maintaining a continuous nuclear bomber patrol?

It is easy to see why Kennedy explained to Khrushchev at once that the overflight was due to a navigational error and added: "I regret this incident and will see to it that every precaution is taken to prevent recurrence." Whether this episode really increased the possibility of war is hard to surmise, but it was probably more of an irritant and a delay than anything else.

As for a technological failure, the chances may have increased slightly simply because there were undoubtedly more planes in the air and more missiles ready for instantaneous firing. But it should be emphasized that the United States, at least, has invested vast sums of money and effort into perfecting a control system that virtually assures that a nuclear attack cannot be launched without approval of the President. It should be added that these measures also protect against the proverbial "mad colonel" who decides to take matters into his own hands. Whether the Soviets have been equally as responsible about creating a control system that cannot be undermined is not known.

The most likely path to total war was—and is—escalation from a smaller conflict into ever larger ones until no limits are observed. During the Cuban crisis, the great fear on the American side was that the Soviets would retaliate somewhere else, most likely Berlin. On no other matter is the fear of escalation so great. Therefore, insofar as the Cuban crisis increased the possibility of a Soviet move against Berlin—or, less ominously, some other limited Soviet retaliation—to that extent the possibility of escalation and ultimately total war was enhanced.

Finally, there is the question of how much a crisis increases the prospects for irrational action. Some light on this might be shed if the precise contents of Khrushchev's Friday, October 26, message were known. On the basis of it alone, it apparently might be reasonable to draw the conclusion that fright induces conciliation, not belligerency. Obviously, however, no such generalization can validly be inferred from a single episode; and it only takes one deviation from such a generalization to bring on the holocaust that neither side wants. Common sense would seem to suggest that causing fright is a risky business and should be avoided whenever possible.

Each observer will add these factors up in a different way. The conclusion of this writer is that the possibility of a total war was only very slightly increased during the missile crisis. All of the compelling constraints that apply in normal times continued to apply during the crisis. Both sides knew then as they knew before and after that to start a thermonuclear war against the other side would be to invite one's own destruction. The worrisome possibilities discussed above cannot be entirely dismissed, to be sure. But the basic constraints applied throughout; and although they may have been threatened slightly, they did prove to be strong enough. Mutual terror is very hard to overcome.

Some Implications   Epochal events of this kind provide scraps of evidence for a vast number of interpretations and alleged implications, many of them mutually contradictory. The most conspicuous area of disagreement is whether this experience indicates that American policy toward the Soviets should be aggressive and demanding ("hard line") or whether it indicates that our policy should be cautious and respectful of Soviet interests and sensibilities.

There is support for both kinds of arguments in this experience. The President did demand that the Soviets remove the missiles, and they removed them. The United States did make a conspicuous show of strength, and the Soviets retreated. On the other hand, President Kennedy did pursue the least aggressive—or most cautious—policy consistent with having the missiles removed, and he did display a great willingness to make it as easy as possible for Khrushchev to back down. Not only did the President not publish that apparently frantic letter that hinted at the compromise finally adopted, but he praised the Soviet Premier generously when the latter capitulated. Moreover, he demonstrated throughout a prudent respect for Soviet strength. According to Hilsman, President Kennedy was determined "to pace events . . . to give the Soviet leaders time to think out the consequences of each move. His purpose was to avoid putting them in a position where their only response could be, in the President's own words, a 'spasm reaction.' "[62]

Arguments about whether American policy should be "hard" or "soft" are, however, badly misleading. They miss the main point, namely that statesmanship consists of being both "hard" and "soft" or neither as the occasion requires. There are no simple lessons to be drawn from the missile crisis, just as there are no simple prescriptions for successful foreign policies. In a speech nearly a year before the event, President Kennedy stated this forcefully:

> In short, we are neither "warmongers" nor "appeasers," neither "hard" nor "soft." We are Americans, determined to defend the frontiers of freedom, by an honorable peace if peace is possible, but by arms if arms are used against us.

Each confrontation or policy choice will involve unique and unknowable factors. Simple analogies from case to case are a gross abuse of history and common sense. Some of the special factors at work in this instance, for example, were the proximity of Cuba to the United States and the resultant overwhelming superiority of conventional forces that the United States could bring quickly to bear as compared with the Soviet Union. The reverse conditions apply, by the way, in Berlin. There was, moreover, in the nature of the issue a considerable span of time within which each side could make its plans and come to its decisions. This condition might not apply during another crisis. Finally, the issue involved was regarded as vital by only one side. The Soviets did not have nearly as much at stake as did the United States, and they seemed to realize this. Under such circumstances, yielding is facilitated. Had it been otherwise—or were it to be otherwise in some future showdown—a very different American policy would have been—or would be—called for. The failure to make distinctions of this kind could be fatal.

In saying that the Soviets had less at stake and seemed to realize it, one presumes to look inside their minds and judge their perceptions and motives. This is a hazardous enterprise. It must be done because virtually all policy is based on implicit or explicit expectations about what one's adversary is likely to do in response. But the failure to recognize that this is an uncertain matter and that a misjudgment could induce a catastrophic response might very well contribute to such a result. In sum, a certain humility and uncertainty about one's adversary is the mark of a statesman, not a weakling. Beyond such nonprescriptive, nonspecific observations,

[62] Hilsman, *op. cit.*, p. 19.

most generalizations about how policy should be conducted or what it should be in all cases are spurious and possibly dangerous.[63]

There were other kinds of grandiose meanings that various observers claimed to be able to see in the missile crisis and its denouement. One was that these events marked "an historic turning point" in the cold war, which signaled its quick—or at least certain—demise. The validity of this argument depends in good measure on how the phrase "turning point" is understood. If the argument is merely that relations between the United States and the Soviet Union in 1963 and 1964, say, were more cordial and hopeful than they were in 1961 and 1962, and that the sobering experience of the missile crisis *contributed* to this new spirit of moderation, most observers would probably agree.

But if the argument is that the missile crisis somehow *caused* the ensuing progress in East-West relations, and guarantees its permanence, its validity is more doubtful. Such an argument assumes that such a mutually frightening event can somehow resolve, and quickly, all the animosities and conflicts of interest that have formed the basis of the cold war. It assumes, basically, that the cold war is subject to a psychological solution that will transcend and render trivial all the political conflicts between the Soviet Union and the United States. But this is not true. The cold war is, to be sure, partly the result of dated grievances and unreasonable and rigid attitudes, but it is based on more than that. It is based also on such things as the conflict over Berlin, the divergent interests and policies regarding Germany, the competing interests and activities in the newly independent areas of the world, the ideological presumptions of the Soviets, and the policies and activities of the Castro regime. None of these matters was resolved by the missile crisis.

---

[63] These observations apply with special force to a word such as "brinkmanship," which occasionally has a revival in the American dialogue about foreign policy. This term, like so many other vivid and controversial phrases—such as "massive retaliation" and "agonizing reappraisal"—was originally based on something written or spoken by John Foster Dulles. In early 1956, in an article in *Life*, Dulles was quoted as saying that "the ability to get to the verge without getting into the war is the necessary art. If you cannot master it you inevitably get into war. If you try to run away from it, if you are scared to go to the brink, you are lost." James Shepley, "How Dulles Averted War," *Life*, vol. 40, no. 3, p. 78, Jan. 16, 1956. By itself, this is a rather unexceptional statement. It is undeniably necessary to display a willingness to use armed force if pushed too far. But as a comprehensive prescription to be applied whenever a controversy arises, it leaves very much to be desired. It is neither necessary nor desirable to rush "to the brink" each time a conflict of interest occurs in international affairs. The test of statesmanship is the ability to distinguish between those many instances when power should be sheathed or used selectively or subtly and those few instances when it is regrettably necessary to threaten its extensive use or actually to use it extensively. Established statesmen are capable of, and are known by their adversaries to be capable of, strong action, but they prefer and usually pursue other and less militant policies. Reckless adventurers regard militancy as the *sine qua non* of policy. They misunderstand and misrepresent Dulles's formula.

The cold war has proceeded in a less tense and dangerous manner since October, 1962, and the missile crisis contributed to this relaxation. But there have been lulls and thaws in the cold war before, and none have proved to be lasting. One may eventually do so, but recent history counsels caution in such matters.

Another dazzling interpretation of the event was that the United States had "seized the initiative in the cold war." The question of which side has the initiative in the cold war at any given moment is among the most favored, most amorphous, and most misleading topics for discussion among newspaper columnists, television commentators, and academic seers.

It is based on some sort of simple analogy with a football game or a boxing match, wherein one side manages to put the other side on the defensive. The analogy is not altogether meaningless in international politics. It is possible, though quite unlikely, that one side or the other in the cold war will cease to be competitive in the political, military, economic, and psychological realms in which the struggle is carried on. But it is far more likely that both sides will maintain a competitive posture and capability for many years to come. Under such conditions, it is usually misleading to talk about "the initiative" in a struggle as complex and many-sided as the cold war. One side will have it one day, the other the next. Even great achievements such as the American success in the missile crisis are not easily convertible into new successes, especially when they are essentially defensive in character.

The Contemporary Problem

At the beginning of this chapter, it was noted that "the Cuban problem" has been the most emotional foreign policy issue facing the United States in the postwar period. It has already figured in two presidential elections, with the Democrats and then the Republicans having the opportunity to suggest that whatever happens in Havana is the fault of the incumbent administration in Washington. This kind of electioneering is for the most part unenlightening, of course, both because it is based on the illusion that the United States is somehow responsible for nearly everything that happens in the world and also because it doesn't come to grips with the hard question of what to do about a problem that assuredly does exist.

What is "the Cuban problem"? To put it another way, why should the most powerful nation in the world be concerned about what happens on that little island? There are, needless to say, nearly as many answers to that question as there are persons answering it, but four stand out. First of all, the Castro regime persists in its destructive efforts to export revolution throughout Latin America. Second, it is a source of embarrassment to the entire nation to have this petty dictator so close to home engaging in repeated and outrageous verbal assaults on the United States. Third, it is a source of political vulnerability for whatever party happens to be in power to have this noisy radical undermining our dignity from "only 90 miles away." Fourth, Castro's Cuba remains a potential source of military trouble simply by virtue of its close ties with the Soviet Union. Even if no missiles are installed again, there remain such unpleasant possibilities as a large Soviet submarine base in Cuba or a Soviet supply depot for use in some nefarious activity or other in the Western Hemisphere.

Of these four concerns, only the first—the exporting of revolution—would appear to be an immediate problem of considerable importance. Embarrassment and domestic partisan concerns are not likely to drive any administration to rash action. As for potential military disadvantages, they can be met as they arise. But the exporting of revolution is something that effects directly and seriously the many interests—public and private, economic and political, idealistic and sentimental—that the United States has in Latin America.

The revolutionary fervor of the Castro regime has expressed itself from the very beginning of its existence. It welcomes Communists and other revolutionaries from all over Latin America to Cuba and trains them in revolutionary tactics, and it periodically supplies guns, ammunition, and literature to radical elements in many Latin countries. It is this activity that most endangers its own survival, and yet the Castro regime is apparently determined to continue it. Whether Castro and his supporters do this out of a sense of obligation to some kind of revolutionary morality (or ideology) or whether they believe that their own survival depends ultimately on the communization of Latin America is an open question. But that they do it cannot be seriously questioned.

In late 1963, the Organization of American States (OAS) appointed a committee to investigate Venezuela's charges that Castro was shipping arms and ammunition to dissident groups in Venezuela and was directing the campaign of sabotage and terror then under way in Venezuela. The five-nation committee reported back on February 18, 1964, and excerpts from their conclusions follow:

A

1. The present Government of Cuba since its institution in 1959 has carried on, supported, and directed in various ways a policy of intervention in the hemisphere through propaganda methods, provision of funds, training in sabotage and guerrilla operations, and the supply of arms to support those movements that seek to subvert national institutions through force in order to install communist regimes.

B

1. The Republic of Venezuela has been the target of a series of actions sponsored and directed by the Government of Cuba, openly intended to subvert Venezuelan institutions and to overthrow the democratic Government of Venezuela through terrorism, sabotage, assault, and guerrilla warfare.

2. A characteristic manifestation of this policy of aggression has been the sys-

tematic and hostile propaganda campaign carried out through information organs that are under the control of the Government of Cuba. . . .

3. Other manifestations of this policy of aggression are found in the supply of funds and the indoctrination and training in Cuba of numerous Venezuelans who later returned to their country to participate in subversive movements.

4. An important element in this intervention in Venezuela directed by the Government of Cuba, was the shipment of arms that was found . . . [in Venezuela] on November 1, 1963, close to the date of the general elections. The shipment was made up of arms originating in Cuba that were surreptitiously landed at a solitary spot on the coast, for the purpose of being used in subversive operations to overthrow the constitutional Government of Venezuela. . . . [64]

After months of haggling and delay, the foreign ministers of the OAS nations met in July, 1964, and endorsed these findings by a vote of 15 to 4. Only Mexico disputed the findings. The ministers then declared that these acts constituted aggression and condemned Cuba for them. They declared that OAS members "shall not maintain" diplomatic or consular relations with Cuba, and "shall suspend all trade" except food, medicine, and medical equipment. Another exception was granted for the airplane flights between Cuba and Mexico. They also threatened Cuba with the use of armed force if the aggression and intervention did not stop.

These measures were adopted by the necessary two-thirds majority to make them "mandatory" for OAS members and will apparently be implemented by all members except Mexico. But the practical effect of the resolution will be minor because less than 10 per cent of Cuba's trade was with Latin America, and most of that was in foodstuffs, an exempted category. The United States and others hailed it as a great achievement, but its value is largely symbolic. It surely will not eliminate the Castro regime and will probably have little or no effect on its behavior.

Given the fact that Castro continues to attempt to export revolution and given the fact that this is widely recognized but not likely to result in significant collective action, what should United States policy be? Let us assume for a moment that the elimination of the Castro regime is an appropriate objective for American foreign policy. Whether it is also a reasonable objective depends upon whether it can be achieved in a manner that involves acceptable risks and costs.

There are essentially four types of action that *might* achieve the objective: an embargo by all non-Communist nations, internal subversion, naval

[64] "Report of the Investigating Committee Appointed by the Council of the Organization of American States . . .," Council of the Organization of American States, Council Series, OEA/Ser. G/ IV, C-i-658 (English), 18 February 1964, pp. 35–36. For a chilling and graphic account of what Cuba was doing in Venezuela—and specifically of what this shipment of four tons of automatic pistols, submachine guns, mortars, rifles, bazookas, recoilless cannon, demolition charges, and thousands of rounds of ammunition was designed to do—see Romulo Betancourt, "The Venezuelan Miracle," *The Reporter*, vol. 31, no. 3, pp. 37–41, Aug. 13, 1964. Betancourt was President of Venezuela from 1959 until 1964.

blockade, and invasion. The United States has been pursuing an embargo policy since October, 1960, on all goods except food and medicine. In recent years intensive efforts have been made to induce the rest of the non-Communist world to stop trading with Cuba. These efforts have met with only limited successes, and the trend is in the direction of more, not less, trade with Cuba by our European allies. But even if we could by some means or other—and it would take a near-miracle, because Britain and France, for example, simply reject our embargo policy and see no reason to change—bring about such an embargo, it would almost certainly fail to achieve the objective. It would still serve the interests of the Soviet Union to maintain the Castro regime, and it would presumably do so. In sum, the embargo route has been tried; and although it certainly has handicapped Castro, it has not brought about, and is not likely to bring about, his downfall. It may be worthwhile for other reasons—to keep the Castro regime economically repressed and therefore less able to export revolution and less attractive to other Latin countries, to serve as an object lesson in the costliness of being anti-American, and to make its support of Castro very costly to the Soviet Union—but it will not achieve the objective of eliminating the regime.

Internal subversion appears to be an equally unpromising method of getting rid of the Castro regime. Reports vary on how popular and stable the regime is, but apparently a combination of genuine enthusiasm by large sections of the population—especially the peasantry—plus the traditional techniques of suppression practiced by dictatorial governments have managed to squelch all sources and manifestations of serious dissent. Without access to classified information, it is impossible to know what efforts, if any, are being made along these lines by the United States, but it would seem safe to surmise that such efforts are being made. But it is highly unlikely that they can be successful.

A total blockade might succeed in forcing Castro to meet some kind of terms or perhaps even in forcing him to capitulate. Cuba is heavily dependent upon imported products and if forced to attempt self-sufficiency, probably could not sustain the effort. There are two kinds of problems associated with a blockade, however, which make it extremely doubtful that such a policy would be either possible or wise. The first problem is that the imposition of a blockade in time of peace is a ruthless enterprise requiring strong wills and stronger stomachs. It is not certain by any means that the democratically elected government of a humane people could sustain a blockade for any length of time. The clamor both at home and abroad against the imposed suffering of the Cuban people would almost certainly have an effect on official Washington, regardless of how callous or determined the President and his advisers might be. There are presumably some things that a United States government simply cannot do, or at least cannot do very well, and one of them is probably the systematic starving of a nation of 6 million people. And if the blockade exempted food, it would almost certainly not be effective because at least the Soviets would see to it that sufficient food was shipped to Cuba. So would other and non-Communist countries, of course, but it is well to underline the fact that such a partial blockade would not work *even if* the United States somehow managed to induce the rest of the non-Communist world to go along.

But suppose that the United States did muster up enough strength of purpose to impose a sustained, total blockade. There would still be serious doubts about the wisdom of such a policy. Leaving aside any legal questions that might arise—and ignoring such things, for example, as the fact that we allegedly entered World War I because of German violations of our neutralist shipping rights—one is still confronted with the inescapable fact that a blockade would involve either the use or the threat of the use of force *against the Soviet Union*. Not even an invasion has this characteristic, unless one believes that the presence of a small number of Soviet troops and technicians in Cuba would render any invasion of Cuba an attack on the Soviet Union. Soviet ships regularly go to Cuba bringing all manner of equipment and supplies. To stop this flow, the United States would either have to sink Soviet ships or threaten to do so. It was one thing to do this with regard to the shipment of offensive weapons to Cuba during the missile crisis. It would be quite another to do it regarding all shipping during peacetime.

It can be argued that such a policy is necessary because of the activities of the Castro regime, but it should be clearly understood what risks and costs such a policy entails. The unavoidable cost would be, as already noted, a widespread and angry disapproval from much of the rest of the world and a sizable portion of the American public. The risks would include some kind of Soviet retaliation. Again, the possibility of a Soviet counter-move aimed at West Berlin comes quickly to mind. And there are other possibilities. The Soviets might decide to try to run the blockade. Then, if a ship were sunk, they might retaliate by sinking an American merchant vessel somewhere else. Or they might even sink a Navy ship with one of their numerous submarines. Where would any of these developments lead us? Nobody knows, but such considerations should be kept in mind. A blockade is neither an easy operation for a democratic government to execute nor an inexpensive one in terms of costs and risks.

Balancing the problems presented by the continuance of the Castro regime against those that would inescapably be involved in a blockade, should the United States institute a blockade? Presumably, an effort would be made to gain OAS approval of such an effort. If such approval were forthcoming, and if the Castro regime continued to attempt to export its revolution in such a brutal fashion, a case could obviously be made for such a policy. How one chooses between the advantages and disadvantages of a blockade versus the present policy of restraint depends on a myriad of factors, including one's assessment of the danger posed by Castro, the likelihood of the risks mentioned above materializing into reality, the depth of disapproval provoked at home and abroad, and so forth. The judgment of this writer is that under existing conditions the disadvantages of a blockade clearly outweigh its advantages and that the present policy is vastly preferable.

That leaves only the alternative of invasion. An invasion by the United States as an option during the missile crisis was discussed above. All of the disadvantages noted for that context would apply contemporaneously: uncertainty about whether the Soviets would honor in some fashion or other (a seizure of Berlin?) their pledges to "defend Cuba"; the high cost in human life; and the heavy loss around the world in terms of prestige and respect. Is the problem presented by the Castro regime serious enough to warrant incurring these costs and risks? Almost certainly not. Moreover, the propriety—or morality—of such an operation under existing circumstances would also be open to serious doubt.

Another option would be another invasion by Cuban refugees, this time afforded adequate air coverage. The complexity of another such undertaking staggers the imagination. The Cuban exiles in this and other countries are divided into an indeterminate number of factions, many of them mutually hostile. Moreover, there is very little assurance that such an undertaking would succeed where the last one failed most conspicuously, namely, in the stirring up of mass support within Cuba. And if it failed to do this, it would merely be another gigantic mistake. Finally, a United States–backed invasion by Cuban refugees would incur the same kinds of disadvantages referred to above in connection with a United States invasion. Some people seem to regard this option as an inexpensive way of getting rid of Castro, waiting only for a sufficiently "courageous" administration in Washington to come along and support it. It should be clear that the matter is not nearly that simple.

Coming back to the original question: Is the elimination of the Castro regime a reasonable objective? Embargo and subversion very likely cannot achieve the objective, and either a blockade or an invasion would seem to involve risks and costs out of all proportion to the objective. The current policy of restraint, combined with aid, trade, and other policies designed to improve living conditions in Latin America, is definitely preferable. Or so it seems to this observer. In this, as in so many other matters affecting foreign policy, dogmatism is unwarranted. The Castro regime is a problem primarily because of its efforts to train and arm revolutionaries from all over Latin America. This problem is probably manageable, especially if the Castro regime continues to experience the serious economic difficulties that it has experienced since seizing power. But if it should prove to be unmanageable—i.e., if Castro's export of revolution should suddenly become more successful—or if some other developments should cause Cuba to become a greater menace than it now is, then United States policy should be reassessed and perhaps changed. The current policy of restraint, like all other policies, should be susceptible to change in the face of new conditions.

The same willingness to adjust policy should, by the way, be evident in response to Castro's periodic intimations that perhaps the time has come to reach some kind of understanding with the United States. The prospects for a genuine *rapprochement* appear dim, but the United States should not be so rigid as to make such a development impossible.

Guerrilla Warfare

The final "defense problem" to be discussed is unorthodox and baffling. It goes by many names—"local defense," "sublimited war," "internal war," and so forth—but its most common designation is "guerrilla warfare." It has been an urgent problem in South Vietnam for years; it is a potential problem in many other areas of the world. The focus herein will be on South Vietnam.

During World War II, the Japanese overran the French colonial empire in Indochina. With the defeat of the Japanese, the French attempted to reimpose their control in the area and were met with much resistance and some open rebellion. The leader of the rebellious forces was a Vietnamese Communist called Ho Chi Minh, who had been educated in France and indoctrinated in Moscow.[65]

He and his fellow Communists, by their zeal, shrewdness, and skills, had managed to gain control of the nationalist forces not only in Vietnam but in the rest of Indochina as well. One of the most unfortunate legacies of colonialism has been the opportunity it affords Communists to cloak themselves and their goals behind the popular appeal of nationalist independence movements. Throughout Indochina, Ho Chi Minh became—and still is—a hero and a liberator. After years of intensifying guerrilla activity, the forces under Ho finally were strong enough to force a more traditional military showdown with the French and to win. In 1954, the Geneva Agreements ended the war and created three independent states out of what used to be French Indochina: Vietnam, Laos, and Cambodia. Vietnam was "temporarily" divided at the 17th parallel between North and South, pending all-Vietnamese elections. It is a measure of the unfavorable circumstances surrounding the whole situation in Vietnam that the reluctance to

[65] On September 2, 1945, Ho Chi Minh proclaimed the Declaration of Independence of Vietnam. The Declaration begins as follows: "All men are created equal. They are endowed by their Creator with certain inalienable rights, among these are Life, Liberty, and the Pursuit of Happiness." The text is in Claude A. Buss, *Southeast Asia and the World Today*, D. Van Nostrand, Company, Inc., Princeton, N.J., 1958, p. 154.

hold elections as a partial means of reunifying the country has come, in this unique instance, from the non-Communist side: in any fair election, Ho and his associates might win. The elections have never been held.

After 1954, the Eisenhower administration, in the name of anticommunism, assumed much of the heavy burden of sustaining South Vietnam economically. It also provided military assistance and military advisers. There were high hopes that South Vietnam, under Ngo Dinh Diem, the postindependence leader, would become a sturdy, anti-Communist bastion. During the struggle for independence, the nationalist forces—called the Viet Minh—had organized resistance all over Indochina, including South Vietnam. After independence and the "temporary" partition, the Viet Minh organization in the south was quiescent for several years. But it did not wither away; it was merely awaiting a propitious moment to resume its activities, this time against the new "imperialists," the United States, and their "lackeys" running the government in South Vietnam.

In late 1958, the opportune moment was deemed to be at hand, and guerrilla action against the Diem regime was begun in earnest. As this is written (June, 1965), large portions of South Vietnam are controlled by the Viet Cong, the name now given to Communist guerrillas in South Vietnam. This bleak situation has come about despite massive infusions of economic and military aid from the United States and an "advisory" American military force that grew from approximately 1,000 men in 1960 to over 15,000 men in 1964, and then multiplied rapidly in 1965 as the United States involvement deepened.

No attempt can be made herein to describe with authority or perspicacity a situation that is undergoing constant and fundamental change as this is written. Consonant with the analytical aims of this book, more modest purposes account for the introduction of this unstable and uncertain crisis into the discussion. An effort will be made to describe briefly the character of guerrilla warfare in South Vietnam and the problems posed for United States policy by this and other guerrilla activity. This much must be attempted because the issues raised are grave ones and have implications well beyond South Vietnam.

The Nature of the Challenge

Guerrilla warfare is irregular and unorthodox. It does not involve mighty clashes between opposing armies. The guerrilla force does not seek victory through decisive military engagements, at least not until the late stages of its overall effort. Instead it seeks to undermine—by means discussed below—the morale of the established order, the regular armed forces, and the population as a whole. It offers itself and its cause as an attractive alternative.

Guerrilla warfare is by no means a new phenomenon. It has been waged from time to time throughout history. It can be employed by a captive population seeking to subvert the rule of an alien power, it can be used by dissident elements opposed to a governing regime, and it can be promoted by a foreign government seeking to overthrow an existing government. The guerrilla war in South Vietnam is a combination of the last two types. Most of the Viet Cong are South Vietnamese, but they are led, trained and partially supplied by the Communist governments in North Vietnam and, more indirectly, China.

Guerrilla warriors are part of a tightly controlled organization, and they are, for the most part, motivated by some common political values, or goals, such as nationalism or communism or—what is more likely, and the case in South Vietnam—some heady combination of the two. Such powerful incentives must be present because the guerrillas live an austere and dangerous life. Most of them live away from the regular population, in mountains or jungles or swamp areas where it is easy to hide but difficult to survive. The necessity for concealment accounts for the central importance of a favorable terrain for successful guerrilla operations. Other guerrillas live in the cities and villages or on farms, engaging in inconspicuous activity during the day and in acts of sabotage, terror, and murder at night.

Guerrilla warfare is often described as being more "political" than military. The meaning of this is not altogether clear because guerrillas assuredly do employ armed force, albeit in a special way. But the "political" emphasis does accurately suggest that the guerrillas seek to seize power by methods other than decisively defeating the regime's armed forces, except as a final measure against an already demoralized and tottering regime. Moreover, the word "political" also suggests the intimate relationship that successful guerrillas establish between themselves and the population. Mao Tse-tung, the Chinese Communist leader and a leading practitioner and theoretician of guerrilla war, has written as follows:

> Without a political goal, guerrilla warfare must fail, as it must if its political objectives do not coincide with the aspirations of the people and their sympathy, co-operation and assistance cannot be gained. The essence of guerrilla warfare is thus revoluntionary in character. . . . Because guerrilla war basically derives from the masses and is supported by them, it can neither exist nor flourish if it separates itself from their sympathies and co-operation.[66]

A guerrilla force depends upon the local population for food, new recruits, intelligence, and concealment. It must have this cooperation or it will be isolated and defeated.

Guerrilla forces employ many and varied techniques. They attempt by propaganda and indoctrination to convince a sizable segment of the popu-

---

[66] As quoted by Brian Crozier in "The Guerillas," *Encounter*, vol. 19, no. 4, p. 61, October, 1962. The quotation is from Mao's *Guerrilla Warfare*.

lation that the existing system is decadent and that its days are numbered. Concurrently, they seek to convince the public that they represent the new order and that their cause is just and/or historically sanctioned. They are fighting, they claim, a "war of national liberation." They seek, in other words, to create an aura of both success and virtue. Selected military action by single guerrillas or small groups—expanding as conditions grow more favorable and less caution is required—is an essential aspect of the guerrilla strategy. Guerrillas engage in hit-and-run raids on military installations and supply lines, seeking to sap the strength and morale of the regular army and, simultaneously, supplying themselves with weapons and ammunition. (Most of a guerrilla force's weapons are taken from the opposition forces.) They engage in extensive sabotage against civilian institutions and facilities, seeking to undermine the economy and the normal governmental processes, thereby spreading discontent. Where propaganda and the more gentle means of enlisting the support, or at least the protective sympathy, of the population do not succeed, terror is employed. Systematic and selective murder of uncooperative persons in the target area has been quite successful in cowing a population. The original response might be anger and a stiffened resistance in a given area, but after a few more selected persons are purposefully murdered, resistance is likely to soften, and accommodations are more likely to be worked out.

There is also an indiscriminate type of terror that can be employed under auspicious circumstances. Such things as throwing high explosives into crowded restaurants and blowing up civilian trains can sap the strength and will to resist of a weary population that sees little to choose between the competing forces and desperately wants peace and quiet. The same can be said for less drastic means of coercion.

In an orderly and stable society, the kinds of acts mentioned above would be considered the most outrageous and intolerable form of banditry, and they would probably be rather quickly and ruthlessly squelched by officialdom supported by a united and loyal population. But in an unstable, disintegrating society, where the government enjoys little popular support, such acts are part of a revolutionary process that will more than likely hasten the end of the old order.

 Successful guerrilla operations, then, have at least four prerequisites: superior organization and discipline; a political cause that not only attracts fanatical activists but is also capable of appealing to broad masses of people; favorable terrain; and an unpopular, unstable established order.

The Policy Problem in Vietnam
Unfortunately, the situation in South Vietnam from the late 1950s on contained all the necessary ingredients for successful guerrilla warfare. The Viet Cong were thoroughly organized and disciplined. Moreover, they were

bound together by the moral fervor that unites all nationalist movements, and this was further supported and inflamed by a heavy program of indoctrination into Communist ideology. And the terrain of South Vietnam lent itself perfectly to guerrilla warfare, especially the swampy delta area of the vital Mekong River.

Moreover, the established order in South Vietnam was a relatively easy target for the guerrillas. The regime of Ngo Dinh Diem was a reasonably progressive and democratic one—by Southeast Asian standards—for a few years after 1954, but by the late 1950s it had degenerated into a heavy-handed despotism, which depended for its survival not on any strong base of popular support but rather on its own waning capacity to impose order. The great majority of the population supported neither the Viet Cong nor the Diem regime. It was a nearly ideal environment for guerrilla activity. Diem was overthrown by a group of army generals in November, 1963— who, in turn, were removed in a bloodless coup by another general in January, 1964, after which there was a bewildering and debilitating series of coups and countercoups—but his successors did not appear to be much more successful in gaining popular support.

In addition to these favorable circumstances, the Viet Cong enjoyed two other valuable assets. One was the friendly sanctuaries and sources of supply in contiguous North Vietnam and that part of Laos controlled by the Communist-led Pathet Lao. It would have been difficult enough to defeat the guerrillas in South Vietnam if the struggle had been limited to that unhappy land. The fact that it was not so limited made the task vastly more difficult and perhaps beyond achieving. The second special asset was the momentum and aura of success that surrounded the Viet Cong. The guerrillas had behind them not only the luster of the original war for independence from France, but also the growing achievements in the struggle in South Vietnam since late 1958. This was reflected in the success of their recruitment efforts. Despite the rigors and dangers, the Viet Cong apparently more than made up for their losses over the years. And as the rebellion spread and became increasingly bold and successful, recruitment apparently became easier and easier.

In sum, it is probably no exaggeration to say that in early 1965, a disciplined, indoctrinated, and growing force of guerrillas was fighting a faction-ridden, dispirited, and fatigued South Vietnamese Army, which was itself merely a reflection of a divided, tired, and stricken people, who wanted peace at nearly any price.

The United States government was thereby confronted with a grave dilemma. There were two basic alternatives to continuance of the limited role then being performed, each of which allowed of many variations: withdrawal and expansion of the United States role. Each of the options had serious drawbacks; none of them seemed very promising. Even a cursory analysis of them shows why South Vietnam posed a most frustrating problem for United States policy makers.[67]

Withdrawal would have had the advantage of cutting United States losses in a deteriorating situation that appeared to be unsalvageable short of a massive United States intervention. But it would have had the serious disadvantage of generally undermining the credibility of United States commitments that had been solemnly and repeatedly made to South Vietnam in the preceding months and years. It wasn't as if the government had to decide whether to intervene *de novo*; we had been there for over ten years and had often and publicly announced our intention not to permit the communization of South Vietnam. The credibility and prestige of a major power are not insignificant factors in international politics.

Moreover, the loss of South Vietnam would very likely have increased the danger to such nations as Cambodia and Thailand, especially the latter. South Vietnam may have been intrinsically insignificant from the standpoint of United States security interests, but its communization could have had serious repercussions.[68]

Finally, American performance under these conditions was bound to affect the portentous struggle going on in the Communist world between China and the Soviet Union. Signs of American weakness were bound to strengthen the hand of the Chinese, who argued that "the imperialists are paper tigers" who should be constantly and boldly challenged. It would seem obvious that the United States had an interest in sustaining the more cautious, less dangerous, Soviet view of how to conduct international affairs in this thermonuclear age.

As for continuing the existing policy, this would have had the advantage of limiting United States casualties and costs and at least making more

---

[67] There were some who argued that there was a fourth alternative, namely, neutralization through negotiations. There were two difficulties with this position. In the opinion of most observers, neutralization under existing circumstances was simply a euphemism for communization. However that may have been, there was an even more fundamental problem: The Viet Cong, with the war going well for them, apparently were not interested in negotiations.

[68] The famous "domino theory" holds that if one nation in Southeast Asia goes Communist, the others will also topple, like a row of dominoes. Aside from the question of whether this theory is sound, there is an additional question, one that lurks in the background of virtually all discussion of the United States role in Southeast Asia: What difference does it make to the United States if all of Southeast Asia goes Communist? Are any vital United States interests involved? One of the usually unspoken convictions of those favoring withdrawal is that the answer to that last question is "no."

A related line of argument is that the communization of Southeast Asia is inevitable and that the best the United States can hope for is that those achieving it will be indigenous and nationalistic Communists, not beholden to the Chinese. Such "Titoist" regimes, it is argued, would constitute no threat to the United States. Therefore, we should be tacitly *encouraging* the success of the Viet Cong rather than forcing them into increasing dependency on the Chinese.

feasible some possible future accommodation and withdrawal. But in early 1965, this policy was—or so it seemed to most observers—simply not working and not likely to work. It was time for a new policy.

The second basic alternative was an expansion of the United States role in the war. This could be done in several ways, but the two most frequently discussed were the introduction of large numbers of American troops in the South and the commencement of large-scale United States–Vietnamese bombings in both the North and the South. The anticipated advantages were three: improved South Vietnamese morale, more effective and skillful overall ground operations against the Viet Cong, and a reduced Northern capability for supplying the Viet Cong with men and supplies. It was hoped that these steps would ultimately lead the Viet Cong—and/or their supporters in North Vietnam and China—to seek a peaceful settlement.

The disadvantages were clear. There would surely be increased casualties and costs, at least in the short run. Moreover, there was no guarantee that the desired results would be achieved, or at least that they would be achieved at a cost commensurate with their worth. Finally, and most ominously, there was the increased prospect of war with China—and perhaps, more apocalyptically, the Soviet Union.

Quite obviously, this set of alternatives was not a pleasant one for the Johnson administration to contemplate. It had delayed any decisive move for a long time. In February, 1965, it made its choice: The war was expanded. As this is written, the outcome is wholly uncertain, and the policy has provoked a storm of controversy at home and abroad.

The General Policy Problem

Whatever may develop in Vietnam, the experience of the United States there in the last decade highlights the challenge posed by guerrilla warfare. Communist attacks on existing non-Communist regimes are likely to take this form elsewhere. What responses are appropriate and practicable?

The most obvious answer is to try to build societies and governments that are not vulnerable to guerrilla assaults. And the United States is engaged in a large-scale foreign aid effort designed, among other things, to serve such ends. But once a guerrilla force takes hold in a given country, what can be done?

The optimists point to the successful postwar antiguerrilla operations in Malaya and the Philippines. These do indeed demonstrate that guerrillas can be defeated, but it is instructive to note how different the attendant circumstances were from those that prevailed in South Vietnam and that may very well prevail in other areas subjected to Communist guerrilla attacks. In Malaya, there were three favorable conditions that may not be present in some future struggle. In the first place, the guerrillas were Malayan Chinese and were therefore more readily identifiable and less acceptable to the rest of the non-Chinese Malayan population. Moreover, the guerrillas in Malaya did not have access to a friendly border through which they could be supplied and replenished. Finally, the counterguerrilla Malayans were promised their independence by the British, and this incentive is no longer available in most of this decolonized world.

As for the Philippines, the communist "Huk" guerrillas there were fighting on an isolated island against a popular and democratically elected government. The number of democratic island nations in the world is not large.

Whether guerrilla forces can be defeated in certain other parts of the world—and there are sporadic signs of guerrilla activity in parts of Africa and Latin America as well as Asia—is an open question. What is not open to much doubt is that such forces will challenge non-Communist governments in the years to come and that these challenges will confront the United States with some painful choices.

This chapter has been a *selective* analysis of some recent and contemporary problems for the defense policy of the United States. It does not purport to be comprehensive, of course, and such important problems as basic strategic doctrine, arms control, and military assistance have been dealt with only partially at best. Moreover, as indicated above, the preceding analysis of the selected problems does not purport to be exhaustive regarding these complex and contentious matters. This chapter, like this book, has not been primarily designed to provide answers. Rather, it attempts to focus on the central questions, to make them meaningful, and to provide some guidelines as to how they might best be dealt with. In defense policy, technological change combines with political uncertainties to make dogmatism even more inappropriate than usual.

Selected Bibliography

Brown, Seyom: "An Alternative to the Grand Design," *World Politics*, vol. 17, no. 2, pp. 232–242, January, 1965. An unusually sensible discussion of and prescription for the complex problem of United States–European relations.

Draper, Theodore: *Castroism, Theory and Practice*, Frederick A. Praeger, Inc., New York, 1965, especially pp. 223–256. The latest book by a leading authority on Castro's Cuba and United States–Cuban relations.

Halberstam, David: *The Making of a Quagmire*, Random House, Inc., New York, 1965. A *New York Times* reporter's account of his experience and United States policy in Vietnam.

Halperin, Morton H.: *Limited War in the Nuclear Age*, John Wiley & Sons, Inc., New York, 1963. An authoritative analysis of a prominent subject.

House of Representatives: *Index to United States Defense Policies from World War II through 1963*, 88th Cong., 2d Sess. (1964), H. R. Doc. No. 371. This is an index of a series of annual House documents dealing with United States defense policies. Both the Index and the annual analyses are prepared by Charles H. Donnelly, Senior Specialist in National Defense of the Legislative Reference Service, Library of Congress.

Janowitz, Morris: *The Professional Soldier, A Social and Political Portrait*, The Free Press of Glencoe, New York, 1960. See especially sec. VI, "Political Behavior: Pragmatic versus Absolutist."

Kissinger, Henry A.: *The Troubled Partnership*, McGraw-Hill Book Company, New York, 1965. A well-known strategist analyzes and prescribes for the NATO alliance.

Larson, David L. (ed.): *The "Cuban Crisis" of 1962*, Houghton Mifflin Company, Boston, 1963. A useful collection of documents bearing on that fateful confrontation.

Levine, Robert A.: *The Arms Debate*, Harvard University Press, Cambridge, Mass., 1963. A brilliant analysis of the various positions being argued for and against in the continuing controversy over defense policy in this country.

Mander, John: *Berlin, Hostage for the West*, Penguin Books, Inc., Baltimore, 1962. A description of a perennial issue and an argument on behalf of existing Western policy

Osgood, Robert E.: *Limited War*, The University of Chicago Press, Chicago, 1957. An early and still relevant discussion of a controversial subject

————: *NATO, The Entangling Alliance*, University of Chicago Press, Chicago, 1962. An authoritative account of the history and contemporary problems of NATO, with an emphasis on the unresolved strategic debates.

Paret, Peter, and John W. Shy: *Guerrillas in the 1960's*, rev. ed., Frederick A. Praeger, Inc., New York, 1962. An able treatment of a vital problem.

Rees, David: *Korea: The Limited War*, St Martin's Press, Inc., New York, 1964. A sober and responsible treatment of a crucial event in postwar American foreign policy.

Rosecrance, Richard N. (ed.): *The Dispersion of Nuclear Weapons*, Columbia University Press, New York, 1964. The best discussion of a fateful problem.

Schelling, Thomas C., and Morton H. Halperin: *Strategy and Arms Control*, The Twentieth Century Fund, New York, 1961. An expert discussion of a vital topic.

Foreign Aid as an Instrument of Policy

*I recommend this program [of foreign
aid] . . . in the belief that it will:
Enlarge the strength of the free world,
Aid in frustrating the ambitions
of Communist imperialism,
Reduce the hazards of
widespread conflict, and
Support the moral commitment of
free men everywhere to work for
a just and peaceful world.
Lyndon B. Johnson*

*. . . I am opposed to foreign aid; it has
been, in my opinion, one of the greatest
foreign-policy failures in history. . . .
Otto E. Passman, Chairman,
House Subcommittee on Foreign
Operations Appropriations*[1]

[1] The Johnson quotation is taken from
his 1964 message on foreign aid to
the Congress, dated March 19, 1964.
The Passman quotation is from a
statement that he prepared for *The
New York Times Magazine*, July 7,
1963, pp. 16–17. The statement was
entitled "Why I Am Opposed to
Foreign Aid."

chapter 8 Both of the opinions quoted above have the support of powerful elements in American politics, and there are many strongly held and supported opinions falling somewhere between them. The result has been that the annual struggle over appropriations for foreign assistance has been prolonged, divisive, and not a little bewildering.

Assisting foreign governments is not a new foreign policy technique. History provides many examples of governments' providing subsidies or paying bribes in an effort to secure the neutrality or cooperation of other governments. Another and more recent kind of foreign aid was the purchase of bonds issued by needy governments. Sometimes these purchases were made by the aiding government itself as a significant diplomatic gesture, and sometimes they were made by private citizens of the aiding nation after having been prompted and influenced to do so by their government. A prominent example of this technique was the large-scale French purchase of czarist Russian bonds prior to World War I. When the French and others sought compensation for these purchases from the new Soviet government after the war, the Soviet response included the observation—by no means without foundation—that the bond purchases had been politically motivated in the first place and would not—for this and other reasons—be treated as involving a normal commercial obligation.[2]

The United States engaged in a massive military assistance program during World War II. These "lend-lease" expenditures came to over $48.5 billion, most of which was not repayable. As the war drew to a close, millions of homeless and/or destitute Europeans desperately needed help merely to stay alive. The United States government contributed over $3 billion to the United Nations Reconstruction and Rehabilitation Administration (UNRRA) to alleviate their plight.

Nonetheless, in terms of scope, objectives, and longevity, the postwar American foreign aid program is unique. In an organized and continuing program, the United States has granted or loaned slightly over $70 billion in money or supplies or services to foreign nations since the end of World War II. Slightly over half of this has been for economic assistance of some kind or other, of which over two-thirds has been in the form of outright grants. The rest of the overall figure has been for military assistance, nearly all of which has been by grant.

These figures are somewhat misleading, especially in terms of current aid programs. Much of the economic aid has been of an emergency nature or in indirect support of the heavy military burdens borne by economically underdeveloped areas such as South Korea. Some of it can be called "aid"

---

[2] For a brief history of foreign aid, see George Liska, *The New Statecraft*, The University of Chicago Press, Chicago, 1960, chap. 2. This book is a pioneering and brilliant attempt to provide a theoretical framework for foreign assistance policies.

only in rather loose terms. Only a small fraction of it has been for the economic development of underdeveloped areas, which is the focus of the current effort. Moreover, most of today's economic assistance is by loan, repayable in dollars, rather than by grant. Nonetheless, the overall figure of "slightly over $70 billion" does appropriately suggest the magnitude of the effort.[3]

Types of Foreign Aid

In this chapter, the central purpose will be to analyze in detail the most criticized and vulnerable aspect of the United States foreign assistance effort, namely, the attempt to promote the economic development of the

[3] There are other and substantially different overall figures that are sometimes used. Anyone attempting to ascertain the "real" figure will encounter a bewildering number of governmental sources and a confusing dissimilarity in their statistics, which grow out of differing sources of information, methods of reporting, and calculations of the dollar value of the goods and services provided. To cite only one example of the problem, the annual executive branch *Summary Presentation to the Congress* for fiscal 1965 used a very different set of figures from those appearing in the fiscal 1964 version. [See *Proposed Mutual Defense and Development Programs FY1965, Summary Presentation to the Congress,* Washington, D.C., 1964, pp. 200–201, and *Proposed Mutual Defense and Assistance Programs FY1964, Summary Presentation to the Congress,* Washington, D.C., 1963, pp. 166–168. These booklets are prepared by the Agency for International Development (AID) as they relate to economic aid and by the Department of Defense as they relate to military aid. They will be referred to hereinafter as *Summary Presentation to the Congress, FY19___.*]In the booklet for fiscal 1964, a table appeared (pp. 166–168) showing a total economic and military assistance figure from July 1, 1945, to June 30, 1962, of $97,133,000,000. In the booklet for fiscal 1965, this overall figure was omitted altogether (perhaps because the awesome figure of $100 billion had been passed). Instead, a table showing aid figures from July 1, 1945, to June 30, 1963, appeared (on pp. 200–201), which not only showed no total figure but the overall military and economic figures of which, calculated independently, totaled only $68.1 billion. What happened to the other approximately $32 billion? A comparison of the details of the two charts indicates that the following categories were deleted for the later table: P.L. 480 (under which agricultural surpluses are sent abroad; the earlier table had a figure of $8.4 billion for this); the Export-Import Bank (earlier table: $7.5 billion); the Social Progress Trust Fund (earlier table: $0.2 billion); and "Other U.S. Economic Programs" (earlier table: $16.8 billion). These categories apparently constituted the difference.

There is a legitimate and meaningful difference of opinion about what should be called "assistance" and what should not be and this dispute will be taken up in greater detail later in this chapter. The fact remains, however, that it is impossible to ascertain any generally agreed upon figures on the magnitude of the postwar aid program and the resultant "numbers game" makes assessment more difficult and by itself creates problems for the aid program, especially in Congress.

It should perhaps be added that any attempt by an independent researcher to clarify the statistics is virtually doomed to failure. Anyone interested in making the attempt is referred, in addition to the sources cited above, to *Operations Report,* a quarterly publication of the Agency for International Development; *Foreign Grants and Credits by the United States Government,* a periodic publication of the Office of Business Economics of the Department of Commerce; and the *Statistical Abstract of the United States,* an annual publication of the U.S. Department of Commerce and its Bureau of the Census.

underdeveloped areas. Before coming to this analysis, however, it will be worthwhile to give a summary description of this and the other major elements of what is, altogether, called "foreign aid." To put the matter into some perspective, the following table shows the types of aid dealt with in the annual Foreign Assistance Act and how much was appropriated for each category for fiscal 1965.

Foreign Aid, FY1965

Category	Presidential Request (in millions of dollars)	Congressional Appropriation (in millions of dollars)
Development loans	922.2	773.7
Technical assistance and development grants	224.6	204.6
Alliance for Progress: Development loans	465.0	425.0
Technical assistance and development grants	85.0	84.7
Supporting assistance	405.0	401.0
Contingency fund	150.0	99.2
International organizations	134.4	134.3
Administrative expenses, AID	52.5	51.2
Administrative expenses, Department of State	2.9	2.9
American schools and hospitals abroad	18.0	16.8
Investment opportunities survey	2.1	1.6
Military assistance	1,055.0	1,055.0
Totals:	**3,516.7**	**3,250.0**

Source: *Congressional Quarterly Weekly Report*, vol. 23, no. 41, p. 2402, Week ending Oct. 9, 1964.

For purposes of the following descriptions, no distinction will be made between Alliance for Progress loans, grants, and technical assistance, on the one hand, and the other development loans, grants, and technical assistance on the other. The Alliance for Progress is administered separately and has somewhat different goals from much of the other development aid provided in Asia and Africa, but it is essentially just another aid program. It will be referred to from time to time below as a distinctive entity when appropriate.

Development Loans

As the table shows, development loans constitute by far the largest element of the economic aid program today, or nearly 55 per cent of the nonmilitary aid appropriation for fiscal 1965. They provide the capital for a wide variety of projects designed to increase the economic productivity of the borrowing nation. Some examples are transportation facilities (roads, railroads, ports, airports, pipelines), electric power installations, mining equipment, textile manufacturing equipment, the establishment of credit institutions, and various schemes for increasing agricultural output.

The terms of these loans have hardened over the years but are still far below commercial levels. Since 1961, all development loans have been repayable in dollars, not nonconvertible local currencies. For many years, the typical interest rate was 3/4 of 1 per cent, but in 1963 Congress required that all development loans have an interest rate of at least 2 per cent, except during the first ten years. Most loans today are for forty years at 2 per cent, with a ten-year "grace period," during which the borrowing government pays nothing on the principal and an interest charge of only 3/4 of 1 per cent per year. Some loans, however, have harder terms, ranging all the way up to 5¾ per cent, with no "grace period," and a much shorter length of time for repayment. Ghana, for example, received a $55 million loan in fiscal 1962 to assist in financing an aluminum smelter in conjunction with its huge Volta River hydroelectric project. Because of the commercial character of this project and its promise of early profits, the loan was for only twenty years at 5¾ per cent interest.

Technical Assistance and Development Grants

In "technical assistance" projects, the United States offers the skills, techniques, and knowledge of modern specialists to underdeveloped areas. The administration's fiscal 1965 request was to provide for 600 projects in fifty-two countries. The projects are designed to do such things as increase agricultural productivity, raise health standards, improve public administration practices, and increase educational standards and opportunities. Technically skilled or professionally trained or managerially skillful people are usually in very short supply in these areas.

Associated with such endeavors there is occasionally a need for limited capital expenditures; hence the additional words "development grants." These, however, are of declining significance, as most capital expenditures are now funded by loans rather than grants.

The preceding categories of aid are the most controversial and will be the focus of the analysis of economic development assistance to be undertaken below.

Military Aid

Military assistance consists of "military equipment, training and related services to help nations protect themselves against external attack or internal subversion."[4] Compared to economic aid, this category of aid is a rather straightforward, uncomplicated, and noncontroversial enterprise. It is given largely to those nations situated on the periphery of the Communist empire (or empires), whose need for protection against aggression and subversion is obvious. Eleven "forward defense" countries—Greece, Turkey, Iran, Pakistan, India, Laos, Vietnam, Thailand, the Philippines, Korea, Taiwan—were scheduled to receive 64 per cent of the military assistance in the proposed program for fiscal 1965. The mere listing of their names suggests why military aid has been relatively popular in Congress.

On the other hand, military assistance is not without its critics. Among the most significant complaints is one suggested by the official definition given above, which notes that one of the purposes of military aid is "to help nations protect themselves against . . . internal subversion." This has a variety of specific applications, some of them not especially ennobling or obviously related to anti-Communist efforts. No knowledgeable observer really believes, for example, that the military aid given to Iran is likely to enable that country to throw back an invasion by the Soviet Union. Its purpose is almost exclusively internal: it helps to keep the Shah in power against the passionately expressed wishes of substantial elements of the Iranian population. Communists, many democrats, and a reactionary aristocracy all oppose the monarch, though obviously for different reasons. Believing that any alternative to the Shah would almost certainly be worse —at least from the standpoint of the United States—we supply military aid that is patently for use against dissident internal elements, not foreign aggressors.

A similar odor of repression attaches to much of our military aid to Latin America. With disconcerting frequency, Americans learn that United States tanks and other military equipment have been used by United States–trained officers to overthrow a Latin government. When the overthrown government was democratically elected—or otherwise bore the imprint of "responsibility" from the standpoint of the United States—these episodes are at the very least embarrassing.

Some critics condemn this usage of military aid altogether and without reservation. The government's position, however, is a delicate one, and policy cannot—or should not, anyway—usually be dictated by abstract principles. The brutal fact is that in many countries the choice is not between repressive rule and democracy, but rather between repressive rule and something far worse, such as anarchy or communism or a progression

---

[4] *Summary Presentation to the Congress, FY1965*, p. 30.

from the former to the latter. All things considered—and unseemly innocence to one side—it is probably a prudent policy for the United States
to provide most of those countries now receiving it with sufficient military
aid to ensure their internal security against elements whose accession to
power would be disadvantageous to the United States. Whether this is true
for a given country at any given time is, of course, an arguable question,
and it goes without saying that the United States should avoid this rather
callous support of repressive elements whenever it can wisely do so.

Another major problem posed by the military aid program is the fact
that the United States becomes embroiled in some bitter, preexisting disputes. We provide the aid for the recipient's internal or external security,
but it is not viewed that way by a neighboring state that has a major
quarrel with the recipient power. The classic case has to do with the long-
standing and deeply felt animosity between Pakistan and India over
Kashmir. As an ally of the United States situated close to both the Soviet
Union and China, Pakistan has received a substantial amount of military
aid.[5] India has always viewed this with grave suspicion. But it is not merely
the difficulties that this poses for United States–Indian relations that casts
doubt on the wisdom of giving military aid to Pakistan. There is the additional fact that India feels called upon to create and maintain a compensatory military establishment, thus undoing some (much?) of the benefit
that derives from our economic aid to India.

Mention of the Pakistan-India dispute raises still another basic question
about military aid: Can recipients be relied upon? After the Chinese
invasion of India in the fall of 1962, the United States began to give India
substantial amounts of military assistance, despite the absence of treaty
ties. This so enraged Pakistan that her rulers began to court the Chinese
and to suggest in unsubtle ways that her alliance with the United States
was at best overrated and at worst an outright liability.

Another vexation for the United States arose with special urgency in
1964 as the possibility of war between Greece and Turkey—both recipients
of massive amounts of United States military aid—over Cyprus appeared to
be quite real. The spectacle of a serious clash of arms between these two
NATO allies is usually discussed in terms of its impact on NATO and
the even more obvious questions it would raise about how the Soviets
might take immediate advantage of such an imbroglio. But another ele-

---

[5] The amount has not been made public. This by itself is an interesting fact since the
figures for military aid through fiscal 1963 were included in *ibid.*, pp. 200–201, for
nearly all countries. The exceptions were Pakistan, Saudi Arabia, Laos, Vietnam,
Morocco, and Tunisia. There must be special reasons why the figures for Saudi Arabia,
Morocco, and Tunisia have been regarded as too sensitive for publication—and one
can guess at them—and there are obvious reasons for not releasing the data regarding
Vietnam and Laos. But Pakistan is another matter. The only reason for withholding
this figure that suggests itself to this writer relates to the one under discussion: India
would probably be appalled and angered.

ment of great importance would be the fact that such a war would involve the use on both sides of huge amounts of American military equipment, which was consigned to those nations for rather different purposes.

Another question that can be raised about our extensive military assistance program is whether its presence and, more particularly, its size do not involve us rather automatically and unthinkingly in some areas where perhaps noninvolvement would be preferable. To raise this question, of course, is to confront again the agonizing problem of Vietnam. But whatever this nation's policy toward that baffling problem should be, or will be, it is a fact that the mere existence of a military assistance program—with its history, its bureaucratic and congressional allies, and the assumptions that it induces—tends to draw us into matters that we might otherwise ignore or touch only lightly.

The preceding paragraphs have touched on some of the problems posed by a military assistance program. On balance, however, the justification for military assistance—or most of it, anyway—is clear enough, and the program is relatively noncontroversial.

Supporting Assistance

"Supporting assistance" is a special kind of economic aid. It is not aimed directly at economic development, but instead is designed to serve four major purposes in selected underdeveloped nations:

(a) to enable maintenance of larger armed forces for the common defense; (b) to preserve reasonable economic stability in critical situations; (c) to encourage independence from [Communist] bloc dominance in sensitive areas; and (d) to assure access to strategic United States military bases.[6]

For fiscal 1965, four countries—South Korea, South Vietnam, Laos, and Jordan—were scheduled to receive 78 per cent (or $273 million) of the proposed supporting assistance program. In South Vietnam, the program is directed toward the rural population in the struggle against the Viet Cong, and it also provides for essential imports. In South Korea, it is primarily to finance the importation of needed raw materials and capital goods. In Laos, it constitutes a rather desperate economic sustaining operation on behalf of a weak and divided non-Communist government. In Jordan, it is used to underwrite the monarchy in an artificial and economically unviable nation.

Other leading recipients of supporting assistance are Thailand and the Congo. In the former, the program is centered on an effort to strengthen internal security in the northeastern part of the country, which is menaced by Communist guerrillas. In the Congo, the assistance is used to "maintain economic stability," because "the economy is going through a transitional

---

[6] *Ibid.*, p. 34.

reconstruction period."[7] This is a diplomatic way of saying that the Congo is, as usual, in a state of disintegration and chaos, both politically and economically, and that the United States is making a sizable contribution toward the effort to feed the population and keep the situation from degenerating into complete anarchy.

Supporting assistance has been declining in amount in recent years as the major recipient nations have developed a stronger economic base for their military expenditures. It seems likely, however, that as long as the military assistance program continues, the supporting assistance program will also, especially in such heavily armed but economically dependent nations as South Korea. Moreover, it also seems likely that since supporting assistance is ordinarily so directly and vitally tied in with the military capabilities of the recipient nations—and therefore, presumably, with the security interests of the United States—it will continue to be a relatively popular program in Congress.

Contingency Fund

The "contingency fund" is an annual appropriation for the President's discretionary use in unforeseen emergencies abroad. In recent years, much of this money has been allocated for military purposes in South Vietnam, but it can be used for a wide variety of purposes, such as propping up the currency of a friendly government or rendering assistance to the victims of a natural disaster.

Partly because of institutional rivalry, and unlike the two preceding categories of aid, the contingency fund is not viewed favorably in Congress. For fiscal 1964, President Kennedy's request was cut by 83 per cent, from a request of $300 million to an appropriation of $50 million. For fiscal 1965, President Johnson heeded this lesson and requested only $150 million; Congress appropriated $99.2 million, a cut of "only" 34 per cent, and an absolute figure nearly double that of the preceding year.

Contributions to International Organizations

The annual foreign assistance bill also includes some of the amounts that the United States *voluntarily* gives to international organizations—primarily agencies of the United Nations—engaged in development and humanitarian programs that can reasonably be defined as "aid."[8] Some

---

[7] *Ibid.*, p. 35.

[8] The amount appropriated does *not* include the regular *assessed* contribution to the United Nations and its peace-keeping operations, which are handled separately. The assessed contributions are nonvoluntary in the sense that failure to make them would result—at least according to a literal reading of the Charter—in the loss of voting privileges in the General Assembly. The "aid" contributions, on the other hand, are entirely voluntary. The assessed contributions of the United States constitute slightly over 32 per cent of the regular United Nations budget. Our voluntary contributions usually constitute somewhere between 38 and 45 per cent of the annual expenditures of the United Nations outside of the regular budget.

understanding of the nature and purposes of these programs can be gained from a partial breakdown of how the United States administration proposed to spend most of its fiscal 1965 request for $134.4 million (virtually all of which was actually appropriated by Congress): the United Nations Expanded Program of Technical Assistance and the United Nations Special Fund, $60 million; the United Nations Relief and Works Agency for Palestine Refugees, $16 million; the United Nations Children's Fund (UNICEF), $12 million; and the World Banks' massive financing—over $1 billion—over a ten-year period of the Indus water project, involving both India and Pakistan, $37 million.[9] Congress has been remarkably willing to make appropriations at roughly this level and presumably will continue to do so at least as long as the overall request stays at this comparatively low level.[10]

Programs Funded Outside the Foreign Assistance Act

There are several other programs of the United States government that are sometimes called "foreign aid" but that are not covered by the annual foreign aid bill and that will merely be cited briefly herein. The one involving the most "money"—at least on paper—and the least generosity is the Food for Peace Program (P.L. 480). Under this program, which began in 1954, the United States gives away or sells for local currencies—or, much less frequently, makes available long-term credits (repayable in dollars) for the purchase of—vast amounts of surplus United States agricultural products. This has developed into an enormous program. In fiscal 1963, for example, agricultural products acquired by the United States government at a cost of nearly $2 billion under the agricultural price support program were shipped abroad under this program. But despite the fact that these products constitute assistance to the recipients, the program scarcely deserves to be called "aid." These products are shipped abroad primarily because they are surplus and storing them is expensive for the government. In other words, the program is motivated primarily by domestic, not foreign policy, considerations. Moreover, the dollar value mentioned can be misleading since it is based on what the government pays under the price support program—for domestic policy purposes—but, by definition, there is not a demand for these surplus products at such prices. Finally, the local currencies that are acquired under the program are partly used for such

---

[9] *Ibid.*, p. 37.

[10] No program, of course, is isolated from the pressures and influences of international politics, not even one as "nonpolitical" as this one might appear to be. In the fall of 1964, as the long-awaited showdown over regular United Nations financing approached, the United States announced that it would not make its annual pledge to either the Expanded Program of Technical Assistance or the Special Fund until the controversy over the peace-keeping budget had been satisfactorily resolved. (The fact that this threat was not finally carried out does not invalidate the point.)

purposes as paying the costs of American diplomatic missions and financing —through loans—the expansion of American business abroad.[11]

Another program that can be called "aid" only in a rather self-deluding manner but that unquestionably is helpful to foreign—as well as domestic —interests is that administered by the Export-Import Bank. Originally established in 1934 by the United States to facilitate purchases by the newly recognized Soviet government in the depression-racked and export-hungry United States, the bank survived a disappointing beginning and now operates on a rather grand scale. It offers credits to foreign purchasers who want to buy American-made commodities. Although it does not operate at a loss, its capitalization is supplied by the United States government, and it does make possible—albeit at commercial rates—the purchase of capital goods that would not otherwise be available to underdeveloped areas. In fiscal 1963, for example, the Export-Import Bank authorized $203.7 million in long-term loans to underdeveloped countries, nearly half of it to Latin America.[12]

The Peace Corps is unquestionably a form of assistance, whether the volunteers are engaged in teaching, road building, health programs, or one of the many other activities undertaken by the Corps. On the other hand, it is generally conceded that the justification for the program is *at least* as much related to the direct benefits that accrue to the volunteers themselves and to the reputation of the United States as it is to the benefits derived by the host countries.[13] Moreover, it is still a comparatively in-

---

[11] The reader may believe that dragging motives into the analysis is illegitimate. By this standard, it might be said, there is little or no "foreign aid," since its ultimate rationale has much more to do with United States interests than with humanitarian instincts. But a meaningful distinction between Food for Peace and, say, economic development assistance can be drawn. Regarding the former, there are direct and immediate benefits to powerful American interests, and it is these benefits and these interests that largely explain the existence of the program. Regarding development assistance, on the other hand, there are direct and immediate benefits to only a small and relatively powerless element of the American body politic, namely, the specific manufacturing, shipping, and other interests involved in transactions paid for by foreign aid funds. These interests could not demand and get a development assistance program; they are merely the happy beneficiaries of a program that is carried on for other reasons.

[12] *Ibid.*, p. 189.

[13] Note, for example, the candid testimony of David E. Bell, Administrator of the Agency for International Development (AID):

The justification for the Peace Corps is partly because of the benefit to the young Americans who are overseas in it. . . .

Secondly, the Peace Corps volunteers do make a direct contribution of type. of skills which are frequently very short in countries where they work, and that is beneficial.

Thirdly, they provide a very significant personal demonstration of the interest of the United States in wanting to help the people of these countries where they work.

I believe those are the three primary values that the Peace Corps serves from the standpoint of the U.S. interest.

Foreign Operations Appropriations for 1965, Hearings before the Subcommittee on

expensive program—the requested appropriation for fiscal 1965 was $115 million, and $87.1 million was appropriated—and is now popular with virtually all segments of American opinion. Like the two preceding programs, the Peace Corps has become an accepted aspect of American foreign policy; peripheral, but accepted.

The United States also participates in other ventures that, in varying degrees, can be regarded as foreign assistance. It contributes by far the largest single amounts of capital to such institutions engaged in international lending as the following: the International Bank for Reconstruction and Development (IBRD, popularly known as the World Bank), the International Development Association (IDA), and the Inter-American Development Bank.[14]

It may have occurred to the reader that one way of making an easier target of "foreign aid" would be to draw together all of these programs funded outside of the regular foreign aid bill, total the annual expenditures, and add that total to the regular foreign aid appropriation. This is, in fact, commonly done. As noted in a previous footnote, for example, the "over $100 billion" figure includes *all* of these programs, even those such as the Food for Peace shipments and Export-Import Bank loans, which are quite obviously more designed to assist domestic interests than foreign recipients.

The annual verbal fireworks in Congress associated with the foreign aid bill invariably involve charges of fraudulent statistics and allegations that "the real cost" of foreign aid each year is much higher than the figures

---

Foreign Operations Appropriations of the House Committee on Approriations, 88th Cong. 2d Sess., 1964, pt. 2, p. 71. (Cited hereafter as *Hearings for 1965 of the House Subcommittee on Foreign Operations Appropriations,* pt. 2, 1964.)

Representative Passman, the most powerful congressional opponent of foreign aid, was so elated by this candor that he interrupted Bell twice to say how much he agreed. At a later point in the hearings, he labeled himself—no doubt facetiously—as "the father of the Peace Corps." (*Ibid.,* p. 1149). Anything so frankly designed to benefit the suppliers of assistance and, what is more, so inexpensive, was bound to appeal to Mr. Passman.

[14] For an account of the activities of these and lesser institutions, see the excellent description and detailed report contained in House Committee on Foreign Affairs, *Staff Memorandum on International Lending and Guaranty Programs,* 88th Cong., 2d Sess., 1964.

Through 1964, the United States had made $635 million available to IBRD (plus "subscribing" an additional $5,715 million, which is not available for the lending operations of the Bank but is subject to call if—as is highly unlikely—it is required to meet the Bank's obligations), $319.9 million to IDA (plus an agreement to provide $312 million more during fiscal years 1966, 1967, and 1968), and $300 million to the Inter-American Development Bank (plus a "subscription" of $200 million, and an appropriation of $525 million for the "Social Progress Trust Fund," which is administered by the Bank). It had also provided $4,125 million for the International Monetary Fund (IMF), an international financial institution of great importance. *Ibid.,* chart opposite p. 82.

associated with the foreign assistance act suggest. In 1964, for example, the dissenting minority views accompanying the Report of the House Foreign Affairs Committee included the following "recapitulation of the various [foreign aid] authorization proposals and appropriation requests during 1964 that can be identified:"[15]

Foreign Assistance Act:	
Economic assistance	$2,461,700,000
Military assistance	1,055,000,000
Peace Corps	115,000,000
Food for Peace (P.L. 480)	2,215,000,000
Inter-American Development Bank:	
Social Progress Trust Fund	750,000,000
Callable capital stock	412,000,000
International Development Association (IDA)	373,656,000
Tax credit proposal	60,000,000
Total:	***$7,442,356,000***

Obviously, if the "true" foreign aid request in a given year were more like $7.4 billion than $3.5 billion, the opposition would have a stronger case.

This is a defensible way of discussing overall foreign aid costs, and the figures are accurate. There is, however, a rather compelling reason for taking the position that the $7.4 billion figure is grossly misleading. For all the reasons indicated above, the $2.2 billion Food for Peace item does not deserve the label "foreign aid." As suggested above, moreover, similar doubts about the appropriateness of labeling the $115 million Peace Corps item as "foreign aid" could be raised.

Another reason for holding that the $7.4 billion figure is misleading has to do with the appropriations for the international lending institutions. These appropriations do undeniably constitute a form of foreign aid, but it is quite appropriate to keep them separate from the calculations affecting the regular foreign aid bill, which is, with the minor exception of the amounts given to international organizations, concerned with bilateral and multilateral enterprises over which our government retains a direct control. The funds provided for international lending institutions are not properly regarded as competitive with or a substitute for our own bilateral aid program. They do constitute aid, but of a different and complementary sort. These enterprises should be judged separately on their own merits. There will presumably always be room for bilateral and multilateral programs, however, and these should also be judged on their own merits. In other words, whether $3.5 billion or $4.5 billion or $1.5 billion should be appropriated for the United States program is a question that is related to

---

[15] House Committee on Foreign Affairs, *Foreign Assistance Act of 1964*, 88th Cong., 2d Sess., 1964, H.R. Rep. No. 1443 to accompany H.R. 11380, p. 49.

but not directly dependent upon the size of our contributions to international lending institutions in any given year.

Finally, it should be emphasized that whatever annual figure one chooses to deal with, there is bound to be some unavoidable confusion about how much of it really deserves to be called aid. In a footnote above, it was suggested that a distinction should be drawn between those elements of the overall program that at best have only indirect, long-range benefits to the United States and those that have immediate and direct benefits to the United States as a whole and that are sustainable on those grounds alone. It was suggested that the former are much more clearly "foreign aid" and that the latter could often more accurately be treated as "self-aid." This distinction applies within the foreign aid bill itself, thereby complicating even more the question of what can reasonably be regarded as "foreign aid" in any given year. Take military aid, for example. Every recent administration has assured Congress that in the absence of this program, much more money would have to be spent on United States defenses. So, if we are saving money with the program, why call it "aid"? And what about the development loans now being offered? They are offered at rates well below what it costs our government to borrow the money, and they therefore do constitute aid in some degree. But they are repayable in dollars, so what proportion of the annual appropriation for these loans is actually "aid"? And these last few sentences do not even raise the wholly unanswerable question of how much security—if any—we are actually buying with this kind of assistance.

It is hoped that the above paragraphs have prepared the reader to understand somewhat better the annual "numbers game" associated with the foreign aid bill and have disabused him of the notion that it is easy—or even possible—to attach a price tag to the foreign aid program. Nonetheless, it will now be necessary to revert to common usage and treat as foreign aid at least all of those items that appear in the annual Foreign Assistance Act.[16]

---

[16] Unfortunately, the categories in the annual bills change almost as often as the arguments for and against them. The Social Progress Trust Fund, for example, was dealt with in the 1963 act, but was funded separately in 1964. In addition, the character of the various categories changes over time. Efforts to categorize the foreign aid expenditures since 1945 are made, but they deal in such broad categories as to be nearly useless.

All this confusion and complexity underlines the fact that the task of a congressman in dealing with this program every year is a most difficult one. One of the primary reasons for the conspicuous congressional distaste for this program is its elusive and imprecise nature. Some complexity is unavoidable, but the executive branch merely deepens the problem by rearranging the figures and using different types of calculations nearly every year. Even when it is done to ease the congressional burden and "simplify" the presentation, these endless changes are bound to irritate congressmen, who have other things to do besides keeping up with the bureaucracy's latest bookkeeping techniques.

Economic Development Assistance

Assistance designed to foster economic development in the underdeveloped areas—i.e., development loans and grants, and technical assistance—is easily the most controversial and vulnerable aspect of the foreign aid program. There are many reasons for this. Perhaps the two most important are that the economic development of these areas has neither a clear nor a direct relationship to the vital interests of the United States and that assistance costs are high. But these are by no means the only criticisms put forward by the many congressmen, intellectuals, journalists, businessmen, and others who are dissatisfied with the program. Some of these critics can be rather easily dismissed as persons who do not understand the modern world, but many of them are experienced, highly motivated, and sophisticated individuals whose criticisms deserve careful attention. What follows is an attempt to set forth the rationale of the program and an analysis of the manifold criticisms being made of it.

The Rationale

Western Europe, South Africa, Great Britain, Canada, the United States, Japan, and parts of Latin America have "developed," industrial economies and "modern" societies. Although the standards of living and levels of productivity vary substantially within and between these nations, these gaps are relatively insignificant alongside the gulf separating such nations from the rest, or economically underdeveloped part, of the non-Communist world. Most of the world's population lives in underdeveloped areas. These conditions have prevailed ever since the West began to industrialize and create radically different societies with vastly increased levels of economic productivity; and the gulf continues to widen. What distinguishes the contemporary situation from that of, say, 25 years ago is the fact that almost all these areas have now become independent, and they therefore have the opportunity to seek—or at least appear to seek—a less depressed or primitive standard of living. They are doing so—or are appearing to do so—and the resultant demands on the developed areas and upheavals in the underdeveloped areas pose a challenge to the diplomacy of developed nations, especially the one that is conspicuously the most wealthy and powerful, the United States.

The proponents of economic assistance believe that such aid is an appropriate response to this challenge. They make essentially the following argument, or some variation of it: (1) The future of the underdeveloped areas is a matter of some considerable importance to the United States. (2) That future can be beneficially influenced—from the standpoint of United States interests—by fostering economic development in these areas. (3) The provision of economic assistance is an effective means of fostering such development. Each link in this chain of reasoning, or rationale, is debatable, and although there is no way of authoritatively proving or disproving the validity of any of them, the next section of this chapter will attempt to analyze them in some depth. Thereafter, the specific but less fundamental questions that have been raised about the American economic aid program will be examined.

An Analysis of the Rationale

United States Interests and the Underdeveloped Nations   What difference does it make to the United States what happens in the populous underdeveloped nations of the world? Does it matter whether the governments of these nations are hostile or indifferent or friendly to the nations of the West? Does it matter what kinds of foreign policies they pursue generally? These kinds of questions are seldom asked any more in any kind of serious or probing manner.[17] Isolationist ideas and attitudes have been thoroughly discredited, and properly so. But the necessary awareness of our unavoidable involvement in international politics should not dull our capacities to distinguish between what is important and what is not. It does not follow from the fact that we cannot isolate ourselves from the rest of the world that whatever happens anywhere is bound to affect significant interests of the United States. In this, as in most matters, it is requisite that a discriminating intelligence separate the vital from the trivial, the important from the unimportant. The significance of our relations with the underdeveloped nations can be as easily overrated as it can be underrated.

There are basically three types of considerations that merit attention in this respect: economic, military, and psychological. The present American economy is, like all modern, industrial economies, increasingly dependent upon trade with and raw materials from foreign nations. Barring some major reversal of contemporary trends, our economy will become more and more heavily intertwined with the economies of other nations. Much of this interdependence, however, will be with other *developed* areas, such as Europe, Canada, and Japan. Moreover, insofar as we are likely to become increasingly dependent upon foreign raw materials, this dependence could probably be selective, concentrating upon such an historically related area as Latin America and avoiding many ties with Africa and Asia. Could we not, therefore, ignore these latter areas and develop no need either for their trade or their raw materials?

Perhaps we could. Given the uncertainty of our future needs and technological developments, it would be foolish to be dogmatic about this matter. But it is certainly fair to say that our economic well-being would be enhanced by continued access to the materials and markets of the under-

---

[17] For a provocative treatment of precisely such questions, see Edward C. Banfield, *American Foreign Aid Doctrines*, a booklet published by the American Enterprise Institute, Washington, D.C., 1963, especially pp. 32–36. Banfield answers these questions rather differently from the present writer.

developed nations. How much we should be willing to spend in an effort to maintain such access—especially when the fate of such efforts is so uncertain—is an open question. A response to it will be easier after examining other elements of the overall problem.

The second of these is military. How would a loss of access to these areas affect our military security? Military technology changes rapidly these days, and it is impossible to predict what raw materials or bases will be requisite for deterrent or defense purposes in, say, twenty years. It would appear to be prudent to try to retain access to all of the underdeveloped world, but how much such an effort is worth is, again, an open question. And it is impossible to answer such questions with any precision or even confidence.

Another military implication of the underdeveloped areas for the United States is the fact that warfare, or even threats of it, anywhere in the world tend to draw in the major powers, thus raising the most ominous possibilities. Of course, the question under consideration is whether the United States *should* be sufficiently concerned about these areas to consider intervention. But at the very least it should be borne in mind that such interventions have occurred in the past, and that whatever their justification in any specific instance may have been, it cannot be ruled out that some future American government might be induced into intervening again. If this is so—and if such interventions are inherently very dangerous, regardless of their merits—it is a matter of some importance to the United States that conditions be fostered whereby such interventions are not induced.

Another military aspect of this problem is whether the huge populations of the underdeveloped world might themselves someday constitute a military threat to the West. Would this preponderance of humanity pose a military threat just by sheer weight of numbers? Under present technological conditions, the answer is probably negative. But one cannot be sure that superior numbers will always be indecisive. The Chinese explosion of a nuclear device in October, 1964, raises, however dimly, the possibility that someday the underdeveloped areas of the world will have a technology somewhat comparable to the West. If they should achieve such a position, could they then exploit their superior numbers by engaging in widespread "conventional" and "guerrilla" military activities against the West? Such a question seems bizarre today; it may not be in the future.

Finally, what would be the psychological consequences of finding the West surrounded by an uncooperative or hostile Asia and Africa (and Latin America) in addition to the Communist nations? It may be true that a mature and self-confident democratic West, led by the United States, *could* deal with such a set of circumstances calmly, sensibly, and successfully. But whether it actually would is highly dubious. Such speculations should not be dogmatically asserted, but no one who has lived through the McCarthy era of the early 1950s or the rise of the radical right in the

1960s should view this prospect with much assurance. These movements were given much of their impetus by a widespread dissatisfaction with the insecurity and uncertainty of the cold war, which was channeled into xenophobic and paranoid activity. If so much extremist, undemocratic, and divisive activity can flourish under such relatively favorable conditions, what would become of the morale and psychological health of the body politic if the democratic West were to find itself encircled by an envious and hostile world?

The preceding paragraphs have raised many more questions than they have answered. A detailed investigation of them would require at least another book, and many of them are simply unanswerable today. Intelligent and conscientious persons can come to diametrically opposite conclusions about the basic problem of how important to the West the under-developed areas are or will become. As indicated earlier, this writer's position is that their importance is considerable and is likely to become more so. It is easy to ridicule the exaggerated claims—sometimes hysterical, often moralizing—that are made about the central significance of Asia, Africa, and Latin America. Some of the most vacuous speeches and writing in recent years have been devoted to such themes. Preposterous and/or glib declamations about how our survival is allegedly dependent upon the political sympathies of the inhabitants of Paraguay or Zambia or Cambodia have afflicted our mass media and even more discriminating channels of communication. The absurdity of such claims and the hyperbolic character of such rhetoric should not, however, blind us to the very real dangers that do exist in the world, including the dangers of living in a world in which the West would no longer be able to deal with the under-developed areas of the world in a mutually satisfactory manner.

Economic Development and United States Interests   Even if it does matter what transpires in the underdeveloped nations and what their foreign policies are, it remains an open question whether the fostering of economic development is an appropriate response. Is there any reason to believe that the economic development of the underdeveloped nations is likely to induce political conditions and policies beneficial to the interests of the West? This is a more difficult question to answer than it might appear to be at first. There just is no simple connection between economic development and either internal stability or moderate and prudent foreign policies.[18]

---

[18] There used to be a good deal more emphasis in the writings and testimony supporting aid about the alleged relationship between economic development and democratic governmental systems. The sobering experiences of the last decade or so have made it abundantly clear, however, that democracy is not easily transplanted and that the alleged correlation between standards of living and democratic processes is at best doubtful.

Consider first the possibilities existing for a nation that is just beginning to develop economically. This is an unsettling and painful process, which generates great tensions and conflict within the traditional society. Far from inducing stability, it may very well create revolutionary conditions, especially as the rising expectations of the populations are frustrated by the harsh realities of continuing economic scarcity.

Next, consider the fact that underdeveloped nations pose a small military and economic threat to the West, whereas developed nations—such as the Soviet Union, for example—pose very real threats. It is, after all, strong nations, not weak ones, that have traditionally endangered or broken the peace. Hitler's Germany, to cite a recent and terrifying instance, had a highly developed economy, which not only did not prevent its rapacious foreign policies but, instead, made them possible. Do we really welcome the economic development of those vast portions of the globe where weakness has been endemic and where the existing and potential manifestations of anti-Western sentiment are so considerable?

A related matter is the relationship between economic development and vulnerability to communism. Although, as the above paragraphs indicate, there are many possible anti-Western developments inherent in the politics of the underdeveloped nations, the most worrisome of all is the possibility that they will come under the control of Communists. Indeed, in its crudest form, the argument in favor of fostering economic development is put in strictly anti-Communist terms: economic development will ward off communism. But, alas, this argument is as dubious as the others that connect economic development with favorable consequences for the West. The subtle and sobering fact is that there is no obvious or necessary connection between economic development—or even standards of living—and susceptibility to communism. It can be argued, on the contrary, that most or all of the successes of communism have been unrelated to the level of economic development in the communized nation. Russia went Communist during a massive upheaval occasioned by its collapse in World War I. China became a Communist nation after a prolonged civil war in which the major issues were not economic. Cuba was among the wealthiest of the Latin American nations when Castro assumed power. Eastern Europe had Communist governments imposed on it by the occupying Soviet Army after World War II, and economics had nothing to do with it.

Each of these statements could legitimately be labeled an oversimplification. It could probably be shown that low levels of economic development played some role in all of these Communist accessions to power, except in Eastern Europe. But these contentions are valid enough to underline the fact that there certainly is no simple relationship between the level of economic development and vulnerability to communism.

For the leaders of the underdeveloped nations in this modern world, the question of whether economic development is a good or bad thing is a nonsense question. It is universally believed to be a good thing, and, with varying degrees of skill and integrity, it is universally being pursued. Moreover, there is a sufficient number of developed nations, including Communist ones, willing to provide at least modest assistance to these efforts to ensure that they will go forward, however haltingly. As a result of these conditions, United States policy makers are not confronted with a choice as simple as whether to approve or disapprove of economic development. The only questions are whether the United States should continue to assist the developing efforts under way and forthcoming, and, if so, to what extent. And since the United States is by far the wealthiest nation in the world, it is in a position substantially to affect the pace and direction, perhaps even the success, of these development efforts.

The arguments in the preceding paragraphs constitute powerful support for the proposition that the United States should do nothing to foster economic development in "the third world." But there are strong reasons for reaching the opposite conclusion. They boil down to the conviction that although economic development may not proceed fast enough, its total or near absence would engender even more dangerous conditions. The demands for development cannot be eliminated; they are bound to grow. The United States may not be able to control the consequences of economic development, and some may be at least temporarily disadvantageous. But to turn our backs on the problem and the people involved would be to ensure not merely that the process would be markedly slowed but that the leaders—who know from first-hand experience the vast and growing disparities in standards of living between their own countries and the developed nations—and masses in these areas would become or remain bitterly anti-American. Although this might be of small consequence for the foreseeable future, it is a handicap of unknown and potentially enormous size to bequeath to succeeding generations of Americans. For better or worse, justly or not, there now exists a nearly universal expectation that the West, and particularly the United States, will help the underdeveloped nations progress economically. To frustrate this expectation in any thoroughgoing and deliberate manner would unquestionably be risky.

If the reader senses that the argument in favor of fostering development is based less on evidence than on faith, he is correct. To talk about the future of the underdeveloped countries—or, indeed, of the world—is to talk about the unknown. But this is true for both sides of the argument. The historical evidence cited above about the nonrelationship between economic development and vulnerability to communism, for example, may be impressive, but it is surely not conclusive. There *are* sensible reasons for believing that, however Communist regimes have seized power in the past, they may very well seize power by more "orthodox" means in the future; that is, as a result of revolutions engendered by economic deprivations. To attempt to blunt this possibility is not foolish; it is a plausible way of confronting a problem that is complex and dangerous. Action may not induce favorable consequences, but nonaction may not either. Nobody knows.

Economic Aid and Economic Development The rest of this discussion is predicated on the judgment that fostering economic development is a prudent policy for the United States in the contemporary world. The next question then becomes: Is economic aid an effective means of fostering economic development? Like the preceding questions, this one is not so simple to answer as it might at first glance appear to be. The following passage from a recent book by Herbert Feis, an experienced and wise participant-observer in international economic affairs for over thirty years, sets the appropriately grim tone for this discussion.

> While listening to statements of what we aim to achieve by foreign aid, the spirit is uplifted. But the spirit may sag when the panorama of poverty we would like to relieve is envisioned. The area of destitution is vast and striated.
>
> The vista is smudged by the sight of the so many dreadful human situations that have so long persisted. The dark, dank existence in the charcoal and fishing villages of Brazil; the shivering and dull-eyed Indians in the mountain towns of Peru, Bolivia, and Ecuador; the huddled destitution in Sicily intensified by searing tempers and cruel violence; the teeming half-starved millions in the dirt and dung of the congested villages and city slums of India, the sickly and hungry jute redders of East Pakistan and the refugees from India huddled in the hovels of Dacca; the teeming, ignorant millions in the tropical villages of Java; the ragged, sickly workers along the Nile, and the beggarly families in the back streets of Cairo; the pestilential, rotting, vermin-infested quarters and alleys in Morocco and Algiers; the ignorant weird congregations in tribal villages and eroded hill-sides of tropical Africa; the sadness and blindness of children in the fly-blown tenements of Bagdad, Tabrix, and Teheran; the displaced families trudging over dusty, bleak roads of Korea, or squatting in smoky huts.[19]

This graphic, tragic word picture and the preceding discussion suggest that economic development is a complex process that requires a good deal more than a supply of outside capital. Experience has sobered both donors and recipients and focused attention on the many prerequisites to economic development. In much of the underdeveloped world, these prerequisites are wholly or largely lacking; they merit some summary attention.

A basic prerequisite to economic development for underdeveloped nations is the will to modernize. Modernization involves changing the entire pattern of life of underdeveloped societies, and such things are not done lightly or without massive resistance from many elements of the popula-

[19] Herbert Feis, *Foreign Aid and Foreign Policy*, St Martin's Press, Inc., New York, 1964, p. 74.

tion. It is one thing to want the benefits of industrialization; it is quite another to accept its demands. It is unreasonable to assume that today's developing nations can escape all or even much of the travail and suffering that accompanied industrialization in the West, to say nothing of the hard work that sustains and expands it today. Are today's underdeveloped nations willing to accept these burdens, which are psychological and even spiritual as well as physical? In those instances wherein the answer is negative, no amount of foreign assistance can transform the nation's economic performance.

Akin to the will to modernize is the spirit of entrepreneurship. Somewhere in the society—either in the private or the public sector—there must be talented people who can and want to organize and concert activity in pursuit of material gains. This may sound commonplace to Western ears, but the fact is that such skills and ambitions are often in scarce supply in underdeveloped areas. Different cultures are based on different kinds of values. Citizens of underdeveloped nations are often scornful of the hard-working, sometimes frantic and neurotic, style of life in much of the West; and there can be no doubt that the quality of life in modern, industrialized societies merits a good deal of criticism. But the pace of modern life and the kinds of values that drive it on are to a large extent necessary concomitants of economic development and growth. Citizens and rulers of nations with highly developed economies cannot escape choices that affect the quality of their lives (e.g., working longer to make more money); neither can citizens and rulers of nations with primitive economies. And development does not come cheaply; enough people in a society must be willing to do the difficult things that generate wealth. In sum, there must be entrepreneurs.

Another prerequisite to economic development is a reasonably honest and efficient government. Corruption is a virtually ineradicable aspect of government, but in developed countries it has at least been reduced to the point where it does not interfere severely with economic progress. In many underdeveloped countries, on the other hand, it is a deeply entrenched practice.[20] Governmental corruption and inefficiency are usually accompanied by the same conditions in the private sector, both being but a reflection of a general absence of social discipline. They will effectively cripple the will and the energy of any would-be entrepreneurs, even where they do not eliminate opportunities for economic creativity entirely.

A related but distinguishable prerequisite to economic growth is a stable governmental system. Investors, both foreign and domestic, and economic managers—be they governmental or private—must have a minimum level of confidence that tomorrow's policies will not be radically different from

---

[20] For a shrewd first-hand description of the sources and effects of corruption in government, see M. McMullan, "A Theory of Corruption," *The Sociological Review*, vol. 9, no. I, pp. 181–201, March, 1961.

those of today. Unfortunately, chronic instability, endless struggles for power, frequent disorders, and occasional civil wars are more typical of conditions in the underdeveloped world than are stability and order.[21]

A developing economy also requires an ever-increasing level and distribution of technical skills among the populace. And it is one of the central facts of the contemporary world that the know-how that pervades and is taken for granted in developed economies is usually in critically short supply elsewhere. It may be difficult to get an automobile repaired properly even in Detroit, but it is virtually impossible in many areas of the world. And the history of the foreign aid program is marred by such episodes as the introduction of modern farm machinery into areas where the indigenous population does not bother to keep it oiled, to say nothing of knowing how to repair it. Such skills and habits cannot be easily introduced into societies where they are alien to the whole pattern of life. This technological gulf sharply separates industrially developed nations from the rest of the world, and it hinders economic development even where the other conditions are most promising.

It goes without saying that certain minimal educational and literacy levels must be reached before a truly modern economy can be created and sustained. It is nearly as obvious that these conditions do not exist in many areas of the world.

We turn now to what may be the most ominous problem of all: population control. Any serious discussion of this issue—as of the preceding ones —is beyond the scope of this book. Presumably, its general outlines are common knowledge today. There are approximately 3.25 billion people in the world today; in 1900 there were less than half that number. By the year 2000, there will probably be 6 billion people in the world. Most of this fantastic increase in the world's population will take place in the underdeveloped areas of the world, and it raises a multitude of profound questions. Our immediate concern, however, is with the implications for economic growth of the especially high birth rates in the underdeveloped areas. In its Report to the Senate on the foreign aid authorization bill in 1963, the Senate Foreign Relations Committee made the following observation:

> Substantial progress has been made in recent years in defining the preconditions of economic growth. . . . The one vital criterion of successful development which has been neglected is that of population control.[22]

---

[21] For a rather different argument—for example: "In the present, as in the past, a resolute and rigorous government is not necessarily essential to economic growth"— see a review article by Mancur Olson, Jr., "Some Social and Political Implications of Economic Development," *World Politics*, vol. 17, no. 3 pp. 525–554, April, 1965. The quoted sentence is on p. 551.

[22] Senate Committee on Foreign Relations, *Foreign Assistance Act of 1963*, Rep. No. 588, 88th Cong., 1st Sess., 1963, p. 14.

The committee inserted an amendment into the bill that called for research into the problems of population growth. The amendment became part of the law, and so, despite religious and other objections, the government is now officially concerned with this vital question.

It would be difficult to exaggerate the seriousness of this problem. One wise and authoritative scholar recently wrote that "no one who looks for very long into the question of population growth in the underdeveloped areas can refrain from a feeling of impending catastrophe." He goes on to note that

> calculations show that Asia, merely to *maintain* her present low level of living standards, must *increase* her aggregate product by 60 per cent between now and 1975, and by an additional 75 per cent between 1975 and 2000. Thus the bulk of any gains from increased productivity is used up merely in sustaining the ever-threatened level of subsistence.[23]

Quite obviously, population control is a *sine qua non* of economic development in underdeveloped areas.

There are other factors that probably do not constitute prerequisites to development but the presence or absence of which usually has a profound bearing on its prospects. Abundant natural resources are clearly a valuable attribute of a nation attempting to industrialize. If it has agricultural or mineral products to sell on the world market, it can begin to acquire the machines and knowledge necessary for development. In the absence of some such salable resources, the outlook is ordinarily bleak. The only exception to this has probably been Israel, where that new state, and for special reasons, was the beneficiary of huge amounts of foreign capital, which permitted its unique and highly skilled citizenry to create a developed economy in a relatively barren land.

Another factor that facilitates development is a favorable climate. But most of the underdeveloped areas are afflicted with distinctly unfavorable tropical climates: too much heat, humidity, and rainfall. The impact of these elements is, of course, not easily demonstrated, especially with anything approaching precision. But it is quite obvious that they adversely affect the tempo and efficiency of work, and therefore of productivity.

Finally, there is the matter of health. It is common to read in the United States about how many hours and days of work are lost each year due to sickness. The figures always sound fantastic, but the comparable figures in most of the underdeveloped areas would be many times higher.

It should be clear from the preceding summary remarks that economic development is not achieved easily or quickly and that in some areas it is

---

[23] Robert L. Heilbroner, *The Great Ascent*, Harper & Row, Publishers, Incorporated, New York, 1963, pp. 67–68, 69. Italics in the original.

not likely to be achieved in the foreseeable future *regardless of how much economic aid is poured in by developed nations.* And the fact is that a typical United States aid program constitutes 1 to 2 per cent of the gross national product of the recipient nation. The process of economic development is complex and subtle, going well beyond the presence or absence of large amounts of capital. There is, in sum, no simple or necessarily effective relationship between economic aid and economic development.

It is surely fair to say that the validity of the basic rationale behind the economic assistance program is challengeable. Foreign aid may or may not be a wise and appropriate instrument of United States policy. But policy makers cannot wait until all the evidence is in; they must act. Despite all the problems outlined in the preceding paragraphs, every postwar American administration has chosen to sponsor an economic assistance program, and every Congress has, with varying degrees of enthusiasm and amounts of money, supported it. In the opinion of this writer, these judgments were and are the correct ones on both moral and practical grounds. In any event, we shall return to this question of what overall policy should be near the end of the chapter.

Beyond the basic questions and criticisms raised above, there is a formidable array of more specific ones that can be raised regarding the contemporary American program. We turn now to an examination of these more specific questions.

An Analysis of the Contemporary United States Aid Program

The Effects of United States Economic Aid   What have been the political consequences of the United States aid program? In the nature of things, there cannot be any clear and differentiated answer to that question for many years. The evidence and the judgments have been diverse and conflicting. The critics have some spectacular examples of what at least appear to be aid programs that yielded the United States little or no political benefit and that, indeed, may have had the reverse effect. France, for example, has received more economic aid in the postwar period than any other nation except Great Britain,[24] yet she is pursuing policies today that are at sharp variance with those of the United States, and her government's attitude toward the United States is often quite negative. Pakistan has received $1.33 billion in economic aid—slightly more than half loans, the remainder grants—which is a very sizable amount of money. Yet in recent years, her government and controlled press have been full of denunciations

---

[24] Through fiscal 1963, France had received $3.19 billion, $2.96 billion of it in grants. The figures for Great Britain were $3.83 billion, of which $3.45 billion was in grants. *Source: Summary Presentation to the Congress, FY1965,* p. 201. Almost all this money was given or loaned during the Marshall Plan period, 1948–1952. All the other statistics cited in this section are from the same table unless otherwise noted.

of the United States, and the Pakistan government has made a special project of courting and praising Red China. Over a quarter of a billion dollars has been provided Indonesia, whose government is engaged in adventures in Southeast Asia that directly endanger American objectives and interests there and whose President told the American Ambassador at a public ceremony in March, 1964, to "go to hell with your aid."[25]

These and other available examples make it abundantly clear that it is fatuous to expect that aid will create feelings of gratitude that will in turn induce cooperative policies on the part of recipient nations. Indeed, it is possible to argue precisely the reverse: aid will create feelings of resentment, especially if conditions are imposed of which some sizable element in the population disapproves. Such disapproval may emerge out of pride and sensitivity or out of a more substantive difference of opinion. And it may come from elements of the population that do not then have, but subsequently assume, power.

But even if few or no conditions are imposed, resentment is at least as likely a response as gratitude. For one thing, economic aid is bound to benefit one element of the recipient population more than another. Whether because of a typical search for scapegoats or because of a legitimate source of grievance, dissident groups—some of whom subsequently seize power—blame the United States aid program for at least part of their difficulties. Through fiscal 1963, the United States had provided Bolivia with $224.5 million in economic aid, most of it in grants. When a coup occurred there in November, 1964, the new leaders denounced the aid program as having aided only the ruling groups. This was almost certainly not a fair allegation, but the important thing is that it was made.

Another sort of problem associated with the aid program is the fact that at least tacitly the donor and recipient nations are not dealing with each other as equals. A recent article by a South Korean law professor exemplified this problem. He complained bitterly about what he believed was a common American attitude, namely that the South Koreans have a "mendicant mentality."[26] His sorrow and anger about this allegedly common American attitude are the inevitable result of a relationship that for so many years has involved a large expenditure of American money in South Korea with no end really in sight. Are such resentments, soundly based or not, worth incurring?

This problem of the psychological fruits of aid programs can be brought much more directly within the purview of many American citizens, particularly those associated in some way with universities. There are many thousands of foreign students in the United States at all times, and many of

---

[25] *Washington Post*, March 26, 1964, as reproduced *Hearings for 1965 before the House Subcommittee on Foreign Operations Appropriations*, 1964, pt. 2, p. 56.
[26] Pyong Choon Hahm, *Foreign Affairs*, vol. 43, no. 1, pp. 165–174, October, 1964.

them are being financed by the United States government. Anyone who has had much contact with them knows that many are hostile to the United States. This hostility grows out of many circumstances, some of the more important ones being an exposure to overt racial prejudice, an isolation—sometimes self-imposed—from ordinary student activities, envy of, or, less often, a genuine contempt for, the material comforts of the United States, and a revulsion against the quality and style of American life. But whatever its sources, this hostility is real and widespread and must be measured against the undeniable benefits of bringing foreign students to this country for technical and professional training.

There is another and rather powerful argument that can be used against economic assistance: the experience of the Soviet Union with such endeavors. It is, of course, well known that Soviet assistance to Red China was once rather substantial and that one of the most momentous developments of the postwar world is the Sino-Soviet split. Not only did Soviet aid fail to prevent the split, it contributed to it.[27] In a feud of this sort it is impossible to distinguish between cause and effect, and the Soviet termination of aid in 1960 was undoubtedly more a reflection than a generation of political tensions having deeper roots. But the Chinese were embittered and angered, and from that point forward attempts at reconciliation were further handicapped. The same remarks apply to the more comical but nonetheless revealing severing of ties between the Soviet Union and Albania.

Of more direct relevance, however, is the Soviet experience with the non-Communist underdeveloped areas. Beginning in the middle 1950s, the Soviets have conducted a modest program of loans for economic development.[28] It is a highly concentrated program, with such countries as Afghanistan, India, Indonesia, Syria, and the United Arab Republic receiving most of it.

There does not appear to be any appreciable connection between these efforts and the internal or external policies of the recipient governments. Moreover, there have been some experiences that must have proved quite upsetting to the Soviet government. The United Arab Republic has been a special target of Soviet assistance and attention, and yet it continues to suppress the local Communists and to pursue an independent, albeit often anti-Western, course in foreign policy. The same can be said of Iraq, where a large-scale Soviet aid effort following an anti-Western coup there in 1958 merely facilitated the later creation of a staunchly independent and effectively anti-Communist regime. But the most spectacular Soviet failure

---

[27] See, for example, David Floyd, *Mao against Khrushchev, A Short History of the Sino-Soviet Conflict*, Frederick A. Praeger, Inc., New York, 1964, pp. 86, 136.

[28] The entire Soviet effort from 1954 to 1964 totaled $3.5 billion. For this statistic and an excellent review of the Soviet aid experience, see Marshall I. Goldman, "A Balance Sheet of Soviet Foreign Aid," *Foreign Affairs*, vol. 43, no. 2, pp. 349–360, January, 1965.

occurred in Guinea, a former French African colony, which gained independence in 1958 at the cost of alienating France and being forced to seek assistance elsewhere. The Soviet Union rushed in with a flashy economic assistance program, and for some time Western observers looked on Guinea as nearly a Soviet satellite. Then, in December, 1961, Guinean President Sekou Toure let it be known that he believed that certain recent internal disturbances had been backed by Moscow, and a few days later the Soviet Ambassador left the country at the request of the Guinean government.

Perhaps even more disconcerting to Soviet leaders is the fact that, like the United States, the Soviets have encountered hostile sentiments among visiting students from underdeveloped areas.[29]

It would seem safe to infer that in a governing elite as hard-headed and practical as the one in the Kremlin there must be at least several Otto Passmans who want to know why scarce capital is being "squandered abroad on ungrateful and even unfriendly foreigners." The opponents of economic aid read this as independent confirmation of their view that these programs are misguided at best and dangerous at worst.

Proponents of aid tend to see rather different kinds of evidence when they assess the effects of aid programs. They dispute the interpretations of the preceding paragraphs, and, in addition, they cite different examples. These differing perspectives are summarized in the subsequent paragraphs.

As for France, the basic response to the argument above is that it is not fair to expect aid to eradicate problems and divergent perspectives that have their roots deep in history, geography, dissimilar experiences, and—in this instance—the personality of a unique and independent leader, Charles de Gaulle. Moreover, it is easy to exaggerate the problem of United States–French relations. De Gaulle's policies are *not* designedly anti-American. He sees the challenges to and within the West in a different light from most Americans. But this does not establish that he is hostile. In many important ways, France's policies coincide with or are complementary to United States policies.

Regarding Pakistan, her government's recent alienation from the United States is based on a sharp disapproval of United States military aid to India. Aid should not be expected to eliminate such possibilities; it is concededly a limited instrument. It assuredly cannot "buy friends" and should not be judged a failure when it fails to do so. Moreover, the long-range results are not known; occasional setbacks are inevitable.

The problem posed by the example of Indonesia is admittedly the most difficult to resolve in favor of our aid program there. Two things, however,

---

[29] One impatient observer suggested that perhaps the wisest thing either side could do would be to subsidize sending students from underdeveloped areas to the universities of the adversary. That way they could learn their professions and skills and develop antipathies toward the *other* side.

can be said in this connection: Indonesia's policies may change, and the United States aid program may turn out to have been a wise long-term investment, after all. Such a development seems remote but cannot be ruled out entirely. Secondly, any program, especially one that is based as much on imponderables, hope, and guesswork as foreign aid, is bound to have some grievous failures. But a balanced judgment would require a more careful look at some of the more favorable experiences of the program.

The proponents of aid do not take very seriously the arguments about an absence of gratitude and the potential for resentment. First, and most importantly, such arguments are essentially beside the point. We are not seeking gratitude, and resentment against the wealthiest and most powerful nation in the world is unavoidable. The aid program is aimed, instead, at creating conditions that will be conducive to international peace and security. Wanting to be loved is as fatuous as it is irrelevant and unattainable.

This is not to say that it is not important, at least in the short run, to conduct our relations—especially those involving aid transactions—with a keen appreciation of the sensitivities and political circumstances of the recipients clearly in mind. But along with this must go an equally acute appreciation of the fact that a certain level of resentment is inevitable, and reverses are unavoidable.[30]

Finally—and here we come to the practical heart of the matter—the economic aid program can be defended in terms of its concrete achievements since its origins in the late 1940s. At this point, we enter into the endlessly controversial area of how much development has in fact been achieved, and how much aid has contributed to it. It should be emphasized that there are no agreed upon standards of success for anything as complicated and having as many unknowable effects as the foreign aid program. Hence, the efforts to defend it in terms of its achievements are necessarily surrounded by uncertainty, dubious statistics, controversy, and about the same amounts of sleight of hand and oversimplification as are employed in the efforts to denigrate the program.

The most striking examples of postwar economic progress helped by United States economic aid are essentially irrelevant, being examples of recovery rather than development. These include fourteen Western European nations (aided by the Marshall Plan) and Japan. The only noteworthy aspect of this as far as the contemporary program is concerned is

---

[30] These remarks about gratitude and resentment raise some interesting questions about the rationale of the Soviet program. Could it be that their resumption of the program—after a lengthy suspension in 1962–1963—suggests that they have essentially the same view as we do, namely, that *in the long run* the economic development of the underdeveloped areas will redound to the advantage of "the right side" and the disadvantage of the adversary? Perhaps so. But who is correct, we or they? Neither?

its demonstration, if any were needed, of the fact that developed economies can occur outside of white, European cultures. Are there other and more instructive examples?

According to the Agency for International Development, there were fourteen countries "in transition" between dependency on outside aid and self-support in 1964.

> For the first time, the transition to self-support is now underway in a number of countries where development has been the challenge, rather than recovery.
>
> In some, it has already been reflected within the AID program, by diminishing levels of assistance, the completion of technical assistance programs, and the hardening of AID loan terms. . . .
>
> The transition from AID economic help to more conventional resources of finance such as Export-Import Bank lending, World Bank lending, and private investment, is now underway in at least 14 countries where AID conducts programs.
>
> In general . . . the transition has been made possible because economic aid has helped accomplish what it set out to do.[31]

Only 2 per cent of all economic assistance funds for fiscal 1965 was scheduled to go to these fourteen nations.[32]

It is difficult to assess these official pronouncements. The administration did not list the names of the fourteen transitional states, but it did indicate that Greece and Israel were among them. There do not appear to be any among the fourteen who could reasonably have been classified as underdeveloped a decade or so ago. At least no such stirring exemplars have been brought forward in support of the contemporary program.

It is in the next-most-successful category of states where the real burden of proof lies, and it will be years before any decisive evidence on them is forthcoming. There are twenty-five nations in this category, and they were to receive 88 per cent of the fiscal 1965 funds for "major programs." And within this group, seven named nations were singled out for preferential treatment. To cite the official presentation again:

> Fifty per cent of the economic program in 1965 is proposed for seven countries— India, Pakistan, Turkey, Nigeria, Tunisia, Colombia, and Chile—each of which ranks high in both assistance needs and self-help performance. They have generally raised savings and investment levels in the past few years and taken steps to allocate investment funds and other resources more effectively. Although their development policies are by no means ideal, these seven countries have made serious and sustained attempts to make better use of both their own resources and the external

---

[31] *Summary Presentation to the Congress, FY1965*, p. 11.
[32] *Ibid.*, p. 21.

funds available to them and have had a substantial measure of success. The share of U.S. assistance going to this group has been steadily rising for the past several years.[33]

Again, it should be remarked that these official versions must be treated circumspectly and that independent verification of their accuracy is most difficult to come by. It is undeniable, however, that the effort is being concentrated in a limited number of nations and that among them are some of the most important ones in the world, ones whose futures are likely to affect the United States noticeably, even sharply. Surely the most obvious such nation is India.

India is far and away the most important nonaligned power in the world. If its nearly 500 million people should come under the control of Communist or other sharply anti-Western elements, it would constitute a disaster of the first magnitude for the West, comparable only to the communization of China in the late 1940s. It is therefore not by accident that India has been receiving large amounts of economic assistance from the West, particularly, of course, the United States. Since its independence in 1947, India has received $1.88 billion from the United States, most of it in loans. In recent years, however, it has bulked even larger in the United States effort. In fiscal 1963, for example, India was loaned $392.3 million and granted $4.9 million, for a total of $397.2 million. This was more than twice the amount provided to the next highest recipient (Pakistan: $174.3 million) and many times more than was provided to any other nation in the world. The entire Latin American program—which, for the most part, is categorized under the much-publicized Alliance for Progress—totaled "only" $551.5 million, and the total loan figure for the seventeen Latin nations that received loans was nearly exactly what India alone received. The loans to India, in summary, constituted over 29 per cent of the total economic aid loans and over 17 per cent of the total economic aid program for fiscal 1963. Finally, it is worth noting that India is by far the largest single recipient of Food for Peace shipments.

Can this massive effort be justified? In the absence of certainty about India's future external policies, one's response to this question necessarily depends upon one's assumptions and expectations about the efficacy of the aid program. But if there is *any* justification for an aid program, India most definitely should be among the major beneficiaries. This impression is reinforced by the generally accepted view that India has sufficient skills and maturity to absorb this aid effectively.

Whatever may be the precise rate of economic development in these countries, there is no room for doubt about the importance of each of them

[33] *Ibid.*, pp. 22–23.

from the standpoint of the long-range prospects for the kind of world the United States hopes to foster.

The following criticisms raise less basic, more technical questions about the United States economic assistance program. They do not, for the most part, in and of themselves challenge the value of the program.

The Cost   At the root of much of the criticism is, not surprisingly, the fact that the program costs a great deal of money. In quieter and more secure days, the instruments of American foreign policy were inexpensive; a glance at today's $100 billion budgets shows how things have changed. The major item, of course, is military expenditure; the current annual rate is roughly $50 billion. Most elements of American society and government accept this as a sad and burdensome necessity. Another costly instrument of foreign policy that enjoys near-immunity from effective criticism is intelligence activity. The amount of money spent for this enterprise is a closely guarded secret, but whatever it is, the few executive branch officials and members of Congress who do know seem to raise little objection; and neither does the public.

Foreign aid is also an instrument of foreign policy, a means to an end. But unlike military capabilities, it is not a traditional or easily understood implement. It is not easy, as the earlier discussion was designed to show, to point to conspicuous "successes" or "victories" attributable to the program. Nearly everyone agrees that the Marshall Plan was such a success and that Europe's renewed strength and self-confidence are, on balance, a good thing. But, as noted earlier, the economic assistance program has shifted entirely to the underdeveloped areas; and not only are the results more dubious, but there is no end in sight. It is one thing to pour $12 billion successfully into familiar old Western Europe, with which the United States has so much in common in terms of history, culture, religion, and goals. It is quite another to go on spending billions of dollars year after year with mixed and uncertain results in nations all over the globe, many of which have sharply differing styles of life and pursue uncooperative foreign policies and whose immediate or long-range relevance to American security interests is often obscure.

Aside from a general disagreement on the utility of the current economic aid program, the supporters endeavor to minimize its costs. They point out, for example, that the fiscal 1965 appropriation for economic development assistance was only $1,488 million, or approximately 0.24 per cent of the gross national product as of June, 1964, and 1.5 per cent of the Federal budget. The Marshall Plan originally constituted 2 per cent of the gross national product and about 11.5 per cent of the Federal budget. Aid supporters believe these figures put the matter in its proper perspective and make a mockery of the notion that the United States cannot afford this program.

The debate about cost is rather general, even amorphous. It is impossible to form an intelligent opinion about whether a program is too costly until one examines what the alternatives are and what some of the related consequences are. The former is really the subject of this chapter: Should there be an aid program or not; and, if so, of what kind? As for "related consequences," we turn to them next.

Domestic Needs and Foreign Aid   Whatever is spent for foreign aid cannot be spent for other projects, such as the domestic "war on poverty." Many millions of Americans do not share significantly in the general affluence that has characterized the postwar United States. Why should scarce resources—and resources are always scarce in the sense that not everyone is wealthy—be spent on foreigners when we continue to have poverty at home?

The only answer to this question involves some rather abstract discussion of the purposes and prospects of the foreign aid program. If it is really a necessary and efficacious means of serving the long-range national interest, it can be justified on traditional grounds. If it is neither necessary nor efficacious, it can only be justified on moral or humanitarian grounds, but this raises again the question of why the well-being of foreigners is a more noble objective than the well-being of Americans. As has been conceded above, the question of whether the economic aid program is serving or not serving the long-range interests of the United States cannot be answered categorically. Most concerned observers seem to believe it is, but they may be wrong. If they are right, however, the answer to the original question is that the welfare of some Americans will have to be postponed—sacrificed?—on behalf of the demands of the nation as a whole. This argument will not appeal to many deprived people in this country, but it has been the considered judgment of both the Congress and the executive branch since the late 1940s that it is a valid one.

Aid and Budgetary Deficits   Another problem, which in recent years has cast a shadow over the advisability of the aid program, is the apparently chronic budgetary deficits being run by the Federal government. Since the beginning of the Korean War, Federal revenues have exceeded Federal expenditures in a fiscal year only three times; and the Federal debt is over $300 billion. This is not the place to discuss the question of how serious this problem is, except to remark that most economists are not particularly concerned about it. Many others are, however, and they have combed the budget each year in search of expenditures that might be curtailed or eliminated. A favorite item, needless to say, is foreign aid. Although it does enjoy the vague and generalized support of the public, it does not have the kind of vigorous and effective support that most other items in the budget do have. Defense expenditures, veterans' benefits, farm subsidies, space exploration programs, welfare programs, educational subsidies—all these and many more have large and politically potent supporters. There are, of course, many firms and individuals that profit from foreign aid expenditures in this country, but they are not well organized, and their stake in the program is not as generally understood by themselves and by others as are the vested interests in more traditional government programs. Foreign aid, therefore, is the ideal target for budget cutters. Its beneficiaries are either far away and without votes (foreign countries) or unorganized (American business firms—and their employees—that do business with recipient governments) or only vaguely aware, at best, of any values accruing to them (the country as a whole).

The proponents of economic aid, like the rest of the population, can be divided into those who are seriously concerned about the size of the national debt and the problem of chronic deficits, and those who are not especially concerned. The concerned ones tend to argue that other expenditures, not economic aid, should be cut, or, as an alternative, that aid should be cut only slightly and proportionately as part of a general reduction in expenditures.

Behind the attitudes and positions of the proponents on this matter is the general conviction that somehow the whole issue is either fraudulent or misconceived. Granted that our resources are finite, and that what is applied toward foreign aid does not, therefore, go into something else, public or private, the United States is, after all, the wealthiest nation in the history of the world, with a gross national product of well over $600 billion. To suggest that such a colossal economic giant cannot afford to share approximately 0.24 per cent of this affluence with less developed nations each year—especially since the sharing is designed to protect American interests and values—is simply preposterous. Aid supporters suspect that some kind of bizarre numbers game is being played in order to confuse and deceive the American public and its representatives in Washington.

Aid and Imbalance of Payments   Still another kind of fiscal concern is the fact that economic aid *apparently* contributes to the balance of payments problem, which has troubled the United States since 1958. Beginning in that year, the United States—including both government and private sources—was spending more dollars abroad than were being brought back to this country. The result has been that dollar reserves have been building up overseas and foreigners—unlike Americans—are entitled to convert their dollars into gold. Many have done so, and the resultant outflow of gold from the United States has become a source of grave concern to the free world, for whom the stability and strength of the dollar is a matter of the highest priority. Because of the complex and archaic practices of international finance, the gold outflow has threatened the value of the dollar. A serious international economic crisis is unavoidable if these conditions persist indefinitely.

The United States government has taken many steps designed to reduce and eliminate the imbalance of payments. For example, tax benefits on overseas investments have been reduced, tourist travel to the United States has been promoted overseas, and the dollar outflow generated by the existence of our vast overseas military establishment has been reduced by such expedients as limiting the conditions under which dependents may be brought overseas. But a favorite object of concern has, of course, been the foreign aid program. And there can be no doubt that it constitutes a potentially serious contributor to the balance of payments problem. How much it in fact does contribute is a matter in some dispute.

Soon after the problem emerged, efforts were made to resolve it. In the foreign aid field, the primary change was to require that more and more of the aid money be spent in the United States, thereby reducing the dollar outflow. By fiscal 1962, 50 per cent of the economic assistance dollar was spent in the United States. By fiscal 1965, the figure was over 80 per cent, and it is hoped that it can ultimately reach about 90 per cent. As Secretary of State Dean Rusk told the Senate Foreign Relations Committee in June 1963:

> We are in effect saying to as many countries as possible, and wherever possible, that what we have to offer basically in foreign aid these days, given our foreign exchange situation, are goods and services. We do not have free dollars to make available in large amounts.[34]

There are at least two other positive things to be said in defense of the economic aid program in this connection. Most such aid today is in the form of loans repayable in dollars. When these payments begin to assume substantial proportions,[35] the United States balance of payments problem will be favorably affected. This may in fact already be happening, at least during selected time periods. In 1964, the Agency for International Development included a lengthy statement on aid and the balance of payments in its testimony before the Senate Foreign Relations Committee. Among other things, this statement purported to show that during 1963, the repayment on earlier loans had the effect of producing a net *inflow* from the aid program of over $400 million.[36]

Moreover, insofar as the aid program helps to induce economic develop-

---

[34] *Foreign Assistance Act of 1963, Hearings of the Senate Committee on Foreign Relations,* 88th Cong., 1st Sess., 1963, p. 25.

[35] There is some reason to doubt that they ever will; this problem will be taken up below.

[36] *Foreign Assistance Act of 1964, Hearings of the Senate Committee on Foreign Relations,* 88th Cong., 2d Sess., 1964, pp. 323-329.

ment, it creates potential export markets for American goods, thereby also affecting the balance of payments favorable.

With this last argument, we approach the other side of the debate. Economically developed nations abroad are not only potential buyers; they are potential competitors. To cite only one of the more conspicuous examples, United States aid was instrumental in bringing about Japan's remarkable economic revival. And now Japanese products compete with domestic goods in many fields, notably finished textiles. Whatever may be the salubrious effects of this condition—and they are many—there can be little doubt that it affects adversely the balance of payments problem. In addition, the taxes that support the foreign aid program raise the cost of American-produced goods, thereby impairing their competitiveness in the world market. Finally, there remains that 10 to 15 per cent that is not spent in this country and thereby constitutes a direct outflow of dollars.

The preceding arguments should make it clear why this section began with the equivocal assertion that "economic aid *apparently* contributes to the balance of payments problem." Until recently, it undoubtedly did. But in view of the nearly exclusive "Buy American" requirements now in effect and with due regard to the great complexity of the matter, it cannot be dogmatically asserted that it either does or does not contribute, or, if so, how much. This would appear, then, to be one of the least substantial arguments against economic aid.

Concern over these fiscal difficulties has expressed itself in a variety of ways. In addition to those already touched on, two merit passing attention: the tightening of the terms of assistance and a heightened concern about the role of other developed nations.

As noted above, the terms of the aid program have changed markedly since the Marshall Plan, which was 90 per cent outright grants. By the late 1950s, most economic aid was in the form of loans, which were, however, repayable in the currency of the recipient nation. Since these currencies were usually not convertible into dollars and since there was usually a limited number of things to do with the currency, such loans came to be regarded suspiciously as disguised grants. In the early 1960s, the loans were made repayable in dollars, but on very generous terms. In 1963, Congress increased the minimum loan from $\frac{3}{4}$ of 1 per cent to 2 per cent, except during the ten-year grace period, during which repayment may still be at only $\frac{3}{4}$ of 1 per cent. This is still a long way from a commercial loan; but it is also a long way from a grant.

This gradual tightening of terms has increased the apprehensions of many that these loans will not be repaid, or at least not fully. Many ambitious new governments are assuming staggering debts in their sometimes unthinking drive toward industrialization. They may or may not prove to have both the will and the capacity to meet these obligations. A country such as India will presumably make every effort to do so, and India's repayment record thus far is good. But as due payments accumulate in other nations that have received large sums of loan assistance, their fragile economies may not be able to support repayment; or their domestic politics may be such as to invite repudiation of the debts. What will become of the American aid program when and if such defaults should become conspicuous is a matter for conjecture. We have come a long way from the cash-register mentality that provoked Calvin Coolidge's revelatory comment about World War I debts—"They hired the money, didn't they?"—but at the very least it can be said that widespread defaulting would seriously endanger the program.[37]

Another consideration that affects our commitment to the aid program is the performance of other developed nations. There has been an increased awareness of the growing affluence of Europe, in particular, and a concomitant interest in sharing the burden with them. It might be said that our desire to share foreign aid responsibilities with European powers is as genuine and lively as is our disinclination to share nuclear responsibilities with them; and for obvious reasons.

American critics have been concerned about both the size and the terms of the European programs. The latter would appear to be the only legitimate concern. Meaningful statistics on the size of various programs are, of course, very hard to come by. Figures given to Congress by the Agency for International Development show total free world aid commitments in 1962 to have been $8.4 billion. The United States accounted for 56 per cent of this, other nations for 29 per cent, and international institutions for the other 15 per cent.[38] These figures are probably about as reliable as any, and they suggest that the U.S. effort is really not so disproportionate after all. As a leading authority on the subject recently wrote:

> The 60 per cent of the total economic aid effort that represents the U.S. contribution is approximately proportional to our share of total national incomes of the aid-giving countries. As a percentage of national income, a number of countries in fact exceed the U.S. contribution, and the contribution of France is more than double. So far as economic assistance is involved, there is then no strong justification for a U.S. complaint of inequitable "burden-sharing."[39]

[37] For an official and impressively documented expression of concern about this problem—it draws the conclusion that minimum loan terms are already hard enough, maybe too hard, and should not be hardened further—see U.S. Department of State, Agency for International Development, *A Study on Loan Terms, Debt Burden, and Development*, April, 1965.

[38] *Ibid.*, p. 155.

[39] Edward S. Mason, *Foreign Aid and Foreign Policy*, Harper & Row, Publishers, Incorporated, New York, 1964, p. 6. Published for the Council on Foreign Relations. Chapter 3 of this book, entitled The Problem of Equitable Sharing of the Foreign Aid Burden, is a dispassionate and persuasive analysis of the problem and makes clear the difficulty of making valid comparisons.

Regarding the terms of non-American assistance programs, a recent Presidential commission established to study the matter made the following observations:

> With the exception of France, assistance from other free nations has to a substantial extent been in the form of hard loans to finance exports from the lending countries.[40]

There are some signs of a loosening of terms in recent years, especially by the British, but non-American terms are still on the average considerably harder than American. Moreover, the trend is not likely to be toward easier terms, either from the United States or elsewhere. Britain's financial difficulties are severe and apparently chronic. As for France, her whole effort began, in 1964, to come under precisely the same kinds of attacks at home as the American program has provoked for years. Not even a government as strong as de Gaulle's is likely to encourage these criticisms by extending its program or easing its terms.

In the final analysis, this issue of burden sharing is largely a phony one. Our exhortations may or may not affect the performance of the other developed nations; probably not. But governments should be careful not to be taken in by their own propaganda. Our aid program is not primarily a humanitarian gesture, but even if it were, its size and character should not be made dependent upon someone else's efforts. This applies with special force when it is considered that our program is in large measure a calculated investment in our long-range security. Viewed in this way, whether the Europeans cooperate or not is essentially irrelevant to our own policy, despite the fact that it would be pleasant and reassuring to have them do so.

The Problem of Waste and Corruption   Turning now from the problems associated directly with the unavoidable costs of the program as now constituted, we encounter one of the special concerns of congressmen and editorial writers, namely, the problem of waste and corruption. In another context, corruption and inefficiency were discussed as contributants to the slowness of economic development. At this point, the basic issue is how valid such matters are as grounds for opposing the aid program.

It is impossible to make any supportable statements about the extent to which waste and corruption characterize the aid program. Waste is endemic

---

[40] The Committee to Strengthen the Security of the Free World, Report to the President of the United States, *The Scope and Distribution of United States Military and Economic Assistance Programs*, March 20, 1963, p. 14. This committee was popularly known as the Clay Committee. Hereinafter, this report will be referred to as *Clay Committee Report*.

in all large-scale operations, but there are grounds for believing that it is uncommonly present in the aid program. Nearly anyone associated with or knowledgeable about the program can cite instances of waste of resources: the building of magnificent highways that lead nowhere in particular or that are too large for any foreseeable needs or that serve no economic or military purpose; the construction of modern manufacturing plants in areas where raw materials are not readily available or where no real need for their products exists or where skilled technicians and capable managers are nonexistent; and excessive costs resulting from incompetent management by American aid officials. Some colorful publicity has resulted, as, for example, when a House Foreign Affairs subcommittee released a report in late 1963 on the aid program in Panama. The report, drawn up by a staff survey team, charged among other things that schools have been "overdesigned" and "badly located," that roads have been built "to standards in excess of need," and that housing has been erected with "major technical faults." The following excerpt provides perhaps the most striking illustration of these charges.

On October 14, 1963, the survey team, accompanied by mission officials, visited that part of the road begun by the Ambassador in 1962. Beginning at Tambo, we managed to travel during 2 hours about 1.5 miles in 4-wheel-drive jeeps outfitted with winches. Most of the time we spent getting ourselves out of the first mudhole less than a mile from the start. We turned back at the first river crossing. Although no doubt we could have forded the river at this particular spot, this is the rainy season and mission personnel felt that if it rained while we were on this road, we might have to remain where we were. Considering the clay composition and very deep ruts in the road, this was a real possibility.

On February 28, 1963, which is during the dry season, AID/mission engineers and agricultural advisers were able to cover approximately 12 miles of the 20 miles that had been constructed. In their report they stated that—

owing to the washout of an extensive fill (made across a narrow ravine without culvert) we left our 4-wheel-drive jeep at mile 8.2—covering the remaining distance of 3.8 miles on foot. Another ravine fill approximately 0.3 of a mile from the Rio Tucue was also washed out, making vehicular traffic impossible.

The road from Tambo to the third crossing of the Rio Tucue, a stretch of approximately 8.5 miles, which was constructed along meandering trails is in very poor condition. The grades are very steep with sections approximating 25 per cent. There are 17 streambeds and small ravines requiring culverts. The Rio Toabre at mile 1.5 and the Rio Tucue at miles 4.2, 4.9, and 8.5 are fordable except during periods of extreme high waters. This entire section of the road will require extensive relocation to effect proper drainage, eliminate the excessive grades, and to avoid two of the Rio Tucue crossings as well as many ravine and small stream crossings.

In view of observations of the mission engineering and agriculture personnel as well as the team's as to the present condition of the road, serious question is raised with respect not only to the need for a road, but also whether or not a substantial part of the money spent in constructing what is now largely a muddy trail was not wasted.[41]

Defenders of economic assistance concede that such blunders have occurred, but insist that they are both rare and inevitable. Any large-scale enterprise is bound to involve some waste and inefficiencies, and the foreign aid program has the added handicap of dealing with many unique and uncontrollable situations. Moreover, it is contended, these matters are a constant worry and object of attention and their incidence is so low that aid administrators should be congratulated rather than ridiculed.

As for outright corruption, that also would appear to be an unavoidable aspect of the program. For the most part, Americans and American officials have not been implicated,[42] but it has proved to be impossible to avoid a certain amount of venality within recipient governments. In many of them, of course, corruption is an accepted method of operation. Supporters of aid make essentially the same response to criticisms regarding corruption as they do to those arising out of waste.

As it is stated above, the argument over waste and corruption glosses over the important point that some of it is, in a sense, deliberate. Foreign aid serves many purposes, some more immediate and ephemeral than its basic rationale would suggest. It almost certainly has occasionally been used for purposes less lofty and lasting than economic development. It can be used as a straightforward bribe, to induce a recipient government to offer some specific *quid pro quo*. Providing expensive yachts for monarchs and jet aircraft for showpiece air forces, and looking the other way when aid money is being administered by the recipient government, are sometimes not as absurd and blameworthy as they might appear to be. If such gestures can induce useful diplomatic support on a given issue or facilitate access to valuable information, for example, they are quite defensible expedients. The fact that it is difficult and usually unwise to defend them in congressional hearings, at least during public sessions, does not detract from this point. This writer has no idea how frequent such transactions are, but some occurrences would seem to admit of no other explanation.

The Quality of Administration   In discussing such "administrative details," one comes rather close to a question that hovers ominously over the entire discussion of foreign aid, or indeed any other program: How

[41] Subcommittee for Review of the Mutual Security Programs of the House Committee on Foreign Affairs, *Report of the Staff Survey Team on the Housing Investment Guaranty Program and the Economic Aid Program in Panama*, 88th Cong., 1st Sess., 1963, pp. 17–18. The entire report bears on the problem under discussion.
[42] For a spectacular exception to this, see House Committee on Government Operations, *Seventh Report, U.S. Aid Operations in Laos*, 86th Cong., 1st Sess., 1959.

good are the administrators? The answer to that question will go a long way toward determining how effective any program is, and foreign aid is certainly no exception. The President sets out certain broad objectives and perhaps promulgates some rather detailed instructions. Congress determines the budgetary limits and also imposes certain kinds of policies on the program. From there on, its value as an instrument of American policy depends heavily upon the quality of the people administering it; and "from there on" covers a lot of distance and most of the decisions affecting the program. These decisions require ingenuity and judgment, together with technical skills, of the highest order.

These sentences merely state the obvious, but they are so centrally important that they deserve mention. And what is the answer to the question as it affects the economic aid program? No authoritative answer is available. One hears and reads many opinions ranging all the way from the view that the Director of the Agency for International Development is a brilliant and effective leader, supported by a dedicated and capable staff, to the view that AID is staffed largely by mediocrities who were unable to get ahead in other Federal departments. The real situation probably falls somewhere between these two views, but if it is very far removed from the favorable one, the foreign aid program—a subtle and complex instrument of United States policy, encountering ever-changing, unique, and unfamiliar circumstances at virtually every turn—is surely doomed to failure and, ultimately, rejection. No amount of reorganization—a favorite palliative—or money or exhortation could save it or justify it.

Too Many Countries?   There is a general sense that emerges from a reading of the congressional hearings that many congressmen feel that the program has been altogether too ambitious, too undiscriminating. Wealthy as we are, the argument runs, we cannot have much impact anywhere if we try to help everyone. What is needed are more carefully drawn eligibility standards, more scrupulously enforced.

Like much of the debate over foreign aid, this argument has an abstract quality to it. When it is buttressed by statistics, they are generally undifferentiated and unenlightening. Recent administrations have, however, become quite concerned about this issue, and efforts are made each year to show that greater selectivity and serious "tightening up" are being practiced. As noted above, for example, in the presentations to Congress for fiscal 1965, the Johnson administration stressed that only seven countries were scheduled to receive 50 per cent of the proposed budget for economic aid, and that "only" twenty-five countries were to receive 88 per cent of the funds for "major programs." The same presentation noted that those seven countries were to receive 67 per cent of the development loans, with forty-one other countries sharing in the remaining 33 per cent.

But are these figures of 25 and 41 still too undiscriminating? Are we still, in the words of the Clay Committee, doing "too much for too many"? Such questions are virtually meaningless when posed in this generalized fashion. A sensible answer would require an analysis of, and then an informed guess about, each of the proposed country programs. It is easy to say that too many countries are receiving assistance; the difficult task is to say which ones ought not to receive it. There are many practical problems in trying to make such distinctions. If a government is uncooperative or unwilling to undertake the kinds of administrative or socioeconomic reforms that are deemed necessary for the proper absorption of aid, there is a strong presumptive case for cutting it off. But these kinds of judgments will always be difficult ones.[43] And what is the hidden cost of denying at least a token amount of aid to a nation that seems to need it and whose neighbors are receiving it?

The Wrong Ones?   Sometimes the complaint about "too much for too many" either masks or takes the form of disapproval of aid to a specific country, or list of countries. Two favorite congressional targets are Nasser's Egypt and Sukarno's Indonesia. Nasser has incurred the wrath of most Americans at one time or another for his adventurist foreign policies in the Middle East and Africa, his threats against Israel, and his sporadic but bilious anti-American pronouncements. In 1963, Congress barred aid to any country that the President determined was engaging in or preparing for military aggression against the United States or any country receiving United States assistance. This action was quite candidly aimed at Egypt.

For his part, Sukarno seems determined to set new records in prolonged international tension building, neglect of internal problems, and truculence regarding the United States. In 1963, Congress took the unusual step of prohibiting aid to Indonesia, unless the President determined that such aid was essential to the national interest and so informed Congress. In this instance, this effectively terminated the already waning program.

Very often, of course, concerns about assistance for specific countries take on a much more ideological aspect. Congress has been especially anxious to restrict assistance to Communist nations, and, in addition, to penalize those nations that in any way facilitate the survival of the Castro regime in Cuba. Actual aid to Communist regimes has been infinitesimal, and most of it has been to Yugoslavia, a non-bloc nation, which received

[43] In a rare moment of drollery, the Clay Committee made the following observation about the difficulties of making long-term projections about which countries should have what kinds of development programs: "Extrapolations of mathematical models based on questionable statistics for debatable base periods seem to have a way of going wrong, even when it is possible to find economists who agree with each other." *Clay Committee Report,* p. 16.

a total of $575.3 million in economic aid in the postwar period but now receives none. The only other recipient has been Poland, which was loaned $61 million.[44]

The debate over any kind of assistance to Communist regimes is largely terminated. Congress was merely pounding another nail in that small coffin when, in 1963, it barred any aid in war or strategic materials to any country "whose government is based upon that theory of government known as Communism," and further barred any economic assistance to such countries unless the President determined that to withhold aid would be contrary to the national interest and so reported to Congress. There is something touchingly naïve about the phrase quoted in the last sentence, especially in this day of polycentrism; such excursions into dogma and definition do not put Congress in its best light. More importantly, they suggest a doctrinaire refusal to treat foreign aid as a political instrument of foreign policy. There may again arise situations such as the one that followed Yugoslavia's break with the Soviet Union in 1948, which offer the West an opportunity to foster still further division in the Communist world. Although existing legislation does not prohibit such tactics absolutely, it forces any President to take unusual and, in terms of domestic politics, hazardous steps to overcome congressional obstacles. Aid is by nature a blunt instrument; this kind of dogmatic posturing makes it still more so. Some day, that may be quite unfortunate.[45]

Aid and Private Enterprise   A somewhat related criticism—since it is heavily imbued with considerations of doctrinal purity—is that the American aid program hampers private enterprise and promotes "socialism." This criticism recurs frequently in the congressional hearings, and, for obvious reasons, it touches a sensitive nerve. It refers to the prospects for both American and indigenous investors and has both practical and "ideological" sources. That is, regarding the latter dimension, a sincere conviction that private enterprise is both a more efficacious and a more humane means of economic development mingles with a more doctrinaire convic-

---

[44] These figures do not, of course, include surplus food shipments, the most important "aid" provided to these two countries.

[45] As so often happens in the contemporary world, the Soviets are confronted with a nearly identical problem. Should the Soviets support only Communists abroad, or should they, in the name of anti-imperialism, support all revolutionary nationalist forces, even if they pursue anti-Communist policies internally? For the most part, the Soviets have opted for the latter policy in recent years, but it is hazardous to predict their next turn, especially with the Chinese denouncing them for allying themselves with the bourgeoisie. For a discussion of these tensions in Soviet and Chinese policy, see Philip E. Mosely, "Soviet Policy in the Developing Countries," *Foreign Affairs*, vol. 43, no. 1, pp. 87–98, October, 1964.

tion that publicly financed and managed development is bad and privately financed and managed development is good.[46]

Aid policy has been adjusted to meet these concerns in several ways. For many years a "specific risk guarantee" program has existed, under which the United States government, after reaching agreements with the governments involved, insures United States investors against the "specific risks" of expropriation and confiscation of private property and inconvertibility of local currencies. In 1963, Congress barred aid after December 31, 1965, to any government that by then had failed to enter into such a "specific risk" guarantee agreement. More recently, an "extended risk guarantee" program has been launched. It was described in the Senate Foreign Relations Committee's report on the authorization bill in 1964 as follows:

> The extended risk guarantee program was designed to attract private capital to areas where instability, administrative inexperience, and various other conditions have tended to discourage investment. Thus, the program offers considerably broader protection than is available under the specific risk program . . . by covering normal commercial risks.
>
> Extended risk guarantees emphasize social development, and fall into two categories: Guarantees against loss of any loan investment for housing projects with appropriate participation by the private investor in the loan risk; and guarantees against loss of up to 75 per cent of other forms of investment.[47]

Both of these programs have attracted considerable interest among United States investors. It is impossible to know how much "aid" is involved because that depends entirely on how often such guarantees will have to be backed up by the United States government. But Congress has seen to it that, however that might be, the guarantee program is to be regarded as inseparable from the aid program itself, and has thereby asserted positively its concern to foster private enterprise in underdeveloped areas. In a similar vein, the 1962 Hickenlooper amendment provided that unless a foreign government takes steps within six months to compensate justly for expropriated property, that government shall receive no further assistance. Other measures designed to facilitate American private investment in underdeveloped areas include assistance in the conduct of investment surveys, and loans—in dollars and in local currencies—to American borrowers for investment.

[46] For some, this doctrinaire conviction grows out of the belief that "socialist" countries are thought to be less friendly and cooperative with the United States. This, of course, is a myth. It arises out of semantic confusion and the inability to distinguish between various kinds of "socialism," which range all the way from the benign and democratic variety of the Scandinavian countries and Britain to the harsh and dictatorial variety of the Soviet Union and Communist China. See above, p. 103.

[47] Senate Committee on Foreign Relations, *Foreign Assistance Act of 1964*, Rep. No. 1188, 88th Cong., 2d Sess., 1964, pt. 1, p. 11.

Despite all these efforts and more, the prospects for widespread private capital investment in underdeveloped areas are anything but promising, as the following table shows.[48]

New United States Private Capital Investment, Net (in millions of dollars)

	1961	1962	1963
All areas	3,953	3,273	4,082
Western Europe	1,110	1,258	1,595
Eastern Europe	3	—3	26
Canada	972	634	773
Latin American Republics	397	227	154
Japan	*	516	833
All other countries	1,506	407	644
International institutions, and unallocated	—35	234	57
Addendum sterling area	(499)	*	*

* Not available.
Source: U.S. Department of Commerce.

And even that gloomy table conceals the magnitude of the disparities. Most of the investment in underdeveloped areas has gone into extractive industries (e.g., oil, minerals); only a small fraction has gone into manufacturing and commerce.

There are some indications that these patterns are being broken, that more private capital is being invested in underdeveloped areas, and that more developmental industries are being nurtured. But the controlling fact for years to come is likely to be that private investors are more likely to go where the need is least—but their investments reasonably safe—and most reluctant to go where the need is greatest.

Oddly enough, it is by no means definite that this state of affairs is undesirable from the standpoint of long-range United States interests. Persuasive as the case may be in the abstract for the utility of private investment in the economic development process, the fact is that extensive United States investments create many problems for this country and will present many more in the future. Bearing in mind the primacy of politics —especially the politics of nationalism—there are bound to be many instances in which foreign-owned (i.e., American-owned) enterprises, no matter how productive and beneficent, come to be regarded as violators of the independence of the nation involved. The contemporary term for a

[48] *Ibid.,* p. 13.

condition in which a substantial portion of a nation's economy is controlled by foreigners is "neo-imperialism." There would appear to be only two ways to avoid attracting this label in today's world. One is to ensure that the governing elites in all underdeveloped areas are "moderate" and "pro-Western"; the other is to avoid investments in such sensitive areas. Since the first alternative would appear to be out of the question, the second one should not be regarded lightly. It is not only the ugly epithet of "imperialist" that would thus be avoided; it is also such sticky problems as not knowing how to react when a revolutionary government nationalizes American-owned industries.

As indicated at the outset of this section, the concern about fostering private enterprise is only in part a concern about the opportunities for United States investors. It is, in addition, a concern about how the foreign aid program might be used to foster indigenous private enterprise. The sources of this concern are essentially the same as those regarding United States private investment, minus the natural interest in creating new opportunities for United States capital: a pride in the manifold blessings of our own "free enterprise" system and an attendant conviction that such an economic system will best serve the underdeveloped areas, too; and an antipathy for anything that resembles or calls itself "socialism."

These convictions, or doctrines, whatever may be their merits, cause many problems for the aid program. Most of the recipient governments are committed in some vague way to "socialism" as the fastest means of developing their economies and the most equitable means of distributing their products. They are not likely to be disabused of these notions by preachments from Washington, or anywhere else. Therefore, if we propose to assist their development, we shall often have no choice but to support their "socialistic" schemes.

The most publicized instance of the triumph of abstract principle over practicality in this connection occurred in 1963 over the proposed construction by the government of India of a steel mill at Bokaro. The Kennedy administration had expressed a willingness to assist in this effort, and it would have been the largest single foreign aid project in history, requiring nearly $1 billion in loans from the United States. When Congress learned of projected deal, a storm of protest arose. A Clay Committee admonition against "projects establishing government-owned industrial and commercial enterprises which compete with existing private endeavors" was cited approvingly. (India then had five steel mills, two of which were privately owned and three of which were owned by the government.) The gigantic cost of the project attracted attention to its "socialist" character. After the House passed an amendment that effectively prohibited American aid for the project, India quietly withdrew its request for the assistance in order to save the administration any further rebuffs on the matter.

But India got its steel mill: The Soviet Union agreed to build it, the second such highly visible Soviet project in that crucial nation. If our purpose in withholding the aid was to induce India to invite private capital to build it—and it is highly doubtful that there would have been enough private capital for such an undertaking—our purpose was frustrated. If our original purpose in appearing to favor the loan was to involve ourselves further and importantly in India's quest for development, that purpose was of course also frustrated. And in the process we gave the Soviets another and much-publicized opportunity to "demonstrate" that they, unlike the United States, were committed only to the progress of India and not to either self-interest or dogma.

However one views the denouement of this particular episode, it seems clear that this fixation on the undoubted benefits of the private enterprise system has handicapped the flexibility and utility of our aid program. For a nation that is so relatively innocent of dogma, so persistently pragmatic— and whose economy, moreover, bears so little relationship to such shibboleths and oversimplifications as either "free enterprise" or "socialist"— this is a peculiarly unfortunate and unseemly handicap.

How Many Strings Attached?   As several of the preceding criticisms have suggested, there are many who believe that aid has been given too indiscriminately and that there is a greater need for United States control over the use of aid. This argument over "how many strings should be attached" is a perennial one in the foreign aid debate. It is as fascinating as it is ultimately unresolvable.

It is quite obvious in the abstract that the United States government has both the right and the duty to take steps to ensure that its assistance is not being squandered or used inappropriately for private gain. At some point, however, this "principle" collides with the even more beguiling one that holds that any "interference in the internal affairs of a sovereign nation" is legally, morally, and practically insupportable. This latter notion is much easier to proclaim than it is to practice or to define in concrete circumstances. The simple fact is that interference in others' affairs is the rule rather than the exception in international affairs, especially for superpowers whose every act affects nearly everyone else. Moreover, the very act of aiding necessarily involves "intervention" regardless of how circumspect the aiding nation may be. Finally, the exhortations regarding noninterference should be understood to cut both ways. As the Clay Committee put it, ". . . they too lack the right to intervene in our national pocketbook for aid to enterprises which only increase their costs of government and the foreign assistance burden they are asking us to carry."[49]

---

[49] *Clay Committee Report*, p. 6.

There are bound to be, and should be, "strings attached." As usual, the difficult problem is not in resolving such an abstract question but in knowing when to attach strings and what kind. The Alliance for Progress provides an excellent example of the problem. Prior to the inauguration of that ambitious effort, the primary conditions for qualifying for aid had to do with a nation's foreign policy. If it accorded with our view of the appropriate way to deal with cold war and other international political problems, aid was much more likely to be forthcoming. There were other considerations, of course, such as whether or not we felt constrained to pay much attention to the area involved, but in any event our primary concerns were international. With the Alliance for Progress, we became— at least ostensibly—more concerned with a recipient's domestic policies than with his foreign policies. The leading questions would be of the following type: Is the tax system being reformed to ensure collection and redistribution of the wealth? Is land reform being vigorously carried out? Are housing and education being provided for the historically deprived but newly awakened masses of Latin America?

Several things need to be said about this policy shift. First of all, it was not as dramatic or complete as it might seem to have been. The emphasis on domestic reform was regarded as being intrinsically desirable, but the real force behind it was, once again, a concern about international politics. Fidel Castro was the "Father of the Alliance for Progress." His Cuban revolution struck fear into the hearts of United States policy makers and many Latin Americans, who shared the desire to avoid additional Fidelista revolutions. Hence, the alleged shift in emphasis was really more tactical than substantive in motive, though it did unquestionably introduce new types of criteria for allocating assistance.

In the present context, however, the more important consideration is the fact that this new emphasis on internal reform rather than external orthodoxy raised with special force the old problem of when acceptable monitoring becomes unacceptable meddling. As the Alliance for Progress experience has shown, and as common sense would suggest, it is no simple thing to try to induce some governments to institute widespread domestic reforms. How much pressure should be applied? What kind? Should aid be cut off if performance is below requirements? If not, of what value is the whole elaborate effort?

It is not surprising that in practice our aid policy has vacillated between great permissiveness and hard bargaining, and has included such gimmicks as creating boards composed primarily of representatives of recipient nations whose job is to establish "reasonable" criteria for aid eligibility and then to judge whether performance meets or fails to meet these criteria. Our frustration over these matters grows from essentially three conditions. We cannot publish all the concessions to our demands that have in fact been made because some would embarrass the yielding governments. Secondly, the problem of inducing reform is indeed a formidable one. And, finally, the whole experience underlines once again the basic fact that foreign aid, whatever its other merits may be, is not often an effective means of gaining control, or even much influence, over the policies —foreign or domestic—of recipient governments.

Should the Administration of Aid be Internationalized?   When Senator J. William Fulbright announced in December, 1964, that he would no longer assume the responsibility of serving as floor leader for the foreign aid bill as then constituted, he reiterated his view that the money for economic assistance should be primarily funneled through international lending institutions such as the International Bank for Reconstruction and Development (IBRD) and its affiliate, the International Development Association (IDA). This is a commonly expressed opinion, and the Clay Committee Report contained the following summary statement of the case for such a use of aid funds.[50]

We . . . believe that the interests both of the United States and of the developing nations will be best served by the gradual shifting to effective international administration, free of the complications arising from membership of the Soviet Bloc, of as large a share of the responsibility for developmental investment as the cooperation of other free world aid-giving nations makes possible.

A multilateral organization, having no political or commercial interests of its own to serve, is able to concentrate on obtaining the greatest possible return, in terms of economic and social development, for each dollar of aid funds invested. It is also better able to limit its assistance to projects which are soundly conceived and executed and to condition the financing of such projects upon appropriate economic performance by the recipient country. Moreover, conditions imposed by an international, cooperative organization are not so susceptible to the charge that they infringe on the sovereignty of the recipient country; even if they offend national sensitivities, they do less damage to the fragile fabric of comity among nations than when such resentment is directed against a single country. Also, to the extent that international administration integrates funds contributed by a number of countries, it avoids the difficult problems of coordination which arise when aid is provided by many independent sources.

[50] *Ibid.*, pp. 15–16. The terms "multinational" and "international" are often used interchangeably, as they are in this excerpt. They will be distinguished in this chapter, however, with "multinational" meaning two or more nations acting cooperatively for some specific goal, and "international" referring to institutionalized activities involving large numbers of nations and designed to achieve some broad goal or goals. An example of a multinational aid effort is the one funded by a consortium of eight Western nations, Japan, and two international lending institutions, which finances most of the aid program for India. An example of international aid is that provided by the International Development Association. There is virtually no debate about the desirability of multinational efforts; it is the proposal for increased reliance on international efforts that is under discussion herein.

International administration of development assistance, of course, will realize the advantages cited only if it is effectively organized. In this connection, we would point out that the International Development Association (IDA), an affiliate of the International Bank for Reconstruction and Development, is a ready-made instrument to accomplish these purposes. To the extent that the U.S. and its partners can agree to increase the use of IDA as a common channel for aid funds, we will have achieved many of our common objectives—a fairer sharing of the burden and the effective and coordinated use of the assistance provided on terms both appropriate to the needs of the recipient countries and impartial as among the commercial interests of the contributing nations.

As noted earlier, the United States already makes substantial annual contributions to such institutions as the United Nations Expanded Technical Assistance Program and the United Nations Special Fund. Moreover, it is the principal source of funds for the major international lending institutions, IBRD, IDA, and the Inter-American Development Bank. These institutions are already playing significant developmental roles, but their resources remain quite limited, and their projects do not approach in magnitude those sponsored by the United States. The arguments in the excerpt from the Clay Committee Report cited above in favor of expanding these programs at the expense of our own unilateral efforts are plausible ones and may be proved sound. Surely no one would deny that it would be highly desirable to avoid charges of infringing on sovereignty and to eliminate the possibilities for offending national sensitivities. And no doubt international agencies are better able to limit their assistance "to projects which are soundly achieved and executed. . . ." Moreover, the goal of an internationally coordinated aid effort, wherein recipients would be allocated funds on some kind of "rational" basis, might appear to be a sound one.

But the quoted excerpt is based on some assumptions that should at least not go altogether unchallenged. It suggests, implicitly but unquestionably, that aid should be depoliticized and that the only appropriate criteria are such things as efficiency, efficacy, and soundness—along with the aforementioned reduction of the risks and costs attendant upon being the donor nation in bilateral arrangements. But these assumptions are quite obviously of dubious merit, as the following discussion seeks to demonstrate.

The basic difficulty, as already suggested, is that aid cannot and should not be depoliticized. However and by whom it may be used, it cannot fail to have political effects, whether consciously sought or not. Indeed, even the quoted excerpt concedes this in a broad way by insisting that the Soviets should be excluded from the proposed efforts. This surely is not because we would object to using their capital. Rather, it is because we do not want a Soviet voice in the allocation of aid, and this is quite clearly and undeniably for political reasons. With a bilateral program, the United States can control the use of its money. It can select which countries will receive aid and how much. It can discriminate on behalf of certain nations whose future it regards as more important than others. It can reward policy complementarity and withhold support from nations pursuing policies inimical to its interests. In sum, it can use aid as an instrument of policy, and use it selectively for various purposes.

But once the aid is turned over to, say, IDA, its distribution would be determined by a management that presumably would not be controlled by the United States. Of course, as a practical matter, the United States would always have a major voice in the decision-making process of any such organization, since our assistance would almost surely be disproportionately large. But there is a considerable difference between being in sole control and having a large amount of influence. Moreover, while Americans usually head up these agencies, and United States citizens are prominent in their bureaucracies, these individuals are not officially representing the United States or its interests. They are not employees of the State Department. Finally, international institutions develop interests and personalities of their own, and, consciously or not, they also develop policy biases. These policy biases are not necessarily at one with those of the United States government.

These considerations should give pause to those who favor the aid program but want it internationalized. But there are many who will argue that the preceding arguments merely reinforce their belief in internationalization. They take the view that one of the worst defects in the current program is its at least allegedly close ties with United States policy, including all the changes and alterations. Long-term interests would be better served by avoiding both the stigma and the nonproductiveness of this close relationship.

Whatever one concludes from the preceding dialogue, there is one other consideration of great importance, namely, the reaction of Congress. One can only speculate, of course, about whether a given Congress would be sympathetic to such a change. It might accept it originally as an apparent way to achieve the ends mentioned in the *Clay Committee Report* quoted earlier. There is, of course, great irritation in Congress at the frequency with which our aid earns us the opprobrium of the recipient governments. Internationalizing appears to many to be a means of avoiding the political liabilities and embarrassments while retaining the essential technique of providing aid. If it is ever sold to Congress, it will probably be on some such basis.

But after it has been tried awhile, a reaction will almost surely set in. It will become clearer and clearer that the United States no longer controls the allocation of its money. Some will doubtless go to nations whose poli-

cies are inimical to our own. Perhaps worst of all, the administrators of
the program will not be United States officials, subject to the call of and
harassment by congressional committees.

How long would Congress continue to be willing to turn over large sums
of money to institutions over which it had very little control? The following episode suggests one quite likely answer to that question. In 1963, it
became known that the United Nations Special Fund planned to assist the
Cuban government in a preliminary survey designed to determine whether
a crop diversification program was feasible. The survey was to last five
years at a total expense to the Special Fund of slightly over $1 million.
The United States contributes 40 per cent of the fund's capital, and a
minor storm developed in Congress. The American director of the Special
Fund, Paul Hoffman, insisted that no United States money was directly
involved, and he went ahead with the project. The issue was soon forgotten
in Congress, at least for the time being. But what if a large amount of
money had been involved, or the administrator had not been an American,
or the specific project had been less innocuous? It may be that as a
prescription for curing the ills that afflict the aid program, its internationalization would turn out to be fatal.

Conclusions

This chapter has been primarily an attempt to analyze in some detail the
arguments for and against the program of providing economic assistance
in an effort to promote economic development in the underdeveloped areas.
It has been designed, like all the other examples in this book, to show
something of the complexity and ultimate unpredictability of the factors
involved and to put contemporary policy into some perspective. What
conclusions should be drawn about United States aid policy?

It should be obvious by now that a powerful case can be made either
for or against economic development assistance. It should be equally
obvious that this writer favors the program, even while conceding the
force of many of the criticisms. Anyone even faintly aware of the pitfalls
in this effort knows what a gamble it is, how uncertain are the consequences. But the same must be said about a policy of curtailment or abolition of the program. Moreover, it should be borne in mind that the choice
is not between starting or not starting an aid program. Rather, the choice
is between continuing or abandoning, or curtailing, the effort. There is
quite a difference between these two kinds of choice. The existence of the
program has given rise to expectations in the underdeveloped areas of
continued assistance. In cutting it off, or sharply curtailing it, we would
incur heavy liabilities in our relations with these nations. Such liabilities
might very well be more costly and/or burdensome in the long run than
the aid program itself.

Who knows? All national policy is based on expectations about what various alternative policies are likely to result in; in other words, policy is based, however implicitly, on predictions. Since no one has the gift of prophecy, all policy making is ultimately based on estimates, projections, guesses, and even hunches, which in turn are based on varying levels of information and varying degrees of shrewdness and wisdom. Because of this, one of the elements of statesmanship is the willingness to expend resources on programs of doubtful efficacy in an effort to hedge against the uncertainties of the future. Economic aid is such a hedge, a limited and not especially costly attempt to exercise some marginal influence in those vast areas of the world that are potentially dangerous as well as underdeveloped.

A key phrase in that last sentence is "marginal influence." If there is one general criticism of United States foreign policy that seems to this writer to be more important than any other, it is that we often seem to view the world with too much anxiety and too many enthusiasms and not enough detachment and perspective. Our aid program needs to be recognized as the limited instrument it is, and we need to take a less excited view of the significance of diplomatic setbacks and project failures. Intemperate rhetoric and virulent anti-Americanism will be elements of international politics for many years. Aid programs will not change this. We should be self-assured enough to avoid the twin errors of expecting too much from and damning too quickly this uncertain effort. Perhaps the best illustration of the necessity for this kind of perspective is the evolution of United States–Indian relations. There have been many occasions when the speeches or policies of the Indian government irritated Americans, and for good reason. But to have reacted with petulance and a severance of aid would have crippled not only India's efforts at development but also the growing opportunities for a cooperative relationship with this crucial Asian democracy. Dignity and a calculation of our long-range interests require that we refuse to be bullied or blackmailed by the frequently intemperate talk and action of the many new and inexperienced governments. But neither should we reciprocate their excesses or lose sight of our longer and larger perspectives and responsibilities.

Finally, any judgment about what our aid policy ought to be should include some consideration of moral responsibilities. This is, of course, an unusually murky and controversial area, and a good deal of foolish breast-beating and many exaggerated feelings of guilt are apt to become involved in any attempt to discuss it. It is important to get the matter into some perspective. Many extravagant denunciations of the West have been made and doubtless will continue to be made. In the colonial era—now virtually ended—economic exploitation did, of course, take place. And continuing Western control of some vital industries in newly independent areas does constitute a troublesome economic and political problem. But Western colonialism did not create economic backwardness in these areas, and in some instances it took useful steps toward its elimination. The former colonial powers offer perfect scapegoats for the political elites in the under-developed areas, but the charges against them have more validity in the area of political liberty and human dignity than in the area of economics. What moral obligations were acquired by this historical experience is not a simple matter to judge.

In any event, the United States is in a different position. Our colonial holdings were more limited, better treated, and more expeditiously given their independence. So what are our moral obligations to the under-developed world? Are we in any meaningful sense morally responsible for the condition of these peoples? Surely we are not responsible in the sense of having caused their condition, although an argument might be made in this connection regarding some parts of Latin America. But are we respon-sible in the sense of having a moral obligation to assist them now as they struggle toward economic development? This is not a book on ethics, but ethical questions have been faced when it appeared necessary. The view of this writer is that such a moral responsibility does exist and should be met. The difficult question is in determining how much is "owed," and any moral calculus of this type is bound to be subjective and therefore debatable. But surely *some* obligation rests upon those whose material conditions of life are so spectacularly superior to the majority of humanity living in the afflictively underdeveloped areas of this shared earth. If this be sound, considerations of morality and self-interest both point toward a continuation of the aid effort.

It is impossible to know what the fate of the economic assistance program will be over the next decade or so. There are too many imponderables involved. Much will depend on the experience of the program itself and the interpretations placed upon that experience. Much will depend upon the extent to which the Johnson and successor administrations continue to support and fight for the program. And, of course, the final arbiter will continue to be Congress. But Congress changes over time, and today's majority may be tomorrow's minority. After 1961, there was a sharp falling off of support among Republicans in Congress. Under certain circum-stances, this could portend the end of the program, but what actually happens will depend on a variety of factors, including what kinds of in-terpretation the party's legislators place, in the long run, upon the over-whelming defeat of Senator Goldwater in 1964.

Perhaps the most hopeful aspect, from the standpoint of supporters of aid, is the continuing support that the program continues to receive from the public. Despite the fact that many legislators feel that their constitu-encies are hostile to foreign aid, reliable polls steadily report solid majori-ties in favor. The explanation of this paradox probably lies in the fact that few people who favor assistance are likely to be very vocal or active about it, whereas the opposition can generate much noise and activity. Yet foreign aid has not become a noticeably effective campaign issue one way or the other. In sum, the public's attitude seems to be of a piece with its general one regarding foreign policy: permissiveness.

What American aid policy should be will continue to be a source of controversy and opportunity for prudent judgment for years to come. It will be neither the most nor the least important policy question before the government.

This chapter has focused on one important aspect of one of the central challenges to contemporary American foreign policy, namely, how to relate to that "third world" of underdeveloped, overpopulated, nonaligned, and profoundly non-Western nations. It is difficult in the mid-1960s to be confidently optimistic about the future of our relations with these areas. We are too rich, too powerful, too conservative, too white, and too foreign to be much appreciated there. Many Americans find this beyond comprehension. Are we not providing generous economic assistance? Are we not a liberty-loving people with a relatively clean record on colonialism? Are we not color-blind in our official dealings and even increasingly so at home? Is not our general record in foreign affairs, historically and contemporaneously, essentially honorable and respectful of the legitimate rights and interests of others? Are not our adversaries in the cold war the enemies of freedom and human dignity?

The fair answer to all these questions is almost certainly "yes." But they are the wrong questions. As put by many (most?) influential persons in the underdeveloped areas, those questions would have a rather different cast, somewhat as follows. Are you not providing aid merely as a means of serving your own interests, some honorable and some less so? Has not your policy regarding Latin America demonstrated that you are also imperialists, albeit more subtle ones? If you love liberty so much, why do you support Franco in Spain and Salazar in Portugal, and why do you not sever relations with South Africa? If you are color-blind, why is it that you feel free to meddle in the internal affairs of African nations in a way unthinkable vis-à-vis your European-colonialist allies? Are Negroes in Mississippi—or Chicago, for that matter—really first-class citizens? If your foreign policy is so honorable, how do you explain the Bay of Pigs invasion, your earlier support of Batista, and your frantic and disapproving response to every revolutionary movement that threatens a decadent *status quo?* Why do you try to drag us into your quarrels by preaching to us about the alleged stakes of the cold war?

It depends on who asks the questions and what his angle of vision is. Even though there are respectable and decent answers to nearly every one of these latter questions, the point at the moment is simply that they tell us more about the state of mind of many of the key people in the elites in the underdeveloped nations than do the earlier questions. The gap between the United States and the underdeveloped areas is not merely economic and will not be bridged by Peace Corps programs, cultural and educational exchanges, or massive propaganda efforts, desirable as all of these assuredly are. This rich, powerful, relatively satisfied, and predominantly white nation cannot expect to be loved. But it can and should attempt to be respected.

Selected Bibliography

Annual *Hearings* and *Reports* on the Foreign Assistance program, House: Committee on Foreign Affairs and Subcommittee on Foreign Operations Appropriations; Senate: Committee on Foreign Relations and Committee on Appropriations.

Feis, Herbert: *Foreign Aid and Foreign Policy*, St Martin's Press, Inc., New York, 1964. A wise and sophisticated—yet humane—treatment by a distinguished historian-economist-diplomat.

Frank, Isaiah: "Foreign Aid and the Liberal Dissent," *The New Republic*, vol. 152, no. 4, pp. 17–22, Jan. 23, 1965. A good summary of the newer criticisms of aid.

Goldman, Marshall I.: "A Balance Sheet of Soviet Foreign Aid," *Foreign Affairs*, vol. 43, no. 2, pp. 349–360, January, 1965. A shrewd and reassuring assessment of the Soviet experience with aid.

Goldwin, Robert A. (ed.): *Why Foreign Aid?* Rand McNally & Company, Chicago, 1963. An uneven collection of essays, pro and con. See especially the contributions by Edward C. Banfield, Hans J. Morgenthau, Max F. Millikan, and Joseph Cropsey.

Heilbroner, Robert L.: *The Great Ascent*, Harper & Row, Publishers, Incorporated, New York, 1963. (Available in a paperback edition, same publisher, 1963.) A sobering discussion of the prospects for economic development in the underdeveloped countries.

Liska, George: *The New Statecraft*, The University of Chicago Press, Chicago, 1960. An abstruse but rewarding theoretical treatment of foreign aid as a political instrument.

Mason, Edward S.: *Foreign Aid and Foreign Policy*, Harper & Row, Publishers, Incorporated, New York, 1964. An authoritative analysis by an experienced economist.

Morgenthau, Hans J.: "A Political Theory of Foreign Aid," *The American Political Science Review*, vol. 56, no. 2, pp. 301–309, June, 1962. A penetrating essay on the theory and practice of United States aid policy.

Summary Presentation to the Congress, an annual booklet prepared by the Agency for International Development and the Department of Defense.

The President's Annual Report to the Congress for the Fiscal Year 19.. on the Foreign Assistance Program.

YANKEES GO HOME

Chapter Nine
Epilogue

chapter 9   This book has dealt *selectively* with United States foreign policy. As noted in the Preface, it is virtually impossible—and is
surely foolhardy—for any one person to attempt to write meaningfully
about the whole range of foreign policy problems that confront the United
States today. Moreover, this book has not had as its central purpose the
transmission of vast amounts of information about current affairs. These
and other issues are changing all the time. Even if it were possible to provide comprehensive information about them, to analyze them thoroughly,
and to suggest "correct responses" at any given time, their characteristics
would be different in a few years or even months or days. Therefore, the
primary aim has been to use selected issues as vehicles for instruction on
how to think intelligently about United States foreign policy.

Nonetheless, the book has focused on many of the crucial foreign policy
problems of the day, and therefore, lest there be any false impression
fostered that it has been comprehensive regarding contemporary challenges,
a few paragraphs below will be devoted to dispelling that illusion by
introducing in cursory fashion some of the other vital problems.

Some Emergent Challenges

Communist China

United States policy regarding Red China has been nearly frozen since
1950. How long this condition will persist is uncertain; how long it should
persist is a hotly controversial question. China is an emerging major power
whose ambitions are shrouded in secrecy but are quite possibly expansionist. It is a nation of approximately 700 million people, and this huge population is a source of both strength and weakness. It has demonstrated the
will and the ability to develop at the very least a primitive nuclear capability. Although it has demonstrated considerable moderation in its actions,
its ideological fervor and rhetorical excesses and bellicosity may someday
be matched by deeds. Meanwhile, despite many internal difficulties, it
casts an increasingly ominous shadow across Asia and has pretensions of
being influential in Africa and Latin America as well. Its split with the
Soviet Union—which is among the most significant and encouraging developments of the postwar era—appears to have stimulated rather than
blunted these global ambitions.[1]

The somewhat surreptitious debate about whether the United States
should recognize Red China tends to obscure rather than clarify the

---

[1] For expert discussions of Red China's capabilities, potential capabilities, and likely
future policies, see Alice Langley Hsieh, "Communist China and Nuclear Force," in
Richard N. Rosecrance (ed.), *The Dispersion of Nuclear Weapons*, Columbia University Press, New York, pp. 157–185; and Samuel B. Griffith, II, "Communist China's
Capacity to Make War," *Foreign Affairs*, vol. 43, no. 2, pp. 217–236, January, 1965.

problem. There are excellent arguments on both sides of that issue;[2] and it is intrinsically important. But the problem of how to deal with Communist China is a much broader one, and recognition would almost certainly not have as dramatic an effect one way or the other as the debaters often imply.

However that may be, the whole agonizing postwar experience with our China policy is among the most discouraging episodes in recent American history. It would be difficult to exaggerate the amount of sentimentality, ignorance, and demagoguery that has characterized official policy and opposition rhetoric on this subject.[3] Anyone interested in arguing that a democracy cannot formulate rational foreign policies can find plenty of evidence in this sorry story. Fortunately, this has been an exceptional case.

We may be approaching the day when American policy can adjust with something like its usual flexibility to these realities and challenges. On December 14, 1963, Roger Hilsman, then the Assistant Secretary of State for Far Eastern Affairs, delivered a public address, which presumably had President Johnson's approval and which suggested that new attitudes might be emerging. Near the end of a remarkably dispassionate analysis of Chinese performance and policies and a defense of nonrecognition by the United States, Hilsman said:

> We do not know what changes may occur in the attitudes of future Chinese leaders. But if I may paraphrase a classic canon of our past, we pursue today toward Communist China a policy of the open door: we are determined to keep the door open to the possibility of change, and not to slam it shut against any developments which might advance our national good, serve the free world, and benefit the people of China. . . .
>
> We hope that, confronted with firmness which will make foreign adventure unprofitable, and yet offered the prospect that the way back into the community of man is not closed to it, the Chinese Communist regime will eventually forsake its present venomous hatreds which spring from a rigid class view of society.[4]

These remarks surely did not reflect any dramatic policy shift, and they explicitly based the hope for improved relations on the views of future, not contemporary, leaders. But the mere fact that they were publicly made

---

[2] For a detailed analysis of this question, see Robert P. Newman, *Recognition of Communist China?* The Macmillan Company, New York, 1961.

[3] For a definitive study of the early period, see Tang Tsou, *America's Failure in China: 1941–50*, The University of Chicago Press, Chicago, 1963. For an insight into the trauma that beset the United States after the communization of China, see Newman, pp. 7–15, 51–103, and *passim*. For a survey of the entire problem, see A. Doak Barnett, *Communist China and Asia, A Challenge to American Policy*, Vintage Books, Inc., Random House, Inc., New York, 1961.

[4] U.S. Department of State, *The Department of State Bulletin*, vol. 50, no. 1280, p. 17, Jan. 6, 1964.

and were so nearly devoid of the usual bombast and preachments which ordinarily characterize United States pronouncements regarding China was noteworthy. Whether new policy directions and contacts will emerge is unclear. What is clear is that Communist China will become an increasingly serious fact of life for the United States in the years and decades to come, requiring American foreign policies of the highest order.

Southeast Asia

Closely related to the Chinese issue is the future of Southeast Asia. Whatever may finally happen in South Vietnam, the extension of Communist influence in the areas to the south and west of that tormented land is unquestionably the long-range goal of the Chinese and North Vietnam governments. There is already evidence of guerrilla activity in Thailand and no reason to doubt that it would expand appreciably if its eastern and northern borders were securely in hostile hands. Should the United States be willing to commit itself fully to the containment of this expansion? President Eisenhower enunciated the famous "domino theory" during his administration. It held that if one of the non-Communist states in Southeast Asia should go Communist, the others would systematically suffer the same fate, falling like a row of dominoes. It would appear that at least Thailand is a candidate for becoming a domino. We have solemn commitments to defend Thailand, and we have made dramatic gestures of support, such as sending in Marines during a crisis in Laos in 1962. Confronted with a situation comparable to the one in South Vietnam, would we or should we in fact be willing to commit vast numbers of American troops to defend Thailand? If not, could Thailand's large army be more successful than has the South Vietnamese?

If Thailand were to go, what would become of Malaysia or Burma? Given Indonesia's apparent determination to destroy Malaysia and its concomitant willingness to cooperate with Communist China, could Malaysia survive, even with British help? Could Burma? If the latter should go, what would then happen to Pakistan and India? Would even the Philippines be immune from such a spread of Communist domain?

And what difference would any of this make to the United States? There are respected voices in this country—such as Walter Lippmann, for example—who have long believed that we are overcommitted and over-involved and who do not regard the fate of these areas as being intertwined with our own. They stress the view that our sea and air power are not sufficient to control affairs on the Asian mainland and that any attempt to commit large numbers of ground forces would be both unnecessary and ineffectual. The Philippines, Formosa, and Japan—and Korea, for obviously special reasons—should be our line of defense, not mainland Asia.

General de Gaulle would seem to have a similar view, with a somewhat different emphasis. In this era of polycentrism, it is no longer helpful and it can be dangerous to think of "communism" as an undifferentiated phenomenon. If one assumes that the victory of the Communist forces in, say, Vietnam is inevitable, the thing to do is to accept this fact and attempt to use it to your advantage. Try to make another Tito out of Ho Chi Minh; this is the only feasible way of checking the spread of Chinese influence. If such unfortunate accommodations must be made in other countries, such as Thailand, for example, then make them. The alternative is to try to conquer and control Southeast Asia, a project that is both breathtaking in conception and almost surely doomed to failure from the outset.

Whoever is in power in Washington in the next decade or so, these questions and dilemmas will need to be faced up to. However sad and frustrating it may be, there are no readily apparent formulas for dealing with them.[5]

Latin America

As in much of the rest of the world, there are revolutionary forces at work in Latin America. In an area never known for its political stability, the entire established order is under attack, and it is a fairly safe assumption that in the not-too-distant future the governments of at least some nations in Latin America will be radically different from what they have been in the past.

What will be the composition and policies of these new governments? Will they attempt to exploit the deep resentments against the colossus of the North, or will they seek to establish cooperative relations with the United States? How successful will "Communist" elements—be they Chinese-supported, Soviet-supported, Castro-supported, or unsupported—be in infiltrating successful radical movements in Latin America?

What should United States policy be in response to any of the various contingencies suggested above?

Belatedly, and with imperfect instincts and limited influence, the United States has begun to adjust to the emergent realities in an area traditionally regarded as a sleepy back yard, to be exploited and ignored or, at best, patronized. The Alliance for Progress is the most tangible evidence of the new appreciation of the significance of and dangers in Latin America. But behind the economic aid is a larger transformation of opinions and priorities. The shock of Fidel Castro was, ironically, instrumental in awakening the United States government and citizens to responsibilities and dangers too long neglected.

The questions for the future are of this kind: Can the Alliance for Progress or any other United States policies manage to channel the dynamics of change into constructive avenues, or will the process neces-

---

[5] For a survey of these problems, see Russell H. Fifield, *Southeast Asia in United States Policy*, Frederick A. Praeger, Inc., New York, 1963.

sarily be violent and anti-Yankee? If the latter, what should we do about it, if anything? Will we be able to distinguish between native radicals and genuine Communists, and even if we can, will we know how to handle either one or the other? To put it more concretely, what should be the United States response if a leftist revolution occurs in, say, Venezuela, and a bitterly anti–United States group seizes power? Would patience or intervention be the appropriate response?

When a rebellion broke out in April, 1965, against a regime in the Dominican Republic which had been installed by the military after the deposition of a democratically elected President in 1963, the United States intervened. Whether this was a prudent decision has been very difficult to determine on the basis of the conflicting and confusing reports out of Santo Domingo and Washington. What is unmistakably clear is that such actions, whether justified or not, are extremely costly in terms of United States relations with Latin America. It is a matter of the utmost importance that United States administrations be able to distinguish between various kinds of leftist revolutions in Latin America and fit their responses to the realities and not to some oversimplified view of what is "Communist-inspired." The formulation of intelligent and far-seeing responses will require subtle and shrewd statesmanship during the next few years and decades.

Atlantic Affairs

Nowhere are change and challenge more conspicuous than in relations among European states and between Europe and Great Britain and the United States. The policy issues go well beyond the defense dilemmas and controversies discussed elsewhere in this book. Is the trend toward economic union in Europe irreversible? If so, what will be the relations between this emerging giant and the United States and Great Britain? What are the prospects for European "political integration"? Will it be de Gaulle's semi-integrated "Europe of Fatherlands" or a single sovereignty called "The United States of Europe"? Or neither? Whatever develops, how will the United States relate itself to the new and constantly changing realities in Europe?[6]

Any observers who might have been complacent about the trend of European–United States relations have had that complacency jolted several times in recent years. Attitudes that take Europe for granted or that

---

[6] The literature on these matters is, needless to say, enormous. As introductory reading, the following books are recommended: Francis O. Wilcox and H. Field Haviland, Jr. (ed.), *The Atlantic Community*, Frederick A. Praeger, Inc., New York, 1963; Alvin J. Cottrell and James E. Dougherty, *The Politics of the Atlantic Alliance*, Frederick A. Praeger, Inc., New York, 1964; Don D. Humphrey, *The United States and the Common Market* (rev. ed.), Frederick A. Praeger, Inc., New York, 1964; and John Paton Davies, Jr., *Foreign and Other Affairs*, W. W. Norton & Company, Inc., New York, 1964, pp. 141–162. For continuing commentary and reporting, see *The Atlantic Community Quarterly* published by the Atlantic Council of the United States, Inc., Washington, D.C.

foster hopes for an early achievement of some kind of institutionalized "Atlantic Community" would appear to be equally misguided. The widespread need for creative and sophisticated United States foreign policies is nowhere more conspicuous than here, at the foundation of United States strength and security. The breakup of the Communist monolith is paralleled in the West by the resurgence and independent impulses of Western Europe. Old assumptions and the policies that have rested on them are daily being undermined and must be replaced by different and sounder ones.

The list of existing and potential challenges to American foreign policy could be extended at great length. The agonies of decolonization and internal change in southern Africa, the potential for mischief inherent in the immature and unstable governments in parts of Africa, the festering Arab-Israeli dispute, the apparently insoluble problems of Cyprus, the ominous strife and hatred between Indonesia and Malaysia, the uncertain future direction of Japanese policy, and—most ominous of all—the likely dispersion of nuclear weapons: these and other challenges ensure that the demands on United States diplomatic ingenuity and policy adaptability will not slacken with time. There is no golden age of security and tranquility just around the corner, regardless of how shrewd and effective our policies may be.

The Future of United States–Soviet Relations

The central issue for American policy makers for the foreseeable future is the same one it has been since 1945, namely, the status of United States–Soviet relations. Neither polycentrism on both sides of the Iron Curtain, nor the emergence of the newly independent nations, nor temporary or even long-standing periods of reduced East-West tension should obscure the truth that the central fact about international politics and American foreign policy is the confrontation between the United States and the Soviet Union. This would be true if thermonuclear weapons did not exist, but their presence converts a primary fact into a preeminent, nearly dominating one. And from one's views of the nature and meaning of that confrontation flows much of the rest of a person's policy predilections.

The basic questions have to do with Soviet intentions. Are their most doctrinaire and militant declarations to be taken at face value, or is it safe to assume that they have lost some or most of their zeal for messianic goals and adventurist policies and are becoming just another nation-state with traditional, not revolutionary, aspirations? As suggested in Chapters 4 and 5, there is no agreement in this country or among specialists in Soviet affairs about the role of ideology in contemporary Soviet policy or about such related questions as those just noted above. But policy must be made whether there is agreement or not, and American policy in recent years has been based on a rather more hopeful set of assumptions regarding Soviet intentions than was the case not many years ago. Although the essential outlines of the policies associated with the word "containment" have not changed, there has been an increasing acceptance of the rather different, though not incompatible, notion of "peaceful coexistence." There has been, in other words, an increasing official and public acceptance of the view that the Soviet Union is here to stay, that it has, in the need to avoid thermonuclear war, an interest in common with the United States which far outweighs those interests that conflict, and that Soviet recognition of this basic fact will increasingly make it possible to build upon this common interest a basis for a mutually satisfactory and even accommodating relationship. Therefore, every opportunity to reduce tension and conflicts of interest must be seized, and new possibilities must be assiduously cultivated.

In what was probably his most memorable speech, President Kennedy spoke to a commencement audience at American University in June, 1963, about United States–Soviet relations. He called upon Americans to reexamine their attitudes toward peace, the cold war, and the Soviet Union. In a passage that in retrospect is as poignant as it was then courageous, he spoke as follows:

> So let us not be blind to our differences, but let us also direct attention to our common interests and to the means by which those differences can be resolved. And if we cannot end our differences, at least we can make the world safe for diversity. For in the final analysis our most basic common link is that we all inhabit this planet. We all breathe the same air. We all cherish our children's future. And we are all mortal.

As this is written, it would seem that a hopeful assessment of Soviet intentions and United States–Soviet relations is essentially sound. Several concrete steps have been taken in the direction of hope and stability, notably the partial nuclear test ban treaty, the "hot-line" agreement, the demilitarization of Antarctica and outer space, and an agreement to expand consulate facilities in each country. Many, including this writer, believe that these small steps have helped induce and also reflect a substantial, perhaps qualitative, change in United States–Soviet relations. It does not seem naïve or foolish to believe that the long hoped-for "thaw" or "normalization" of United States–Soviet relations has finally taken on something more than a temporary or aberrant character. After all, both sides have exhibited a healthy awareness of the dangers that inhere in the opposite trend and even in an indefinite prolongation of the postwar confrontation with all its animosities, recriminations, suspicions, dogmatic affirmations, and fixed positions. We have, as it were, become rather accustomed to each other and, in the process of avoiding the holocaust, have even developed a certain respect for the other side's essential sanity, if not good will.

There are even some signs that each side is beginning to sense, however dimly, common interests transcending the elemental one of survival. There is every reason to believe, for example, that the Soviets are just as alarmed by the presence of a nuclear China as we are. And there is even some reason to suspect that the Soviets are beginning to sense that the incessant fostering and exploiting of revolutionary movements all over the tragically poor and unstable portions of the globe are not clearly in either their interests or the interests of world peace. Dogma and Chinese charges that the Soviet Union has degenerated into an imperialist state have thus far blunted such instincts in the Soviet leadership. But the relatively weak and inconstant Soviet efforts in such areas as Latin America do suggest that the Soviets do not operate as grandiose a subversive network around the world as one would expect or as they presumably could afford.

There are many, and some respectable, observers in this country who regard the above position as dangerously misguided and likely in the long run to create an atmosphere of opinion in this country that will make the nation vulnerable to Soviet pressure or even ultimatums. One does not have to be a dogmatic believer in the irredeemable perniciousness of Soviet leaders to take a very cautious view of any purported change in Soviet behavior or intentions. There is plenty of evidence for this side of the argument. The Soviet attempt to install long-range missiles in Cuba occurred as recently as 1962 and contravened nearly all official United States expectations at the time. Such marginal accords as the partial test ban treaty may not be lasting and, more importantly, are intrinsically not decisive events. Soviet tactics have always been flexible; Soviet intentions have remained. As for the manifest reduction in tension, this has happened before only to be rudely overturned by some new twist in the Kremlin line. And if the Soviets have become so passive in the underdeveloped world, why are they expending so many scarce resources in sustaining the Castro regime in Cuba, and meddling in the internal affairs of such nations as Iran and Iraq?

These two strains of thought, and the infinite number of variations and differing emphases that occur within them, have always been competitive in American political thought, and neither one has ever routed the other. They usually coexist within incumbent administrations, and to some extent within most individual observers. According to some interpretations, for example, John Foster Dulles and Dwight D. Eisenhower, despite their close relationship, tended to make rather different assumptions about the mainsprings of Soviet policy, with the President usually taking a more hopeful view.[7]

[7] See, for example, Emmet John Hughes, *The Ordeal of Power*, Atheneum Publishers, New York, 1963.

The only time in the postwar period in which either party has nominated a candidate for the presidency who flatly rejected the "hopeful" view and emphatically embraced the "pessimistic" view was in 1964 when the Republicans nominated Senator Barry Goldwater. There would seem to be little reason to doubt that *one* of the factors contributing to his overwhelming defeat was precisely this unyielding dogmatism about the Soviet Union. Public opinion polls have repeatedly and consistently shown that the American people, in and out of season, favor attempts at accommodation and believe them to be something other than hopelessly futile. Each postwar administration has reflected this view, but it became much more pronounced in the Kennedy and Johnson administrations.

But majority votes do not determine the course of international politics, especially that element of it known as Soviet policy. United States–Soviet relations may deteriorate again rather than, as seems more likely, gradually improve.

Meanwhile, the biggest question is unchanged: Regardless of whether United States–Soviet relations improve or deteriorate, will there be a major war between them? For all the reasons discussed in Chapter 7 (especially pages 285–286), this writer believes the chances are extremely remote. But there can be no certainty about this matter. It is as absurd and indefensible to argue that such a war cannot happen as it is to argue that it is inevitable. Although it is possible to assess the prospects with some intelligence, it is impossible to be certain about what will happen. This book has quite clearly been written on the basis of a rather optimistic set of assumptions about the likelihood of all-out war. If one does not make or arrive at these assumptions, much of the rationale and rationality of this book and of official policy is undermined. For clearly, if our present policies are leading us toward thermonuclear extinction, all such questions as Soviet intentions or American intentions are transcended by other considerations. It remains, therefore, to discuss briefly a point of view that dissents radically from the basic characteristics and rationale of official policy, namely, nuclear pacifism.

Nuclear Pacifism

Contemporary American policy is rooted in the belief that we are not faced with the choice between "Red or dead," that there is a strong chance of being neither. If this belief is erroneous—and it cannot be proved or disproved in any definitive manner—some rather stark choices should be made, and made quickly.

Pacifism has a long and honorable tradition. But its essence has always been much more moral than tactical, much more concerned with doing what is believed to be intrinsically right than with doing what might have desirable consequences. To be sure, some pacifists have always grounded their position in the essentially amoral view that this was the best means of preserving their own lives or nations. But for the most part, pacifism has sprung from religious and/or moral convictions which hold that violence is intrinsically immoral and should not be engaged in regardless of the circumstances. And with this latter view it is difficult to argue on tactical or pragmatic grounds, though it might be possible to convince a pacifist that such an ethic is utopian or irresponsible. Strong moral convictions are notoriously hard to reason about, and beliefs sanctioned by religion are even less touched by calculations of consequences and implications. Right is right and wrong is wrong. If violence is wrong, that is all that can be said about it.

There is a new kind of pacifism today, however, which is only tangentially related to the type referred to above. It grows less out of moral sentiments than an implicit or explicit calculation about the probabilities of a thermonuclear war. It will be referred to herein as "nuclear pacifism."

Most people do not think much about whether a major war is likely. The thought is so horrifying and the feeling of being unable to do anything about it anyway is so widespread that the issue is seldom discussed, even in sophisticated and knowledgeable circles. But some people do think about it, and not everyone expresses the confidence of this writer that a major war will be averted. To repeat, it is impossible to determine what the likelihood of a major war is. Too many unknown and unknowable factors are involved. Even if, as seems likely, both sides are expending much energy and resources in parallel efforts to avoid such a war, it *might* happen anyway.

It makes a good deal of difference to one's policy position how he views this matter. In very crude terms, one could range the entire concerned population along a continuum from those who believe that a thermonuclear war in, say, the next twenty-five years, is "extremely unlikely" to those who believe that it is "extremely likely." For clarity's sake, add four more positions: "quite unlikely," "unlikely," "likely," and "quite likely." Among those who hold the "extremely unlikely" position, the incentives for adopting a pacifist position on tactical grounds—i.e., in order to save one's own life or nation—are minimal. But as one moves across the continuum, the incentives increase. By the time the "extremely likely" position is reached, the incentives for adopting the pacifist position are powerful.

Calculations about the likelihood of a thermonuclear war are not the only factors affecting one's inclination or disinclination toward the pacifist position. Some people who believe that such a war is "extremely likely" still favor our present policies. They are either heady gamblers or they would genuinely prefer being exterminated to being at the mercy of the Soviet Union, or both. And a few who believe that such a war is "extremely unlikely" nonetheless favor a pacifist policy. Aside from religious/moral pacifism, this position could be based on the view that no risk of such a war is tolerable.[8]

But such calculations are probably decisive for most of those who bother to think about the matter. This is, at any rate, surely true for a typical nuclear pacifist. Whether his threshold is "likely" or "extremely likely"— or even "extremely unlikely"—he is a nuclear pacifist because he believes the risks are simply too great to persist in a policy that involves the maintenance of nuclear weapons.

This position is an eminently rational one. If it is accepted that no one really knows what the likelihood of a major war is, it is not absurd— especially in the light of what we know about human nature and human history—to conclude that such a war may be "likely." It would hardly be "in the national interest" to have this nation annihilated. If this prospect is not a dim one—and maybe even if it is—perhaps the risk should be reduced by ceasing to pursue the policy of deterrence.

Nuclear pacifism has been embraced by only a small fraction of the American population and virtually none of its influential elements or persons. But the same cannot be said for those nations, such as Britain, that have long been within range of Soviet planes and missiles. Will it grow in this country as the realization sinks in that we are as vulnerable as anyone else? If the "thaw" continues, the answer is quite probably negative. But if United States–Soviet relations worsen, and a war scare or two envelopes the nation, it is likely that nuclear pacifism will attract many converts. The Cuban missile crisis in October, 1962, induced a temporary reaction of this kind in many people, who believed that the suppressed nightmare might become reality.

Each person has his own values and calculations to harmonize. Very few do it in a consciously systematic way, but most people do it, at least in a sort of instinctive manner. Most observers, including this writer, believe that such a war is "extremely unlikely," and their preference for a policy of deterrence is therefore rather undisturbed. But if that belief could be extensively undermined, some rather wide-ranging changes in American policy would probably ensue, at least after a period of time.

There is a kind of ghoulish asymmetry to the argument as it now stands, because as long as we are still around to discuss the matter, the "unlikely" proponents have at least most of the evidence on their side. If the "likely"

---

[8] This kind of argument can become very involved, of course. It can be argued that even a pacifist policy would not guarantee survival. The other side might simply bomb you anyway. But would the policy nonetheless preserve life on the other side and therefore be worthy anyway? This gets one back to the moral dimension. For an insightful examination of the implications of unilateral disarmament, see Louis J. Halle, "Animal Instincts and Pacifism," *The New Republic*, vol. 146, no. 23, pp. 13–15, June 4, 1962.

proponents should ever be shown to be right, the argument would probably be silenced forever.

Concluding Remarks

This book has several themes, some more explicit than others. It stresses the continuity in essentials of American postwar foreign policy—under Republicans and Democrats alike—and suggests that those essentials have been an enlightened and appropriate response to the international political environment in which we have found ourselves. It stresses the great complexity of foreign policy problems and the all-too-real dangers in the modern world. We can afford neither dilettantes nor crusaders in policy-making roles, but instead require men possessed of intelligence, sophistication, imagination, patience, courage, steady nerves, and—above all—mature judgment.

For the world beyond our borders is an intractable arena, being submissive neither to our wealth, nor our immense power, nor even our abundant good will. Those who would have us believe otherwise—who declare or imply that if we simply had the courage and strength of character to assert ourselves, all would be well—deceive us and betray their own ignorance. But we are not alone in being at once immensely powerful and yet conspicuously without controlling influence nearly everywhere; the Soviets are discovering the same thing. With all its weaponry and ideological preeminence in the Communist orbit, the Soviet Union cannot impose its will on tiny Albania, to say nothing of China. In the thermonuclear age, great military power has great deterrent value, but is not capable of achieving many more positive objectives. Such are the paradoxes of the modern world, and a failure to grasp them could be fatal. As a distinguished diplomat-historian declared in the midst of the demeaning and dispiriting witch hunts of the early 1950s, "the first criterion of a healthy spirit is the ability to walk cheerfully and sensibly amid the congenital uncertainties of existence, to recognize as natural the inevitable precariousness of the human condition, to accept this without being disoriented by it, and to live effectively and usefully in its shadow."[9] More recently, President Johnson, in his January 4, 1965, State of the Union Address, touched on a related theme when he said that "a President's hardest task is not to do what is right, but to know what is right. Yet the Presidency brings no special gift of prophecy or foresight. You take an oath—step into an office—and must then help guide a great democracy."

The future is open. No one knows what the world will be like in ten or

---

[9] George F. Kennan, "The Illusion of Security," *The Atlantic Monthly*, vol. 194, no. 2, p. 34, August, 1954.

twenty years. A great deal will depend on the quality of United States foreign policy.

Selected Bibliography

Brzezinski, Zbigniew: *Alternative to Partition*, McGraw-Hill Book Company, New York, 1965. A prominent American scholar analyzes contemporary United States policy regarding divided Europe and puts forward some ideas on how it might be changed.

Bull, Hedley: *The Control of the Arms Race*, 2d ed., Frederick A. Praeger, Inc., New York, 1965. A literate and informed discussion of an important issue.

Davies, John Paton, Jr.: *Foreign and Other Affairs*, W. W. Norton & Company, Inc., New York, 1964. A wise and witty polemic on the assumptions and implementation of United States foreign policy by a former Foreign Service Officer.

Kennan, George F.: *On Dealing with the Communist World*, Harper & Row, Publishers, Incorporated, New York, 1964. Three essays by a shrewd and experienced—but not jaded—man.

Luard, Evan (ed.): *The Cold War, A Re-appraisal*, Frederick A. Praeger, Inc., New York, 1964. A series of intelligent essays dealing with a wide range of topics by a group of British scholars.

Schlesinger, Arthur M., Jr.: *A Thousand Days, John F. Kennedy in the White House*, Houghton Mifflin Company, Boston, 1965.

Sorensen, Theodore C.: *Kennedy*, Harper & Row, Publishers, Incorporated, New York, 1965.

Turner, Arthur C., and Leonard Freedman (ed.): *Tension Areas in World Affairs*, Wadsworth Publishing Company, Inc., Belmont, Calif., 1964. An excellent collection of articles dealing with many of the vital issues of the day.

Wolfers, Arnold (ed.): *Changing East-West Relations and the Unity of the West*, The Johns Hopkins Press, Baltimore, 1964. An impressive collection of essays by reputable scholars.

INDEX